TIME AS A HUMAN RESOURCE

for NICK

from your old friend

with best regards —

Eli

TIME AS A HUMAN RESOURCE
TIME AS A HUMAN RESOURCE
TIME AS A HUMAN RESOURCE
TIME AS A HUMAN RESOURCE
TIME AS A HUMAN RESOURCE
TIME AS A HUMAN RESOURCE
TIME AS A HUMAN RESOURCE
TIME AS A HUMAN RESOURCE

Edited by
E. J. McCULLOUGH & R. L. CALDER

The University of Calgary Press

TIME AS A HUMAN RESOURCE. © 1991 by Ernest J. McCullough and Robert Calder

The University of Calgary Press
2500 University Drive NW
Calgary, Alberta
Canada T2N 1N4

Canadian Cataloguing in Publication Data

Main entry under title:
Time as a human resource

Includes bibliographical references and index.
ISBN 1-895176-04-2

1. Time. I. McCullough, Ernest J., 1925-
II. Calder, Robert Lorin, 1941-
BD638.T55 1991   115   C91-091578-4

Cover design: Eli Bornstein, *Multiplane Structurist Relief IV,
No. 2, Arctic Series*, 1987-88.

Text edited and designed by Terry Teskey

All rights reserved. No part of this work covered by the copyrights hereon may be reproduced or used in any form or by any means—graphic, electronic or mechanical—without the prior permission of the publisher. Any request for photocopying, recording, taping or reproducing in information storage and retrieval systems of any part of this book shall be directed in writing to the Canadian Reprography Collective, 379 Adelaide Street West, Suite M1, Toronto, Ontario M5V 1S5.

Printed and bound in Canada by Kromar Printing Ltd.

∞ This book is printed on acid-free paper.

Contents

Acknowledgements *vii*

Introduction *1*

PART I THE CONCEPT OF TIME

The Emergence of Clockwork Society
Robert Banks 23

Time and Life's Meaning
Richard Taylor 45

Change and Uncertainty
David Skelton 55

PART II FUNCTIONAL ACCOUNTS OF TIME

The Human Lifespan as a Functional Framework
Duncan Robertson 65

Some Economic and Demographic Implications
of Canadian Life Cycle Changes
Frank T. Denton and Byron G. Spencer 75

Social Time Clocks: Transforming Later Life
Joseph A. Tindale 103

Ethics and the Handicapped Newborn Infant
Helga Kuhse and Peter Singer 121

The Days of One's Life and the Life of One's Days
Bernard M. Dickens 151

PART III THE TIME OF ONE'S LIFE: SPECIAL ISSUES IN SOCIETY

Indian World View and Time
Cecil King 183

Gender and the Value of Time
Margrit Eichler 189

Women, Time and Societal Values: Lessons from the Farm
Seena B. Kohl 205

Spending Time
Andrew S. Harvey 227

Time-Budget Research: Methodological
Problems and Perspectives
Jiri Zuzanek 243

PART IV TIME IN ART AND MUSIC

Time and the Drama
Ronald Mavor 251

Of Time in Art and Nature
Eli Bornstein 257

Michael Praetorius on Time and Tempo
Robert Solem 265

PART V. FOCUS ON THE FUTURE

Time and the Power of Law
Donna Greschner 273

The Creative Imagination
R. L. Calder 277

Concluding Comments
E. J. McCullough 281

Epilogue: Narrative and Time *289*

Bibliography *309*

Index *343*

Contributors *351*

Acknowledgements

This book is the result of the efforts of many people. First, the conference on time that inspired this volume had its origins in the seventy-fifth anniversary celebrations of the founding of the University of Saskatchewan. University president Leo Krisjanson provided the initial inspiration for the conference. It was his hope that an international conference could be convened that would, first, consider a topic of universal interest and, second, create a climate for a fruitful research program. No topic could be more fundamental than that of time, which, in one form or another, underlies every research program.

A committee chaired by legal scholar Donald Clark was enlisted to work on this project. The members were Donald Bailey, Physical Education; Robert Calder, English; John Crawford, Medicine; Naomi Herson, Education; Ernest McCullough, Philosophy; and Gwenna Moss, Administration. The planning for the conference took many weeks of work; work on the projected volume took some years. The committee played the central role in the realization of the conference's objectives.

Special credit for the work of producing the volume goes to Terry Teskey, freelance editor. Her careful work on the book was crucial to the success of the project. Donald Ward, a Saskatoon editor, did outstanding work on the volume in its formative stages. Eli Bornstein did the major work on the cover, including providing his own artwork for the front cover. Roly Muir of the Research Office of the University of Saskatchewan provided important support for the volume. Kathy Swann of the French Department of the University of Saskatchewan gave invaluable time to the manuscript, and Steven Snyder of North Dakota State University was of great assistance in providing time references.

Special credit goes to the staff of the University of Calgary Press, and particularly to John King, Production Coordinator. Sharon Boyle ably assisted in gathering permissions to reprint material, and Linda Cameron,

Acknowledgements

Director of the University of Calgary Press, provided support throughout.

This book has been published with the help of a grant from the Canadian Federation for the Humanities, using funds provided by the Social Sciences and Humanities Research Council of Canada. The following graciously agreed to reproduction of previously published materials:

"Ethics and the Handicapped Newborn Infant," by Helga Kuhse and Peter Singer, first appeared in *Should the Baby Live?* by the same authors (Oxford University Press, 1985). Reprinted by permission of Oxford University Press.

Excerpt from "The Connection between Paid and Unpaid Labour and its Implications for Creating Equality for Women in Employment," by Margrit Eichler, forthcoming in Royal Commission on Equality in Employment, *Equality in Employment*, vol. 2 (Privy Council Office, 1984). Reproduced with the permission of the Minister of Supply and Services Canada, 1991.

Excerpt from *The View from Eighty*, by Malcolm Cowley. © 1976, 1978, 1980 by Malcolm Cowley. Used by permission of Viking Penguin, a division of Penguin Books USA Inc.

Excerpt from *The Tyranny of Time*, by Robert Banks. © 1983 by Robert Banks. Used by permission of InterVarsity Press, P.O. Box 1400, Downers Grove, Ill. 60515 (U.S. and Canadian rights) and Anzea Book House Ltd., Homebush West, NSW, Australia (world rights).

Figures reproduced from *Fertility in Canada: From Baby-Boom to Baby-Bust*, Statistics Canada catalogue no. 91-524E (Statistics Canada, 1984), p. 121, and from *Labour Force* and *Vital Statistics*, catalogue nos. 84-204 and 84-001 (Statistics Canada, 1984). Reproduced with the permission of Chief, Author Services, Publications Division, Statistics Canada, Ottawa, Ontario K1A 0T6. Readers may obtain copies of related publications by mail from Publications Sales, Statistics Canada, Ottawa, Ontario K1A 0T6, by phoning 1 613 951-7277 or national toll-free 1 800 267-6677, or may facsimile their order by dialing 1 613 951-1584.

Figures from *Fact Book on Aging in Canada* (Supply & Services, 1983), pp. 17, 27, 67, 77.

Excerpt from "Days," by Philip Larkin, in Larkin, *The Whitsun Weddings* (Faber & Faber, 1964), by permission of Faber & Faber Ltd.

Canadian Time Use Pilot Study results, first reported in Brian L. Kinsley and T. O'Donnell, *Marking Time*, vol. 1 of *Explorations in Time Use*, edited by Brian L. Kinsley and M. Catherine Casserly (Employment & Immigration Canada, 1983).

Excerpt from *Preface to Shakespeare*, Vol. 1, by Harley Granville Barker (Princeton University Press, 1974). © 1974 by Princeton University Press. Reprinted by permission of Princeton University Press.

Introduction

E. J. McCULLOUGH

"Have you guessed the riddle yet?" the Hatter said turning to Alice again.

"No, I give up," Alice replied. "What's the answer?" "I haven't the slightest idea," said the Hatter.

"Nor I," said the March Hare.

Alice sighed wearily. "I think you might do something better with the time," she said, "than wasting it in asking riddles that have no answers."

"If you knew Time as well as I do," said the Hatter, "you wouldn't talk about wasting it. It's him."

"I don't know what you mean," said Alice.

"Of course you don't," the Hatter said, tossing his head contemptuously. "I dare say you never even spoke to Time."

Lewis Carroll, Through the Looking Glass

T HE MAD HATTER's claim that time is something more than is immediately evident, that it can be personified, was not understood by Alice; she yearned for clear, unambiguous language and concepts. Can time be understood in such a way? If it can, then one might imagine a conference based on time and celebrating the seventy-fifth anniversary of an academic institution would reveal such an understanding. In fact, the proceedings of the conference on time at the University of Saskatchewan reveal four distinct notions of it: foundational, functional, social, and artistic.

The foundational approach is conceptual and involves the theological and philosophical dimensions of time; the functional approach reveals time in its physical, economic, and moral dimensions; the social approach brings out the lived and operational aspects of time-consciousness and of community perceptions; the artistic approach reveals an imaginative world of human experience. Each section of the conference raised major questions related to the existence of time, the use of time, and perception of time. It did not end in the startling ambiguity seen in *Alice in Wonderland*, but there remain differences in understanding at all four levels. These point to the need to consider time, at least initially, from a broad cultural standpoint that integrates myth, conceptual attitudes, and technological applications in a lived social setting.

Chronos, the Greek word for time, is personified in myth as Kronos, the youngest son of Gaea, daughter of Chaos. Gaea signified the earth. Uranus, the father of Kronos, was both son and husband of Gaea; he signified the heavens. Kronos castrated his father with a sickle, thus separating the earth from the heavens. The dark wraith with a sickle—the grim reaper—is more than a symbol of time or a messenger of death. From the severed genitals of Uranus cast into the sea rose Aphrodite, the goddess of sensual love. Eventually, Kronos was himself overthrown by his son Zeus, who escaped Kronos's attempt to swallow his sons.

Chronos, in the early Greek philosophers such as Plato and Aristotle, is no longer a personified reality but an impersonal reality. In their conceptual approach, time is seen as the moving image of eternity, or as the measure of motion. *Chronos* is tied to the movements of astronomical bodies and the relationship between them. There is, however, another sense of time in Greek understanding, which escapes a clear English expression: time as the point of decision. We might designate this sense of time as *kairos*, the time of ordination or of appointment, and consider it as "event" or "decision" time. Thus, time for the Greeks had at least three distinct senses: personal, functional, and eventful.

Confusion as to the precise nature of time led Augustine to note in his *Confessions* that time appears to be clearly known until one reflects on it, at which point it loses its immediate clarity.[1] Late mediaeval writers looked at time in relation to eternity, in relation to motion, and in relation to events; the passion for univocal terms was not a mediaeval passion. Contemporary men and women care little about mythical, theo-logical, or philosophical characterizations of time. Historian David Landes writes:

The ordinary man (or woman) thinks he knows what time is but cannot say. The learned man, physicist or philosopher, is not so sure he knows but is ready to write volumes on the subject of his speculation and his ignorance. The ordinary man could care less. What matters to him is that he can measure time.[2]

Landes writes of the technological revolution that the invention of time-pieces brought to western Europe. The technology of mechanical clocks was a five-hundred-year monopoly; it "turned Europe from a weak, peripheral, highly vulnerable outpost of Mediterranean civilization to a hegemonic aggressor." Against historians Needham and Price, who argued for a Chinese connection, Landes maintains that the technology was uniquely European. The Chinese failed to move beyond primitive water clocks; Europe, in contrast, developed an elaborate technology perhaps beginning with the Canon Gerbert (later Pope Sylvester, 999–1003) in the late tenth century. These developments culminated in Roger Stokes's clock tower for Norwich Cathedral (1321–25), Richard Wallingford's astronomical mechanisms at St. Albans around 1330, and the planetarium of Giovanni de' Dondi in Padua around 1364. Dante, in the early 1300s, wrote of "wheels in clockworks" (*Paradiso*, canto 24), indicating the advance from primitive to mechanical clocks. Landes argues that the technological revolution, stimulated by the desire for punctuality within the monastic system, took place between 1100 and 1300.

The hundreds of years of technology that form the backdrop for our consciousness of time lead us to a studied indifference to the nature of time and its relation to eternity, to functional moral and economic issues, and to the social dimensions of time as it works in our lives. It is for this reason that the conference on time at the University of Saskatchewan is significant. It began with an exploration of time from a variety of perspectives. Perhaps only in Saskatchewan, with a large aboriginal population and a university system dedicated to relating Native culture to modern society, could the stark contrasts between ancient cultures and contemporary technology be observed so dramatically. The sensitivity of Natives to the rhythms of the seasons and their openness to a more personal time-consciousness can be contrasted with the modern indifference to time as a personal and a metaphysical reality. The conference provided a beginning of both an interdisciplinary and a cross-cultural concern with time—an unusual accomplishment in an era dedicated to specialization, to the unambiguous use of terms and concepts.

This collection comprises the best of the conference papers. The theoretical and philosophical concepts of time are treated in three foundational discussions by Robert Banks, Richard Taylor, and David Skelton. The more functional questions of the human lifespan are examined by Duncan Robertson, Byron Spencer and Frank Denton, and Joseph Tindale. Helga Kuhse, Peter Singer, and Bernard Dickens present ethical and legal arguments arising from the growing problems with the beginnings and the end of life. The particular importance of time to society in general and to special-interest groups is examined by Cecil King (the Native community), and Margrit Eichler and Seena Kohl (women's issues). Andrew Harvey and Jiri Zuzanek provide surveys of time use and analyses of time-budget research. The applications of time consciousness in art are examined by Ron Mavor (drama), Eli Bornstein (fine arts), and Robert Solem (music). The book concludes with summations of the issues and comments on the future of time research by legal scholar Donna Greschner, English professor Robert Calder, and philosophy professor Ernest McCullough.

Robert Banks, a theologian, points to the importance of the clock as the key mechanical discovery of modern times. It brings inestimable blessings; it grounds industrial and scientific progress. At the same time, it brings psychological suffering of a unique kind, particularly to those who are not attuned to the rhythms of an industrial society. Banks deals with changes wrought in contemporary life from two perspectives: historical and theological.

A historical shift took place at the beginning of the Enlightenment—from the religious world view that related time and eternity in a "cosmic drama," to a secular world view that was more individualistic and subjective in the arts, in music, and in politics, and at the same time more objective in science and in economics. Technological changes came rapidly; more and more sophisticated clocks were developed for increasingly complex industrial applications. In the process, individual lives were transformed; society found itself radically changed in its approaches to both work and leisure. With social changes came shifts in values and a greater emphasis on possessions than on agency and activity. As these processes gained momentum, theological studies shifted in perspective as well.

For Banks, the Hebraic sense of time involved a linear progression from a beginning to an end. Further, time was perceived as a gift from a personal Creator. The concept of linear progression worked against the cyclical notions of time present in the ancient world, and favoured human progression through freedom to an end. Modern evolutionary and determinist models have once again raised difficulties for the religious model, and for the notions of freedom implicit in it. Time, in the modern view, has become a resource and a commodity rather than a gift. Early resistance by the romantics to time as measurement was expressed in their focus on felt time and the affective order. Accelerated temporal rhythms make it difficult to sense life rhythms and therefore extremely difficult to relate time to affectivity. Even the rhythms of personal birth and death are ignored, with the result that the human condition is no longer understandable. Banks calls for a re-examination of the essential meaning of time, and a recognition of the need for personal transformation in time. He suggests a return to a more primitive religious intuition about the nature of time.

Philosopher **Richard Taylor** sees an equally serious crisis in the current misunderstanding of time, but argues for what might be popularly called a non-religious, existentialist interpretation of time. He begins with a brief historical survey of the philosophical notions of time, beginning with the Greek philosopher Parmenides, who regarded time as unreal or an imitation of the real. This view became part of a long tradition in Western thought. But Taylor agrees with Banks that it does not accord with our intuitions and with the sense of time that we acquire as we age. There is a felt dimension of time that the romantics recognized and that every person experiences. Henri Bergson, the twentieth-century French philosopher, metaphorically points to time as "leading us to death." For Taylor, the proper understanding of time is as an element in the creative world of man. Without creativity, time loses its meaning and its relation to a lived world.

In a lived world, history comes alive; it is part of the reflective universe of men and women who live feeling the passage of time, but grasp it initially in a cyclical fashion. The mortal Sisyphus, son of Aeolus, sentenced to an eternity of rolling a stone up a hill only to have it roll down again, symbolizes the seeming meaninglessness of human existence. But once Sisyphus sees the task as beautiful and creative then it and his life are endowed with meaning. His reason is able to apply itself to understanding that beauty.

Reason, in Taylor's view, is more than functional; it is contemplative and it sees meaning in the human works of many creative persons. Does this mean that we all share in the creative human tasks? Not at all, for we are not all equally worthy or equally creative. Taylor maintains that as we achieve greatness we rise above the mass of men and women; a Picasso, a Keats, a Byron are unique and not to be replicated. Great artists, scientists, and philosophers give meaning to history by their creative contributions. This account runs counter to the received wisdom of our time in which men and women are all regarded as of equal worth. In Taylor's view, it is the creative thinkers who give meaning to life and history. In this position, Taylor joins such thinkers as Nietzsche, Sartre, and Camus, who share the conviction that meaning comes through human endeavour and not through any shared metaphysical essence or theological perspective.

David Skelton, an Anglican clergyman and a medical doctor specializing in geriatrics, provides yet another point of view. His concern with the physical, social, and spiritual aspects of aging, his function as a teacher and researcher in the science of geriatrics, and his role as an Anglican priest inform his conceptual view that change and time are intimately related. This view, as old as Aristotle, puts a particular stamp on an era in which change occurs at such a rapid rate that stress is inevitable. Again, the ancient Greek notion of time as cyclical conflicts with the interpretation of time as linear, a perception that arises both from personal experience of our mortality and from overarching religious attitudes. These two conflicting models lead to stress and uncertainty but also to the fruitful speculations of science. Science looks for symmetry and predictability; until recently, it sought certainty as well. Certainty, as Skelton sees it, provides the highest ideal for men and women. The conflicting models for change and the current integration of uncertainty in change are a source of greater stress for individuals, yet this stress stimulates discovery and new understanding.

Four factors increase the level of stress beyond individual ability to cope: the degree of change, the rate of change, the predictability of change, and the ability to control change. In modern life, the degree, rapidity, unpredictability, and uncontrollability of change produce enormous stress and uncertainty. Such things as pollution, population pressures, technological change, and economic shifts must be responded to at the individual level in science, political and social life, religious life, and in art by leaders in the fields. But this is not enough. The ordinary person must also be involved.

The ordinary person, as Skelton sees that individual, has enormous resilience under stress. The devastating experience of Hiroshima, the tragedy of South Africa and other troubled areas of the world point to the resilience of ordinary people in the face of tumultuous change. The aged, who are so often seen as passive observers of these changes, respond to them actively as well. The individual shares in the creative response in order to cope with change. From the demands made on the individual emerges a functional account of time, which centres on the proper activities that agents perform in response to the demands of temporal existence. The two key functions are understanding of and active participation in the day-to-day decisions and social contexts in which we live. From understanding the degree and rate of change, some predictions can be made and some control can be exercised. Social and artistic implications follow, and certain crucial research areas are identifiable.

Duncan Robertson, a physician, discusses the shifting patterns in aging in humans. He begins with a general portrayal of life stages and then discusses how the reduction of infectious diseases has affected patterns of aging and resulted in what Robertson calls a „rectangular society": the aging curve has shifted graphically towards a linear model, with the termination of life coming at the time of the biological comple-tion of the internal systems of the organism. The shifts in the causes of death and patterns of aging have resulted in a more positive approach to aging, which had been regarded as a pathological condition. He points to the psychiatrist Erickson's division of life stages into three quests: the search for identity, the search for conflict resolution between stagnation and generativity, and the final search for personal integration in opposi-tion to despair as life comes to an end. The process is manifested in the physical signs of aging.

Three physical factors give clear indications of aging: bodily appear-ance, body composition, and organ efficiency. We are familiar with the differences in appearance and in composition of the body, but organ deterioration does not become severe until the eighth decade. Hence, with the elimination of some of the more serious causes of disease in early life, there is a more rectangular population profile at the beginning of life. With the decline in infectious diseases effected through preven-tative medicine, the profile in later life becomes more linear. On the one hand, there has been an increase in the Western world in life expectancy of from three to four years; on the other hand, there has been a dramatic increase in lifestyle-related diseases, which could reverse the trend. Bad habits of nutrition, sleep, and physical inactivity coupled with stress contribute to increased morbidity in later years.

Despite the reduction in deaths due to infectious diseases and a pos-sible reduction of diseases resulting from choice of lifestyles, there is no sign that there can be an increase in the maximum human lifespan. The real causes of aging lie in the molecular and the genetic order. If this is so, can late-life decline be slowed by diet, work, or exercise? It seems not. The effect of such factors is to make life more enjoyable and fruit-ful, not longer. The result is that the rectangular population profile will be the norm in Western society, if we avoid such disasters as nuclear war. The new profile will make geriatric medicine more and more impor-tant. The university will play a major role in the shifts in emphasis in health care and in the creation of new opportunities for the aged. The functional framework goes beyond the physical description of aging to statistical interpretations, and the social and historical applications of time are vitally important.

Economists **Byron Spencer** and **Frank Denton** provide data on life-cycle patterns over the past few decades in Canada and consider the economic implications. Fertility swings, life expectancy, overall population, post-war labour participation, labour projections, and large-scale economic implications are the major items studied.

The dramatic fertility swings of the past forty years have resulted from the post-war "baby boom" and the post-pill "baby bust." A long-term downward trend that began early in this century was only interrupted by the surge of births following the war. Furthermore, there were a variety of significant shifts in the birth patterns and life patterns, such as the number of single women giving birth. Life expectancy has changed dramatically for both men and women, with a growing gap between them and a lengthened period of life for the very aged. Mortality rates have also decreased. The results have been a steady growth in population, with a rising percentage in the sixty-and-over category. This growth can be expected to continue until around the year 2030. There are economic implications, including reduced education costs as a percentage of government expenditures, but increased health care costs.

Labour participation has also changed with a dramatic increase in female participation and a large overall increase in participation within the labour force. Projections for the future vary widely. Dependency ratios diminish as the population ages. Spencer and Denton develop a number of models based on varied assumptions of fertility and labour participation. Projections for supply and demand and the cost of health care are contingent on these assumptions. But in their view a crisis in budgetary policy need not be anticipated, as the rises in health-care costs will be accompanied by a reduction in education costs.

Economist **Joseph Tindale** considers the effects of modernization on the elderly in a social and historical perspective. Controversies concerning the effects of aging on indigent populations and the influence of aging on the entry and egress from the work force of secondary school teachers provide the framework for Tindale's study. Demographic shifts in Canada over the past century are instructive as a preliminary consideration. The dramatic increase in the population of people over 55 years of age in the past one hundred years has two basic causes: better health care and lower fertility. There is also the phenomenon of longer life expectancy for women; two interesting consequences of this are an increased proportion of the population in the category over 55 and a disproportionate number of older women in that population. This results, some argue, in isolation from the workplace and the family, and reduced status. In Tindale's view, neither has been a result of industrialization. Sociological data indicate, rather, that the aged generally maintain a good relationship with their families, and maintain their status in the community.

Studies of skid-row populations seem to oppose this thesis, since they provide an obvious example of alienated victims of an industrial society. It is the common view that indigent men and women have come to their condition as a result of socio-economic forces that destroyed their sense of identity. Tindale discovered, however, that there is a strong sense of identity and community among these unfortunate men and women, and he found that they are more affected by family status than by socio-economic forces. Most are unmarried; and those who have been married developed little sense of family identity.

Tindale's study of Ontario secondary school teachers focused on the relation between declining enrolment and on questions of seniority. The former could be expected to result in increased tension between age groups, more early retirement, and a curtailment of promotions. The problem of seniority provided a focus for these questions and revealed that there were tensions both in early retirement and in promotion. There are many dimensions to time-related social problems; both skid-row inhabitants and secondary school teachers are affected by social and historical conditions that make generalizations about aging hard to substantiate. Tindale's conclusion is that there the effects of modernization on the elderly is a much more complex phenomenon than has been thought.

Australian ethicists Helga Kuhse and Peter Singer and legal scholar Bernard Dickens examine the moral and legal features of the functional account of time and human experience. Kuhse and Singer deal with the ethical dimensions of time as it relates to the beginnings of human life. They point to the famous Baby Doe case in the United States as an instance that highlights the key ethical issues. Baby Doe's parents decided, in consultation with their doctor, that routine surgical procedures should be denied to their child, who had Down's syndrome. As a result, the child died. In Kuhse's and Singer's view, arguments against such actions centre on notions concerning the equal worth of all human life, the infinite value of human life, and the idea that equal rights apply in the same way to all members of the human species. Using these principles, the United States government attempted to curtail any similar actions as those taken in the Baby Doe case by imposing restrictive guidelines on all hospitals in the United States.

Kuhse and Singer raise practical and theoretical objections to the equal-worth principle. Medical practitioners argue that "hard cases," such as those involving anencephaly, intra-cranial haemorrhage, and intestinal deficiencies, involve medical judgements that cannot be easily related to the federal guidelines. On practical grounds, exceptions are

10 INTRODUCTION

made that undermine any general principles. The authors object, as well, to the arguments for equal worth based on the infinite value of human life. Inconsistencies in their application are evident to the most enthusiastic supporters of the guidelines. The common way of avoiding such inconsistencies, in the view of Kuhse and Singer, is to introduce the notion of "extraordinary means." There is a difficulty here, however, in distinguishing between ordinary and extraordinary means when sophisticated modern technology is involved. Furthermore, interpretations differ in each case and borderline cases blur the distinction. Behind the arguments for this distinction lie the notions of benefits to the patient that, in Kuhse's and Singer's view, involve decisions about the quality of life. These practical considerations are enough to undermine the arguments for the distinction.

There are theoretical objections that need to be faced as well. The central concept that enters into decisions with respect to human life is that of personhood. Kuhse and Singer define a person as a being with the power of self-awareness. Using this definition, some infants and all foetuses might be excluded, and some animals included. They discount the claim that there is value in potential life, as they discount the moral relevance of the distinction between acts and omissions. They would reduce the possibility of abuse by granting some value to the needs of parents and society; infants could also be granted rights of a minimal kind. They argue that practical decisions about abortion already recognize this situation.

A final question is that of the choices between handicapped and normal, healthy children. Again, Kuhse and Singer argue that these choices are already being made in abortion cases and should be given moral sanction by society. Their views introduce the complicated problem of the legal state of the question as it influences moral and ethical decisions in the contemporary world.

Legal ethicist **Bernard Dickens** considers the functional aspects of time from the perspective of legal debates about the qualitative, as opposed to the quantitative, aspects of temporal life. The courts uniformly refuse to introduce more subjective qualitative distinctions. They do, however, admit the notions of extraordinary and ordinary care, which depend on standards of expected care and the availability of resources. The Quinlan case in the United States and the Dawson case in Canada have been instrumental in providing practical legal guidelines. In the Quinlan case, a respirator was removed from an unconscious patient in accord with the parents' wishes; in the Dawson case, a shunt was implanted against the wishes of the parents. The minimum condition for extraordinary care in the Quinlan case was a functioning conscious life. In the courts' view, necessary care involved the provision of basic comfort. The Dawson case involved a child who was conscious but in a severe state of physical disability; in this case, more drastic intervention was ordered by the courts.

Dickens introduces two further problems that give rise to legal complications: the surgical correction of intestinal blockages in Down's syndrome children, and "wrongful life" suits in which patients claim the right not to be born with congenital abnormalities. In the Down's syndrome cases, the law appears to be moving towards acceptance of the removal of even normal nutritional care in cases in which the prognosis involves suffering; but life cannot be actively terminated. In "wrongful life" cases, there have been awards made by the courts, but the general inclination is to resist such claims.

Natural death provides a further test of legal precedents. The law protects both long-term survival and quality of life. A natural death may be preferred to a death prolonged by intrusive means. The law protects the right of patients to refuse unusual treatment, but it does not allow the individual to opt for direct action to terminate his or her life. As Dickens notes, terminal illness involves an incurable condition that can only be prolonged by aggressive intrusion. Conscious life of some kind remains an important condition for the maintenance of care.

Ideally, life-determining decisions are not left to the discretion of the doctor alone, but involve the patient and the patient's family. Additional factors, such as psychic and spiritual well-being, may sometimes put patient and doctor at odds, with legal consequences. Family involvement further complicates consultations, particularly those that bring in a "living will" or a statement of the patient's wishes as to the limits of care. In cases such as Stephen Dawson's, where the parents opted for the removal of basic care, the parents' preferences are often overruled by wider community concerns. The general rule is to follow the patient's preferences where they are ethically and legally acceptable. When these preferences are unknown, the patient's best interests form the standard. Parents and family, health professionals and ethics committees may all play an essential role in these decisions. Outside parties can also enter into the process, as was the case in both the Baby Doe decision and the Dawson case, where there was a legal intervention by outside advocates. Dickens' main point is that patients should have the right to play a determinative role. At present, however, professional, institutional, and societal needs are equally significant.

The functional accounts of time applied in the physical and moral order lead to concern with time from perspectives of particular elements in society, such as Natives and women. They also lead to consideration of the economic aspects of time in society.

Cecil King, a professor of North American Indian and Northern education programs at the University of Saskatchewan, writes of the vast differences between native Indian and western European time-consciousness. The differences follow from a distinct set of notions of human existence and the place of humanity in the universe.

In the Indian view, the human species is not the dominant and most important in the universe. Humans, rather, lie at the end of an animist chain and are entirely dependent on that chain. Animism is a life-giving force that transcends death and encompasses past, present, and future. The Indian derives moods from the surroundings rather than imposing them on the surroundings. As a result, attitudes to studies and work are shaped by a non-linear or circular view of the universe. This cyclical view is represented in Indian time-perception.

In the broad picture, there is an intermediary between humanity and its Maker. This intermediary, such as Waysahayjak, possesses the power of the Maker. Humans, plants and animals admit of levels of superiority. The set of values that follows involves being in harmony with nature and our fellow humans. In King's view, Western views are quite different.

In the Western world, competition, punctuality, and self-discipline are all characteristic features that are represented most fully in the system of education. The core disciplines of mathematics and science and the centrality of English seem to submerge the natural Indian values.

The Indian resists excessive analysis, segmentation of learning, specialization, and many other features of the Western spirit. King argues for a world in which "Father Sun punctuates each day, with light and darkness. . . . The Moon, our Grandmother, punctuates the months into their seasonal distinctions. . . ." The Native Indian is conscious of time, but only in the wider perspective of animate heavenly bodies. Life takes on a circular character following the circular motions. Time is thus more generational than clock-like, more seasonal than calendar-like, more circular than linear.

The place of women in time-consciousness provides a further dimension to the study of time and human society. **Margrit Eichler,** a sociologist, approaches her topic from the perspective of time allocations to women. She begins with a thesis enunciated by sociologist B. Schwartz that power and the value of time are intimately related. As an example, we can imagine a doctor's office, where time is of enormous value to the doctor but of little value to the patient. In order to deal with the Schwartz hypothesis, Eichler considers three questions: the problem of time wasted waiting, the monetary value of time, and the position of those who count time as money. She then turns to the relationship of gender to each of these areas.

Schwartz argues that waiting is a key indicator of power. Servants are in a relationship of "waiting on" people; the greater the dependency, the greater the time spent waiting. The person in power waits a minimal amount compared to the servant or the dependent person. There are economic consequences, since the powerful in society can demand a higher return on time invested. Health needs, for example, put the dependent in a state in which large amounts of time are wasted waiting. This dependency can be viewed in monetary terms.

Time and money are economically associated in an economic exchange of work for pay, such as is involved in the sale of medical services and skills. In client relationships, the skilled person has a marketable power as doctor, professor, or tradesman. The skilled activity is not always as valuable as the value perceived in its social context. The role of the person whose time is perceived as valuable is vital. Managers, physicians, dentists, judges, and lawyers score high on the value scale; babysitters, waitresses, farm and textile workers score low. Individual roles play a vital part in the evaluation: children, prisoners, and the mentally handicapped are perceived to have less valuable time. A negative economic value is assigned to those with no power or with little power. Three factors are identified as crucial: a power-to-time relationship, a value assigned to time based on the role of the individual, and a negative value assigned to time based on dependency.

Insofar as they exercise little power, women are more often in a position of waiting. Their time is less valuable in the common view; hence, it is more likely to have a negative economic value. Using statistical data, Eichler argues that on all three criteria, women hold positions which are characterized by waiting: child care, restaurant work, and textile and farm labour. Finally, there is a negative value assigned to time experienced by women in the home; the wife is often seen as totally dependent (though recent studies of the value of housework could alter the common perceptions of its value).

Eichler concludes that women wait more on men, fill less valued occupational roles, and suffer from a negative valuation of time. The idea that role assignment is a social convention indicates, in Eichler's view, that negative time valuation can be changed by recognition of women as independent and involved in work of equal value with men.

Sociologist **Seena Kohl** examines women's issues in the more specific context of the family farm. She uses a case study of rural family life—in an area she calls "Jasper"—to examine time allocation, society's attitudes towards farm women, and men's roles on the farm. Jasper was settled first by cattlemen in the late nineteenth century and later by home-steaders. It is sparsely settled, the main town having a population of twenty-four hundred. Significant changes in attitudes towards women and the roles of farm women have emerged there over the past twenty years.

The prevailing values in Jasper appear similar to those of Canadian society in general. Women are seen as homemakers. Families strive for succession within the family; the apprenticeship is served by sons but not often by daughters, save through marriage. Young women generally leave the region as a part of their process of maturation, while young men tend to remain in the region if there is an opportunity for succession to the family farm. Women who return to the region or who continue to live there are expected to take the full responsibility for household duties, but they also share in the economic decisions of the enterprise. They play a major role in connecting this enterprise to the outside community. In recent years, women have taken a larger role in activities such as fenc-ing, feeding animals, book-keeping, and clerical work. In general, prior to entering the farm enterprise, women had a broader business experi-ence than men. Kohl's study reveals that both men and women share in the farm duties, but women alone do the household duties.

In common with other segments of society, homemaking is considered of lesser value on the farm than activities that are economically rewarding. The participation of women in the farm enterprise is often regarded as an additional service and is not calculated as part of the partnership. Recent economic research has recognized the value of women's work in the farm enterprise; accurate assessments of the value of this work are now available. Legal precedents have established that men's and women's contributions to the farm enterprise are to be regarded as equal. Disputes have been settled by the division of property; control over the matri-monial home has been accorded to women. In spite of these changes, however, federal and provincial farm assistance programs do not credit the contributions of women to the farm enterprise. A continuing political struggle goes on to gain that recognition.

Changes in Jasper arise from the advances in research and in legis-lation. Between 1962 and 1982, there were dramatic shifts in attitudes with respect to equality of opportunity. The possibility of women succeeding to farm ownership was acceptable to many; the participation of women in farm labour was more acceptable; the notion that women could be "farmers" was also received favourably. These facts indicate a new respect for women's rights and a recognition of equality of opportunity for men and women in the farm enterprise. These dramatic changes are well documented in Kohl's studies of the region. Economic factors also provide insight into society's use of time.

Andrew Harvey, an economist, takes the view that time, like money, can be spent. He analyzes how time-use studies have proceeded and how they have been used in economic research, and speculates on their future direction. The standard approach to time use has been through observation, questionnaires, diaries, and time budgets. Until the mid-seventies, little attention was paid to the subjective use of time. This dimension of time study has recently been analyzed in studies carried out in a number of countries, including Canada.

Time studies have been used to look critically at several subgroups in society—working mothers, children, the elderly, the handicapped—and also to examine the nature of leisure activities. In urban planning, time shifts have been studied as they apply to traffic patterns and urban development. Harvey provides useful data on subgroups, such as students and the unemployed, as models; settings for time allocation are considered, with the notable fact emerging that a heavy proportion of time is spent at home. Harvey deals, as well, with the amount of time spent alone and in groups. The fact that 70 percent of free time at home is spent viewing television points to a serious breakdown in family involvement both with-in the family and with the outside world.

In Harvey's view, there are two useful areas for future research: the first deals with activities and contextual settings, the second, with the relation of settings to individuals. There is a need still to develop fruitful theoretical constructs to aid in time allocation.

Commenting on Harvey's paper, economist **Jiri Zuzanek** suggests that there is a need to consider methodological problems in time-budget research. The value of time research is evident as an indicator of life preferences, since the research is based on universal, holistic, and objective measurements. The problems with such research include faulty recollection of details, lack of motivational research, and a certain arbitrariness in calculations. The difficulty with faulty memory does not apply to more sophisticated contemporary research practices, but problems still remain with the classification of activities and with motivational research. Activities are enormously complex, and their classification depends to some extent on the research program and its objectives. The structure of the activities themselves is also of serious concern.

As Zuzanek sees it, three factors are essential to successful research programs: conceptual analysis based on functions, statistical analysis isolating common properties, and application of meaning to various activities. Recent studies indicate, for example, that older males enjoy household duties much more than older females. Because so much depends on the meaning attached to these activities, Zuzanek contends that it would be more fruitful for the researcher to focus on the functional, structural, and purposeful aspects of daily life.

The conceptual, functional, and social aspects of time studies lead to a consideration of time as it applies to artistic concerns. It is here that the deeper meaning of human activity is most vividly expressed. Even the viewing of television, which tends towards the most superficial of the musical and dramatic arts, reveals an inner hunger for the purposeful application of leisure time. When the arts are at a high level, the purposeful elements are most clearly revealed.

The artist moves through the foundational, the functional, and the social aspects of time to the order of time-perception and experience. The artist lives time intensely and expresses this life in a temporal framework. As drama professor **Ron Mavor** sees it, the dramatist illustrates time experience vividly in imagery and in symbol. The familiar depiction by Yeats of an aging man as a "paltry thing, a tattered coat upon a stick" or a soul "fastened to a dying animal" gives substance to an experience of aging. It is thus that we live out moments passing and to come. But the artist is not entirely beholden to time. The artist shapes and bends it. As Mavor reads the classical Aristotelian picture of art, it represents or imitates reality; this applies to time as to all it depicts. The modern artist, however, inspired by Shakespeare and others, "bends" both time and space. Musicians bend the time in early performances of a work to fit their deficiencies. So also artists bend time to fit their purposes.

Shakespeare's use of time in *Hamlet* provides a notable example. Hamlet's initial resolve and determination quicken the pace; later irresoluteness slows the pace. Time slows as Hamlet loses touch with the ordinary temporal order, until Ophelia brings him back to the present and the reality of the lived experience.

The segmentation of time into moments, minutes, hours, days, weeks, months, and years is overshadowed by the attempt to ask where we live in an atemporal existence. The doctor presses for more time for reflection on the future; the priest offers an eternity of time ahead; the dramatist provides a perpetual present against the inexorable end and the remote eternity. For Mavor, it is the eternal present that drama brings to life through memories, feelings, and emotions. The theatre enriches by recreating in the present. This immediacy brings back our own experience, in spite of our temptation to dwell in the past and future. Perhaps the master of the immediate was Marcel Proust, who consciously aimed at recreation of the intensity of the moment. The "realist" writes of objects past and future; the artist reunites us with the present—caught ultimately in the deeper and deeper intensity, in the words of poet-philosopher T. S. Eliot.

Artist **Eli Bornstein** places the fine arts in the context of temporal change: time is the "ultimate medium of all the arts." It is the element common to all. Within time, art is created; similarly, within art, time is created. It is an elemental symbiosis of two life forms. Art shapes time as artists strive for immortality through their creations. The artist knows time as both saviour and destroyer: a saviour as da Vinci brought together past and future, a destroyer as his murals decayed before his very eyes. The artist knows that historic or natural time and the time of artistic creation rarely coincide. The interplay between lived physical time and creative artistic time spurs the emergence of works of genius that may be unrecognized in the lifetime of the artist.

A crucial claim of Bornstein's is that as clock time (*chronos*) and decision time (*kairos*) differ, so also do clock time and the artistic time of creation. The difference can stimulate creation, or it can inspire neglect of art and the artist. Fashion is the dominance of historical and natural time over art, and one of the sources of the neglect of true genius. Our age, more than any other, is an age in which art is threatened by fashion and its corollary, novelty, which flows from fashion and serves to embellish and nourish it. Our age, Bornstein argues, needs time to assimilate the vast changes in art of the past two centuries, but there is no such time available. Monet sought to bring continuity into his art, in a gallant effort to set time's continuum against the dominant episodic, fragmented approach to art and existence characteristic of our age. Cubism reflects the same sort of temporal concern.

As no other people in history, we are able to recapture the past and imaginatively picture the future through photography, film, and television. We are able to see the progression of art through "representation," to transformation, to translation and then to abstraction-creation-invention." We stand at an unusual moment in history. As Bornstein sees it, part of the difficulty in modern assimilation of contemporary art lies in the inability to see the link between art and time. Modern art embodies an experience of the closeness to the evolutionary sources of nature, which the artist captures. Time, nature, and art are closely linked in harmony in cinema, in music, and in the visual arts. Thus, art and

18 INTRODUCTION

history, human creativity and nature, work towards a kind of natural juncture in a marriage of process and dynamic creation.

Musician **Robert Solem** provides a graphic example of changing time-consciousness in the work of seventeenth-century musician Michael Praetorius. Two of Praetorius's published works form the basis for his study: the *Syntagma musicum*, Volume 3, and a set of compositions called the *Polyhymnia caduceatrix et panegyrica*. Analysis of these two works reveals an interesting contrast in the tempo or pace of his work and the duration or practical matter of timing. At a moderate pace by modern standards, the *Polyhymnia* seems to take considerably less time than is described in Praetorius's instructions. The contemporary moderate tempo is considerably slower than that described by Praetorius, indicating that contemporary performance of renaissance and baroque music proceeds at a pace up to a third faster than was in the mind of the composer. Solem tests his observations against the interpretations of several musicians and through analysis of various recordings. Does this case indicate a general shift in the musical approach to time-consciousness since the seventeenth and eighteenth centuries? Solem's study indicates that there is such a change in the musician's time-perceptions. On the whole, as Bornstein, Mavor, and Solem show, fine art, drama, and music reveal a remarkable shift in the artist's consciousness of time in the contemporary period.

Concluding remarks by legal theorist **Donna Greschner**, author and literary critic **Robert Calder**, and philosopher **Ernest McCullough** focus on time in general research areas connected to law, literature, and philosophy. Greschner points to the notion of natural justice as interpreted in modern law as concerned with procedures rather than with metaphysical or theological notions of justice. The use of "fair procedures" is designated in modern law as natural justice. The use and misuse of time is a crucial factor in the profession. Interminable procedures, as illustrated in Dickens's *Bleak House*, point to the need for legal reform. The reforms come in assessing the values of current procedures and in the achievement of distributive justice through reflective research and political action.

Robert Calder looks at the experience of the artist as the way through which changes in approaches to time are *felt*. Early classical artists pointed to the feeling of the brevity of lifespan and of time as short; hence, the need to enjoy the moment. Contemporary lifespan is more extended, as we have seen in these papers; hence, the artist is less likely to point to the need to seize the moment. Calder points to the poetry of Malcolm Cowley and the fiction of Margaret Laurence as evidence of the awareness of the extension of time. Cowley depicts a child riding through a series of lived segments of life culminating in old age. Laurence gives us a poignant picture of the ninety-year-old Hagar, who lives her past in her memory and struggles through the present in an attempt to maintain her dignity. The artist provides an avenue to the felt world of temporality.

Ernest McCullough summarizes some of the basic themes of the volume and points to positive and negative features. The positive features are the identification of key research areas in foundational, functional, social and artistic understanding of time. He maintains that there are three vital research areas to consider: logical, social, and metaphysical. The use of the word "time" in multivocal senses needs closer examination by scholars; the historical application of time in communities has undermined the notion of equal worth as a central feature of Western society; and finally, the identification of being and function has undermined another central insight in civilized thought, that being and doing are significantly different concepts, and hence that the person is not appropriately defined by function. McCullough holds that failure to deal with these three research areas effectively will result in a new and destructive barbarism, which is individualistic and anticommunitarian.

This volume brought a number of disciplines together and succeeded in providing a unified theme beginning with foundational accounts and proceeding through some of the functional, social, and artistic consequences of these positions. Such conferences are rare because of the difficulty in bridging gaps in a society bent on specialization. If such attempts are not made, however, the distance between disciplines will widen and the classical idea of a *university* will be lost. Similarly, in a world bent on distinctions and difference, the essential unity of humanity will be obscured.

Notes

1. Saint Augustine, *Confessions*, Book XI (London: J. M. Dent, 1949).

2. D. S. Landes, *Revolution in Time: Clocks and the Making of the Modern World* (Cambridge, Mass.: Belknap, 1983), 1.

THE CONCEPT OF TIME

I

The Emergence of Clockwork Society

ROBERT BANKS

ACCORDING TO LEWIS MUMFORD, the celebrated historian of urban and technical development, "the clock, not the steam engine, is the key machine of the industrial age."[1] Every advanced industrial society is dependent upon the clock, watch, and other timekeeping devices. These orchestrate and pace all the other technological inventions upon which our civilization depends. They integrate workers, employers, and machines so that they function in an orderly and efficient way. They coordinate other sectors of the economy, for example, service industries, the professions and even primary production, with the whole industrial process. They largely determine the way we spend our leisure as well as working hours, the lives of children as much as adults, even—in a negative way—the existence of the unemployed, disadvantaged, and aged. In fact, the wristwatch and clock regulate the lives of people not only more than any other machine, but more than any other individual agency, corporate institution, or political structure.[2]

The pivotal place of the watch and clock in our society is both a blessing and a curse. Without them the economic development we take for granted and the material benefits we value so highly would not have come our way. Because of them we have sophisticated transport and communication systems that allow us to extend the number and speed of our activities. Through them we have access to a greater number of people and broader range of experience than ever before. But we have paid a heavy price for these advantages. We are determined by the watch and the clock more than we determine our movements by them. We are forced to live at a rate faster than most of us would prefer. We are pressured to work too late and too long.

Most people regard this regulation by the clock, stepped-up pace of life, and over-filled daily routine as normal. It does not occur to them that life could be different. Some people, less affected by the forces that have shaped modern society, know better. Those living in rural areas, those who come from a non-European background, those who do not belong to the middle class, and now those who have opted for a counter-culture way of life, in varying degrees, move to a different rhythm. But the majority of people increasingly find that their time is not their own, that everything is happening too fast and that there is just too much to do. Like Lewis Carroll's Alice, they find that it takes all the running you can do, to stay in the same place.

This ambiguous role of the watch and the clock is related to some of the puzzling contradictions in our society. We have shorter working hours than our forefathers, yet some people work longer hours than those who lived earlier in the century.[3] We have more free time than our parents and grandparents, yet a larger proportion of our free time is programmed or booked up in advance.[4] We are more concerned about health and fitness than previous generations, yet are suffering more, both physically and psychologically, from stress-related illnesses.[5] We have smaller families and can be more selective about our relationships, yet give less time to children and friendships, even to spouses, than people did earlier.[6] We have greater opportunities to pursue cultural and spiritual interests, but give less time to these than the previous generation.[7] Although, over the past ten to fifteen years, a small but increasing minority has protested against this state of affairs, the general situation continues to deteriorate.

How have we come to this position? What are the chief factors that have shaped our present attitude to, and use of, time? Why are we so different in this respect from all pre-modern and non-Western cultures? In attempting to answer these questions I will not provide a chronological outline of how these changes took place. I have done this elsewhere and it would take too long to do so here.[8] Instead I will give a summary account of the chief historical factors bearing on the matter. Before doing so, however, I need to say something about how I am using the word "time" in this paper. By "time" I mean primarily the experience we have at an everyday level of present, past and, future, the consciousness we have of the moments, duration, and passing of time, and our awareness of various internal and external rhythms affecting our bodies and environment. I am not talking about time, therefore, primarily in a philosophical, sociological, historiographical, or scientific way, though I will draw on all of these at points in the discussion that follows.[9]

A Historical Perspective

Conceptual Changes

Among the basic changes that have taken place in people's world view or *de facto* understanding of reality, several are relevant to a discussion of time. Perhaps the most significant conceptual changes in this connection took place between the Reformation and the period of the Enlightenment. Decisive here were the shift from a theocentric to an anthropocentric view of the universe and the weakening of belief in an eternal dimension. As a result, humankind came to occupy the centre of the stage rather than God, and the events of this life were detached from any supra-temporal significance they might have.[10] For individuals this generally led to a preoccupation with personal affairs at the expense of the cosmic drama in which they, spiritual beings, and God were involved. It also led to a concentration on the period of time that made up the natural span of a person's life, with little reference to its interpenetration and ultimate transformation by the life of God's present and coming realm. While most people in every age have probably placed their own affairs and the affairs of this life at the centre of their interests, the supernaturalist framework of mediaeval and reformation society did exert some influence on the way people organized and conducted their lives. After Darwin, people gradually became more aware of the apparently random way in which life evolved on this planet and of the ultimately entropic fate that awaits the universe.[11] Though few dwelt on such things, many began to feel a pervasive sense of cosmic meaninglessness and personal insignificance. These changes in worldview or in the boundaries of life have tended to place pressure upon the more limited amount of time people now feel they have at their disposal. Since this world and the period between birth and death is all that they have, they are inclined to make as much of this world as they can in the limited time they have available. As A. Mendilow comments in his article "The Time Obsession of the Twentieth Century":

Urged to look for some solution, to find some way out of the *impasse* of modern living, filled with a general sense of transition from one cultural or social cycle to another not as yet fully determinable, we become more appetitive. While the final goals tempt us on and yet evade us, we can on the other hand look to the realisation of more and more immediate desires which modern technical achievement render possible more and more quickly. . . . It is the appetitiveness that makes Time so emphatic for us on the level of everyday life. The more we

26 THE CONCEPT OF TIME

have or can get, the more we want; the quicker we can get what we want, the more we become aware of change and movement (not necessarily synonymous with improvement in progress), that is, of Time.[12]

Other significant changes in attitude to and use of time have their source in mathematical and utilitarian ideas. Newton's formulation of the concept of abstract time, which is divisible into equal units, was a scientifically and technologically fruitful notion.[13] In effect, he simply put into words the view of time embodied in the clock. Despite attacks upon this view by the romantics in favour of a subjective view of time, or one more closely associated with natural rhythms, the notion of artificial, objective time continued to grow in prominence. Utilitarian ideas, which had their philosophic origin in Bentham and others, gradually permeated the worlds of business, education, and bureaucracy.[14] As a result work, learning, and social administration became tied to notions of efficiency, sometimes at the expense of such qualities as craftsmanship, creativity, and humanity. Given greater precision by the introduction of time-and-motion studies, these ideas led to the exact measurement of various operations in industry and commerce and consequent regulation of the workers' movements according to carefully calculated time units.[15]

Utilitarian ideas and time-and-motion studies spread far beyond the world of work. Many people, particularly in North America, now find that they have to justify their pursuit of leisure in terms of its usefulness. Instead of doing certain things for their own sake, or not doing anything in particular at all, these people have to find some advantage in or benefit from them in order to enjoy them, for example, greater knowledge, skill, experience, fitness, or refreshment. Otherwise they feel guilty and worry that they are wasting time.[16] Meanwhile sport has become dominated by the clock and by time-and-motion studies. The training of sportsmen and women, their performance and achievements now take place within "the prison of measurement," as one writer calls it, measurement down to one-hundredths of a second.[17] Utilitarian values, therefore, and ever more sophisticated measurements of efficiency, have increased the pressure upon both work and free time, and narrowed the range of legitimate activities associated with them.

Technological Changes

Devices for the measurement of time and other inventions enabling people to use time more profitably have been with us for thousands of years. For example, the water clock, sand glass, and sundial were considerable technical inventions in comparison with earlier methods of calculating the passage of time.[18] Other basic inventions like the wheel and alphabet also speeded up the amount people could do and communicate. But during the last few hundred years we have seen a qualitative change in the precision of time-keeping devices and in technological innovations increasing the number, rate, and duration of many human operations.[19] This is true even in the area of clock-making, which preceded the Industrial Revolution by several centuries. Compare, for example, the way in which public clocks functioned in the fourteenth century and their counterparts today. In the fourteenth century clocks had only hour hands, the length of the hours varied seasonally according to the amount of daylight, the calculation of time differed from one region—even one village—to another, and accuracy was a relative affair. Or consider the difference between the first personal clocks, in the sixteenth and seventeenth centuries, and the latest wristwatch. Originally only the wealthy could afford personal clocks, they regarded such clocks primarily as sophisticated gadgets or as fascinating ornaments, the clocks themselves had only hour and minute hands, and their operation was always mechanically based. Quite apart from changes in public and personal time-keepers, we now have standardized time-zones all over the world. Clocks have been built into other mechanical and electrical inventions such as the Bundy clock at work and radio clock at home. Stopwatches and computerized clocks make possible the calculation of very small fractions of time. Atomic and quartz clocks are accurate to an almost unimaginable degree. The mass production of watches has extended the influence of the clock into the most private arrangements of the majority of people. The advent of the digital watch is taking us a step further, altering our perception of measured time. No longer is time portrayed as a cyclical (or earlier as fluid) but as a purely atomistic affair.

Other modern inventions that have altered our approach to time include railway travel, the electric light, telephone, and car. Before the introduction of gas, and especially electric light, few people worked at night or, if they did so, did not work for long. The risk to their eyesight was too great. But the invention of the electric light began what one writer has described as the last great act of "colonization," the colonization of time, that is, the spreading of work throughout the night-time as well as day-time hours.[20] The increasing number of people involved in shift work is the clearest indication of this, and the growing awareness of the risks associated with this a reminder of its ambiguous consequences. The telephone and other communication inventions from the telex to the computer have greatly multiplied the number of things we can do, and accelerated the speed at which we can do them. The extent to which the telephone intrudes upon our private lives, and the over-supply of information that is now adversely affecting the efficiency of many business operations, point up the double-edged nature of these technological advances. The car, along with the airplane and rapid transport systems generally, has enabled us to diversify our activities and relationships to a remarkable extent. For all the benefits of these—and our conference on time is one of them—the car has cost us dear in terms of physical injury, stress, and environmental pollution. All of these inventions have contributed both to the smoother running and to the more hectic pace of our society, to its maximization but also exploitation of time use, and to the more accurate calculation but also greater fragmenta-tion of the time we have.

Social Changes

We are shaped not only by our ideas but also by the relationships and structures in which we are involved. The decisive changes that have taken place in Western society over the last two centuries, generally referred to as the industrial and technological revolutions, have further changed our conceptions of reality and radically affected our use of the inventions we have created.[21] It was, as I said at the beginning, the Industrial Revolution that placed the clock at the centre of working life, first in the factory, then in the office, lecture hall, and consulting room. In order to fulfil its function in such places it had to be central in the railway station, and later in the tram or bus terminal, airport, and even car. It had to be present in the home as well—beside the bed and on the mantelpiece—and finally in the pocket or on the wrist of every individual. Without this distribution of the watch and the clock throughout the industrial economy, the economy itself could not work properly. No clock, no organized workforce. No organized workforce, no surplus labour. No surplus labour, no capital accumulation. No capital accumula-tion, no mass goods and services, and so forth.

How revealing is it that the first item a non-Westerner wants to own is a watch and that a watch is often the first adult present we give to our children? In both cases we induct people at the beginning of their social or personal development into the heart of the industrial and technological process. The watch is not only—if you will forgive the pun—the main-spring of those revolutions in our way of life, but the doorway to the enjoyment of its benefits and suffering, of its disadvantages. That is, a revolution in economic and social structures provided both the *means* for meeting, and further defining, the new goals of life associated with changes in world view over the last few centuries, and also the *dynamic* enabling the possibilities inherent in technological invention to unfold to their fullest extent. The information revolution that we are experiencing at present is only heightening the forces unleashed by the Industrial Revolution two centuries ago. The bureaucratization and computerization of life now taking place demonstrate the victory of what Ellul refers to as *la technique*, of instrumental reason, as typified by the administrator and engineer, welfare department and hi-tech firm, committee meeting and calculator respectively, though once the entrepreneur and clock were its main embodiment.[22]

However, we are only looking at half the picture if we fail to understand that our modern socio-economic revolution has transformed free time as much as patterns of work. The large-scale commercialization of sport and industrialization of leisure are clear examples of this. Sport today goes hand-in-hand with both speed and precision timing, as we have already mentioned. The Olympic Games is the most dramatic illustration of this, but it occurs in all levels and facets of sport. Leisure is now subject to widespread scheduling and speeding up. From media programming to packaged tours on the one hand, and from high-paced television ads to thrill-a-minute leisure experiences on the other, regulation and pace are the name of the game. While the introduction of video machines and noncompetitive games has reduced the amount of external regulation and hyperactive pace inherent in so much leisure time today, they have not decreased the amount of actual busyness in people's lives. The reason for this is that there is a deeper link between the rhythms of work and free time than those carried over through the application of business methods or technology to leisure activities. So addictive are the rhythms of many work situations that some people can only cope during their time off by reproducing them. Not to do so is to go into withdrawal, with all the pain associated with that. Too long an addiction to high-pressure work and leisure rhythms results in burn-out, physical breakdown, and coronary disease.

Value Changes

So far I have talked of ideas, inventions, and socio-economic arrangements and the part they have played in the emergence of our wristwatch society. What about the private ambitions and priorities of the average person? While these are not independent of the ideas, inventions, and socio-economic arrangements that form people's broader cultural environment, they cannot simply be reduced to them either. As the historian Herbert Butterfield has tirelessly stressed, the individual is not just a plaything of the historical process but a creative agent within it. Even where individuals are heavily conditioned by their social environment they have a capacity—strong in some, reduced in others—to resist the pressures around them and march to the beat of a different drummer. Social disadvantage is a very real, at times frighteningly destructive, affair but, except in certain extreme cases, individual capability and responsibility are no less real. Among the changing goals and priorities of Western men and women during the last two centuries, two stand out as particularly relevant to the issue of time.

Perhaps the most obvious aspiration has been "to have" rather than "to do," to use Erich Fromm's terminology.[23] The quest for possessions, but equally the quest for experiences, services, qualifications, success, and status, are evidence of this acquisitive instinct. Even the preoccupation with dress, appearance and style, or with personal development and relational skills, partially rests upon it. But in order to have, it is necessary to buy, for these days acquiring such things generally involves paying for them. In order to buy, one must earn, and the more one wants to have certain things, the more one needs to earn. This puts pressure upon one's time at work and frequently involves spending more time there, or working in a more intensive way. A desire to have, therefore, puts pressure upon the time spent in production. As the Swedish economist Staffan Linder points out, however, it puts pressure upon consumption time as well. If you have more to consume—whether goods, services, experiences, relationships, or other—you have to expand the time you have available to consume more things in the same time: multiple consumption, one might call it. The end result of the drive to have is the emergence of what Linder calls "the harried leisure class."[24] In other words, "conspicuous consumption," to resort to Thorstein Veblen's phrase,[25] leads inevitably to time scarcity. And so we have inverted the situation in the Two-Thirds World. There, material poverty occurs, but time is in rich supply. We have gained the benefits of affluence, but only by becoming poverty-stricken with respect to time.

The other aspiration that has markedly affected attitudes towards time over the last two centuries is the desire "to do" rather than "to become." In our advanced industrial society we have become obsessed with doing. Indeed, what we do largely governs our understanding of who we are.[26] Our sense of identity is significantly shaped by the work we do. But what we do also strongly influences our estimate of one another. "And what do you do?" is one of the first questions we ask when meeting someone for the first time. The answer helps us to place the persons to whom we are talking and helps us know how—or how much—to relate to them. Our desire to do affects our approach to free time. It involves us in various degrees of activity in clubs, causes, churches, and charitable work, or in leisure activities of various kinds rather than in less doing-oriented ways of spending our time. Even the new concern for "being," as reflected in self-awareness and group therapy approaches, tends to be pursued through courses and programs, or with the aid of techniques. Children's development is largely defined in terms of their involvement in activities such as after-school or weekend sports, music, dance, and art classes, Scout, Guide, and other groups. The point is this: so long as "doing" is regarded as having more value than anything else—there is nothing more socially unacceptable than to confess to, or be accused of, "doing nothing"—additional pressure is placed upon our time. The trage-dy is that so much of this activity fails to produce the goal aimed at. It does not necessarily secure for people a firmer sense of their own iden-tity, of acceptance by others, of making a contribution to society, of developing one's own or one's children's character. Even where it does achieve these things it may do so in ways that are at odds with our inner nature or actual capacities. In fact, activism is at times a substitute for a proper understanding of who we are, mature relationships with others, genuine social change, or the cultivation of a well-rounded personality.

A Theological Perspective

These four levels of historical explanation do not exhaust the analysis of why we live in a haste-ridden, booked-up, clock-regulated society. We have to probe deeper if we are to expose the root causes of our situation. It is no longer fashionable to ask whether a theological perspective would assist us to do this. In these post-Feuerbachian, post-Marxian, and post-Freudian days, theology is regarded as leading us further away from reality rather than penetrating it more acutely. Since a good deal of theology is a flight from reality, a mystification of it, or too general in its approach to life, I cannot blame those who hold such a view. To the extent that theology turns its back on reality or obfuscates it, however, it disqualifies itself as genuine theology. A genuine theological per-spective can deepen our understanding of the situation in which we find

32 THE CONCEPT OF TIME

ourselves and, more than that, should help to change it. It has done this before with respect to the issue of time. As I have argued elsewhere:

The ancient Hebrews had a distinctive awareness of their presence in time and history, and this was a direct consequence of their experience of God. The early Christians took over and intensified this approach to time and through them, it came to have an important place in Western thought. This view of time gave the West its peculiarly forward-looking, dynamic character. By contrast, Greek and Roman thought lacked a strong sense of progress. Only in very limited respects could historians discern development taking place. Every few thousand years the cosmos decayed and a new start had to be made all over again. But in the biblical writings there was a movement from a definite beginning (the Creation) to a definite end (the Last Days), with certain novel and decisive events along the way (e.g., the Exodus, the Covenant, the Incarnation and Resurrection). This conception of a forward movement in time gave impetus to social change in succeeding centuries and ulti-mately produced a new type of individual—it fashioned what we call "modern man." Our emphasis upon will rather than contemplation, our belief that change, development and reform are possible in personal and social life, our drive toward what lies ahead rather than preoccupation with what lies behind, our confidence in our ability to shape and plan the future, all have their origins in the biblical attitude towards time and history.[27]

But what does theology have to say now? This is more important than providing an overview of biblical attitudes towards time in com-parison with their Greek and ancient Eastern counterparts. So, paralleling the four factors already considered from a historical perspective, I would like to draw attention to four others of a theological kind that illuminate and extend them.

The Gift of Time

As explained earlier, changes in worldview from mediaeval to modern times have both shortened the amount of time people feel they have at their disposal, and put pressure upon that time as they seek to extract the maximum out of it. This has led to one of the most common ways of thinking about time today: as a "resource." Compare the title of our conference, where "time" is qualified by the term "human." Time-management approaches to the question of time-use characteristically describe time as a resource that is "scarce," or in "limited" supply.[28]

sometimes stressing the fact of its "equal" distribution.[29] In such contexts time is apt to be discussed in the same way as any other resource. We are able to "utilize" or "waste" it, "maximize" or "accumulate" it, use it "inefficiently" or "productively." While there is some value in viewing time as a resource, and as a human one at that, certain other ways in which time is commonly talked about are more questionable, namely, as a "commodity" or as a "means of exchange." Both the Puritans and Wesley used the language of commerce in exhorting their hearers to use their time wisely,[30] and it was Franklin who started the identification of time with money.[31] It is because we view time as a commodity that we can talk of "buying" or "selling" it, and of "using" and "consuming" it. It is because we view it as a "means of exchange," like money, that we speak of "earning" and "spending" it, "adding," "calculating," and "dividing" it, "using," "stealing," and "losing" it.[32] The greatest danger in thinking about time in these ways is the encouragement they give us to develop an acquisitive and possessive attitude towards it, just as we do with any commodity, and to regard it in a purely commercial way, just as we do any means of exchange.

While Marx criticized Western society for its idolatrous attitude to business and commercial values, he did not call for a revised estimate of its understanding of time—only for a more just recognition of its worth. Marx, as much as any capitalist, tended to think of time as a "resource" and to place a "monetary" value upon it. Even in his vision of the ideal socialist society, the analogy with the production of commodities remains in the background.[33] According to the Judaeo-Christian outlook we do time and ourselves an injustice when we view it as a commodity or means of exchange. Even to view it as a resource has its dangers, for we have a long history in the West of exploiting the resources we have available to us; and time, in any case, does not exist for the pursuit of purely human ends. Time is, in the first instance, a gift from God: like our natural environment, it is a divine present. As such it is to be valued, appreciated, and celebrated, not just used or exploited. Time also offers us the opportunity to enter into a relationship with the author of the cosmos and history, to introduce God's knowledge, justice, and love into the world in which we live, and to cooperate in the construction of the new world God is fashioning.

Unfortunately, we have tended to lose appreciation of time itself and simply take it for granted. We do not see it as a generous gift, but as a possession that is under our control. We do not realize that time has divine as well as human ends, and that human ends can only be defined in relation to divine ones.[34]

The Quality of Time

It was the romantic movement that first protested against the proliferation of time-keeping devices and increasingly totalitarian intrusion of the clock in modern life. In literature, authors as diverse as Baudelaire and Rousseau, George Eliot and Matthew Arnold, William Faulkner and D. H. Lawrence, all attacked external, objective clock time in favour of inner, subjective, unmeasured time. Others such as Proust and Joyce, Woolf and Priestley, also sought a new understanding of time.[35] In their different ways all these writers felt after a less quantitative and abstract, more qualitative approach to time. Despite these protests and explorations, the mathematical use of time continues to dominate everyday behaviour. Such voices have spoken at too theoretical and elitist a level to make much impression upon the average person. That person is as inclined to attach a carefully measured period of time to some activity and experience as a price to some object or service. We do not look at our activities and experiences, or for that matter at the aspirations we have and persons we love, and ask them when and for how long they, by virtue of what they are in themselves, require our attention. Instead we look at what time it is, and how much time we have, and then fit them in or not according to that external standard. We do not allow such things to determine the time appropriate to them, but allow the clock to do so whether this does justice to them or not. Instead of asking "How much time do my children need?", "How much time do I need to recover from the stress I'm under?", "How much time do I need to keep in touch with my basic concerns, values, and longings?" we ask "How much time do I actually have?" for any of these things.

In approaching time in this way, in treating it as a predominantly quantifiable affair, we transgress its purpose as surely as we still tend to transgress the delicate eco-systems in our environment. That is why our relationships with our children, our physical and psychological health, and our sense of self-identity are so much in jeopardy in our kind of society. During the last decade or so we have seen a reaction against this quantifiable attitude to existence in the growing interest in the "quality of life." The biblical writers also speak of a quality of life, but go further than current counter-culture or concerned middle-class attitudes by linking this specifically to our treatment of time. As the writer of Ecclesiastes declares, "There is a time for everything under the sun" (Eccles. 3:1). As he goes on to suggest, the passages of life through which we pass, from birth to death; the experiences we encounter, both good and bad; the activities we engage in, both domestic and employment related; the relationships we enter into, both intimate and alienated; the responsibilities we have, both personal and political—all have their proper time. So far as we are able to do so—and we cannot always see as clearly as we would like—our task is to discern when that time comes and how long it should last. When we do that we begin to develop a more balanced approach to time. Such an approach does not overlook the legitimacy of calculating and measuring time, or fail to reckon with the fact that time is not always under our control. The biblical writings themselves recognize the value of the one and reality of the other.[36] But this approach does not allow calculation and measurement, or the force of circumstances, to determine the way we live. We could put it this way: a theological perspective on time is not against the watch and the clock, it just wants to put them in their rightful place. The watch and the clock, like the sabbath day, were made for us, not we for the watch and the clock (cf. Mark 2:27). They are to be regarded as servants not masters, as means not ends, as tools not tyrants. Only then do they fulfill their proper function.

The Rhythms of Time

Instead of being sensitive to various temporal rhythms, we have substituted a fascination with speed. Indeed, as A. Mendilow says:

The keynote of modern existence is speed, which is relation of distance to time. It is significant that "speed" originally had the meaning of "success"; western civilization measures success today by the increase in the rate of movement towards some spatial point or towards some goal we set up before us. Achievement is estimated in terms of the length of time taken to accomplish our purposes, for time is money, and in a changing universe we have no time to waste or lose.[37]

So, for example, as a result of increased mobility, we move through a large number of high-stimulation environments and travel in and out of various time zones, both of which throw the body's rhythms out of sequence. Shift and night work, increasing in all industrialized countries in the name of efficiency, is upsetting the fundamental pattern of work by day and sleep by night. Previously many kinds of work were taken up and laid down according to opportunity, monthly cycles, and the seasons, and people tended to carry out a variety of tasks; nowadays the work has to be done irrespective of variable factors, and most people do the same thing day in and day out. As mentioned earlier, the compulsive, heightened, and regulated rhythms of many work situations also carry over into the free time of many people. In particular, genuine restful-ness—with the opportunity it offers for disassociation, meditation, contemplation, and reflection—has become increasingly rare. So too, as Johan Huizinga and Joseph Pieper remind us, have genuine play and lei-sure, with all their crucial cultural by-products.[38] In fact, for many people in our society, movement itself, an addiction to "doing" or "pace," has become an end in itself. Instead of being a means for reach-ing some goal, it has become a substitute for having an aim in life.

The study of biological rhythms has unearthed a fascinating amount of information about how our bodies work and the connection between them and the temporal rhythms of our environment.[39] But to date this has not made much inroad into the work situation of the majority of people. From a theological point of view the link between creature and creation is fundamental, and it has a temporal dimension. The creation has major circadian, monthly, seasonal, and annual rhythms as well as a great variety of minor ones, and these rhythms are also planted in our bodies. We function best when we live in accord with these rhythms, and not with some uniform, generally fast-paced, speed. We are capable of over-riding these natural rhythms and sometimes find it legitimate to do so. We have also been freed from an unhelpful determinism by some of these rhythms. However, if we remove ourselves too much from them, they take their revenge and we suffer fatigue, illness, or breakdown. This consequence suggests that we need an "ecology" of *time* to match the emerging respect for the intricate eco-system of the *environment* that has taken place in recent years.[40] Among other things, such an ecology of time should help us establish a proper balance between rest and work, that is, taking note of the "sabbath principle" at a weekly, annual, and life-stage level. It should help us alternate slower and faster rhythms of work and leisure, corresponding to the alternating speeds at which God is said to work in human lives and affairs. It should help us create room for flexibility as well as order in the way we arrange our time, parallel-ing the freedom and form built into the main institutions and celebrations of Israelite and early Christian life. An approach to time-use along these lines would benefit us more than the resort to mystical attitudes towards time implicit in so much stress-management and meditation today. At the occupational level the mystical approach leads people to compensate for activism, not challenge it or the structures that engender it. At the private level it encourages people to seek for "*timeless*" experiences discon-nected from their daily responsibilities rather than enter a new and "*timeful*" reality that, at one and the same time, refreshes and transforms everyday existence. So far as I am aware, only the Judaeo-Christian understanding of time enables the latter.

The Subversion of Time

We need to take further the analysis of individual goals, priorities, and values undertaken earlier. Attempts have been made to do this from both a psychological and sociological perspective. In going beyond the approach of Fromm here, the work, inter alia, of the Swiss psychologist Paul Tournier and the Australian sociologist John Carroll may be mentioned. The former explores the connection between guilt and activism, the latter the connection between consumption and the quest for transcendence.[41] A theological perspective is explicit in the one and implicit in the other. Let me attempt to sharpen it. One major catalyst of the "having" or "doing" as opposed to "being" or "becoming" mode of life is "insecurity." We live in an insecure age and our age is full of very insecure people. These people feel insecure about themselves—who they are, what their roots are, and where they are heading. They also feel insecure about others' attitudes towards and acceptance of them. If this uncertainty does not paralyse them—and therefore lead to procrastination—it can provoke them into a restless doing, through which they hope to find their own identity, justify their lives to themselves, and gain social acceptance. A second major catalyst of the activism that characterizes our age, whether it aims at possessions, power, and prestige or engages with issues, causes, and organizations, is "fear." This fear has many faces. There is fear of oneself, leading to an unwillingness to remain still long enough to discover something that one is unwilling to confront. There is the fear of loneliness, which constantly doing something, or the company of others, attempts to keep at bay. There is the fear of failure, resulting in a perfectionist approach to work and a tendency towards workaholism. There is the fear of death: since this is too terrible to contemplate, it is better to keep as busy as possible. Of course there are other catalysts of activism apart from these, for example, an over-refined sense of obligation, too highly developed a view of one's indispensability.

A theological perspective locates the root of this insecurity and fear—or the sense of obligation and indispensability—in the absence, underdevelopment, or distortion of a relationship with God. "We are restless," as Augustine said "until we find our rest in Thee." From a theological point of view it is only in God that people discover fully who they are and come to appreciate their full dignity.[42] However, in our so-called enlightened world such a belief is less frequent than was once the case. Indeed, it was partly the post-Puritan rejection of the view that God fully justified and accepted the individual through Christ's work that provoked the attempt by many people to justify themselves, and to seek others' acceptance, through their own work instead. It is here that the socalled Protestant work ethic has its ideological origins, not in the Puritans themselves but in the attitudes of the religiously lapsing, upwardly mobile middle class of the period. The modern experiment, already so penetratingly analyzed by Kierkegaard, encourages people to distract themselves from themselves, to avoid being by themselves, to secure themselves against failure, or to insulate themselves against thoughts of death through burying themselves in activities of varied kinds. But theologically speaking, it is precisely through recognizing and confronting human weakness that divine power becomes available to transform it into strength. It is through coming to terms with one's essential alienation that the capacity is given to commit oneself to others. It is through the experience of failure and doubt that achievement and confidence eventually come. It is through the reality of death that new life begins, life that has an eternal quality to it.[43]

From a theological point of view, therefore, the deeply rooted insecurity and fear in our society are due not merely to an intellectual, social, or psychological but ultimately to a spiritual loss of nerve. It is the weakening or loss of this perspective, or the preoccupation with it at the expense of the others and thus falsification of it, that lies at the base of our problems with time today. Once such things as activism, addictive busyness, time-regulation, and speeded-up social change become widespread phenomena, however, they begin to become autonomous. Theology recognizes the enormous power such forces can obtain, power that is capable of manipulation by other forces, too mysterious to identify, that work against humanity, even if their effect is diminished and their days are numbered by the cosmic implications of the divine breakthrough into our history.[44]

Conclusion

I have only two things to add. As has become increasingly apparent in this paper, our problems with time are only symptomatic of other problems. Those other problems are intrinsic to the kind of society we inhabit—with its accompanying world view, technology, and social organization—and the kind of people we are—at the level of both conscious desires and unconscious drives. It is not over-regulation by the clock, too busy a lifestyle, or rapid social change that fundamentally bedevils us, but rather the intellectual, technological, socio-economic, psychological, and above all spiritual conditions that have brought this situation into being. Only as we confront these conditions—all of them, not just this one or that—and do something about them, can we make any progress in the area of time. But to penetrate to their core and have the ability to change them we require greater discernment and power than we possess ourselves, whether as individuals, groups, institutions, or societies. As Jacques Ellul says: "We can redeem the time only if we conduct ourselves in these times . . . with a wisdom in that hope which comes . . . from revelation. Then, and only then, is time set on its true course."[45]

This brings me to my second, and final, point. Unfashionable though it is to say so in an academic context, despite Marx's reminder about the true goal of philosophy and Jesus' emphasis upon the primacy of doing over merely knowing the truth, it is imperative that we go beyond analyzing the situation to concretely transforming it. For it is the very quality of what it means to be human that is at stake. As a corollary of turning time into a commodity, into something numerical and quantifiable, into a purely instrumental and technological affair, the status of the self is in danger of becoming of "purely instrumental, technological value, just like any other commodity. Caught within the formidable pressure of time, and the social world . . . the self is reduced to the status of what it can provide, accomplish and achieve."[46]

Increasingly we ourselves are being talked about as a resource and treated as a commodity. Increasingly we are being treated as numerical and quantifiable. Increasingly we are being regarded as instrumental to some corporate or national end, and as a necessary, even expendable, component in a technological universe. It was said of the Victorian Age— and it was said as a compliment—that it produced people who were "as regular as clockwork." They had adapted so well to the mechanism around which their society revolved that they had become like machines themselves. Our danger is that, no less clockwork in our habits and becoming smaller and ever more interchangeable units in the social machine—a number on a card, a statistic in a report, a case in a file, an entry in a computer— many of us will find ourselves wound up with nothing to do, left on the shelf to stand and stare at the precisely timed, automatically controlled technical and bureaucratic machines we have created.

Notes

1. L. Mumford, *Technics and Civilisation* (New York: Harcourt, Brace, 1934), 14. More generally, see D. S. Landes, *Revolution in Time: Clocks and the Making of the Modern World* (Cambridge, Mass.: Belknap, 1983).

2. See further G. A. Woolcock, "The Tyranny of the Clock," in *An Introduction to Social Science*, ed. A. Naftalin et al. (Chicago: Lippincott, 1953). From a different perspective, see the overlapping conclusions of J. Rifkin, *Time Wars: The Primary Conflict in Human History* (New York: Holt, 1987).

3. On the question of working hours, see J. O. Owen, *Working Hours: An Economic Analysis* (Toronto: Lexington, 1979) for the North American situation; M. A. Bienfeld, *Working Hours in British Industry: An Economic History* (London: Weidenfeld & Nicholson, 1979); and for Australia, J. P. Robinson and P. E. Converse, "Social Change as Reflected in the Use of Time," in *The Human Meaning of Social Change*, ed. A. E. Campbell and P. E. Converse (New York: Russell Sage Foundation, 1972), 46–61. (More generally, see A. A. Evans, *Hours of Work in Industrialised Countries* [Geneva: International Labour Organisation, 1975].)

4. For an interesting comparison of the situation today and a century ago, see S. de Grazia, *Time, Work and Leisure* (New York: Doubleday, 1964), 62–71.

5. The work of H. Selye, e.g., *The Stress of Life* (London: Longmans Green, 1956) and *Stress Without Distress* (London: Hodder & Stoughton, 1974), is fundamental here, but there are now many writings on this question, e.g., L. Levi, *Stress: Sources, Management and Prediction* (New York: Liveright, 1967); M. Friedman and R. H. Rosenman, *Type A Behaviour and Your Heart* (New York: Knopf, 1974), and R. L. Woolfolk and F. L. Richardson, *Stress: Sanity and Survival* (London: Futura, 1979).

6. See further J. Holt, *Escape from Childhood: The Needs and Rights of Children* (New York: Dutton, 1974), 32–33, and F. Hirsch, *The Social Limits to Growth* (London: Routledge & Kegan Paul, 1976), 77–78.

7. As the well-documented downturn of people attending artistic productions and churches or synagogues indicates.

8. See R. Banks, *The Tyranny of Time* (Downer's Grove: IVF, 1983).

9. A useful recent attempt, by various authors, to present a phenomenological view of time is H. M. Yaker, H. Osmond, and F. Cheek, eds. *The Future of Time: Man's Temporal Environment* (London: Hogarth, 1972).

10. On this development see generally C. Cipolla, *Clocks and Culture, 1300–1700* (London: Collins, 1967); R. Glasser, *Time in French Life and Thought* (Manchester: Manchester University Press, 1972); and G. J.

Whitrow, *Time in History: Views of Time From Prehistory to the Present Day* (New York: Oxford University Press, 1988).

11. See F. C. Haber, "The Darwinian Revolution in the Concept of Time," in *The Study of Time*, ed. J. T. Fraser, F. C. Haber, and G. Müller (New York: Springer, 1972).

12. A. Mendilow, "The Time Obsession of the Twentieth Century," in *Aspects of Time*, ed. C. A. Patrides (Manchester: Manchester University Press, 1976), 73.

13. See the definition in I. Newton, *Principia Mathematica, Definitions*, Scholium I (Berkeley and Los Angeles: University of California Press, 1962), I, 6.

14. On Bentham see, inter alia, the fine discussion in E. Halévy, *The Growth of Philosophic Radicalism* (London: Faber & Faber, 1952).

15. On time and motion studies there is a helpful anthology, edited by A. Tillett, T. Kempner, and G. Wills, *Management Thinkers* (Harmondsworth: Penguin, 1970), 75–197. See also J. P. Clark, "Temporal Inventories and Time Structuring in Large Organisations," in *The Study of Time III*, ed. J. T. Fraser, N. Lawrence, and D. Park (New York: Springer, 1978), 391–418.

16. See W. Kerr, *The Decline of Pleasure* (New York: Simon & Schuster, 1965).

17. J. M. Brohm, *Sport—A Prison of Measured Time* (London: Ink Links, 1978).

18. Interesting here is M. P. Nilsson, *Primitive Time Reckoning* (Lund: Gleerup, 1920).

19. On what follows see, inter alia, K. Welch, *Time Measurement: An Introductory History* (Newton Abbott: David & Charles, 1972).

20. The phrase was used by M. Melbin, "The Colonisation of Time," in *Human Spacing and Human Time II: Human Activity and Time Geography*, ed. T. Carlstein, O. Parker, and N. Thrift (London: Edward Arnold, 1978).

21. A fundamental text here is that of E. P. Thompson, "Time, Work-Discipline and Industrial Capitalism," in *Essays in Social History*, ed. M. W. Flinn and T. C. Smoot (Oxford: Clarendon, 1974), even though he tends to exaggerate the Puritan preparation for later industrial attitudes. See also S. de Grazia, *Time, Work and Leisure*, 181ff. on the development from agricultural to industrial patterns of time.

22. J. Ellul, *The Technological Society* (New York: Random House, 1964).

23. E. Fromm, *To Have or To Be* (London: Cape, 1978).

24. S. B. Linder, *The Harried Leisure Class* (New York: Columbia University,

1970), and the development of his argument by F. Hirsch, *The Social Limits to Growth*, 74.

25. Th. Veblen, *The Theory of the Leisure Class* (London: Unwin, 1970), 60-79.

26. See S. Terkel, *Working: People Talk About What They Do All Day & How They Feel About What They Do* (London: Wildwood House, 1975), passim.

27. R. Banks, *The Tyranny of Time*, 171-72. Further to this see A. Th. van Leeuwen, *Christianity in World History* (London: Edinburgh House, 1964).

28. E.g., P. Drucker, *The Effective Executive* (London: Pan, 1970), 26-27, or E. C. Bliss, *Getting Things Done: The ABC's of Time Management* (New York: Scribner, 1976), 104.

29. As G. M. Lebhar, *The Use of Time* (New York: Chain Store, 1958), vi, 14, 124.

30. R. Baxter, *A Christian Directory* (London: 1673), 274-77, and John Wesley, "On Redeeming the Time," in *The Works of John Wesley* (London: Cordeaux, 1811), 181.

31. B. Franklin, "Poor Richard's Almanac," in *The Papers of Benjamin Franklin*, ed. L. W. Labaree and W. J. Bell (New Haven: Yale University Press, 1961), 86-87.

32. On the use of this metaphor for time, see G. Lakoff and M. Johnson, *Metaphors We Live By* (Chicago: University of Chicago Press, 1980), 6-8.

33. See Marx's comments to Engels in his letter dated January 28, 1863, in *Karl Marx and Friedrich Engels: Selected Correspondence 1846-1895* (New York: International Publishers, 1942), 42, and the conclusion of J. T. Fraser in *The Study of Time II*, ed. J. T. Fraser and N. Lawrence (Berlin: Springer, 1975), 337.

34. Some of the best writing on time as a gift, and on the importance of celebrating time, may be found in A. Heschel, *The Sabbath: Its Meaning for Modern Man* (New York: Farrar, Strauss, 1951). See also M. J. Dawn, *Keeping the Sabbath Wholly: Ceasing, Resting, Embracing, Feasting* (Grand Rapids, Mich.: Eerdmans, 1989).

35. Relevant here are the works of R. Glasser, *Time in French Life and Thought*; D. H. Higdon, *Time and English Fiction* (London: Macmillan, 1977); J. H. Buckley, *The Triumph of Time: A Study of Victorian Concepts of Time, History, Progress and Decadence* (Cambridge, Mass.: Belknap, 1967); and, more generally, H. Meyerhoff, *Time in Literature* (Berkeley and Los Angeles: University of California Press, 1960). For a contemporary example of the attitudes explored in these works, see R. Grudin, *Time and the Art of Living* (San Francisco: Harper & Row, 1982).

36. Corrections to one-sided, purely qualitative understanding of time in the biblical writings as, for example, in J. Marsh, *The Fulness of Time* (Lon-

don: Nisbet, 1952), were made by J. Barr, *Biblical Words for Time* (London: SCM, 1962). Quite magisterial is S. de Vries, *Yesterday, Today and Tomorrow: Time and History in the Old Testament* (London: SPCK, 1975). There is nothing comparable on the New Testament, though see O. Cullmann, *Christ and Time: The Primitive Christian Conception of Time and History* (London: SCM, 1951), but only in light of criticisms by J. Barr, *Semantics of Biblical Language* (Oxford: Oxford University Press, 1961), esp. 46–88.

37. A. A. Mendilow, "The Time Obsession of the Twentieth Century," 73.

38. T. Huizinga, *Homo Ludens* (London: Paladin, 1970), and J. Pieper, *Leisure: The Basis of Culture* (London: Faber, 1952).

39. Excellent introductions are provided by G. G. Luce, *Body Time: The Natural Rhythms of the Body* (St. Alban's: Paladin, 1973), and by D. Saunders, *An Introduction to Biological Rhythms* (Glasgow: Blackie, 1977).

40. One might begin to do this from the material discussed by H. Wolff, *Anthropology of the Old Testament* (London: SCM, 1974), 119ff.

41. P. Tournier, *Guilt and Grace: A Psychological Study* (New York: Harper & Row, 1962), and J. Carroll, *Sceptical Sociology* (London: Routledge & Kegan Paul, 1980), 95–105.

42. C. S. Lewis, "The Weight of Glory," in *Screwtape Proposes a Toast* (London: Collins, 1965), 109.

43. See J. Moltmann, *Theology and Joy* (London: SCM, 1970), 69.

44. See further H. Berkhof, *Christ and the Powers*, trans. J. H. Yoder (Scottdale, Pa.: Herald, 1962).

45. J. Ellul, *Hope in a Time of Abandonment* (New York: Seabury, 1972), 232.

46. H. Meyerhoff, *Time in Literature*, 114–15.

Time and Life's Meaning

RICHARD TAYLOR

IT HAS BEEN characteristic of metaphysics, since the beginning of philosophy, to deny the reality of time. The characteristics ascribed to it by unreflective people, particularly that of passage, have seemed so puzzling and paradoxical that the metaphysical temperament has preferred to banish time altogether rather than embrace those paradoxes. Thus Parmenides, the earliest metaphysician, denied reality to all time and becoming, leaving his bleak and changeless conception of reality to be perfected by his pupil Zeno. Plato, too, declared that reality can only be the eternal, describing the strange passage of time in which we mortals live as nothing but that eternity's moving image. Among modern philosophers Spinoza sounded the same note, being unable to think of any reality in which time, by itself, could make a difference, while Immanuel Kant reduced it to a mere form of sensibility. Among recent thinkers McTaggart comes at once to mind, with his proofs that the concept of time is simply self-contradictory.

Time, which seems to move, but in only one direction and at no assignable rate, *is* paradoxical, to be sure, but no declaration of its unreality can alter the fact that we feel it. With each setting sun we see our lives shortened, see the events that we felt so lively just moments ago begin receding into a fading past, gone forever. And with each rising sun we see hopes unfold in fulfillment or, perhaps more often, collapse with finality, to be replaced by new ones. These things are too close to us, too keenly felt, to be declared illusory. To suggest that our rejoicings and sorrowings rest upon illusion, out of deference to metaphysical requirements, would seem to rob our lives of all meaning.

A few philosophical thinkers, aware of this, and starting from experience rather than reason, have found in time and its passage the most basic of realities, real to the point of being unalterable in its course and

THE CONCEPT OF TIME

in its effects. Henri Bergson comes at once to mind, with his notorious declaration that "time eats into things and leaves on them the mark of its tooth." The metaphor is an outrage to reason, but perfectly captures the way time is felt. We feel it eating into things, into ourselves, and its marks are all too visible. We are, it has often been noted, the only beings in creation who can contemplate in thought our own graves, make plans upon that anticipated calamity, and, it should be added, can actually sense its approach.

Time, then, it would seem, is very real to contemplative beings. But I am going to go farther than this, suggesting that time is not merely something to be understood and described, as has been done by number-less philosophers and poets. Time, I shall contend, has little significant reality except in the context of beings who not only think and feel, but who *create*. It is this capacity for creation that not only gives time its most fundamental meaning, but gives our lives whatever meaning they have, as well.

Time in a Lifeless World

To begin to see this, let us think of the whole of inanimate reality, that is, the entire world, considered as devoid of life. It is a world without history or meaning. What happens in that world has happened before and, considering any event by itself, it makes no difference when it happens, nor even any sense to assign it a date. Time is here irrelevant. The earth turns, for example, but it makes not the least difference whether a given rotation is the millionth, or hundred millionth. Each turning is the same as the others, and no assigning of a number to this one or that has any significance. And so it is with everything else that happens in that lifeless world. A mountain rises gradually and is gradu-ally eroded, but it makes no difference when this happens. And raindrops fall, but that a given raindrop should fall at one time rather than at another does not matter, nor is it even easy to make such temporal dis-tinctions. Each drop is just like any other, and no newness is introduced by supposing that it falls earlier, or later, or even millions of years earlier or later. Such a world is without novelty. Combinations of events might occur which occur at no other time, to be sure, but they are already contained in what has gone before. What happens is but a conse-quence of what has already happened. Such a world could not, to any god contemplating it and capable of understanding it, contain any sur-prises. Nothing, in short, would ever be created in such a world. There would be novelties of sorts—for example, a snowflake that resembled no other—but these would not be creations in any sense. They would be but novel combinations of what already existed and then pointlessly fell into those combinations. That lifeless world, in short, resembles a clockwork, but one from which the moving hands are missing. What interests us about a clock is that it tells time, but the lifeless world we are now imagining tells us nothing of the sort. On the contrary, the very image of it is enough to exclude considerations of time. The god we imagined a moment ago would discover nothing from the prolonged contemplation of such a world other than what he already knew, and what he could anticipate in it would be nothing not already implicit in his memories of it. Time, to be sure, would exist for such a god—otherwise his contemplation could not be prolonged nor would it make sense to speak of his memories. But then, by introducing such a being we have, of course, abandoned our premise of a lifeless world.

Life and Time

Let us next, then, add to this lifeless world, in our imaginations, the whole of living creation, excluding only rational beings, that is to say, beings like ourselves who are in the broadest sense capable not only of understanding, but of creative thought and action. What we have now is still a world without history. Except for the long and gradual changes wrought by biological evolution, nothing new or different occurs in this world. The sun that rises one day illuminates nothing that was not there the day before, or a thousand or million days before. It is simply the same world, age after age. The things in it exactly resemble those that went before. Every sparrow is just like every other, does exactly the same things in the same way without innovation, then to be imitated by every sparrow to follow. The robin or squirrel you see today does nothing different from those you saw as a child, and could be inter-changed with them without discernible difference. Each creature arises and lives out its cycle with an invariance that is almost as fixed as the clockwork we imagined a moment ago, and it is, again, a clockwork without hands. That such a creature should live today or a hundred years hence makes no difference. There are days in this world, but no dates. And each such creature then perishes, leaving it behind nothing whatsoever except more of the same kind, which will do the same things again, and beget the same, these unchanging cycles then to be repeated over and over, forever.

Time as Something Felt

The introduction of living things into our imaginary world has, however, resulted in one significant difference, and that is the rudimentary *sense* of time, at least among some creatures. Irrational beings do not, of course, contemplate in thought their own graves, reflectively make provision for their descendants, mark anniversaries and so on, but they must nevertheless sometimes feel time's passage. A trapped animal feels its life ebbing and senses the approach of death, and perhaps birds, however mechanical or instinctive their behaviour may be, have some anticipation of what is going to be done with the nests they build. Our pets anticipate their meals and look forward to them, and possibly the hours drag for them when we leave them alone for the day.

So to that extent time has, in a significant sense, been introduced into our world by the addition to it of living things. But there still remains this huge difference, that these creatures have no history. Each does today what was done by those that went before, and will be done by those to come. The world we are imagining thus resembles an endless play in which the acts are all identical. Every stage setting is the same as every other, the lines spoken are the same, the costumes the same, and the things done the same. Only the actors change, but none introduces any innovation. It would make no difference to any audience which act they saw, nor would there be any point in numbering the acts, or noting which followed which.

The world just described is not, of course, an imaginary one. It is the very world we live in, considered independently of ourselves and our place in it. It is a world in which there is a before and after—the sun, for example, must have risen in order to set—and it is one in which the passage of time is felt. Yet it is timeless in another significant sense, that it has neither history nor meaning. Its meaninglessness is precisely the meaninglessness of the play we were just imagining. There is never any-thing new, no purpose, no goal; in a word, nothing is ever created.

An Ancient Image of Meaninglessness

This sense of eternal meaninglessness was perfectly captured by the ancients in the myth of Sisyphus. Sisyphus, it will be recalled, was condemned by the gods to roll a stone to the top of a hill, whereupon it would roll back to the bottom, to be moved to the top once more by Sisyphus, then to roll back again, and so on, over and over, throughout eternity. Here, surely, is existence reduced to utter meaninglessness. Nor does that lack of meaning arise from the onerousness of Sisyphus's task. It would not be redeemed if the task were made easier, by representing the stone as a very small one, for example. Nor does that meaning-lessness emerge from the sheer boredom of the task. It would still be there even if we imagined Sisyphus to rejoice in it—if we imagined, for example, that he had a compulsive and insatiable desire to roll stones, and considered himself blessed to be able to do this forever.

The meaninglessness exhibited in this myth is precisely the meaning-lessness of the world as it has been described up to this point; namely, that of a world without history, a world that is in this significant sense devoid of time. It is, like the cycles of Sisyphus, a world of endless and pointless repetition.

The Introduction of Meaningfulness

If we now modify the story of Sisyphus in certain ways we can take the cru-cial step needed to transform it from an image of meaninglessness to one of meaning. In so doing, we can finally see what is needed to give the world and human existence, or the life of any individual person, meaning.

Let us first suppose, then, that Sisyphus does not roll the same stone over and over again to the top, but moves a different stone each time, each stone then remaining at the top of the hill. Does this make a differ-ence? Hardly. One stone does not differ from another, so what Sisyphus is now doing is essentially what he was doing before, rolling a stone, over and over, to the top of a hill. The stones, for all we know, merely accumulate there as a huge and growing pile of rubble.

So let us next imagine that this is not so, that the stones, having been moved to the top of the hill, are one by one, over a long period of time, assembled into something beautiful and lasting—a great temple, we might suppose. Has Sisyphus's existence now gained meaning? In a sense it has, for his labour is no longer wasted and pointless. Something important does come of it all. But that existence might still be totally meaningless to Sisyphus, for what we have imagined is consistent with supposing that he is totally ignorant of what is happening, that he is aware only of roll-ing stones, one after the other endlessly, with no notion at all of what becomes of them, the temple being entirely the work of others and out of his sight and ken. From his point of view, then, nothing has changed at all. We next imagine, then, that this latter is not so, that Sisyphus sees the fruit of his toil gradually take shape, is aware of its importance and beauty, and thus has at least the satisfaction of understanding what is happening and realizing that what he does is not totally in vain. Something important does come of it all, something that is great and beautiful, and it is something that is understood.

Now have we invested his existence with meaning? In a sense we have, for Sisyphus has been converted from a mere beast of burden to a being who understands. But there is still a lot missing. For what we have now have before us is consistent with the idea that Sisyphus is a mere slave, a rational slave up to a point, to be sure, but still one who goes through endless and repetitive motions over which he has no choice, these being entirely dictated by others, and for a result in which he has no hand, but can only passively observe. To revert to our image of the endlessly repetitive stage play, Sisyphus is here like an actor whose luck it is to be cast in the leading role, but with this difference, that an actor can at least reject the role. Such an existence is not without fulfilment of a sort, but we must remember that it still corresponds to the meaningless and, in a significant sense, timeless existence into which the whole of animal creation is cast. The vast array of living cycles today resemble those of a thousand years ago, and those of a thousand years hence. Nature, so conceived, is not without grandeur and beauty, just as we can imagine the temple that rises from Sisyphus's labours to have the same qualities. But that image still lacks an essential ingredient of meaningfulness, unless, of course, we are willing to ascribe a fully meaningful existence to a merely productive machine, or to a slave who has no voice whatsoever in his own fate or even his own actions from one moment to the next.

One final modification is needed, then, and that is to imagine that Sisyphus not only moves this prodigious quantity of stones to the top of the hill, but that he does so for the very purpose of seeing them converted to a beautiful and lasting temple and, most important of all, that this temple is something of his own, the product of his own creative mind, that it is of his own conception, something which, but for his own creative thought and imagination, would never have existed at all.

Creation, Meaning and Time

It is at this point, then, that the idea of a fully meaningful existence emerges, for the first time. It is inseparable from the concept of creativity. And it is exactly this that was missing from everything we have imagined up until now. Nature, however beautiful and awesome, exhibits nothing of creative activity until we include in it rational beings, that is, beings who can think, imagine, plan, and execute things of worth, beings who are, in the true sense, originators or creators. Rational beings do not merely foresee what will be; they sometimes determine what will be. They do not, like the rest of creation, merely wait to see what nature will thrust upon them. They sometimes impose upon nature herself their own creations, sometimes creations of great and lasting significance.

Rational beings are the very creators of time itself, in the historical sense, for without them there would be only a meaningless succession of things and no history at all. An animal can, perhaps, anticipate its own death, as can a person. And an animal can bring about works, sometimes of considerable beauty and complexity, as can a person. But what the animal thus does has been done in exactly that way millions of times before. One thinks of the complex beauty of the spider's web, the intricate basketry of the oriole's nest, the ingenious construction of the honeycomb—all things of impressive intricacy, sometimes arresting and marvellous, but also things that disclose not the least hint of creative power. They are, like Sisyphus's labours, only endless repetitions. Human beings, or at least some of them, are capable of going a crucial step further.

What a creative mind brings forth is never something merely learned or inherited, nor is it merely something novel, like the snowflake that resembles no other. It is what a creative mind intends it to be, something to which the notions of success or failure can apply, and sometimes something of such extraordinary originality that no other person, not even a god, no one but its very creator, could ever have foreseen it. And if that creative mind possesses, in addition to this, the rare quality of creative genius, then what is wrought is not merely something that others could neither do nor foresee, it is something they could not even imagine. Thus we see the aptness of Schopenhauer's dictum, that while talent is the ability to hit a target that others miss, genius is the ability to hit a target that others do not even see.

The ancients, in their philosophies, were fond of describing their gods as rational. This idea of divine rationality has persisted among metaphysicians, but the concept of rationality has become narrowed. We think of rationality as care and precision in thought, a due regard for evidence and consistency, and sometimes as mere restraint in conduct. But the ancients quite properly associated it with the contemplative life in the broadest sense. The creation of things beautiful, profound, and unprecedented expressed for them the essence of human rationality. Sisyphus displayed his ultimate rationality, not merely in understanding what he was doing—something that would be within the power of a mere slave—but, as we have modified the myth, in the display of strength and genius that took the form of a beautiful and lasting temple, born first in his own imagination. That was something

THE CONCEPT OF TIME

that no mere slave, and indeed no mere human being, and in fact no other being under the sun except this one, could ever have done. The creative genius of a particular person is something that by its very nature cannot be shared. To the extent that it is shared, such that what it brings forth is also brought forth by others, then it is not only not genius, it is not even a creative power. It is but the capacity for fabrication, which, however striking it may be, is quite common throughout nature.

The Creation of Things Great and Small

Lest the impression be given that the creative thought and work that I am here praising is something rare, the possession of only a few, let it be noted that it exists in degrees and is, in one form or another, far from rare. What is rare, I think, the proper appreciation of it. We tend to think of creative works as spectacular achievements, particularly in the arts, but in fact the human capacity to create something new is sometimes found in quite mundane things. Thus, for example, the establishment of a brilliant position in a game of chess is a perfect example of creativity, even though the result is of little value. Things as common as gardening, woodworking and the like give scope to the originality of those who have the knack for them, and are probably the most constant source of life's joys. Intelligent, perhaps witty conversation and the composition of clear and forceful prose are just as good examples of creativity as the making of a poem of great beauty or depth of meaning, however much they may differ in worth. My own favourite example of a creative work, and one whose value as a creation is rarely appreciated, is the raising of a beautiful family, something that is reserved for the relatively few who can, as a natural gift, do it well. Of course, the mere begetting of children is no act of creation at all. It is something that can be done by anyone. And other creatures sometimes with great skill convert their young to self-sufficient adults. They succeed, however, only to the extent that these young exactly resemble themselves, whereas rational human parents should measure their success by the degree to which their children become self-sufficient and capable adults who do *not* resemble themselves, but express instead their own individualities. This is an art that is neither common nor easily learned.

Two Opposing Conceptions of Meaningful Existence

It would be gratifying if, in the light of what I have been saying, we could now rest upon the comfortable conclusion that our lives derive their meaning from the fact that human beings, and they alone, impose a history upon nature, that the world does not merely persist from age to age, nor does it merely change in the manner of the endless recurrences we see throughout the rest of creation, but that changes are imposed upon it by the creative power of humankind. That would be true, but too general, for in truth, creative power is not something particularly sought and prized by most people. Our culture has taught us to regard all persons as of equal worth, and religion tells us that this is even God's estimate. Indeed, we are taught that we are, each and every one, created in the very image of that God, so that no one can claim for oneself more importance than anyone else. Our lives, it is implied, are invested with great meaning just by virtue of our common humanity. We need only to be born, and our worth is once for all assured. We are, to be sure, set apart from the remainder of creation, according to this tradition, but what sets us apart is not necessarily anything we do. We are set apart by what is merely given to us, so that a human life, and a valuable and meaningful life, are presumed to be the one and the same.

That conception of meaningful existence, which is so familiar, is very sadly at variance with the conception of meaningful existence that I have developed. For in truth, creative power is no common possession. Creative genius is in fact rare. The work of the vast majority of persons does not deviate much from what others have already done and from what can be found everywhere. There seems even to be a determination in most people that this should be so, a determination to pattern their lives after others, to seek as little originality and individual self-worth as possible. People tend, like apes, to mimic and imitate what they already find, absorbing the ideas, manners, values, even, indeed, their religions, from those around them, as if by osmosis. They appropriate virtually everything, returning virtually nothing of their own creative power. The lives of most persons are like the clockwork to which I have so often alluded. They are born, pass through the several stages of life, indulging, for the most part, only trivial thoughts and feelings, absorbing pleasures and distractions, fleeing boredom, conceiving no significant works, and leaving almost nothing behind them. It would be sad enough if this were merely so. What is far sadder is that it is thought not really to matter. Religion then reinforces this by proclaiming that no one can, in God's sight, rise above others anyway, that the fool is already as blessed as the wise, and that the greatest possible human worth has already been bestowed upon us all by our merely being born. It is a hard notion to overcome, and weighs upon us like lead. It tends to render even the exemplary among us weak and hesitant.

We take much comfort in that part of the Bible, the very first book, which assures us that we are all the veritable images of God. We tend to overlook the first five words with which the Bible begins: "In the beginning,

THE CONCEPT OF TIME

God created. . . ." That the result of that act is heaven and earth may be overwhelming, but the emphasis is wrong if we dwell on that. What is signi-ficant is that the original description of God is as a *creator*. And it is this, surely, that endows one with the divine quality. That human beings exist is not, in itself, a significant fact. That this or that being is possessed of human form, or is of that biological species, is likewise of no significance, whatever may be the teaching of religion and custom to the contrary. What *is* signifi-cant, what gives any human existence its meaning, is the possibility that thus arises of creative power. But it is no more than a possibility, realized here and there, more or less, and fully realized only in exceptional persons.

In Praise of Greatness

One brings to consciousness the indescribable worth of creative power by imagining specific instances. Consider, for example, that on a given day the sun rose, as usual, and that throughout that day most of the world was much as it had been the day before, virtually all of its inhabitants doing more or less what they were accustomed to doing; but, in a minute part of that world, a nocturne of Chopin's came into being, or a sonata of Mozart's. On another day, otherwise much like any other, Lincoln composed his address for the visit to Gettysburg, or Matthew Arnold wrote the concluding lines of his *Dover Beach*, or Gray his *Elegy*, or Plato his *Symposium*. That a little-known woman gave birth to an infant in Malaga, Spain, one October day in 1881 means very little, but that the child was to become Picasso means much. And to complete this kind of imaginative exercise, one needs to fix in one's thought some significant creation—something—as small but priceless as a prelude of Chopin or a poem of Keats—and then realize that, if a parti-cular person had not at just that moment brought forth that utterly unprece-dented thing, then it would never have existed at all. The thought of a world altogether devoid of music or literature or art is the thought of a world that is dark indeed, but if one dwells on it, the thought of a world lacking a single one of the fruits of creative genius that our world actually possesses is a depressing one. That such a world would have been so easy, so inevi-table, but for a solitary person, at a single moment, is a shattering reflection. This, I think, is the verdict of philosophy. One wishes it were the theme of religion as well, for the voice of religion is always louder than that of philosophy. That a world should exist is not finally important, nor does it mean much, by itself, that people should inhabit it. But that some of these should, in varying degrees, be capable of creating worlds of their own and history, thereby creating time in its historical sense, is what gives our lives whatever meaning they have.

Change and Uncertainty

DAVID SKELTON

M Y PARTICULAR CONTRIBUTION to this volume focuses on the foundational approach to time. It is my task to consider the problem of change and uncertainty following on the philosophical approach to time by Richard Taylor and the theological approach by Robert Banks. Inevitably when one approaches such an analysis, the subject is perceived from a peculiarly personal perspective, and this of necessity influences the arguments developed and introduces a bias into the interpretations given, of which the listener or reader should be fully cognizant. I should perhaps therefore begin with a brief enlargement upon my own credentials, which will allow you to identify some of my prejudices and biases from the outset.

Firstly, I am a geriatrician: a physician engaged in the practice of the new (at least in Canada) specialty of geriatric medicine. This branch of general internal medicine is concerned with disease as it affects the more aged members of our society; their physical, emotional, social, and spiritual reactions to the pathological processes active within and upon them; the several factors integral to the prevention of illness and the maintenance of health; and the problems involved in the delivery of health care to this especially vulnerable section of the population.

Secondly, I am a university teacher and researcher, and as such I am responsible for the inculcation of appropriate knowledge and attitudes within a new generation of physicians and other health-care professionals. In this way I hope to contribute a little to the sound foundations upon which they will build their own professional lives, perhaps also to benefit indirectly those whom they serve, and even to reach beyond them to the minds of further-flung generations of students—as my teachers' teachers have influenced me. I am, however, continually haunted, as an educator, by the spectre of William Gerhardi's warning (to be found in his book

The Polyglots) that "there are as many fools at a University as else-where—but their folly, I admit, has a certain stamp—the stamp of university training, if you will. It is trained folly!"

Finally, I am an Anglican priest. Not, I hasten to add, a theologian, nor a philosopher, but rather a simple-minded Christian physician, commissioned within the church to fulfill a particular personal witness and ministry.

My bias is therefore not inconsiderable, for in some modest way, like Plato, my personal credo acknowledges the presence of a spiritual dimension that interdigitates powerfully and inextricably with our world—a world that is otherwise constrained by the material, the spatial, and the temporal limits with which we are all so familiar. I do not myself believe that our human existence is worked out exclusively within a closed rational and physical system, nor that our lives are influenced only by our experiences, our senses, or our intellect and reason. For me, and those like me, the ultimate reference point in our lives is God, and God may be said to represent for us the final "certainty." We believe that it is to God that we are ultimately accountable and that God is our creator, redeemer, and sustainer.

But what sort of "certainty" does this represent? Clearly it is not a certainty in the strictly scientific sense. It is not, and never will be, possible to prove the existence of God beyond all doubt by means of objective experimental methodology. For the theist, "certainty" is still an issue of faith. Therefore I would argue that I am as open-minded about the subject of change and uncertainty as the next person.

Gilbert Ryle said of Plato, "He was perhaps an unreliable Platonist, because he may be considered too great a philosopher to think that any-thing he said was the last word. It was left to his disciples to identify his footmarks with his destination." This could also be adopted as a desirable hallmark, if not an absolute prerequisite, of all Christian physicians (especially those without disciples) invited to lecture at universities—that they should be prepared for nothing they say to be taken as the last word on any subject. This cautionary note may of course be extended to all other lecturers and audiences alike.

Time in many ways remains one of the greatest mysteries known to humanity. In our modern world most of our sophisticated and highly integrated activities would be impossible without an ability to measure the passing of time with some considerable degree of accuracy. Since the earliest days of our species' existence, efforts appear to have been made to measure time, and today the precision of this measurement is almost beyond belief. Despite these advances, however, we cannot even now say exactly what time is.

SKELTON / Change and Uncertainty

If we could imagine a world existing totally without time, it would exist as an immutable, suspended or "frozen" environment. If a change did then occur in that timelessness, the world would be different than it had been before that alteration occurred. The period elapsing between the "now" and the "before," however brief, would indicate that time had indeed passed and timelessness had ceased to exist. It is therefore logical to assume that time and change may safely be considered to be intimately inter-related and generally inseparable.

To our forebears time probably appeared as a cyclical phenomenon. Changes occurred regularly and rhythmically; day proceeded to night and returned again to day; the sun and the moon followed each other through the heavens with a reassuring regularity. Season followed season in a predictable fashion and in a manner that allowed human life to continue. But this very changeability, inherent in the passage of time, we now know led to considerable uncertainty about its continued unalterability. What would happen to life if these cycles ceased? An indication of the degree of anxiety produced by such questions as this, reaches across the centuries to us as we unravel the details of the religious practices, sacrificial customs, and fertility rituals of earlier peoples.

Some events, however, must always have appeared to be once-and-once-only happenings: the leaf falling from a tree, or a life proceeding from birth through growth to maturation and then onward again by way of involution to death. In such circumstances the changes produced with time lacked a cyclical nature and could be perceived as a linear or asymmetric phenomenon. The individual affected by these changes appeared to be a player moving across a stage and highly vulnerable to change and chance, and consequently suffering the pangs of uncertainty regarding his fate.

Michael Guillen, a brilliant young mathematical physicist from Harvard, has recently pointed out that scientists, unlike artists, have always struggled to preserve a perfect symmetry in their theories. For the scientist symmetry makes for statistical perfection, since fundamental laws of behaviour or an inherent predictability may then be delineated. Scientifically speaking, therefore, a symmetrical universe is most desirable. If it were not spatially symmetrical, the earth's orbit around the sun would change its configuration as the solar system rotated about the Milky Way. This would disrupt the regular succession of seasons, possibly leading to conditions that would not, or could not, support human life. Chaos and irregularity would exist in place of highly ordered and predictable conditions. Yet our universe is certainly not symmetrical; indeed, asymmetry exists at the macroscopic, microscopic, and submicroscopic levels.

In 1964, I remember being greatly impressed by Bertrand Russell during a radio program carried on the British Broadcasting Corporation network in the United Kingdom. Russell stated that in his opinion what man really fundamentally desires is not knowledge but certainty. I have come to feel very deeply, through my professional experiences, that uncertainty is the root cause of much genuine suffering and morbid or anxious reflection among human beings. Perhaps also, if Bertrand Russell is correct, a primordial fear of—and inability to consciously deal with—uncertainty is a major driving force for all of our learning and enquiry.

Change, by definition, disrupts or disturbs the fixity or invariability of our surroundings and introduces unpredictability into our world, and may even threaten us with fallibility. Conscious or unconscious stresses are engendered in those who are aware of such changes, and these may have either positive or negative results. I use the analogy of a pendulum-driven grandfather clock (possibly an appropriate analogy for a gerontol-ogist) to illustrate this situation, in which the effect of gravity is likened to timelessness or total predictability; when no motion of the pendulum occurs, time is not noticeably passing and the system is physically at rest—immobile and safe. When the pendulum is set into motion, change obviously exists and time is seen to pass, as attested to by the movement of the hands on the clock face. A potential for failure has also been introduced into the system. It is true that the clock may run down or undergo some mechanical failure, but it is only when the pendulum swings that the clock's mechanism transforms that physical stress into a desirable end product.

So it is, I theorize, with change and uncertainty. Change will always produce some uncertainty, and since our human condition strives uncon-sciously for absolute predictability, stresses will be produced that allow us either to fail or to mature and develop. As a physician I have spent a large portion of my professional life helping people to deal with pain and dis-ease, in other words, helping them to reduce the impact upon them of negative influences. I believe this to be a most worthwhile objective in medicine, but I also now recognize how frequently we fail to appreci-ate and exploit the considerable positive potential that may exist in such circumstances. It is only when people deviate from their normally stable emotional "baseline" that they are stimulated to grow. If pressed, I would even suggest that it is only by way of pain, in its broadest sense, that we can grow at all. As Augustine wrote, "God whispers to me in my plea-sures, he speaks to me in my conscience, but he shouts to me in my pain."

Most psychologists would now agree that some degree of stress is necessary in our lives if we are to be normally functioning and resource-ful human beings; it is also true that excessive stress is harmful to our physical and emotional well-being. Under extremes of stress an individual may become destructive to himself and to those around him or perpetual in general. This clearly introduces a new consideration into our examination of change and uncertainty. This new dimension is the individual upon whom the stresses produced act.

I suggest that at least four factors relating to change must be considered when studying an individual's response to the stresses produced. First is the degree of change occurring; the more radical and extreme the change, the more stress developed, and the greater the chance that this will be disruptive and harmful to the individual. Second is the rate at which change occurs; the more rapid the change, the more likely the effects are to be adverse, and indeed, when extreme, such change may precipitate a crisis. Third is the predictability of the outcome of change; the stresses engendered depend upon the individual's previous experience of similar or related events. The acquired knowledge and inherent wisdom possessed by the individual are characteristics that will moderate the impact of uncertainty. A fourth factor is the influence or control that we have over the change; the extent of an individual's power to control a change in his environment is usually inversely related to the amount of stress that results from that change.

Our modern world is full of examples of extreme change, and often the rate at which these changes are occurring is unprecedented in the history of our species. Similarly, they are unique occurrences, never before witnessed by humankind, and most of us feel entirely powerless to influence their course or reduce their impact upon our lives and our society. Many of these illustrations will occur to you rapidly enough, but perhaps I can mention some of the more obvious: exhaustion of our mineral wealth, and deforestation; pollution of our atmosphere, waters, and land; the unequal distribution of food, wealth, and power, and the exploitation of populations; increasing technology with its attendant problems of rising unemployment, an enhanced capacity for self-destruction, and difficult ethical issues. Such changes produce stresses upon us that affect the ecological and environmental, the economic and political, and the scientific, social, and educational domains. No sphere of our human lives is inviolate from the onslaught. I suggest to you that these changes and their associated uncertainties are producing stresses of a magnitude never before experienced.

What then is our potential to respond adequately to this bleak and disturbing situation? I make no apology for my own belief that this question must be addressed at the level of the individual. It has become increasingly clear to me that no single political or organizational philosophy or system will provide satisfactory answers to these giant contemporary dilemmas; the greater the rhetoric proffered by proponents of such groups, the clearer their misconception or deliberate duplicity seems to become. My contention is that it is only when the individual is given an adequate opportunity to act, develops appropriate abilities, and conducts himself in an appropriate way, that these changes and this uncertainty will be mastered without destructive stresses being unleashed upon our society.

Because I am a geriatrician and gerontologist, the questions of opportunity and ability have a special significance to me. The accumulated resource of the experience and wisdom of our senior citizens lies largely untapped in the Western civilized world. This results in part from our societal attitudes and mores, and in part from inadequacies in planning and reward systems. Unfortunately, undisguised lack of interest is also a contributing factor. This nation's greatest natural resource is not to be found in its forests, its oceans, or its mineral wealth, but in its people. Unlike many others, I do not believe that it is the youth in our population who alone hold the key to the future, but rather that the major contributions can and should be made by the elderly. The young can be likened to a crude oil requiring further fractionation and refinement, whilst the elders are already a high-grade product.

I believe that, given the opportunity to react constructively to the stresses that present themselves to us, we have abilities equal to our problems. What causes me the greatest concern is whether we can conduct ourselves in ways commensurate with the need. Descartes based a philosophical argument and system upon the premise *cogito ergo sum*, but I believe that what we are is determined by what we see, what we do, and what we think—not by thinking alone. We cannot truly be ourselves apart from our relationships with ourselves, others, the world around us, and with God. It is in these relationships that our lives have true human value.

The most basic of our responses to time and to change and uncertainty is therefore at this individual level, and we should not feel impotent in the face of the stresses produced. I said earlier that those with the same belief system as myself view God as their creator, but most would agree that we have been charged with the role of co-creators with Him. As such, we have an incredible inherent dignity, and worth beyond imagining. This translates into every person's having rights—rights to ego-satisfaction, an independent identity, freedom, and security. Such a belief system, however, imposes on everyone great responsibilities—responsibilities not only for oneself but towards all of humanity, towards one's environment, and towards one's God.

As Henry Ward Beecher has said, "God asks no man whether he will accept life, that is not the choice. You must take it. The only choice is how." Or if you prefer not to invoke the deity, then you may feel more comfortable with the words of George Bernard Shaw, "Life is no brief candle to me, it is a sort of splendid torch which I have got hold of for the moment, and I want to make it burn as brightly as possible before handing it on to future generations."

II

FUNCTIONAL ACCOUNTS OF TIME

The Human Lifespan as a Functional Framework

DUNCAN ROBERTSON

W HILE SEARCHING FOR an appropriate point from which to embark on an exploration of the human lifespan as a functional framework, I was fortunate in locating a literary quotation that encapsulates the concept of time and the characteristics of an older person—all in a Saskatchewan setting! In the definitive biography of Sarah Binks—sweet songstress of Saskatchewan—Paul Hiebert says of Sarah's grandfather Thurnow, that for him:

The three dimensions of space were much more than abstractions; they were something to be lived, something to be realized in one's everyday life. . . . But in the matter of time he was a complete philosopher. Past, present, and future were inextricably blended, and his mastery of them was such that he was able to use all three of them interchangeably.[1]

In this paper I shall first touch on the "ages and stages" of the human lifespan, present some descriptions of stages of life from English literature, and extend these observations of human aging with contemporary biomedical observations. In the body of the paper I will address the concept of lifespan, and how the near conquest of major infectious diseases has changed human life expectancy. I shall conclude with a glimpse of what the future may hold in a "rectangular society," of which more later, and present some of the ways in which our university can prepare for life in such a society.

Until the middle of this century, human growth and development were viewed by many as processes that commenced in embryonic life and continued into post-natal life with increments in stature and strength and the acquisition of functional competence. The passage from dependence to independence, the establishment of reproductive capacity, and the attainment of a "plateau" in measurable physical and psychological indices marked the onset of adulthood—the endpoint of development. Late adulthood has no place in this schema. Old age was viewed as a state quite apart from growth and development, a state inseparable from disease.

Old age has been viewed as a pathologic state by writers from Seneca, who considered "old age a disease which we cannot cure," through to Metchnikoff, who considered old age to be "an infectious chronic disease." In his eighth decade Samuel Johnson listed his three diseases as "asthma, dropsy, and, what is less curable, age seventy-five."

The confusion between aging and disease continues in the minds of public and professionals—the challenge for those providing health care for the elderly is to tease out remediable disabilities caused by disease from irreversible time-dependent changes. A concept of life course appears in Shakespeare. In the seven ages of man he describes both age-related roles—the lover, the soldier, the justice—as well as anatomic, physiologic, and psychological features of older characters. Among the anatomic markers of antiquity he identifies changes in the skin and hair: "the dry hand, yellow cheek, white beard"; changes in the eye: "the full eye waxes hollow"; changes in posture and in muscle bulk: "the straight back will stoop, the shrunk shank"; and changes in the distribution of body fat: the "fair, round belly" of the justice in the fifth age.

Adding to Shakespeare's seven ages, Erickson proposed eight. Defining stages by anatomic and physiologic decrements, Erickson advanced key polarities appropriate to each stage from infancy to maturity. Personal growth, he proposed, is a quest for identity and depends on successful resolution of conflicting polarities at times of transition. While at any stage of life we may still have to grapple with tasks left incomplete from earlier stages, the main developmental tasks of middle adulthood are to resolve the conflict "stagnation vs. generativity," and for maturity the task embodied in the polarity "integrity vs. disgust and despair." Thus he proposes that growth and development in old age deal with the meaning of life for an individual. Through a process of life review a lifetime of experience can be integrated; self-realization, reconciliation, acceptance, magnanimity, and wisdom may be achieved, resulting in satisfaction with a life well lived. Old age can be more than a season of losses: accumulated biologic deficits, disease, disability leading to functional impairment, and increasing decrepitude that, compounded by loss of role, status, friends, make it not worth living; rather, it's our very last chance to "get it all together." How much more appealing to anticipate the closing chapter of life as a stage, like any other stage in the lifespan, with a purpose.

Aging in a biological sense is the obverse of growth and development;

however, the decremental changes onset not in the senium but in the third decade of life and are already well established by middle adulthood. Age-related changes in skin and hair are too well known to need further description. Some changes, such as reduced light transmission through the optic lens, are clearly time dependent, but others—for example, diminished high-frequency auditory capacity—may be influenced as much by accumulated effects of environmental noise as by the passage of time. Studies of body composition of individuals of different ages show, in general, a reduced lean body mass (that is, proportion of body weight comprised of bones, muscle, and viscera) and an increase in body fat with advancing age. Although these data are based on cross-sectional comparisons and may be influenced by cohort and other effects, there is accumulating evidence to support longitudinal change in individuals as a function of time. Other musculoskeletal changes that are time dependent include loss of bone mass in the thoracic vertebrae and thinning of the intervertebral discs. This normally results in a loss of height approximating one and a half inches between early adulthood and late maturity.

When we measure physiologic indices in individuals free from clinical and biochemical markers of diseases we may observe a near-linear decrease in organ function of around 1 percent per annum from the third decade onwards. Since most organs and body systems have reserve capacity six to ten times that required for basal function, incremental losses usually do not reach a critical level until the eighth decade or beyond. Loss of functional capacity of organs or of the whole organism before the eighth decade usually results from disease. This is an important distinction, since biologic age decrements in function owing to disease are not universal, and are potentially preventable and often modifiable.

It is only in recent years that we have had the opportunity of observing time-dependent changes in our fellow citizens in a relatively pure form uncontaminated by disease. Prior to this century, exceptional individuals achieved advanced age by surviving the acute illnesses to which their contemporaries had succumbed. Disability, disease, and premature death resulting from an inadequate food supply, accidental or natural violence, and infectious diseases were everyday hazards, and in old age survivors would exhibit not only aging changes but also the markers of past disease.

Until comparatively recently, the "fevers"—infectious diseases—were poorly differentiated and their natural history was poorly understood. Observers from Hippocrates through to Sydenham classified and described the fevers, and although the germ theory of contagion was proposed by Fracastoro in 1546, not until 1880 was Koch able to demonstrate that specific bacteria were responsible for the occurrence of certain diseases. Fortunately, advances in preventive and clinical practice did not wait upon the laying of the scientific base. Preventive intervention such as quarantining, variolation, and sanitary reforms had already made an impact on mortality prior to unequivocal demonstration of the responsible infectious agents.

At the turn of this century, acute infectious diseases such as diphtheria and scarlet fever contributed to the high infant mortality rate, and for those infants surviving to adulthood, tuberculosis and septicemia resulting from trivial injury were ever-present risks. In Saskatoon the City Hospital was founded to treat the victims of a typhoid epidemic in the first decade of this century. The last great plague—the influenza pandemic of 1918/19—was responsible for over three thousand deaths in Saskatchewan and is still within living memory. Small wonder that within living memory humans bred like rabbits, for they died like flies.

At the turn of the century, Canada's premier physician and teacher, Sir William Osler, could say, "Humanity has but three great enemies: fever, famine and war; of these the greatest, by far the most terrible is fever." How dated this sounds to our ears only eighty years later. In the Western world at least, the abundance of food, relative freedom from violent accidental death, and the near-conquest of infections that formerly killed one-quarter or more of the population before their tenth year have resulted in a dramatic increase in mean life expectancy. By 1971 in Canada, the life expectancy at birth was 69 for males and 76 for females; that projected for Canada for 2001—73 for males and 79 for females—already obtains in Saskatchewan.

Figure 1 is a mapping of the population survival curve for the United States. The percentage of those born alive surviving appears on the Y axis, and years since birth on the X axis. In 1900 a sharp decline in percentage surviving the first ten years of life reflects the high infant and child mortality of that era—a phenomenon that has altered strikingly by 1980. Compare also the portion of the curve from age ten to age sixty. In 1900, 50 percent of those born had died by age sixty, whereas in 1980 approximately 90 percent of those born alive were still alive at age sixty. The acute infectious diseases that were responsible for deaths of young, fit, otherwise healthy people have been replaced with other disorders. The so-called chronic diseases are long in evolution, multifactorial in origin, chronic in course, and often result in long periods of disability and dependency. Many of these disorders—the so-called diseases of choice—are influenced by lifestyle and voluntary exposure to toxins, yet our folk sayings have not yet caught up with changing patterns

ROBERTSON / *The Human Lifespan as Framework* 69

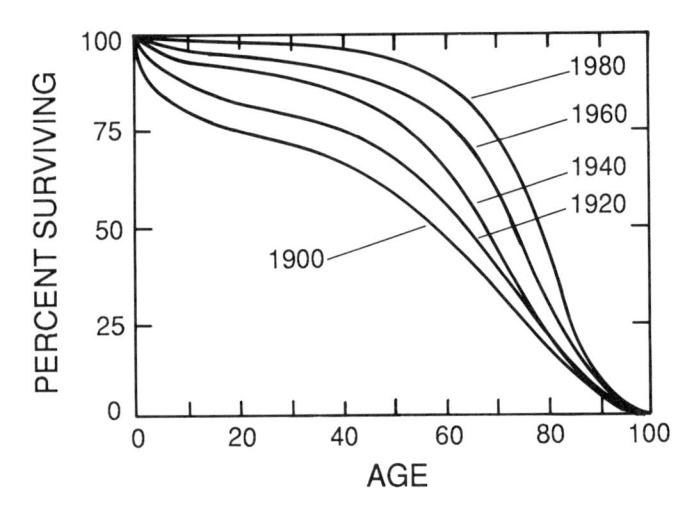

FIGURE 1. SURVIVAL CURVES FOR SELECTED YEARS

Human survival curves for 1900, 1920, 1940, 1960, and 1980. These curves are correct. They converge at the maximum age, thereby demonstrating that the maximum age of survival has been fixed over this period of observation. *Source:* National Bureau of Health Statistics.

of morbidity. The life approach embodied in "Eat, drink and be merry, for tomorrow we die," while appropriate to a time when acute infections lurked in the shadows ready to carry off young and old alike, is inappropriate to an era when most of us can reasonably expect to live long enough to develop diseases associated with unhealthy lifestyles. "Eat sparingly, drink moderately, do not smoke or use toxic substances recreationally, buckle your seat belt, and handle stress appropriately, for you will live long enough to develop diseases of choice" seems more in tune with the time, if less pithy.

Would we be immortal if major certified causes of death—disorders such as atherosclerosis and its complications, diabetes, cirrhosis, emphysema and some forms of cancer—could be eliminated? Some have estimated that elimination of the three major killers of the 1980s—cardiovascular disease, cerebrovascular disease, and cancer—would add perhaps five to seven years to our life expectancy. Why is this?

Closer examination of the population survival curve will explain this unanticipated prediction. While mean survival has increased, there has been no increase in maximum human lifespan. Indeed, there is nothing to suggest increasing maximum human lifespan over recorded history. Biblical accounts of exceptional human longevity notwithstanding, the longest authenticated human survivor is Shigechiyo Izumi, who at last report was alive in Japan at an age of 119 years. In most Western countries, life expectancy at birth is around 72 years for men and around 76 for women, centenarians are unusual, and super-centenarians (over 120 years of age) are unknown. Mean potential human lifespan lies somewhere between today's life expectancy, which, of course, is influenced by premature death due to preventable disease, and age 100. We should not be distracted by long-living outliers on the population survival curve for only one in ten thousand of those who reach age 85 are still alive at 110.

In some animal species, lifespan may be extended by modulation of environmental temperature and by restriction of total calories during the growth period. Supposed anti-aging agents—vitamins, antioxidants, Gerovital H_3, and cell implants—have their proponents, but all appear to be founded on limited understanding of aging processes. Claims of exceptional longevity in Vilcabamba in Ecuador, the Hunza Highlands in the Himalayas, and in the Caucasus, attributed to lifestyles, do not bear close scrutiny and reflect inadequacies in collection and recording of vital statistics. The human lifespan appears to be fixed as indeed is the lifespan of other living things.

Our current understanding of aging is that it results from several processes at work at a variety of levels, from the molecular level within and between cells to the integrated function of organ systems within the body. It has been argued that lifespan is under genetic control since it appears fixed and species specific. A "senescent gene" that confers some undefined benefit in youth and that has its expression as deteriorating function in late life has been postulated. However, evidence to support this is not strong; aging may be genetic only in the sense that genes determine the species—either human or gopher—and since the gopher ages faster than humans, genes in this sense determine aging. The observation that longevity is familial does not really support the genetic hypothesis, since longevity in families may be attributed to relative freedom from diseases that might cause premature death, and relative protection from these may be conferred by dietary and lifestyle patterns that are shared by family members.

In summary, aging occurs at a number of levels—molecular, intercellular, and cellular. The result of these biologic time-dependent changes is to reduce the organism's capacity to recover from perturbations of the internal physico/chemical environment. Reduced organ reserve impairs coordinated and integrated response to stress; "homeostasis" becomes "homeostenosis," and what for a younger person may be a minor or trivial stress is for an older individual the final straw that leads to decompensation or death. In a physiologic sense, the net effect

of aging is to reduce the capacity of the organism to respond appropriately to stress, resulting in increasing mortality from all causes with
advancing age.

Are all decremental changes observed in late life the result of either
biologic aging or of disease? For completeness we must include two
other important factors, disuse or deconditioning and socio-cultural
aspects of aging. Physical training of the cardio-respiratory and musculoskeletal systems may have a salutary effect on physical work capacity,
and some authors have cited this as evidence of "plasticity" of the aging
process. I believe it is more helpful to see disuse and deconditioning
quite apart from intrinsic biologic age changes, since the former are not
universal and are preventable or reversible. Disuse, like disease and
biologic aging, impairs organ function; however, improving physical or
functional capacity by participating in strenuous exercise does not make
us younger, it makes us fitter. By reversing deconditioning caused by a
sedentary life, we may improve capacity to respond successfully to
environmental challenges. Space does not permit adequate discussion of
social and environmental factors that influence functional capacity.

As the upper right corner of the population survival curve approxi-
mates a right angle, we move towards what Fries has called the "rectangular society." No longer is sickness and disability spread across the
lifespan; rather, infirmity and its resultant disability is compressed into
the last one-tenth of the lifespan. Individual variation in biologic
phenomena prevent precise squaring of the corner of survivorship; however, preventive and therapeutic inroads into major killers of the late
twentieth century—cardiovascular disease, stroke, and cancer—would
leave only the hazards of early childhood and accidental death due to
trauma as the main impediments to the whole population's achieving full
potential human lifespan.

Can we glimpse what life may be like in the "rectangular society"
when survival to late adulthood is achievable by all? Each of us may
speculate on the implications these demographic changes may have for
us in our many roles as individuals, as parents, as children, as citizens
and taxpayers, and as members of an educational enterprise. The area
that I know best, the health-care delivery system, is already experiencing
symptoms resulting from a reluctance to accept that programs and institutions that evolved to treat acute disease in young people are inappropriate
to the health problems of the aged. While the young are frequently unim-
paired and healthy prior to acute illness, the problems of the aged are
infrequently amenable to "cure" and often involve continued disability
and dependency. Institutional rigidity and symptomatic rather than radical

response have been compounded by lack of appropriate preparation of health professionals to meet the changing needs of the major consumers of health services—the elderly. Acknowledging the need for new skills for the physician of tomorrow, the faculty at the College of Medicine at the University of Saskatchewan has shown enlightened leadership by finding within the undergraduate medical curriculum forty hours for didactic and clinical teaching in health care of the elderly. This program includes the first mandatory clinical training in geriatric medicine for undergraduates in North America.

The organizers of the conference on time invited us to direct our thoughts towards development of the human resource for the betterment of society. I propose three ways in which, I believe, our university can contribute to this end.

The first, naturally enough considering my professional role, concerns the role of the university in training health professionals. Health-related issues at the end of life increasingly touch us as individuals, family members, and taxpayers. It would be truly ironic if, having achieved the goal of conquest of premature, avoidable mortality, we offered survivors health-care services and a quality of life that made them doubt the wisdom of survivorship. To prepare all trainee health-care professionals and those already in practice for their patients or clients of tomorrow, we need to design and provide educational experiences that increase the student's or practitioner's knowledge and understanding of the meaning of old age and the problems encountered by the elderly. A vital part of such training is work experience in a setting that facilitates the development of appropriate clinical skills.

The second concerns the role of the university in posing and addressing research questions that arise from changing demography. Such issues arise not only in the health disciplines, but also in such disciplines as law, education, anthropology, sociology, and psychology, to name but a few. The findings of research in biologic gerontology may be transferable from elsewhere; however, health-care and social research is context specific. The principles of health care of the elderly may be the same, but their application is greatly influenced by local factors such as ethnicity, health beliefs, place of residence, life experience, and existing programs and services, and so some research questions can only be answered in our province. In 1981 the Division of Geriatric Medicine carried out the Saskatchewan health status survey, in which one thousand elderly residents of long-term-care facilities and over twelve hundred elderly subjects living at home were interviewed and assessed to determine the prevalence of major health problems such as dementia, urinary incontinence, dependency for ADL, and health-service utilization. Data such as these and that from other academic disciplines will be required for rational planning of programs and services to meet changing needs.

Finally, the human resource of the university—the faculty—has a vital role in grappling with complex issues resulting from unprecedented survivorship:

• Resource allocation both between and within publicly supported programs
• Individual accountability for preventable health problems
• Ethics of the prolongation of life—or the prolongation of death
• The ignorance and prejudice that surround the process of aging

From our vantage point at this, the seventy-fifth anniversary of the foundation of the University of Saskatchewan, let us look forward seventy-five years. What will have become of us? We can fairly confidently expect that we shall all have died. We may have died prematurely from a "disease of choice," or more optimistically, we will have escaped premature mortality and have completed a full human lifespan of 85–100 years. We will have lived long enough to develop time-dependent biologic changes and the infirmities associated with great age; we hope our health-care delivery system will have been able to provide us with the human and material resources necessary to identify and rectify remediable causes of disability and dependency.

Enough of the liabilities of aging—old age can be far more than a season of loss. Survival to the ninth and tenth decades presents the opportunity to enter the final stage of growth, an opportunity denied most of our predecessors.

Note

1. Paul Hiebert, *Sarah Binks* (Toronto: McClelland & Stewart, 1971), 71.

Some Economic and Demographic Implications of Canadian Life Cycle Changes

FRANK T. DENTON and BYRON G. SPENCER

OUR AIM IN this paper is to describe some of the major changes in life cycle patterns that have occurred over the past few decades in Canada, and to consider the effects that these changes are likely to have on the population and macro-economy in the decades ahead. The changes in the life cycle on which we focus are those relating to fertility, to longevity, and to labour force activity. As the descriptions that follow make clear, each of these aspects of the life cycle has undergone substantial change in Canada, as in the United States[1] and in other countries. There can be no question that such developments have important implications for the future size and age distribution of the population and the labour force, and hence for the nation's productive capacity—the supply side of the economy, that is. They also have implications for the expenditure or demand side. To take some of the more obvious ones, reductions in the numbers of young people tend to lower the aggregate costs of education, while increases in the number of elderly tend to raise pension and health-care costs. However, the combined net impact of these changes and others is apt not to be immediately evident.

We start with a review of the major changes in fertility rates, and relate these to changes in the annual numbers of births. In the second section we turn to the changes which have occurred in longevity, as measured by life

---

The computer programming and related work for this paper was carried out by Christine H. Feaver. The study on which the paper is based is part of a larger one supported by the Social Sciences and Humanities Research Council of Canada under the terms of a grant awarded jointly to the authors and to Peter C. Pineo for research on the social and economic implications of an aging population.

76   FUNCTIONAL ACCOUNTS OF TIME

expectancy), giving attention to developments at various ages as well as
to the substantial gap which exists between male and female life expectancies. A review of historical growth and change in the overall
population is provided in the third section, where we also offer some
projections of the population to the middle of the next century. In the
fourth section we consider changes in the labour force since World War
II, and in the fifth section, projections of the labour force. The sixth
section draws out some of the more important macro-economic implications that the projected changes in the population and labour force can be
expected to have over the next several decades. Some concluding remarks
are provided in the final section.

Post-War Fertility Swings: Baby Boom to Baby Bust

The dominant demographic events of the past forty years have been the
post-war "baby boom" that took place in Canada as well as in several
other developed countries, and the subsequent "baby bust." An indication
of the magnitude of the swings in Canada is provided by the total fertility
rates, shown in Figure 1. The *period total fertility rate* tells us the
number of children that the average woman would have if she were to
experience the current-period fertility rates over the childbearing age
range, which is taken to be the 15–49 years of age. As can be seen from the
figure, by the late 1930s the period total fertility rate had been on a long
downward trend since 1921, albeit with some short-lived and minor up-
swings. In fact, the downward trend commenced long before 1921, and
it was generally expected to continue. What happened, of course, was
quite different. Instead of a further fall there was a substantial and
prolonged upswing that took the rate from 2.6 births per woman just
before World War II to 3.4 by 1946 (at that time its highest level in
more than twenty years), and then to 3.9 by 1959. Since 1959 the rate
has fallen in every year, with only one minor exception. By 1967 it had
dropped below 2.6, and attained the lowest rate ever recorded in Canada;
by 1972 it had fallen below the long-run replacement level, which is
about 2.1, and ten years later it stood at less than 1.7. Such changes as
these clearly reflect major shifts in the life cycle patterns of Canadian
families. The impact of these shifts on the size and age distribution of the
Canadian population and on the Canadian economy has already been
enormous, and there is much more to come.

While the total fertility rate in any one year relates to a cross-section
of the fertility experience of women in that year, no actual cohort of

DENTON & SPENCER / *Economic and Demographic Implications* 77

FIGURE 1. PERIOD AND COHORT TOTAL FERTILITY RATES

Based on data from A. Romaniuc, *Fertility in Canada: From Baby-Boom to Baby-Bust,* catalogue no. 91-524E (Ottawa: Statistics Canada, 1984), p. 121.

women ever has exactly those rates at each age throughout its own child-bearing years. Instead, the fertility experience of a cohort is better summarized by the *cohort total fertility rate,* also depicted in Figure 1, which tells us the average number of children actually born to a group of women of the same age. Of course, such rates cannot be stated for those cohorts of women who have not yet reached the age of 50. However, for women now of age 35 and over, estimates of completed fertility will probably not be far wrong. For such women, the indications are that their average lifetime fertility will exceed the replacement level of 2.1 children. For younger cohorts now 25 to 34, though, unless there is a very marked shift in the age pattern of childbearing towards more births at older ages, completed fertility will be below the replacement level. Whether the lifetime rates will be as low as 1.7 or possibly even lower, as recent data would suggest, only time will tell.

There are other characteristics of Canadian fertility rates that have changed over the years. For example, based on available annual time series, it appears that the median age of women at childbirth has fallen relatively steadily, from 29.4 in 1931 to 26.6 in 1981. The age interval during which births occur has also become more concentrated: roughly

78 FUNCTIONAL ACCOUNTS OF TIME

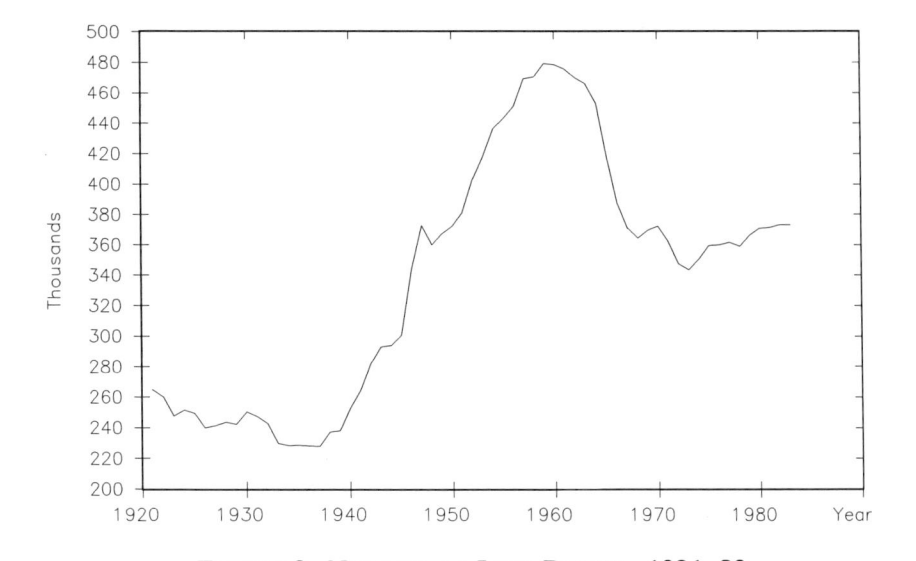

FIGURE 2. NUMBER OF LIVE BIRTHS, 1921–83

Source: Statistics Canada, *Vital Statistics,* catalogue nos. 84-204, 84-001.

50 percent of all births now occur within a seven-year interval about the median age, compared to an interval of almost ten years half a century ago. Another fact of interest is that the median age at first birth has increased by more than one and one-half years in the last decade, and now stands at 24.8. Also, the proportion of births accounted for by single[2] women has increased markedly: in Canada, in the period from the 1930s to the 1960s, there was approximately 1 birth to a single woman for every 24 births to other women. Since then the proportion has increased sharply, and for 1982 it is estimated that the ratio was about 1 to 5.5. Among the provinces, Saskatchewan has the highest ratio—about 1 to 4.[3] The increase in the number of such births has not been limited to young women: whereas in 1974 57.6 percent of all births to single women were to 15–19 year olds, by 1982 this age group accounted for only 32.4 percent. Over the same period the proportion accounted for by women 25–34 increased from 12.0 percent to 26.8 percent.[4]

Changes in fertility rates imply changes in the numbers of children born. Figure 2 records the number of live births annually, starting with 1921. Births increased sharply during the war and in the immediate post-war period, and by 1956 there were 50 percent more than in 1945. The number continued to rise until 1959, when 479,000 births were recorded. Then it fell for a decade, and in 1968 it was 115,000 lower than it had been in 1959 and the lowest it had been in twenty years. Since then the number of births has been relatively constant, the result of an offset between larger numbers of women and continually declining fertility rates.

The magnitude of the impact that the baby boom and the subsequent baby bust have had on some parts of the educational system is obvious and well known. Aside from mortality and emigration, which are relatively unimportant in this context, those born in any year reach the primary schools some five or six years later, the secondary schools in another eight years, and then the post-secondary level in a further four or five years. Each level of the educational system, in turn, had first to absorb and accommodate huge increases, and subsequently to adjust to much smaller inflows. For example, just to accommodate those born six years earlier without increasing class size, the numbers of desks, classrooms, and teachers allocated to the first year of primary school would have had to have increased by 24 percent between 1951 and 1956, a further 19 percent by 1961, and then a further 8 percent by 1966. By 1971, though, contraction was the order of the day: 13 percent fewer places would have been needed in 1971 than in 1966, 11 percent fewer again in 1976, and 3 percent fewer than that in 1981.

The impact at the secondary level came later. There were also substantial increases in enrolment rates, which made the expansionary phase somewhat sharper but the contractionary phase less severe. Similar comments apply at the post-secondary level, where it appears that for the past few years the continuing increase in enrolment rates has more than offset the fall in the number of those newly reaching age 18.

We conclude this section by making assumptions, for use in subsequent population projections, about the future course of fertility rates. For convenience, the assumptions are made in terms of the period total fertility rate, rather than the cohort completed rate. The fact is that no one knows what will happen to fertility in the future. Some expect a continuing decline while others anticipate an increase—not a baby boom of the magnitude just described, but a return to fertility rates above the replacement level. Still another possibility is that of continuing fluctuations, with the rate sometimes above the replacement level and sometimes below it. Faced with such uncertainty, a reasonable approach is to consider a range of alternatives and to assess and compare their implications. In the projections reported below, we consider three alternatives: a continuation of the total fertility rate at its current level of 1.7 (our "standard" assumption); a fall to 1.4 by 2001, with the rate constant thereafter (our "low" assumption); and a rise to 3.0 by 2001, again with the rate constant thereafter (our "high" assumption).

Changes in Life Expectancy

Some major features of the changes in life expectancies that have occurred in Canada over the last fifty years are evident from Table 1, in which are recorded the average numbers of years of life expected at ages 0, 1, 65, and 80 for decennial census years from 1931 to 1981. A number of points stand out, and are relevant in assessing some of the implications of past and future population change. The first point to note is the magnitude of the increases in life expectancies that have occurred for both males and females, and at virtually all ages. For example, male life expectancy at birth increased from 60 years in 1931 to almost 72 in 1981, or by nearly a quarter of a year of age for each calendar year passed; for females it increased from just over 62 in 1931 to 79 in 1981, or by more than a third of a year for each year passed.

The second point follows from the first: there has been a growing gap between female and male life expectancies. Whereas in 1931 a woman who reached the age of 65 could expect, on average, to live only 0.7 years longer than a man of the same age, by 1985 she could expect to live 4.3 years longer. The increases in longevity for both sexes will add to the size of the elderly population of the future, and the fact that the increases for women have outstripped those for men will mean that the growth of the elderly population will be disproportionately greater for women than for men. The life expectancy gap, coupled with the fact that women tend to marry men somewhat older than themselves, suggests a very substantial increase in the number of elderly widows. One leading demographer has expressed concern "about the physical and emotional isolation of older women,"[5] a problem that is very likely to become more widespread in the future for the reasons just noted.

The third point has to do with the numbers of years of life remaining for those already in old age. The average male who reaches age 65 today can expect to live to be almost 80, while the average female can expect to reach 84, based on 1981 life expectancies—and indeed, the expectancies are very likely to increase further in the future.

Underlying the changes in life expectancy are changes in annual mortality rates. Three points are of special note in this regard: (1) when comparing successive life tables over a fifty-year period, we find that mortality rates have declined in every decade at almost every year of age; (2) female mortality rates have been consistently below (and often far below) male rates; and (3) the differences between the male and female rates have generally increased from decade to decade. The general decrease in mortality is presumably associated mainly with better

TABLE 1. LIFE EXPECTANCIES OF MALES AND FEMALES AT SELECTED AGES, CANADA, 1931–81

	Life Expectancy		Change in Life Expectancy (Years)		Difference Between Male and Female Life Expectancy
	Male	Female	Male	Female	
Age 0					
1931	60.0	62.1	—	—	2.1
1941	63.0	66.3	3.0	4.2	3.3
1951	66.3	70.8	3.4	4.5	4.5
1961	68.4	74.2	2.0	3.3	5.8
1971	69.3	76.4	1.0	2.2	7.0
1981	71.9	79.0	2.5	2.6	7.1
Age 1					
1931	64.7	65.7	—	—	1.0
1941	66.1	68.7	1.5	3.0	2.6
1951	68.3	72.3	2.2	3.6	4.0
1961	69.5	75.0	1.2	2.6	5.5
1971	69.8	76.6	.3	1.6	6.8
1981	71.7	78.7	1.9	2.1	7.0
Age 65					
1931	13.0	13.7	—	—	.7
1941	12.8	14.1	-.2	.4	1.3
1951	13.3	15.0	.5	.9	1.7
1961	13.5	16.1	.2	1.1	2.5
1971	13.7	17.5	.2	1.4	3.8
1981	14.6	18.9	.8	1.4	4.3
Age 80					
1931	5.6	5.9	—	—	.3
1941	5.5	6.0	-.1	.1	.5
1951	5.8	6.4	.3	.4	.5
1961	6.1	6.9	.3	.5	.8
1971	6.4	7.9	.3	1.0	1.5
1981	6.9	8.8	.4	1.0	2.0

Note: Prior to 1951, figures exclude Newfoundland.

82   FUNCTIONAL ACCOUNTS OF TIME

nutritional and health-care practices, but the growth of the male-female differential seems not to be well understood.

In order to project the population, it is necessary to make specific assumptions about the future course of mortality rates. We make three alternative assumptions in this regard. Each is based on the age-sex-specific average annual proportionate rates of reduction of mortality rates between 1961 and 1981. In our "high mortality" scenario, we assume that the annual proportionate rates of reduction decline gradually to zero by 2011 with all mortality rates constant thereafter; in the "medium mortality" scenario, we assume that mortality reductions continue (at a decel-erating pace) until 2031; and in the "low mortality" scenario we assume that reductions continue until 2051.

The Overall Population

Population change in Canada has reflected the two basic life cycle changes that we have discussed so far: the shifts in fertility patterns that gave rise to the baby boom and the baby bust, and the lengthening of life that resulted from the general decline of mortality rates. It has also reflected the changing patterns of immigration and emigration.

Some basic information about population change over the period 1921 to 1981 is provided in the top panel of Table 2. Between 1921 and 1981 the total population increased about three-fold—from 8.8 million at the beginning to 24.3 million by the end of the period. While the population grew during each decade, the rates of growth were very uneven. The rap-id growth experienced in the earlier part of the century gave way to much slower growth during the depression of the 1930s, when the continuing fall in fertility combined with negative net immigration to cut the rate of growth by about half. More rapid growth resumed in the 1940s, but most-ly in the later part of that decade, when the beginning of the baby boom coincided with sharply higher levels of net immigration. Growth was extremely rapid during the 1950s, with the baby boom in full swing and net immigration levels also very high; the total population increased by almost one-third during that decade. Then, as fertility started to fall during the 1960s, the population began to grow much less rapidly; from 1961-71 it grew by 18.3 percent, and from 1971-81 by only 12.9 percent.

These changes in the rate of growth of the population have been accompanied by changes in its age distribution. For example, the popula-tion under 5 fell from 12.1 percent in 1921 to 9.1 percent in 1941, in response to the continuing long-term decline in fertility. The proportion then increased sharply with the advent of the baby boom; it reached

TABLE 2. POPULATION OF CANADA, 1921-81, WITH PROJECTIONS TO 2051: ALTERNATIVE FERTILITY ASSUMPTIONS

Year	Total (1,000s)	% Growth, Previous Decade	Distribution by Age (%)					Women 65+ per 1,000 Men
			0-4	5-19	20-64	65-74	75+	
1921	8788	21.9	12.1	31.5	51.6	3.3	1.5	953
1931	10377	18.1	10.4	31.3	52.8	3.9	1.7	955
1941	11507	10.9	9.1	28.4	55.8	4.6	2.1	964
1951	14009	18.6	12.3	25.7	54.4	5.3	2.4	970
1961	18238	30.2	12.4	29.5	50.6	4.9	2.8	1064
1971	21568	18.3	8.4	31.0	52.5	5.0	3.1	1231
1981	24342	12.9	7.3	24.7	58.3	6.1	3.6	1336
— standard projection —								
1991	27048	11.1	7.1	20.5	60.8	6.8	4.8	1426
2001	29205	8.0	5.9	19.8	61.5	6.9	6.0	1466
2011	30805	5.5	5.5	17.4	62.6	7.8	6.8	1479
2021	31977	3.8	5.3	16.4	59.7	10.8	7.8	1456
2031	32398	1.3	4.9	16.0	55.9	12.5	10.7	1458
2041	32132	-0.8	4.9	15.4	55.8	10.6	13.3	1522
2051	31420	-2.2	4.9	15.5	55.7	11.0	12.9	1531
— high-fertility projection —								
1991	27466	12.8	8.4	20.3	59.9	6.7	4.7	1426
2001	31489	14.6	8.9	22.1	57.0	6.4	5.6	1466
2011	35760	13.6	8.7	23.7	55.1	6.7	5.8	1479
2021	40767	14.0	9.4	23.6	52.4	8.5	6.1	1456
2031	46539	14.2	9.6	24.9	49.4	8.7	7.4	1458
2041	52851	13.6	9.7	25.5	50.3	6.4	8.1	1522
2051	60468	14.4	10.0	25.7	51.8	5.8	6.7	1529
— low-fertility projection —								
1991	26952	10.7	6.8	20.6	61.0	6.8	4.8	1426
2001	28798	6.4	5.1	19.2	62.6	7.0	6.1	1466
2011	29677	3.5	4.7	15.6	64.6	8.1	7.0	1479
2021	30122	1.5	4.3	14.3	61.6	11.5	8.3	1456
2031	29673	-1.5	3.8	13.6	57.3	13.6	11.7	1458
2041	28453	-4.1	3.8	12.6	56.6	11.9	15.0	1522
2051	27621	-6.1	3.7	12.7	55.5	12.9	15.2	1532

levels in excess of 12 percent in both 1951 and 1961 before falling to record lows in 1971 and 1981.

The population 65 and over, and more especially 75 and over, increased rather steadily as a proportion of the total population during the period 1921-81. Whereas the population 65-74 accounted for only 3.3 percent of the total in 1921, by 1981 it accounted for 6.1 percent. The proportionate increase in the fraction of population 75 and over was even greater—from 1.5 percent to 3.6 percent of the total. These increases reflect the gains in longevity noted above, as well as changes in the birth rate and the changes in population age structure for which the varying birth rate was largely responsible.

The sustained increase in the ratio of elderly women to elderly men is of interest too: in 1951 and earlier, there were fewer women 65 and over than men; by 1981 there were 1.3 women for every man in that age category. This striking reversal seems to be the result mainly of the growing gap between female and male life expectancies.

What of the future? What can be expected to happen to the overall size of the population and its age-sex distribution in the coming decades? To provide a range of possible answers, we offer five alternative projections of the population under different assumptions about fertility and mortality. In addition, assumptions are necessary with regard to immigration and emigration. The five sets of assumptions underlying the five projections are as follows:

1. *Standard projection:* The total fertility rate continues at 1.7 births per woman; mortality rates at each age for each sex continue to change in accordance with the experience between 1961 and 1981, but the rate of change declines to zero by 2031; net immigration is set at 80,000 per annum throughout the projection period (120,000 immigrants minus 40,000 emigrants).

2. *High fertility projection:* The total fertility rate is assumed to increase to 3.0 births per woman by 2001, and to remain at that level thereafter; otherwise, same assumptions as the standard projection.

3. *Low fertility projection:* The total fertility rate is assumed to decrease to 1.4 births per woman by 2001, and to remain at that level thereafter; otherwise, same assumptions as the standard projection.

4. *High mortality projection:* The rates of change of mortality rates are assumed to decline to zero by 2011 rather than 2031; otherwise, same assumptions as the standard projection.

5. *Low mortality projection:* The rates of change of mortality rates are

assumed to decline to zero by 2051 rather than 2031; otherwise, same assumptions as the standard projection.

The standard projection appears in the second panel of Table 2, followed by the high fertility and low fertility projections in the lower two panels. The high mortality and low mortality projections appear in the lower two panels of Table 3.

Consider first the standard projection. Under the assumptions made, the population would grow by 20 percent between 1981 and 2001, and a further 11 percent by 2031. The growth is largely the legacy of the baby boom: even though each woman, on average, has too few children to replace the population in the long run, the members of the baby-boom cohorts and their daughters represent a sufficiently large fraction of the population that it continues to grow for several decades. However, the rate of growth falls throughout the projection period, becoming negative by the fourth decade of the next century.

What are the major implications in terms of the age distribution? One would expect that if fertility rates remained at recent levels or lower, the proportion of the population under 5 would continue to fall, and this we find. By the turn of the century the population under 5 accounts for less than 6 percent of the total, and by 2031 for less than 5 percent, compared to more than 12 percent in 1961 and more than 7 percent in 1981. The fraction of the population 5-19 also decreases. That age group accounted for 31 percent of the population in 1971, but less than 25 percent by 1981. Under the given assumptions, the projected proportion of 5-19 year olds is less than 20 percent by 2001 and some 15 or 16 percent by the middle of the next century.

While the proportion of young in the population falls, the proportion of old continues to grow. In 1981 those 65 and over accounted for 9.7 percent of the population. By 2001 they account for almost 13 percent and by 2021 for 18.5 percent, based on the standard projection. The age group 20-64 grew from 52.5 percent of the total population in 1971 to a high of 58.3 percent by 1981, reflecting the aging of the baby-boom generation. In the standard projection it continues to grow, reaching 62.6 percent by 2001. The proportion then declines slightly, but remains high throughout the projection period, by historical standards.

These projected changes in the age distribution are particularly important in light of the general concern about the anticipated burden associated with the aging of the population. The very substantial prospective increase in the proportion of elderly dependents is likely to be offset by the decrease in the proportion of young dependents, and potentially accommodated by the relatively large fraction of the population of working age.

TABLE 3. POPULATION OF CANADA, 1921-81, WITH PROJECTIONS TO 2051: ALTERNATIVE MORTALITY ASSUMPTIONS

Year	Total (1,000s)	% Growth, Previous Decade	Distribution by Age (%)					Women 65+ per 1,000 Men
			0-4	5-19	20-64	65-74	75+ (65+)	
1921	8788	21.9	12.1	31.5	51.6	3.3	1.5	953
1931	10377	18.1	10.4	31.3	52.8	3.9	1.7	955
1941	11507	10.9	9.1	28.4	55.8	4.6	2.1	964
1951	14009	18.6	12.3	25.7	54.4	5.3	2.4	970
1961	18238	30.2	12.4	29.5	50.6	4.9	2.8	1064
1971	21568	18.3	8.4	31.0	52.5	5.0	3.1	1231
1981	24342	12.9	7.3	24.7	58.3	6.1	3.6	1336
— standard projection —								
1991	27048	11.1	7.1	20.5	60.8	6.8	4.8	1426
2001	29205	8.0	5.9	19.8	61.5	6.9	6.0	1466
2011	30805	5.5	5.5	17.4	62.6	7.8	6.9	1479
2021	31977	3.8	5.3	16.4	59.7	10.8	7.8	1456
2031	32398	1.3	4.9	16.0	55.9	12.5	10.7	1458
2041	32132	-0.8	4.9	15.4	55.8	10.6	13.3	1522
2051	31420	-2.2	4.9	15.5	55.7	11.0	12.9	1531
— high-mortality projection —								
1991	27043	11.1	7.1	20.5	60.8	6.8	4.8	1425
2001	29167	7.9	5.9	19.8	61.6	6.9	5.9	1461
2011	30675	5.2	5.5	17.4	62.8	7.7	6.6	1466
2021	31685	3.3	5.3	16.5	60.1	10.7	7.4	1437
2031	31929	0.8	5.0	16.2	56.5	12.4	10.0	1436
2041	31524	-1.3	5.0	15.6	56.6	10.5	12.3	1490
2051	30752	-2.4	5.0	15.8	56.6	10.9	11.7	1492
— low-mortality projection —								
1991	27050	11.1	7.1	20.5	60.8	6.8	4.8	1426
2001	29221	8.0	5.9	19.8	61.5	6.9	6.0	1468
2011	30858	5.6	5.5	17.3	62.5	7.8	6.9	1484
2021	32100	4.0	5.3	16.3	59.5	10.8	8.0	1464
2031	32643	1.7	4.9	15.9	55.6	12.5	11.1	1468
2041	32559	-0.3	4.9	15.2	55.2	10.6	14.1	1543
2051	31977	-1.8	4.8	15.3	54.9	11.0	13.9	1561

DENTON & SPENCER / *Economic and Demographic Implications* 87

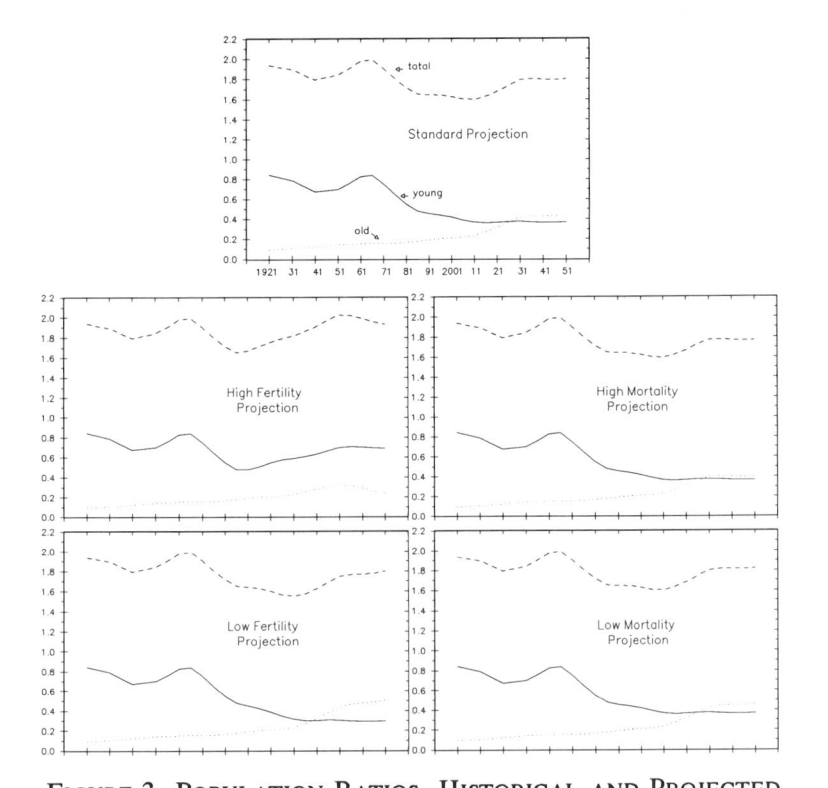

FIGURE 3. POPULATION RATIOS, HISTORICAL AND PROJECTED

Note: The plot labelled *total* is the ratio of the total population to the population 20–64; *young* is the ratio of the population under 20 to that 20–64; *old* is the ratio of the population 65 and over to that 20–64.
Source: Ratios for 1921–81 based on data from census sources; ratios for 1986–2051 based on projections by the authors.

These points are illustrated further in Figure 3, which presents three series of population-based "dependency" ratios for each of the five projections: a "young dependency" ratio (the ratio of those under 20 to those 20–64); an "old dependency" ratio (the ratio of those 65 and over to those 20–64); and a "total dependency" ratio (the ratio of the total population to those 20–64).

Consider the top panel of Figure 3, which relates to the standard projection. It shows a continuing decline in the young dependency ratio from the very high levels of the mid-1960s, and a continuing rise of the old dependency ratio. The overall dependency ratio continues to decline for some three or four decades. It then rises as members of the baby-boom generation reach age 65, but even then the total ratio is below the levels experienced during much of the period since World War II.

Prospective changes in the sex ratio among the elderly are of interest. During the period 1921 to 1981, and especially after 1951, this ratio increased very sharply, as already noted. In the standard projection it continues to increase: by the middle of the next century the number of women exceeds the number of men by more than 50 percent in the age group 65 and over. This suggests again that special attention should be paid to the needs of elderly women, many of whom will be widows living alone.

We turn now to the projections based on alternative assumptions. It is not surprising that the overall size of the future population should vary greatly, depending on the chosen fertility assumption: under the high fertility assumption, the population increases to more than 60 million by 2051, compared with 26.7 million under the low fertility one. There are also marked differences in the age distribution: the proportion of young rises sharply with high fertility and falls with low fertility. Nonetheless, the proportion of elderly people in the population increases for half a century, whatever the fertility assumption, reflecting the aging of the baby-boom generation. However, the extent of increase is substantially affected by the fertility assumption: by 2031 the proportion of elderly is about 16 percent with high fertility, about 23 percent with standard fertility, and somewhat above 25 percent with low fertility. The implications for dependency relations within the population are evident from Figure 3. Much higher overall dependency ratios result when an early return to high fertility is assumed than when the assumption is sustained low fertility.

Changes in mortality rates are likely to be much less critical than changes in fertility rates in determining the major characteristics of the future population, as the bottom two panels of Table 3 make clear. Under the high mortality assumption the overall population reaches 30.8 million by 2051, compared to 32.0 with low mortality—a difference of less than 4 percent. The associated changes in age distribution are correspondingly small. There are relatively fewer young people and more elderly with low mortality than with high, but the differences are minor compared with those associated with the alternative fertility assumptions. The female-male sex ratio for the elderly is also little affected by the mortality assumption, although the increase in the ratio is somewhat less under high mortality than under low.

Post-War Labour Force Participation

The final life cycle changes that concern us here are those reflected in labour force participation rates. In the past several decades there have been marked changes in the labour force behaviour of various groups in

DENTON & SPENCER / *Economic and Demographic Implications*   89

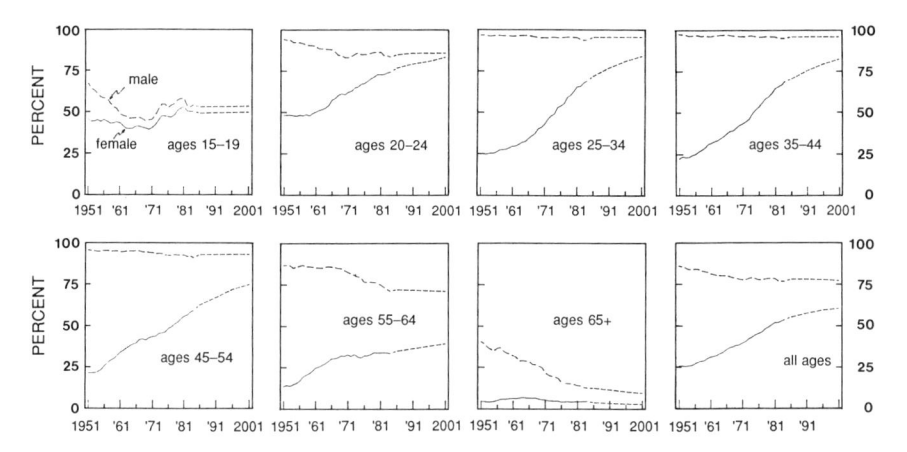

FIGURE 4. PARTICIPATION RATES, HISTORICAL AND PROJECTED

Note: Historical annual average labour force participation rates plotted for 1951–84, and projected rates for 1985–2001. *Source:* Rates for 1951–84 based on Statistics Canada, *Labour Force,* with estimates prior 1976 adjusted to make them consistent with the new definitions introduced into the labour force survey in that year; rates for 1985–2001 projected by the authors.

the population. The most notable ones have been the sharp increases in female participation and the reductions of male participation associated with later labour force entry and earlier retirement.

Labour force participation rates are plotted in Figure 4, for seven age groups and for all ages combined, for each sex, annually over the period 1951–84. Also plotted are the rates that we have assumed to the year 2001 for purposes of projecting the labour force, as discussed below.

As can be seen, there was a reduction in the labour participation rates of males 15–19 of more than 10 percentage points during the 1950s, and a lesser reduction in female rates. The subsequent fluctuations and relatively small increases appear to be associated mostly with the increased holding of part-time jobs by students.

Among males 20–24 there was also a reduction in participation of more than 10 percentage points during the 1950s and 1960s. This reduction, which was associated with increased enrolment in universities and colleges, implied a rise in the average age of labour force entry. For males between the ages of 25 and 54 the rates of participation have remained relatively constant. In the age group 55–64 there has been a trend towards lower participation and earlier retirement, especially since the mid-1960s. In the group 65 and over the downward trend has been strong and persistent.

The pattern of change in participation among women 20 and over has been very different. Whereas the rates for men 20-24 fell, those for women in this age group increased substantially—from less than 50 percent at the end of the 1950s to almost 75 percent by 1984. For women 25 and over the increases have been even greater: in 1951 the participation rate was less than 25 percent for women 25 to 54; by 1984 it was just short of 70 percent for women in the range 25-44, and just short of 60 percent for women 45-54. Even among women 55-64 there have been strong increases in participation during a period when the rates for men were declining. Most of the gains in female participation have been among married women, and a substantial portion of it has been in the form of increased part-time work, which is easiest to coordinate with continuing home responsibilities. Certainly this dramatic growth in the labour force attachment of women, taken in conjunction with the equally dramatic decline in fertility, is a reflection of one of the most significant and far-reaching social changes of this century.

An alternative representation of the increase in female participation rates is provided in Figure 5, which shows the average age-participation profiles for selected years from 1951 to 1984. The rising levels of lifetime participation are evidenced by the continuing upward shifts of the profiles. What of the future? Again, no one can say with confidence what will happen to labour force participation rates in the coming decades. However, a plausible set of assumptions would include further increases in female rates, bringing them closer to male levels, and further declines in the labour force activities of older males. Such a set of assumptions is depicted in the projection portions of Figure 4. Changes in the rates are assumed for the period extending to the end of the present century, the rates being held constant thereafter. We use these assumed future rates below to make projections of the labour force.

The Labour Force: History and Projections

The upper panel of Table 4 provides historical information about the overall labour force, its age distribution, and the ratio of women to men for the period from 1951 to 1981. The labour force has grown rapidly, more than doubling its size between 1951 and 1981. Indeed, its rate of growth increased from one decade to the next over this period, reflecting especially the marked increase in female participation and also, in the

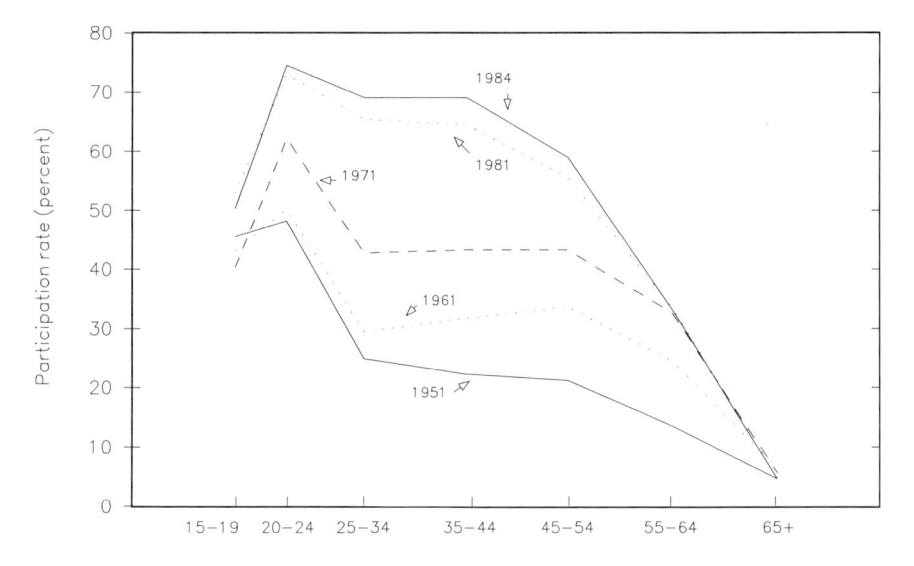

FIGURE 5. FEMALE LABOUR FORCE AGE-PARTICIPATION PROFILES

Source: Rates for 1951–84 based on Statistics Canada, *Labour Force,* with estimates prior 1976 adjusted to make them consistent with the new definitions introduced into the labour force survey in that year; rates for 1985–2001 projected by the authors.

latter part of the period, the entry of the baby-boom generation. While there were fewer than 300 females per 1,000 males in the labour force in 1951, there were almost 700 per 1,000 by 1981. The underlying increases in female participation, which have occurred in virtually all age groups, have dominated the changes in age distribution, with the result that net changes in the age composition of the labour force have been rather small.

The situation promises to be quite different in the future. We provide five alternative labour force projections, each one combining the projected participation rate assumptions depicted in Figure 4 with one of the five population projections described earlier. The standard projection and projections based on the high fertility and low fertility assumptions are shown in Table 4; projections based on the high and low mortality assumptions are shown in Table 5.

Under the assumptions of the standard projection, the labour force continues to grow in this decade and the following two, increasing by more than a third between 1981 and 2011. However, the rate of growth in the 1980s is less than half that of the 1970s; the rate drops sharply in

TABLE 4. LABOUR FORCE OF CANADA, 1951-81, WITH PROJECTIONS TO 2051: ALTERNATIVE FERTILITY ASSUMPTIONS

Year	Total (1,000s)	% Growth, Previous Decade	Women per 1,000 Men	Distribution by Age (%)					
				15-24	25-34	35-44	45-54	55-64	65+
1951	5351	—	296	24.6	23.9	21.0	15.6	10.3	4.6
1961	6677	24.8	387	21.9	22.9	22.6	18.2	10.7	3.8
1971	8737	30.9	523	25.7	22.7	19.9	17.8	11.3	2.5
1981	11985	37.2	689	25.8	27.9	19.8	15.4	9.6	1.6
— standard projection —									
1991	14101	17.8	765	17.9	29.7	25.8	16.4	8.8	1.4
2001	15793	12.0	816	16.2	23.0	28.1	22.1	9.5	1.2
2011	16512	4.6	797	16.1	22.3	22.5	24.7	13.0	1.4
2021	16182	-2.0	780	14.9	23.2	23.3	21.2	15.6	1.9
2031	15673	-3.1	780	15.4	21.9	24.4	22.2	13.6	2.4
2041	15419	-1.6	778	15.4	22.5	22.9	23.0	14.0	2.3
2051	15012	-2.6	776	15.1	22.5	23.7	21.7	14.6	2.4
— high-fertility projection —									
1991	14101	17.8	765	17.9	29.7	25.8	16.4	8.8	1.4
2001	15805	12.1	816	16.3	23.0	28.0	22.1	9.5	1.2
2011	17231	9.0	801	19.4	21.5	21.5	23.7	12.5	1.3
2021	18671	8.9	794	21.1	25.3	20.2	18.3	13.5	1.7
2031	20774	10.7	801	21.3	26.5	23.2	16.9	10.3	1.8
2041	24161	16.3	806	22.3	25.6	23.1	18.4	9.0	1.5
2051	28184	16.7	805	21.9	26.5	22.2	18.3	9.8	1.3
— low-fertility projection —									
1991	14101	17.8	765	17.9	29.7	25.8	16.4	8.8	1.4
2001	15791	12.0	816	16.2	23.0	28.1	22.1	9.5	1.2
2011	16346	3.5	796	15.3	22.5	22.7	25.0	13.2	1.4
2021	15587	-4.6	776	13.1	22.5	24.1	22.0	16.2	2.0
2031	14533	-6.8	773	13.7	20.4	24.8	23.9	14.7	2.6
2041	13627	-6.2	769	13.5	21.2	22.4	24.4	15.8	2.6
2051	12556	-7.9	766	13.1	21.3	23.8	22.5	16.5	2.8

Note: Women per 1,000 men and distributions by age for 1951-81 refer to civilian labour force only; projected figures include members of the armed forces, but the effects of this are very small.

the 1990s, sharply again in the first decade of the next century, and thereafter is negative. The labour force thus stops growing two decades before the population.

The labour force ages rapidly as its growth rate falls. The proportion under 35 declines from 54 percent in 1981 to 38 percent by 2011, while the proportion 45 and over increases from 27 percent to 39 percent. Such changes have implications for the promotion prospects of individuals, and also for labour force mobility; these we discuss below.

Even with slower growth, the sex composition of the labour force continues to shift in the earlier part of the projection period; by the turn of the century there are more than 800 women per 1,000 men. The ratio then declines slightly, but remains high, relative to historical levels.

What happens under alternative assumptions? With high fertility, as we have seen, the population grows rapidly. This rapid growth is reflected, with a lag, in relatively high rates of labour force growth. Even so, the labour force grows much less rapidly over the next several decades than over the past few. Nonetheless, after three or four decades its size is markedly greater, and the fraction of young people significantly higher. When the low fertility assumption is invoked, the impact on population growth is immediate, but the impact on the labour force is again negligible until the early years of the next century. Under all three fertility assumptions—standard, high, and low—there is a strong tendency for the average age of the labour force to rise. For example, the proportion of the labour force 45 and over increases from 27 percent in 1981 to 38 percent in 2011 if high fertility is assumed, to 39 percent if the standard assumption is made, and to 40 percent with low fertility.

Alternative mortality assumptions have little effect on the projected labour force—either its size or its age distribution—as can be seen from Table 5. Even by 2051 the overall size of the labour force differs by only 1 percent as between the low and high mortality projections.

We should, then, anticipate a substantial aging of the labour force over the next few decades. To the extent that job promotion for younger members of the labour force depends on the upward movement and then retirement of older members, the process of promotion will be slower in the future than it has been in recent decades. Because of the increased competition of persons of the same age or older, a smaller fraction of the baby-boom group will reach the most senior positions, and those who do will reach them later in life than did those who came before them. Also, the propensity of individuals to move among industries, occupations, and geographic regions tends to decrease with age, and this suggests that the

TABLE 5. LABOUR FORCE OF CANADA, 1951–81, WITH PROJECTIONS TO 2051: ALTERNATIVE MORTALITY ASSUMPTIONS

Year	Total (1,000s)	% Growth, Previous Decade per 1,000	Women per 1,000 Men	Distribution by Age (%)					
				15-24	25-34	35-44	45-54	55-64	65+
1951	5351	—	296	24.6	23.6	21.0	15.6	10.3	4.6
1961	6677	24.8	387	21.9	22.9	22.6	18.2	10.7	3.8
1971	8737	30.9	523	25.7	22.7	19.9	17.8	11.3	2.5
1981	11985	37.2	688	25.8	27.9	19.8	15.4	9.6	1.6
— standard projection —									
1991	14101	17.8	765	17.9	29.7	25.8	16.4	8.8	1.4
2001	15793	12.0	816	16.2	23.0	28.1	22.1	5.5	1.2
2011	16512	4.6	797	16.1	22.3	22.5	24.7	13.0	1.4
2021	16182	-2.0	780	14.9	23.2	23.3	21.2	15.6	1.9
2031	15673	-3.1	780	15.4	21.9	24.4	22.2	13.6	2.4
2041	15419	-1.6	778	15.4	22.5	22.9	23.0	14.0	2.3
2051	15012	-2.6	776	15.1	22.5	23.7	21.7	14.6	2.4
— high-mortality projection —									
1991	14100	17.8	765	17.9	29.7	25.8	16.4	8.8	1.4
2001	15787	12.0	817	16.2	23.0	28.1	22.1	9.4	1.2
2011	16489	4.4	797	16.1	22.3	22.5	24.7	13.0	1.4
2021	16133	-2.2	781	14.9	23.3	23.3	21.2	15.5	1.9
2031	15605	-3.3	781	15.5	22.0	24.5	22.2	13.5	2.3
2041	15335	-1.7	780	15.4	22.6	22.9	23.0	13.9	2.2
2051	14916	-2.7	778	15.1	22.6	23.7	21.7	14.6	2.3
— low-mortality projection —									
1991	14102	17.8	765	17.9	29.7	25.8	16.4	8.8	1.4
2001	15796	12.0	816	16.2	23.0	28.0	22.1	9.5	1.2
2011	16522	4.6	796	16.1	22.3	22.5	24.7	13.1	1.4
2021	16202	-1.9	780	14.8	23.1	23.2	21.2	15.7	1.9
2031	15707	-3.1	779	15.4	21.9	24.4	22.2	13.6	2.4
2041	15472	-1.5	777	15.3	22.4	22.8	23.0	14.1	2.4
2051	15080	-2.5	775	15.0	22.5	23.6	21.7	14.7	2.5

DENTON & SPENCER / *Economic and Demographic Implications*   95

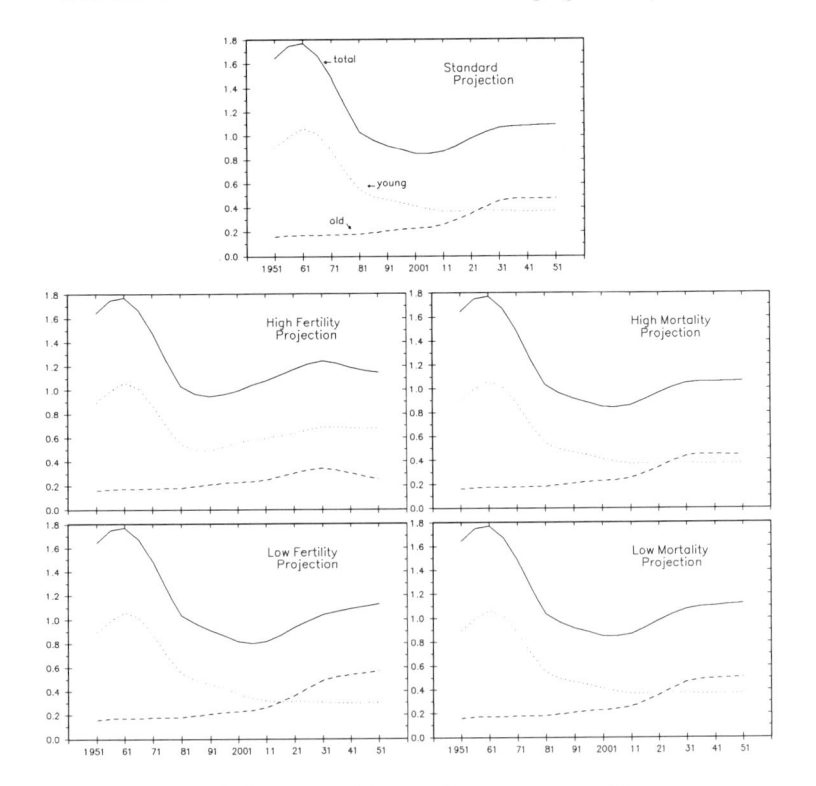

FIGURE 6. LABOUR FORCE DEPENDENCY RATIOS,
HISTORICAL AND PROJECTED

Note: The plot labelled *total* is the ratio of the total non-labour force to
the total labour force; *young* is the ratio of the non-labour force under
20 to the total labour force; and *old* the non-labour force 65 and over
to the total labour force. *Source:* Ratios for 1951–81 based on Statistics
Canada, *Labour Force*; values for 1986–2051 based on projections by
the authors.

labour force may be less mobile in the future than in the recent past—less
willing to change jobs, and generally more conservative.

Having considered above some dependency ratios based on the
population age distribution, we now consider some that are based on the
labour force. Figure 6 shows three such ratios for each projection: the
ratio of the total non-labour force to the total labour force, and the ratios
of those under 20 and those 65 and over but not in the labour force to
the total labour force.

Each of these three ratios was low in 1981, by historical standards,
implying that an average member of the labour force had relatively few
dependents to support. The old dependency ratio is seen to rise in the

future under all five projections, but it rises more the lower the fertility rate and the lower the mortality rate. The young ratio continues to fall, except under the assumption of high fertility, and even then it does not reach the 1976 level until some three decades into the next century. The overall dependency ratio is lower throughout the projection period than it was during the 1960s and 1970s, whichever projection is considered. Again, this observation should provide some reassurance for those who are concerned about the future burdens associated with the aging of the population.

Implications for the Macro-economy

Population change affects the potential size and age distribution of the labour force, as we have seen, and hence affects the productive capacity or potential supply of output of the economy. At the same time, popula-tion change affects the composition of the aggregate demand for goods and services. For example, education expenditures are associated mostly with younger age groups while major expenditures on health care are associ-ated largely with the older population. In general, we might anticipate some important population-related effects on the macro-economy over the next several decades, reflecting the basic changes in life-cycle patterns that have taken place.

An assessment of the probable impact of projected population and labour force change on the macro-economy is facilitated by the use of a computer-based model that incorporates key relationships linking the population and the economy. We have developed several such models, and made use of them in various attempts to anticipate at least the broad out-lines of future population effects.[6] The model that we use here to obtain some illustrative results abstracts from changes in unemployment and inflation levels in order to concentrate on longer-run developments associ-ated with demographic events. The model is designed to simulate the im-pact of population change on the productive capacity of the economy, and to suggest the fraction of that capacity that would have to be allocated to the public pension and old age security system, to health care, and to edu-cation if current levels of services at each age were to be maintained.

Let us expand briefly on what is meant by maintaining "current levels of service." Consider pension costs first. Transfers of purchasing power to Canada's elderly from public sources consist of payments made under the Canada and Quebec Pension Plans, old age security (OAS) payments, and the guaranteed income supplement (GIS). We assume the average amount received by those 65 and over from these sources together to be roughly one-quarter of the average wage of the working population. In the case of pension expenditures, then, a constant level of service means maintaining the average transfer to those 65 and over at one-quarter of the average wage. In the case of health care and education, we have constructed age-profiles of average expenditure levels. Based on these profiles, together with total expenditure data relating to a recent year, the average costs for each age-sex group are estimated, in constant dollars. These costs are assumed to represent the base level of service for the given age and sex, and the aggregate expenditures required to maintain the base levels as the population changes are projected.

Projections are made separately for each of pension costs, health-care costs, and education costs, based on each of the five population projections. The aggregate costs so calculated are compared to the productive capacity of the economy, which itself depends on the future population. The results of the projections are tabulated in Table 6; values are also provided for 1981, for purposes of comparison.

Three measures of productive capacity are reported in the table: total output capacity, capacity per capita (i.e., per population member), and capacity per unit of labour (a concept that is discussed below). Each of these is indexed at 100.0 in 1981. Four cost measures are reported: one for each of pensions, health care, and education, each expressed as a percent of total productive capacity, and the sum of all three, again as a percent of capacity. The pension cost is set at 3.4 percent of capacity in the base year 1981. This is the level required with the 1981 Canadian population and labour force, in combination with our model of a hypothetical economy operating at full capacity, to provide to each person 65 and over an amount equal to one-quarter of the average wage. The other measures—health-care costs at 7.0 percent of capacity and education costs at 7.5 percent—are based on estimated Canadian proportions for 1981. The initial levels themselves are realistic, but our focus is on how the levels would change over time as the population changes.

In the standard projection, the total output of the economy rises by 24 percent by 2001 even, as is assumed here, without the benefit of general improvements in productivity levels. This gain results from the continued growth in the labour force in the 1980s and 1990s. Output per capita also grows, but only very slowly, and output per labour unit actually declines. The "labour units" on which the calculations are based are not simply labour force counts; they take account also of differences in average productive characteristics associated with men and women of

TABLE 6. HYPOTHETICAL PRODUCTIVE CAPACITY AND EXPENDITURE RATIOS UNDER ALTERNATIVE POPULATION PROJECTIONS, 1981–2051

Year	Productive Capacity			(% of productive capacity)			
	Total	Total per capita	per labour unit	Pension Costs	Health-care Costs	Education Costs	Total
1981	100.0	100.0	100.0	3.4	7.0	7.5	17.9
— standard projection —							
1991	113.2	101.8	94.4	3.8	7.3	6.0	17.1
2001	124.2	103.6	91.8	4.1	7.5	5.6	17.2
2011	130.7	103.2	91.6	4.7	8.0	5.1	17.7
2021	131.0	99.7	93.1	6.4	8.8	4.8	20.0
2031	128.5	96.6	94.5	8.3	9.5	4.9	22.8
2041	127.1	96.3	95.0	8.6	9.9	4.8	23.3
2051	124.8	96.7	95.6	8.7	9.9	4.7	23.3
— high-fertility projection —							
1991	113.1	100.3	94.4	3.8	7.5	6.0	17.4
2001	124.1	96.0	91.7	4.1	8.1	6.3	18.6
2011	132.6	90.3	90.5	4.5	8.8	7.3	20.6
2021	141.0	84.2	89.5	5.5	9.6	7.9	23.0
2031	152.1	79.6	87.8	6.3	10.2	8.7	25.1
2041	170.7	78.6	85.0	5.5	10.1	9.1	24.7
2051	194.3	78.2	82.8	4.7	9.9	9.2	23.8
— low-fertility projection —							
1991	113.2	102.2	94.4	3.8	7.2	6.0	17.0
2001	124.3	105.5	91.8	4.1	7.3	5.4	16.8
2011	130.2	106.8	91.8	4.7	7.8	4.5	17.1
2021	128.6	103.9	94.0	6.6	8.6	4.1	19.4
2031	122.9	100.8	96.4	9.0	9.5	4.1	22.5
2041	117.2	100.3	97.9	9.8	10.0	3.9	23.6
2051	110.0	100.2	99.6	10.4	10.2	3.8	24.4
— high-mortality projection —							
1991	113.1	101.8	94.4	3.8	7.2	6.0	17.1
2001	124.2	103.7	91.8	4.1	7.4	5.6	17.1
2011	130.5	103.6	91.6	4.6	7.9	5.1	17.6

TABLE 6. HYPOTHETICAL PRODUCTIVE CAPACITY AND EXPENDITURE RATIOS UNDER ALTERNATIVE POPULATION PROJECTIONS, *continued*

Year	Productive Capacity			Pension Costs	Health-care Costs	Education Costs	Total
	Total	per capita	per labour unit	(% of productive capacity)			
2021	130.7	100.4	93.2	6.2	8.6	4.9	19.6
2031	128.2	97.7	94.7	7.9	9.3	4.9	22.1
2041	126.8	97.9	95.3	8.1	9.5	4.8	22.4
2051	124.4	98.5	96.0	8.1	9.5	4.7	22.3
			— low-mortality projection —				
1991	113.2	101.8	94.4	3.9	7.3	6.0	17.1
2001	124.3	103.5	91.8	4.1	7.5	5.6	17.2
2011	130.7	103.1	91.6	4.7	8.0	5.1	17.8
2021	131.1	99.4	93.0	6.5	8.8	4.8	20.2
2031	128.7	96.0	94.4	8.5	9.7	4.9	23.1
2041	127.3	95.2	94.8	9.0	10.1	4.8	23.9
2051	125.0	95.2	95.4	9.2	10.2	4.7	24.2

different ages. The implication of the decline in output per labour unit, then, is that the anticipated labour force growth includes disproportionate numbers of people in the relatively less productive age-sex groups in the population.

What of costs? Both pension costs and health costs are seen to rise fairly steadily over the next two or three decades, as proportions of the economy's output capacity. The proportions then increase sharply as the baby-boom generation reaches old age. The initial increases are offset by declines in education costs, leaving the total cost ratio in 2011 somewhat below that of 1981. Thereafter education costs remain approximately constant while the other two costs rise, causing the overall proportion to increase by more than 5 percentage points—from 17.7 percent of capacity in output in 2011 to 22.8 percent in 2031, and then to 23.3 percent in 2041. These figures suggest that significant population-induced changes in overall public expenditure requirements are still some decades off, and that even when they arrive they will be of a magnitude that the economy should be able to sustain without major distortion. Moreover, there is every likelihood that increases in productivity will far outweigh population-induced increases in such costs by the time they materialize. In addition, there may well be cost-reducing technologies available in health care, and possibly in education, that would offset further the population effects.

Alternative population projections naturally lead to somewhat differ-ent outcomes. Pension costs will rise by more in relation to productive capacity, the lower are future fertility and mortality rates; the health-care costs proportion will rise by more, at least over the next few decades, the higher are fertility rates and the lower are mortality rates; the educa-tion cost proportion will rise more with high fertility and will be virtually unaffected by mortality change. At the overall level, only with a return to high fertility would the total cost ratio rise above the 1981 level before 2021, and even then the cost differences, while substantial, would not be of such a magnitude as to constitute a "crisis."

Concluding Remarks

The concern of this paper has been to draw out some of the main demo-graphic and economic implications of three major categories of life-cycle change: shifts in fertility rates, increases in life expectancy, and changes in patterns of labour force participation. We have discussed the nature of the changes that have occurred in recent decades, and the likely range of future changes. The various threads of the discussion have been brought together in the context of a computer-based model of the overall economic-demographic system, and this model has been used to provide illustrative projections of the possible effects of population change on future levels of public expenditure in relation to the future productive capacity of the economy. We would certainly not suggest that our projec-tions anticipate with any precision the future course of events. Our aim has been, rather, to provide some very general indication of the problems at the macro-level with which the economic system will have to cope over the next several decades as a consequence of population and labour force change.

A particular concern is the future pension and health-care costs associated with the elderly. As we have seen, these can be expected to grow, and to grow markedly. However, the major population-induced in-creases in the required shares of the gross national product will not occur for another two and one-half to three decades. In the meantime, an off-setting reduction in the share going to education expenditures can be anticipated, unless of course there is an early (and, one would think, unlikely) return to high fertility levels. Even if fertility levels were to rise sharply, the anticipated burden of overall costs would still be manageable. Thus the major conclusions that stem from the analysis can be viewed as optimistic: the gains in longevity, which most of us would consider highly desirable in their own right, are not likely to produce "crises" in the costs of supporting the elderly; the historical swings in fertility rates and the continuing changes in patterns of labour force participation will certainly have their impact on the future economy, but there is no reason to believe that the economy and the governments of the future will not be able to take the coming changes in stride, and to adjust to them without major economic disruption.

Notes

1. Victor R. Fuchs, *How We Live* (Cambridge: Harvard University Press, 1983), provides an insightful discussion and analysis of recent changes in U.S. life cycle patterns.

2. It should be noted that there is some inconsistency in the use of the term "single" over time. Before 1974 it meant that the parents were not married to each other at the date of birth or registration. Starting with 1974 it has meant that the marital status of the mother is single, widowed, divorced, or not stated.

3. Based on A. Romaniuc, *Fertility in Canada: From Baby-Boom to Baby-Bust*, catalogue no. 91-524E (Ottawa: Statistics Canada, 1984), 144.

4. Based on ibid., 37.

5. Jacob S. Siegel, "On the Demography of Aging," *Demography* 17 (1980): 348.

6. The interested reader is referred to Frank T. Denton and Byron G. Spencer, "A Simulation Analysis of the Effects of Population Change on a Neoclassical Economy," *Journal of Political Economy* 81, no. 2 (1973); idem, "Health-Care Costs When the Population Changes," *Canadian Journal of Economics* 8 (1975); idem, "A Macroeconomic Analysis of the Effects of a Public Pension Plan," *Canadian Journal of Economics* 14 (1981); idem, "Population Aging and Future Health Costs in Canada," *Canadian Public Policy* 9 (1983); and Frank T. Denton, Byron G. Spencer, and Christine H. Feaver, "OASI and the U.S. Economy: A Model and Some Long-Run Projections," in *Social Security and Pensions: Programs of Equity and Security*, Joint Economic Committee of the Congress of the United States, Special Study on Economic Change, Vol. 8 (Washington, D.C.: Government Printing Office, 1980).

Social Time Clocks: Transforming Later Life

JOSEPH A. TINDALE

WHEN SOMEONE ASKS you "What time is it?" their meaning is clear and you typically respond with the time of day according to your wristwatch. However, when asked "Are you having a good time?" or "Has your expenditure of time been well rewarded?" the questions and the answers are more complex. This is because the difference between the first question and the second and third questions is the difference between simply counting time and making sense of time.

McPherson, in an address to the Canadian Association on Gerontology, made two fundamental points about the relationship of time to later life.[1] First, studies of the meaning and use of time across the life cycle are very rare. And second, those studies of time in later life that do exist concentrate, with few exceptions, on the allocation of time in terms of frequency and almost ignore questions of the meaning and perception of time. McPherson's interests lay with the allocation, perception, and meaning of time held by older persons along the work-retirement-leisure continuum. My interests lie not with the application of time to particular pursuits, as with leisure for example, but with the social situations and historical conditions that shape the boundaries of possibility in time use. In that sense I am taking one of McPherson's concluding remarks as my point of departure. He notes that where studies of the meaning and perception of time have been carried out, one finds that meaning and perception vary not only by age cohort, but by marital status, education, income, gender, and the presence or absence of children. These reflect both ascribed and achieved statuses that have meanings that vary with the passage of historical time and with social situation and condition.

What I want to focus on, then, are some of the changes that have taken place in terms of socio-historical time—for example, the much debated issue of modernization. Second, I want to draw your attention to ways in which the changing social conditions are tied to demographic shifts to affect how people perform and transform roles as they progress through the latter third of the life cycle.

Proponents of the modernization thesis suggest that the status of older persons is inversely related to the degree of social, technological, and economic modernization that characterizes their society. Adherents to this thesis and their detractors have for the last twenty years been collecting the data they hope will confirm their respective positions. The debate, I might add, is not purely academic. The future direction of social policy for older persons, including the question of universality, is inextricably tied to how one interprets the modernization material.

Throughout this paper I will be invoking an interpretive theoretical framework that directs our attention to the social construction of meaning. As such, the meanings attributed to the timing of role transitions are processual. That is, they are ongoing, dynamic, and require negotiation between the individual actor, his or her fellow actors or immediate participants, and the audience or community.[2]

The interpretive perspective is also complemented by the historical life course perspective.[3] This perspective focuses on the interaction between individual, family, and historical time over the life course. It examines how the timing of entry into and exit from social roles is influenced by this interaction, and specifically, how macro social conditions bear on the choices available to individuals.

The specific questions I will address revolve around the modernization debate within the areas of work and the changing nature of family structure. Work and family phenomena interact with each other as populations evolve, and so, in addition to providing a brief demographic background to some of these questions, I will also try to illustrate the linkages. I will do this by briefly discussing two of my research projects.

One of these projects deals with the maintenance of identity among old men on skid row as their cohort grows older and the community they live in develops around them. The other has less to do with family, and more to do with generational succession in the work setting and how historically emergent social conditions affect the timing of entry into and exit out of work roles, and the quality of the relationship involved in this succession. The context for the latter develops the concept of seniority via a discussion of the situation Ontario secondary school teachers have experienced as a result of enrolment declines in a period of economic restraint.

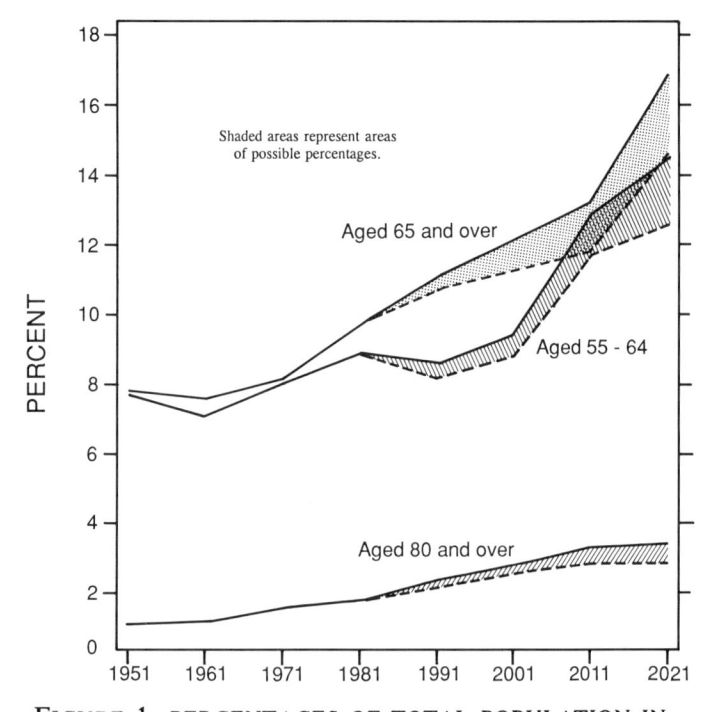

FIGURE 1. PERCENTAGES OF TOTAL POPULATION IN
SELECTED AGE GROUPS, CANADA, 1951–2021

Source: Government of Canada, *Fact Book on Aging in
Canada* (Ottawa: Supply & Services, 1983), Figure 3.1.

Setting the Demographic Stage

In considering, for example, the arguments and counter-arguments regarding the legitimacy of the modernization thesis, it is necessary to
know how the overall population structure has changed over the last century in Canada. As a case in point, are we now talking about a different
group of people relative to the rest of the population than we were prior
to the modern era? Similarly at the more micro end of the spectrum, before we can appreciate the ways in which grandparenting is evolving as
a dimension of intergenerational family life, it is helpful to see graphically how a phenomenon like the potential availability of family support
is being transformed over the life course of the baby-boom generation.

First, consider Figure 1, a comparison of the proportion of the total
population represented by particular age groups between 1951 and 2021.
We can see that with the exception of the decade 1951–1961, the proportions for each of the three cohorts have risen. The exception is explained

by the birth of the baby-boom generation pulling down the aged proportions. The jump occurring around 2011 represents the entrance of the
baby boomers into later life. The growth of the 80-plus cohort is equally
dramatic, although it may not appear so at first glance. We have, then,
in this seventy-year period a doubling of proportions that had taken all
of recorded time to reach the 8 percent level in 1951 for those persons
65 years of age and over.

At the same time as the proportion of the population that is aged is
growing, principally because of declining fertility rates, the life expectancy of individuals is expanding because of declining infant mortality,
better nutrition, and a plateauing of lifestyle diseases such as heart disease owing to reduced rates of smoking. Statistics Canada reported in
December 1984 that life expectancy at birth for men is 72, and women
can now expect to live 79 years. The gap between the sexes is still siz-
able, and it is too soon to tell whether women will curb their recently
acquired habits as quickly as men so as to maintain the gap. If they do,
a biologically explained gap of at least several years will persist.

Current projections of gender-related life expectancy produce some
startling images of male-female ratios and gender-based proportions of
the populations having particular marital statuses at different points of the
life cycle. Each of these has a direct bearing on the transformation over
time of later-life family structure.

Figure 2 illustrates how, for overall ages, the shift from male to
female domination of the gender ratio has not been enormous. It is when
one accounts for differences in life expectancy that one sees significant
differences in the female-to-male ratio. As the projections suggest, we do
not expect to see changes in life expectancy that would dramatically alter
the ratio of women to men in the later years of life.

The differences in life expectancy producing a high female-to-male
ratio in later life have implications we might anticipate for marital status.
Figure 3 reveals that as one ages, the proportion of widowed women climbs
much earlier in the life cycle than the proportion of widowed men. At
age 70, for example, 10 percent of the male population over age 50 is
widowed. At the same age approximately 45 percent of women are widowed.
This reflects a shorter life expectancy for men and a greater likelihood
that men widowed once can remarry.

I will conclude this abbreviated demographic excursion by using Figure 4 to note that with declining fertility and increased life expectancy,
the potential availability of family support is generally declining. The
exception occurs for the over-80 cohort when the parents of the baby-
boom generation achieve this age beginning around the turn of the

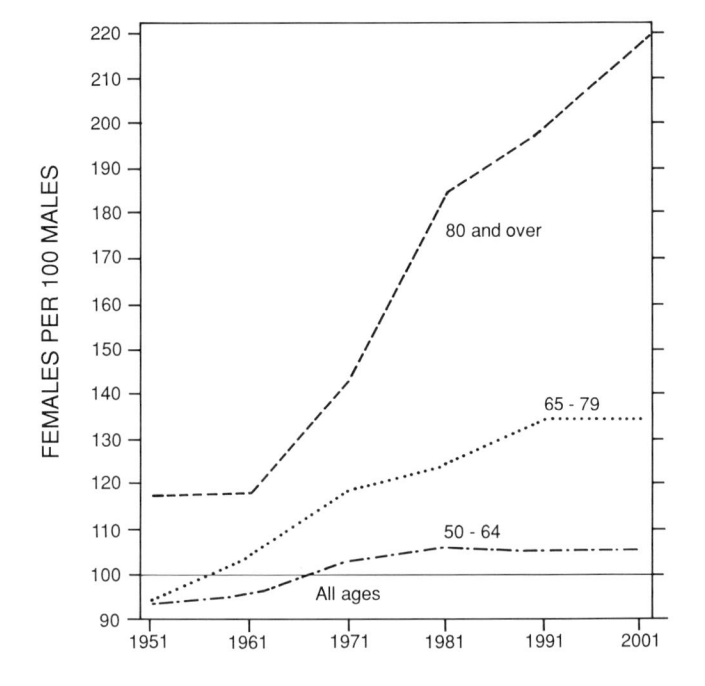

FIGURE 2. RATIO OF FEMALES TO MALES IN
SELECTED AGE GROUPS, CANADA, 1951–2001

Source: Government of Canada, *Fact Book on Aging in Canada* (Ottawa: Supply & Services, 1983), Figure 3.3.

century. At about the same time, however, the index drops for the 65–79 cohort because these are the baby-boom children entering later life, and they are having fewer children than their parents did.

Taken together, the available demographic data suggest a number of things that are relevant in our attempt to understand how the aged experience the passage of time over the course of their own life cycle and as one cohort of older persons succeeds the next. We note, most generally, that the population structure is changing. It is changing in that the proportion of the overall population that is older is growing. As well, the ratio of women to men has increased over the last several decades, and increases over the life course of an individual. This in turn has an impact on family structures.

Overall, the experience of any individual within an older cohort, or that cohort as a whole, is different from the experience of individuals within cohorts before and after it.[4] This is important because it helps demonstrate the falsehood of any claim to universality in terms of what

108   FUNCTIONAL ACCOUNTS OF TIME

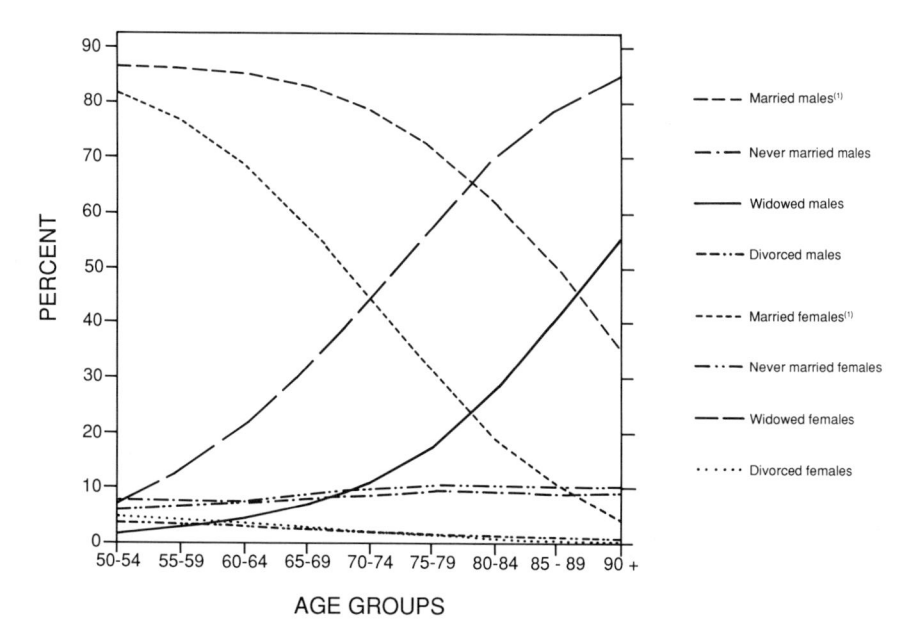

FIGURE 3. PERCENTAGES OF POPULATION AGED 50
AND OVER IN SELECTED MARITAL STATUS GROUPS,
BY SEX AND AGE, CANADA, 1981

Source: Government of Canada, *Fact Book on Aging in
Canada* (Ottawa: Supply & Services, 1983), Figure 9.1.1.
[1] Includes separated.

the experience of aging is all about. Historically different conditions and
attitudes continue to alter patterns of fertility and life expectancy. If we
take this a step further and apply it to the modernization issue, we find
the issue of universality debated and found wanting.

Are the Experiences of Socio-Historical Time Universal?

Modernization theory is presented by its creators, Cowgill and Holmes,[5]
as a theory of social change that purports to document that the passage of
social and historical time from pre-industrial to industrial times has
caused a steady and inevitable decline in the role and status of the aged
at the same time as the society modernized. In fact, as Quadagno[6] has
argued, rather than being a theory of social change it could more properly
be termed a sometimes accurate description of contemporary society.

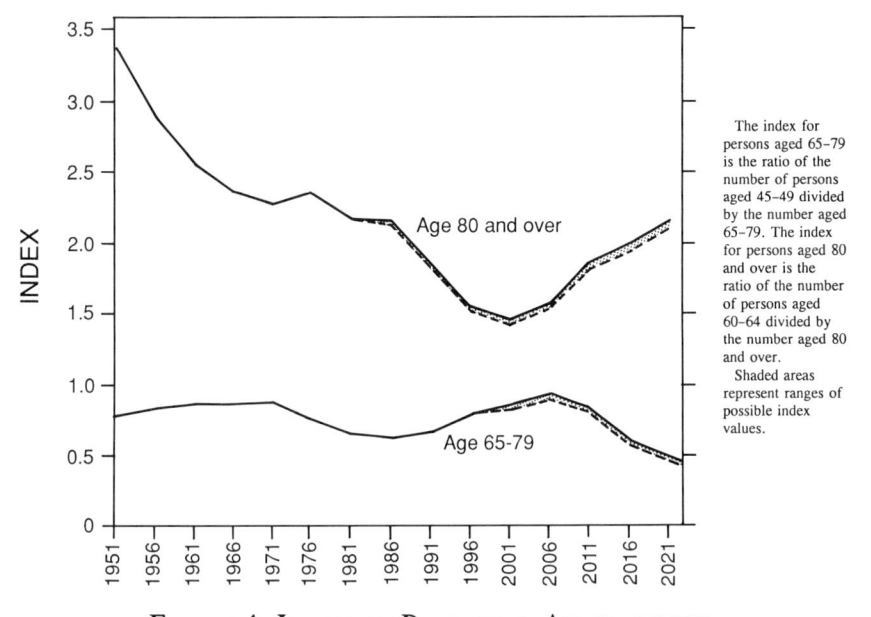

The index for persons aged 65–79 is the ratio of the number of persons aged 45–49 divided by the number aged 65–79. The index for persons aged 80 and over is the ratio of the number of persons aged 60–64 divided by the number aged 80 and over.

Shaded areas represent ranges of possible index values.

FIGURE 4. INDEX OF POTENTIAL AVAILABILITY
OF FAMILY SUPPORT, CANADA, 1951–2021

Source: Government of Canada, *Fact Book on Aging in Canada* (Ottawa: Supply & Services, 1983), Figure 9.2.

It is the failure of Cowgill and associates to adequately document a universal and inevitable decline in status that is the basis for the most fundamental fault historians, sociologists, and anthropologists find with the theory.[7]

Researchers have not found the transition from before to after that Cowgill asserts occurs with the onset of industrialization. The context for before and after is in the areas of work and family life. Laslett, Fischer, and Achenbaum[8] separately argue that there is no good historical evidence of a shift in either the world of work or family. There are, rather, a complex series of social changes that are neither universal nor simply linear.

If one considers the world of work, the evidence suggests that people were not forced into an obsolescent retirement with the arrival of ever newer technologies during industrialization.[9] Neither do the available data present the pre-industrial elderly as wanting to work late in their life, and being able to do it. And while there is some coercion in the form of mandatory retirement today, people in the pre-industrial era only worked until very late in life when financial necessity required it. Those with capital and property did retire earlier, just as they do today. In fact one can argue, as Fischer does,[10] that today's social welfare measures and increased national wealth present opportunities for easier and more comfortable retirement than was the case in the past. In sum, we do not see evidence of a before and after in the experience of retirement. We do see consistency in the desire to retire when one's financial resources allow. As well, there was no golden age of generally revered retired persons. There were some highly respected retired and working people, as there are today.

A parallel situation exists when one considers the evidence for the modernization thesis regarding the family. It posits that there has been a before and after, from closely knit extended households to atomized nuclear ones, in the process of modernizing intergenerational family relations. Laslett refers to this as the "world-we-have-lost syndrome."[11] In fact this is not a world lost, because it was never a world gained. While it is true that eighteenth- and nineteenth-century western European and North American families were more interdependent, flexible, and somewhat more likely to share residences than is the case today, this comes in large part as a result of "economic necessity rather than from tender sentiments."[12] The reality for both past and present seems to be that a modified version of the nuclear family has dominated both the pre- and post-modernized world.[13]

The related myth of abandonment, or that of the alienated elderly, which suggests families are unwilling or unable to care for their older members, has been admirably refuted by Shanas[14] and others. The stereotypical statement that "poor Mrs. So-and-so is in the Golden Pastures Nursing Home because her good-for-nothing family has deserted her," is simply not borne out by the facts. Contact with at least some of one's children or siblings is frequent and of reasonably good quality.

And finally, with regard to distortions in the reported experience of the interaction between individual, family, and historical time as laid out by the modernization theorists, we should briefly dispense with the myth of the empty-nest syndrome. "Empty nest" refers to the feelings of loss that are presumed to afflict mothers when their children mature and leave their parents' home. As Glick argues,[15] the empty nest has emerged because of the combination of earlier marriages, fewer children being born earlier in the family life cycle, the departure of those children from the home earlier than was the case in the eighteenth and nineteenth centuries, and greater life expectancy.

The empty nest is traumatic for some women who have invested a great deal of themselves in mothering, but for the majority of women, it cannot be said there is a crisis when children leave home.[16] And Troll[17] cites the work of Barber[18] and Hagestad and Snow[19] to argue that while both mothers and fathers report feelings of loss and gain at the time of child launching, the studies of these researchers, in Pennsylvania and Chicago respectively, emphasize an overall positive sense of gain as a result of experiencing new freedoms once the children have moved out of the parental nest.

In sum, this discussion of the modernization model has demonstrated, via an explanation of the work- and family-related myths the model has given rise to, that time is experienced both as individual biography and as a social process with others. We know that past demographic changes have contributed to the emergence of phenomena like the empty nest, and that projected future demographic developments have implications for family support structures, as people are expected to live longer and have fewer children than was the case previously. Taken together, we know the experience of time is not simply how you fill the hours of the day and night, but as well, how you interact with your family and community and how you fit into the history of your community.

I want now to briefly discuss two examples from my own work, which illustrate, in an expression of everyday community and work life, how individual, social, and historical time interact in a dynamic fashion that gives meaning to the lives of the participants and does not relegate these older people to an ahistorically assumed low status.

Identity of Older Men on Skid Row: Development and Process Over Time

In 1973 and 1974 I was engaged in a participant observation study of old, poor men in Hamilton, Ontario. The study employed the concepts of career[20] and stigma[21] to help me understand the sort of identity these men had, and how they developed and maintained and maintained it.[22]

This ethnographic study was also a consideration of the meanings of time Hareven speaks of.[23] I gathered material on individual time in terms of these men's personal careers and their current everyday lives. Family time was investigated to determine how "normal" or abnormal their relations with family were. Social and historical time was intertwined with their personal and family experiences as I sought to locate these phenomena in the fabric of the larger community.

One example of how these meanings of time fit together is revealed in an informal hypothesis I initially made, and that did not prove true.

I thought because the Great Depression emerged just as most of these men were coming into young adulthood, it could have had a severe impact on their lives in objective and subjective ways. Objectively, I speculated that they missed opportunities to continue their education, to gain meaningful employment, and to establish families at a point in their lives when preceding and succeeding cohorts of young people typically would do so. Subjectively, I expected that because of these missed opportunities their young adulthood, and its association with the period of the depression, would have made a great impression on them. That is, I expected some bitterness, and some attribution of blame for missed opportunities to be placed on the depression. In fact, this was not nearly so much the case as I had anticipated.

Had I known more about career and identity as it was experienced by these men, I would not have made that initial hypothesis. I think my intuitive hypothesis was logical, and it might have been more accurate with a more middle-class sample because their life-course expectations are more conventionally upscale. My intuition was off the mark because the sense these men had of their careers and identities did not incorporate nearly so much a perception of missed opportunities as I had expected.

In terms of identity, these men, ranging in age from late 50s to early 70s, had an identity that, in their view, was quite respectable. This perception of respectability was not shared by the larger community because of differences in expectations and meaning associated with career. The men I talked with were poor before the depression. They were poor during the depression and continued to be poor after the depression. The difference was that they had more company and were not considered deviant by the larger community during the decade of the 1930s. Apart from the depression, however, they have been considered deviant.

In response to this, the men have developed mechanisms of stigma management. These allow them to take a sense of respectability based on expectations that were not high, and were therefore not greatly diminished during the depression, and seek to maintain it by establishing their own community standards and meanings.

I should say here that the period of the 1930s was painful for these men, and they typically did ride the rails and live in the government work camps known as Royal Twenty Centres, where the pay was twenty cents a day. The point is that they did not see this as overwhelmingly pivotal in their lives.

Stigma is managed and respectable identities are maintained by controlling vulnerability. These old men did this by refusing to accept the perceptions of the larger community whenever possible. Contact with the

TINDALE / *Social Time Clocks*   113

larger community was kept at the perfunctory level, usually to the satisfaction of all parties concerned, and any acceptance of things like food, clothing, or shelter was seen as an exchange. In return for the food, for example, the men might attend a church service, or simply allow the soup kitchen staff to control the environment during the course of the meal.

Old men who violated the skid rowers' standards were perceived as having lost the respect of their fellow skid row community members. Old men who accepted the hostel staff's perception of them as down-and-outers in need of salvation, and demonstrated this by becoming permanently dependent on the hostel as a live-in resident, were termed "mission stiffs" by their fellows and no longer considered members of the community.

In these ways we can see how the old men managed and interpreted the interaction between their individual time and their work careers as they were seen both by themselves and by the larger community. And for the most part, the men were successful in maintaining their respectable identities pretty much intact when the issue was personal-care needs or their work careers. This was not the case when the issue under examination was family.

Only 50 percent of these men had ever been married, as compared with more than 90 percent of the general adult public, and none of these men were still with their wives. Some of them had children, and siblings who were still alive, but they were very infrequently seen or discussed. It was here, in the experience of family time, that these men felt especially vulnerable and because of this had a diminished sense of identity that was correspondingly difficult to maintain. The primary defence they used was to talk about family as little as possible, and to say as little as possible when they did have to talk about family.

In sum, the old men on skid row are a unique example of how individual, family, and social time interact. Their struggles to develop and maintain a strong sense of identity over the life course reveal the complexity of what is involved in later-life status. Their roles as workers and family members are intertwined, and the role transitions they have experienced in later life are consistent with their overall biography.

In my second example there is not the same sense of historical time in terms of career, although it is similar. What is more important than the sense of career overall is the more particular issue and concept of seniority. And seniority is important because it too meshes one's own individual time relative to that of others' in the same workplace, and then ties this to the external circumstances that help shape the nature of the seniority relationships among professional teachers.

Seniority and Redundancy: The Politics of Experience

My research with teachers involves data collected in 1979 on a 1 percent random sample of Ontario Secondary School Teachers Federation (OSSTF) members, with whom I examined the relationship between external social conditions and the internal issue of seniority.[24] The external conditions combined provincial budget restraint with enrolment declines associated with the baby-boom generation's passing through secondary school. The result was surplus teachers. The method chosen to resolve this was to drastically restrict new hiring and in many cases to use seniority as the justification for not renewing a teacher's contract. The lay-off process employed a mechanism termed "bumping" whereby a teacher who finds him or herself redundant in a school can bump another, less senior teacher in the school board. In short, the more junior teacher is not renewed and the teacher with seniority takes the job.

My central hypothesis concerning this relationship was that if there was not age-based tension prior to bumping, there likely would be after it began. And if there already was some age-related tension, it would be exacerbated by bumping. One secondary hypothesis was that older teachers would perceive some pressure on them to take advantage of early retirement options where they were available. A third hypothesis was that promotion opportunities would be greatly curtailed because the people hired to accommodate the baby boom would still have ten to twenty years left in their careers. And finally, I suggested that the ability of teachers to resolve the internal question of surplus teachers was constrained by their position as a quasi profession, because of which they were unable to exercise sufficient control over the work process to moderate the redundancy problem.

My results revealed that whether one is discussing surpluses, alternative promotion plans, or early retirement scenarios, age is a relevant factor. And because of this, the age-based tension that I found existed already to some degree, was heightened by the problems resulting from enrolment declines. It is primarily young teachers who are subject to redundancy job loss. With the exception of some young women seeking to retire to raise children, the great majority of those who are subject to pressure to take early retirement are older teachers. And it is those who have gained enough experience to secure their jobs who breathe a sigh

TINDALE / *Social Time Clocks*

of relief, only to discover opportunities for career advancement have been greatly diminished by the collapse in promotion opportunities.

Space does not permit me to go into these results in detail. I therefore want to briefly discuss the relationship between external conditions and the above-mentioned internal age-related situation. I will then tie the relationship between the external and internal to the concept of seniority. My research suggested that teachers belong to an occupation that has historically sought professional status and to some degree achieved it. At the same time, in periods of challenge such as the one we are discussing, teachers have found themselves reminded that control of the work environment, the feature that in many ways defines a profession, has largely eluded them. While they exercise considerable decision-making authority on a day-to-day basis in the classroom, the ultimate control of curricula, working hours, hiring, and salaries rests with the provincial government. In terming teaching a quasi profession, or a profession under challenge, I am placing it in good company. As the work process generally becomes more differentiated, there is more competition for control over particular job tasks. This occurs both for occupations trying to be defined as professions, such as policing, and traditional professions, such as medicine, whose practitioners are fighting to retain the position they have held at least for most of this century.

Throughout this struggle over redundancy that teachers have been engaged in, we see the interaction again of individual, social, and historical time. This interaction is played out in the operationalization of the concept of seniority. Seniority can most simply be defined as "status ascribed by birth order."[25] when the context is age grading. And because we find that younger teachers are most vulnerable because of their lack of experience, birth order is relevant. At the same time, there are examples of people entering teaching later in life, and so the cohort they enter with may be younger than themselves.

Seniority is associated with experience, where experience is "the application to contemporary problems of previous solutions or modes of solution."[26] Now clearly, solutions are not simply repeated verbatim; it is the knowledge that comes from dealing with similar modes of problems and solutions that makes a teacher with experience more valuable than one who is a relative newcomer. Seniority also rewards people for the time, as part of their own life course, that they have invested in the job and "given to the company."

At the same time, generally younger and certainly less experienced teachers are frustrated. They do not have the same opportunity to acquire this valuable experience because of the accident of birth and the socio-historical conditions that have accompanied their cohort's passage through the life course. Those persons maturing as the baby-boom children began to enter secondary school had vastly greater opportunities for successfully gaining employment, experience, and upward mobility in the profession than those people maturing and starting their teaching career just as the baby-boom children finished secondary school and moved on.

In sum, the experience of the secondary school teachers reveals, in a different context from that of the old men on skid row, how the meaning of time is perceived. Individual time experienced as career is involved in a struggle about seniority, where experience is the key. This has happened because the social progression of demographic patterns has meshed with the historically evolving social condition of economic restraint. The drama is acted out on a social level that combines the internal issue of seniority with the external one of the relationship between teachers and the larger community in terms of being able to control their work futures. Taken together, the centrality of seniority has been heightened because of social and historical processes that have had an impact on the timing of entry and exit from the work role. As conditions change over historical time, and as the size of child and adult cohorts varies, so will the importance of seniority and the meaning of time at the individual, social, and historical levels.

Conclusions: The Dynamics of Social Time Clocks

In sum, the experience of old men on skid row and teachers illustrates how the status of older persons cannot be presumed to be linear or universal over historical time. It is the playing out of time in a social context, as social time clocks if you will, that gives the lie to this myth. We have seen that it is the decisions individuals make throughout their life course, in response to how they "fit" with broadly based demographic and socio-economic patterns, that makes time meaningful.

In the case of the old skid rowers, it is the construction of a community of fellows that makes the passage of time meaningful in a manner not appreciated by society at large. The interpretation of work situations and the struggle to make sense of family life course patterns shape the identities these old men develop. And identity is processually maintained as they and their cohort move along in step with the flow of history.

All of the same components are at work in the case of the secondary school teachers. Their current situation is, first of all, a moving picture.

The enrolment declines and tight budget conditions of the 1970s and 1980s to date, are socially based historical phenomena that interact with the social and historical growth of the OSSTF. These two sets of macro phenomena are dynamically interwoven with the internal structure of sur-plus school staff and the declarations of redundancy leading to bumping and lay-offs. The process of bumping exacerbates existing levels of age tension by frustrating junior personnel and pressuring older ones to consider early retirement when they might otherwise not have done so. I have used the examples of the teachers and old men on skid row to document, in a concrete way, the error in the contention of the modern-ization theorists that the experience of time for older persons is universal, and linearly downward in status. Specifically, several points can be iden-tified in this documentation.

Our point of departure was to show that it is how one perceives and makes sense of time that is important. We found that this sense and per-ception are influenced by the individual's passage through social and his-torical time. The passage is one of constant interaction and negotiation among the parts.[27] This process, in turn, affects the number, kind, and timing of roles one will perform over the life course. And finally, the degree of meaning you can ultimately attribute to your life, in the last period of reminiscence, will depend on your assessment of whether the constraints and opportunities you encountered, yours is a life's time well spent.

Notes

1. B. McPherson, "The Meaning and Use of Time Across the Life-Cycle: The Influence of Work, Family and Leisure" (Keynote address presented to annual meeting of the Canadian Association on Gerontology, Vancouver, 1984).

2. Victor W. Marshall, "No Exit: An Interpretive Perspective on Aging," in *Aging in Canada: Social Perspectives*, ed. V. W. Marshall (Toronto: Fitz-henry & Whiteside, 1980), 51-60.

3. T. Hareven, "The Life Course and Aging in Historical Perspective," in *Aging and Life Course Transitions: An Interdisciplinary Perspective*, ed. T. Hareven and K. J. Adams (New York: Guilford, 1982), 1-26; M. Kohli, "Aging as a Challenge for Sociological Theory," *Aging and Society* 8 (1988): 367-94.

4. L. D. Cain, Jr., "Life Course and Social Structure," in *Handbook of Modern Sociology*, ed. R. E. L. Farris (Chicago: Rand McNally, 1964); idem, "Age, Status and Generational Phenomena: The New Old People in Contemporary America," *The Gerontologist* 7 (1967): 83-92.

FUNCTIONAL ACCOUNTS OF TIME

5. D. O. Cowgill and L. D. Holmes, *Aging and Modernization* (New York: Appleton-Century-Crofts, 1972); D. O. Cowgill, "Aging and Moderniza-tion: A Revision of the Theory," in *Late Life: Communities and Environ-mental Policy*, ed. J. F. Gubrium (Springfield, Ill.: Thomas, 1974), 124-146.

6. Jill Quadagno, *Aging in Early Industrial Society: Work, Family and Social Policy in Nineteenth Century England* (New York: Academic Press, 1982).

7. Nancy Foner, "Age and Social Change," in *Age and Anthropological Theory*, ed. D. Kertzer and J. Keith (Ithaca: Cornell University Press, 1984), 195-216.

8. P. Laslett, "Societal Development and Aging," in *Handbook of Aging and the Social Sciences*, ed. R. Binstock and E. Shanas (New York: Van Nos-trand Reinhold, 1976), 87-116; D. H. Fischer, *Growing Old in America* (New York: Oxford University Press, 1978); Andrew W. Achenbaum, *Old Age in the New Land* (Baltimore: Johns Hopkins University Press, 1978).

9. Laslett, "Societal Development and Aging"; Quadagno, *Aging in Early Industrial Society*.

10. Fischer, *Growing Old in America*.

11. Laslett, "Societal Development and Aging."

12. V. L. Bengston and J. Treas, "The Changing Family Context of Mental Health and Aging," in *Handbook of Mental Health and Aging*, ed. J. E. Birren and R. B. Sloane (Englewood Cliffs, N.J.: Prentice-Hall, 1980), 405.

13. P. Laslett, *The World We Have Lost* (London: Methuen, 1971); Howard P. Chudacoff and Tamara K. Hareven, "From the Empty Nest to Family Dissolution: Life Course Transitions Into Old Age," *Journal of Family History* 4 (1979): 69-83; Hareven, "The Life Course and Aging."

14. E. Shanas, "Social Myth as Hypothesis: The Case of the Family Relations of Old People," *The Gerontologist* 19 (1979): 3-10.

15. Hareven, "The Life Course and Aging."

16. Bengston and Treas, "The Changing Family Context."

17. L. Troll, "The Family in a North American Context," in *Canadian Geron-tological Collections III: The Family of Later Life*, ed. J. Crawford (Winni-peg: Canadian Association on Gerontology, 1980), 17.

18. C. Barber, "Gender Differences in Explaining the Transition to the Empty Nest: Reports of Middle-Aged Women and Men" (Paper presented at meet-ing of the Gerontological Society of America, Dallas, 1978).

19. G. Hagestad and R. Snow, "Young Adult Offspring as Interpersonal Resources in Middle Age" (Paper presented at meeting of the Geronto-logical Society of America, San Francisco, 1978).

20. E. Hughes, *The Sociological Eye: Selected Papers* (Chicago: Aldine, Atherton, 1971).

21. E. Goffman, *Stigma* (Englewood Cliffs, N.J.: Prentice-Hall, 1963).

22. Joseph A. Tindale, "Identity Maintenance Processes of Old Poor Men," in *Aging in Canada: Social Perspectives*, ed. V. W. Marshall (Toronto: Fitzhenry & Whiteside, 1980), 88-94.

23. Tamara K. Hareven, "Historical Changes in the Timing of Family Transitions: Their Impact on Generational Relations," in *Aging: Stability and Change in the Family*, ed. Robert W. Fogel et al. (New York: Academic Press, 1981), 143-165.

24. Joseph A. Tindale, "Generational Conflict: Class and Cohort Relations Among Ontario Public Secondary School Teachers," Ph.D. diss., York University, 1980; idem, "Age, Seniority and Class Patterns of Job Strain," in *Aging in Canada: Social Perspectives*, 2d ed., ed. V. W. Marshall (Toronto: Fitzhenry & Whiteside, 1987), 176-92.

25. Ronald Cohen, "Age and Culture as Theory," in *Age and Anthropological Theory*, ed. D. Kertzer and J. Keith (Ithaca: Cornell University Press, 1984), 244.

26. Ibid.

27. Victor W. Marshall and Joseph A. Tindale, "Notes for a Radical Gerontology," *International Journal on Aging and Human Development* 9 (1978-79): 163-75.

Ethics and the Handicapped Newborn Infant

HELGA KUHSE and PETER SINGER

On April 9, 1982, a baby was born in Bloomington, Indiana. Examination immediately after birth revealed that the infant had Down's syndrome, also known as mongolism. In addition, there was a blockage in the baby's digestive system. Without surgery to remove the blockage, the baby would be unable to obtain nourishment and would die. In such cases surgery is usually, though not invariably, successful and the child grows up to be able to eat in the normal way without serious difficulty. The surgery does not affect the underlying mental retardation that, though varying in degree, is an inevitable result of Down's syndrome.

In this instance the parents refused to consent to surgery. Their stance was supported by their own doctors, but opposed by the hospital paediatricians. The hospital took the case to court. The county court upheld the parents' right to refuse consent to the surgery. So, on appeal, did the Indiana Supreme Court. Preparations were made to appeal to the United States Supreme Court, but Baby Doe's death prevented the litigation from being taken any further.[1]

In a case of this sort, are the parents justified in refusing to consent to surgery? We are not concerned so much with the specific circumstances of the Baby Doe case—details of which are in any case unobtainable because the court records were sealed—as with the ethical issues that must be tackled before a soundly based answer can be given.

This article is drawn from Helga Kuhse and Peter Singer, *Should the Baby Live?* (Oxford: Oxford University Press, 1985). Sections of the article also appeared in *The New York Review of Books*, March 1, 1984.

Is All Human Life of Equal Worth?

When confronted with complex ethical questions it is tempting to look for a simple answer; and in this case, a simple answer seems to be available: that all human life is of equal worth. On this view, the life of a Down's syndrome baby is no less valuable than the life of a normal baby. The life of the most revered statesman, the most generous philanthropist, or the most brilliant scientist, is not worth more than that of a handicapped infant. Since all human life is of equal worth, it is as wrong to let a Down's syndrome baby die, when it could be kept alive, as it would be to let any of these other human beings die when they could be kept alive.

The Sanctity of Human Life

The simple answer gains support from two quite distinct sources. One is the traditional doctrine of the sanctity of human life. Those who speak of "the sanctity of life" hold a cluster of related ideas, rather than a single doctrine; nevertheless, they agree in rejecting claims that one human life is more valuable than another. The central idea is well expressed by Sanford Kadish, writing on the view of human life taken by Anglo-American law: "All human lives must be regarded as having an equal claim to preservation simply because life is an irreducible value. Therefore, the value of a particular life, over and above the value of life itself, may not be taken into account."[2] Here the key claim is that life is an irreducible value; that is, the value of life cannot be reduced to anything else—such as the happiness, self-consciousness, rationality, autonomy, or even simple consciousness, that life makes possible. Life is not valuable because of the qualities it may possess; it is valuable in itself. It is easy to see how this claim leads to the conclusion that all human life is of equal value.

The traditional sanctity-of-life doctrine is also sometimes supported by the claim that human life is of *infinitive* value. The Chief Rabbi of Great Britain, Rabbi Immanuel Jakobovits, has referred to this idea as the ground for opposition to euthanasia:

The basic reasoning behind the firm opposition of Judaism to any form of euthanasia proper is the attribution of *infinitive* value to every human life. Since infinity is, by definition, indivisible, it follows that every fraction of life, however small, remains equally infinite so that it makes morally no difference whether one shortens life by seventy years or by only a few hours, or whether the victim of murder was young and robust or aged and physically or mentally debilitated.[3]

Dr. Moshe Tendler, a professor of Talmudic law, confirms this position:

Human life [is] of infinite value. This in turn means that a piece of infinity is also infinity, and a person who has but a few moments to live is no less of value than a person who has 60 years to live . . . a handicapped individual is a perfect specimen when viewed in an ethical context. The value is an absolute value. It is not relative to life expectancy, to state of health, or to usefulness to society.[4]

The Protestant theologian Paul Ramsey, professor of religion at Princeton University, takes a similar view:

There is no reason for saying that [six months in the life of a baby born with the invariably fatal Tay Sachs disease] are a life span of lesser worth to God than living seventy years before the onset of irreversible degeneration. A genuine humanist would say the same thing in other language. It is only a reductive naturalism or social utilitarianism that would regard those months of infant life as worthless because they lead to nothing on a time line of earthly achievement. All our days and years are of equal worth whatever the consequence; death is no more a tragedy at one time than at another time.[5]

A value might be irreducible without being infinite, and if human life is of irreducible rather than infinite value, there may not be great value in prolonging human existence by a few moments. On the other hand, if human life is of infinite value, every second of prolonged life would be as valuable as a lifetime. This is, on the face of it, implausible: most of us are indifferent to the prospect of our life being shortened by one second, but we are very far from indifferent to the thought that our life might be cut short by thirty years. So far as the treatment of Baby Doe is concerned, however, the difference between irreducible value and infinite value does not matter. Baby Doe could, with appropriate care, have lived for many years, possibly a near-normal lifespan. (The life expectancy of people with Down's syndrome is less than normal, but some do live into their forties or even fifties.) So if human life is in itself a value, irrespective of the quality of the particular life, the presence of Down's syndrome is not relevant to the value a life has.

Human Rights

Whereas the traditional doctrine of the sanctity of human life has its roots in ancient times, the second source of support for the view that all human life is of equal worth is relatively recent. It is the acceptance of the belief that there are human rights, and that all humans share these rights equally. Public support for this belief goes back no further than the eighteenth century, and the "Declarations of Rights" that figured so prominently in the American and French revolutions. Today the human-rights movement is a major force against violations of individual rights by repressive regimes. In the struggle against discrimination, too, it has been important to insist that human rights are possessed equally by all humans. The idea of equal human rights stands as a barrier against those who use some irrelevant or totally spurious ground, such as a difference of race or sex, as an excuse for denying the rights of those who do not belong to their own group.

It is not difficult to see how belief in equal human rights can lead to the view that every human life is of equal worth. The right to life is the most basic of all rights, for if one's right to life is violated, one cannot enjoy any other rights. The idea that all humans are entitled to the same rights thus can be used against making distinctions between the rights to life of different categories of human beings.

This is precisely what happened in the United States, in the aftermath of the Baby Doe case. Barely two weeks after Baby Doe's death, President Reagan sent a memo to his secretary for health and human services instructing him to ensure that laws prohibiting discrimination against the handicapped were "vigorously enforced." Reagan was referring to Section 504 of the Rehabilitation Act of 1973. This section states that "no otherwise qualified handicapped individual shall solely by reason of handicap, be denied the benefits of, or be subjected to discrimination under, any program or activity receiving Federal financial assistance." The language of this statute is similar to that of other United States civil-rights legislation. The section was an extension to the handicapped of the movements to protect the civil rights of blacks and women. It was based on the principle of human equality, and opposition to discrimination on irrelevant grounds. It is so broad, however, that it can be invoked to support the view that all human life is of equal worth, irrespective of the characteristics of the particular life. This is what the secretary for health and human services did when, in accordance with the president's instructions, he sent six thousand, eight hundred American hospitals a "Notice to Health Care Providers." The notice reminded hospital administrators that it was

unlawful for a recipient of Federal financial assistance to withhold from a handicapped infant nutritional sustenance or medical or surgical treatment required to correct a life-threatening condition if

(1) the withholding is based on the fact that the infant is handicapped; and

(2) the handicap does not render treatment or nutritional sustenance contraindicated.

Hospital administrators were told that they would have federal government funds cut off if they allowed handicapped infants to die when non-handicapped infants in similar circumstances would be saved. The notice was saying, in effect, that no matter how severe an infant's handicap might be, the efforts made to preserve its life must be no less than the efforts that would be made to preserve the life of a non-handicapped infant in an otherwise similar condition.

Hard Cases for the Simple Answer

The view that all human life is of equal worth may well be the simplest way of answering questions about the treatment of infants born with major handicaps; but there are two questions that need to be asked about this simple answer. First, does it give us acceptable practical guidance? Second, does it have a sound ethical basis? For the moment we shall focus on the first question, leaving the theoretical issues for later.

The question of whether the simple answer gives adequate practical guidance was raised very directly by the "Notice to Health Care Providers" issued by the Reagan administration, and it is interesting to examine it in this context. First, however, we need to take the story a step further. Strong as its language might seem, the notice was not sufficient for the White House. In March 1983 the Department of Health and Human Services therefore issued a more forceful follow-up regulation. Officially, the new regulation had the contradictory title "Interim Final Rule," but it has become known as the "Baby Doe guidelines." These guidelines specified that a poster was to be conspicuously displayed in each delivery ward, maternity ward, paediatric ward, and intensive care nursery. The poster was to read as follows:

NOTICE

DEPARTMENT OF HEALTH AND HUMAN SERVICES
OFFICE FOR CIVIL RIGHTS

Discriminatory failure to feed and care for handicapped infants in this facility is prohibited by federal law. Section 504 of the Rehabilitation

Act of 1973 states that "no otherwise qualified handicapped individual shall, solely by reason of handicap, be excluded from participation in, be denied the benefits of, or be subjected to discrimination under any program or activity receiving federal financial assistance."

Any person having knowledge that a handicapped infant was being denied food or customary medical care was invited to phone, on a toll-free hotline, the Department of Health and Human Services in Washington:

Handicapped Infant Hotline
US Department of Health and Human Services
Washington, D.C. 20201
Phone 800-368-1019 (available 24 hours a day)
TTY Capability

In Washington, D.C. call 863-0100 — or —
Your State Child Protective Agency.

Federal Law prohibits retaliation or intimidation against any person who provides information about possible violations of the Rehabilitation Act of 1973.

Identity of callers will be held confidential.

Failure to feed and care for infants may also violate the criminal and civil laws of your state.[6]

The Baby Doe guidelines incensed many of the nation's most senior paediatricians—not surprisingly, since it invited all and sundry to make confidential complaints about the way those doctors treated their patients. As a result the American Academy of Paediatrics, an association of twenty-four thousand paediatricians, joined with the National Association of Children's Hospitals and the Children's Hospital National Medical Center, in Washington, D.C., to contest the regulations in the courts. Among the grounds for opposition to the guidelines was the question of their scope. The American Academy of Paediatrics submitted affidavits describing medical conditions in newborns that are, it said, "simply not treatable"; should efforts still be made to prolong the lives of these infants, as they would be, of course, if the infants did not have the conditions in question? In other words, the academy was asking, are doctors now supposed to do everything in their power to prolong all infant lives, no matter what the prospects?

The affidavits referred to three conditions. The first is anencephaly. This means "no brain" and refers to a condition that occurs approximately ly once in every two thousand births. The infant is born with most or all of the brain missing. Many of these babies die at birth or very soon after, but some have lived for a week or two, and it would be possible, with modern artificial support systems, to keep them alive even longer. The absence, or virtual absence, of a brain means that even if such infants could be kept alive indefinitely, they would never become conscious or respond in any way to other human beings.

The second condition is an intra-cranial haemorrhage—less technical-ly, bleeding in the head, which in some cases means that the infants will never breathe without mechanical respiratory assistance and never will have the capacity for cognitive behaviour.

The third condition is one in which an infant lacks a substantial part of its digestive tract, for instance, its intestine and bowels. The infant cannot be fed by mouth, for it will not obtain anything of nutritional val-ue. It is not possible to correct the condition by surgery. Feeding such infants by means of a drip directly into the bloodstream will keep them alive, but nutritional deficiencies are likely and the long-term prospects are poor.

In mentioning these three conditions, the academy was suggesting that the guidelines were, at best, unclear as to whether in these in-fants might be allowed to die without receiving life-sustaining treatment; or, at worst, the guidelines would direct that such life-sustaining treat-ment be given, despite the apparent futility of such treatment.

At the court hearing, the Department of Health and Human Services denied that the Interim Final Rule would compel doctors to provide life-sustaining treatment in these extreme cases. The chief spokesman for the department's position was Dr. C. Everett Koop, surgeon general of the United States and an experienced paediatric surgeon. Referring to a child having "essentially no intestine," Dr. Koop said:

These regulations never intended that such a child should be put on hyper-alimentation [i.e., be artificially nourished] and carried for a year and a half.

Incidentally, I was the first physician that ever did that, so I know whereof I speak. We would consider customary care in that child the provision of a bed, of food by mouth, knowing that it was not going to be nutritious, but not just shutting off the care of that child . . . nor do we intend to say that this child should be carried on intravenous fluids for the rest of its life.

Dr. Koop made a similar remark about one of the other cases men-tioned by the academy: "When you talk about a baby born without a brain, I suspect you meant an anencephalic child and we would not

128   FUNCTIONAL ACCOUNTS OF TIME

attempt to interfere with anyone dealing with that child. We think it should be given loving attention and would expect it to expire in a short time.'"

To Dr. Koop, it was apparently plain common sense that one did not attempt to prolong the lives of infants born with such serious conditions. We agree. But is not this "plain common sense" at odds with the view that all human lives are of equal worth? Can it be squared with an insistence that a handicapped infant must not be refused life-sustaining treatment that would be offered to an infant without the handicap?

Certainly the non-treatment of these infants must be incompatible with the idea that all human life is of infinite value. Anyone who believed this would have to say that the life of an anencephalic infant is also of infinite value. Since any part of infinity is, as Chief Rabbi Jakobovits said, still infinite, one would have to hold that prolonging the life of an anencephalic infant by a single day—or even a second—would still be of infinite value. Since it clearly is possible, by means of artificial feeding and respiration, to prolong the lives of anencephalic infants by several days, perhaps even weeks or months, anyone who believes that all human life is of infinite value would have to consider it wrong not to decide not to take any steps to prolong life in these cases.

What of those who, without necessarily believing that all human life has infinite value, support the principle that all human lives are of equal worth, irrespective of their quality? Those who hold this view would also seem to be committed to advocating life-sustaining measures for infants born without brains or without intestines. For example, in the passage quoted above, Dr. Koop referred to the possibility of "carrying" an infant without an intestine for "a year and a half"; yet Dr. Koop did not advocate that infants born without an intestine should be kept alive for as long as possible. (In fact it is possible for children being artificially fed to survive considerably longer than this, but the precise period is not relevant here.) Why does Dr. Koop not think such infants should be kept alive as long as possible? Would he not think an eighteen-month extension of life worthwhile for a normal child? Would he not think it worthwhile for a normal adult? If he would, the obvious explanation for his different view in the first case is that he does not regard the life of an artificially nourished infant as being of the same worth as that of a normal infant or a normal adult.

Getting Around the Hard Cases: (1) "Medical Decisions"

Is there any other possible explanation for the views expressed by Dr. Koop? The Department of Health and Human Services soon had a second

chance to explain its stance on the type of case we have been considering. Judge Gerhard Gesell found in favour of the Academy of Paediatrics
and its co-plaintiffs on the ground that the department had, by issuing the
regulation without allowing a period for public comment, failed to com-
ply with the requirements of the Administrative Procedure Act, an act
designed to curb bureaucratic actions taken without consultation and
notice to those affected. The department therefore issued, on July 5,
1983, a new "Proposed Rule." The new rule was essentially similar to
the ill-fated Interim Final Rule, but it was issued with considerably more
information on the circumstances in which it was to apply. In particular,
it was stated that:

Section 504 does not compel medical personnel to attempt to perform
impossible or futile acts or therapies. Thus, Section 504 does not
require the imposition of futile therapies which merely temporarily
prolong the process of dying of an infant born terminally will [sic],
such as a child born with anencephaly or intra-cranial bleeding. Such
medical decisions, by medical personnel and parents, concerning
whether to treat, and if so, what form the treatment should take, are
outside the scope of Section 504. The Department recognizes that reasonable medical judgments can differ when evaluating these difficult,
individual cases.

Here the department takes the commonsense view that it is not obligatory to keep alive infants with anencephaly or intra-cranial bleeding.
It is interesting to see how the department tries to take this view without
basing it on the fact that infants with these conditions have no prospect
of a reasonable quality of life. What the department suggests is that in
these cases treatment is "futile" and will "merely temporarily prolong the
process of dying" of an infant born terminally ill. Whether a treatment
is futile in this way is, the department states, a "medical decision" and
"reasonable medical judgements can differ" in these cases. The department seems to be saying that it does not wish to interfere in these "medical decisions."

This will not do. As we have seen, sophisticated modern medical
techniques could indefinitely prolong the lives of children with anencephaly or intra-cranial bleeding. The judgement that someone whose life
could be indefinitely prolonged by available medical means is "terminally
ill" and therefore should not have his or her life prolonged is not a
medical judgement; it is an ethical judgement about the desirability of
prolonging that particular life.

Could the department defend its view by saying that whether a patient is dying is a medical judgement, based on the fact that the patient can survive only with the help of medical treatment? Such a test would be far too broad. By this standard, a patient suffering from diabetes would be "terminally ill" and it would not be required to provide "futile" insulin therapy. The fact that no one in his right mind would regard insulin therapy for a diabetic as "futile" should make us realize that judgements about the futility of treatment are not purely medical judgements based on the prospect of the underlying condition being cured. It is no more possible to cure diabetes by administering insulin than it is to cure anencephaly, an intra-cranial bleeding, or the absence of an intestine. In all these conditions, the patient must currently expect to remain, for his or her entire life, dependent for survival on continuing medical treatment. The difference between diabetes and the other three conditions is, of course, that the diabetic will be able to enjoy a near-normal life, while no matter how much we prolong the life of the infant with massive intra-cranial bleeding, for instance, the infant's life will always remain devoid of everything that we regard as making life worthwhile.

As we read on through the "supplementary information," issued by the Department of Health and Human Services, it becomes still more clear that, despite protestations to the contrary, the department's position is based on thinly veiled judgements that some lives are not worth living. The department's statement continues:

Section 504 simply preserves the decision-making process customarily undertaken by physicians in any treatment decision: will the treatment be medically beneficial to the patient and are those benefits outweighed by any medical risk associated with the treatment? It is only when non-medical considerations, such as subjective judgments that an unrelated handicap makes a person's life not worth living, are interjected in the decision-making process that the Section 504 concerns arise.

The problem with this way of putting it is that we need to decide what treatments are "medically beneficial to the patient." The simple answer, and the only answer that is consistent with the idea that all human life is of equal worth, is that all treatments that prolong life are beneficial. Yet this is clearly not the answer the department would give: it does not regard it as beneficial to prolong the lives of infants born with virtually no brain, or who have suffered intra-cranial bleeding. Why is this not "medically beneficial to the patient" in the same way that giving insulin is medically beneficial to the diabetic? Once again, the answer must be that it is not medically beneficial to prolong the lives of infants who will never experience anything, and will remain alive but in a state without feelings or awareness, unable to enjoy their lives in any way. Plainly, the prolongation of such a life is not "medically beneficial" because it is not beneficial in any sense. Karen Ann Quinlan, the New Jersey woman who has been in an irreversible coma since 1975, has not benefitted from the fact that her life has been prolonged for many years. She has not been aware of the extra years of life she has had, and has had no benefit from them. Similarly, prolonging the life of an infant without a brain does the infant no good because it is not possible for the infant to benefit from the additional period of life. This is not, however, a medical judgement. It is quite obviously a "non-medical consideration" based on the judgement that the handicap—in this case, the virtual absence of a brain—"makes a person's life not worth living." The department seems to think that such judgements are "subjective" and must not be "interjected in the decision-making process"; yet its own position is based on just this type of judgement.

Admittedly, the department does refer to judgements about "an unrelated handicap," and in criticizing its position we have not taken account of the stipulation that the judgement be about a handicap that is "unrelated." But it is difficult to see exactly what this means or how it can make a difference. Presumably it is supposed to be wrong to take account of a handicap unrelated to the treatment needed to keep the infant alive; but how do we define what the handicap is? This may seem clear enough in a case like a Down's syndrome baby with a blocked intestine, where Down's syndrome is the reason for not operating on the blockage; but what about the case of, say, an intra-cranial bleeding? The treatment needed to keep the infant alive might be artificial respiration. A baby who was having breathing problems, but was otherwise normal, would certainly be put on a respirator; the baby who, as Dr. Parrott put it, "never will have the capacity for cognitive behaviour," would not be put on a respirator. If the lack of any "capacity for cognitive behaviour" is a factor in the decision to put it on the respirator, this would have to be a "subjective judgement that an unrelated handicap makes a person's life not worth living." As such, it should give rise to what the department calls "Section 504 concerns." Yet apparently the department does not think it does. On the other hand, the department would presumably think that Section 504 concerns arise even in some cases where the decision not to sustain life is made because of a handicap that *is* directly related to the form of treatment—for instance, if a doctor did not give insulin to a diabetic patient because in the doctor's judgement diabetes is a handicap that makes life not worth living. Thus whether the life-sustaining treatment is or is not related to the patient's handicap cannot be, even in the department's view, a crucial factor in whether a decision not to pro-long life is a case of discriminating against the handicapped.

Getting Around the Hard Cases: (2) "Extraordinary Means"

One frequently used tactic by which those who wish to uphold the tenet of the equal worth of all human lives can try to argue that we do not always have to prolong life in cases like those we have been discussing, is the claim that there is no moral requirement to use "extraordinary" means of treatment; our obligations extend only to the provision of "ordinary" means of prolonging life. Since "extraordinary" means would be needed to keep alive an infant with virtually no brain, with very severe bleeding in the brain, or without an intestine, it is ethically acceptable to provide only "ordinary" care, and allow the infant to die.

The view was the basis of testimony by a Roman Catholic bishop, Bishop Lawrence Casey, in the much-publicized case of Karen Quinlan. Bishop Casey supported the request by Karen Quinlan's parents to have artificial means of life support removed from their comatose daughter. He told the court:

The continuance of mechanical (cardiorespiratory) supportive measures to sustain continuation of her body functions and her life constitute extraordinary means of treatment. Therefore the decision of Joseph . . . Quinlan to request the discontinuation of treatment is, according to the teachings of the Catholic Church, a morally correct decision.

Consistently with this teaching, when Karen Quinlan was taken off the respirator and, to everyone's surprise, continued to breathe, her parents did not seek to discontinue artificial feeding. Providing nourishment they presumably regarded as an "ordinary" means and hence one that could not be withdrawn.[8]

In a recent "Declaration of Euthanasia" issued by the Vatican, the Roman Catholic church has reaffirmed its view that the principle of the "extraordinary means" criterion "still holds good," despite the impreci-sion of the term and the progress made in the treatment of sickness. The American Medical Association has also invoked the principle in a much-discussed attempt to distinguish "the cessation of the employment of extraordinary means," which it allows, from "the intentional termination of the life of one human being by another," which it describes as "mercy killing" and "contrary to that for which the medical profession stands."[9]

The distinction between ordinary and extraordinary means is so frequently invoked that it may seem surprising that the Department of Health
and Human Services did not refer to it in its explanation of why Section
504 does not require doctors to keep infants without brains alive.
Although the department did not use the terms "ordinary" and "extraordinary," it appeared to be appealing to a version of the distinction
when it included a reference to "customary medical care" in the key
sentence of the notice to be posted in hospitals, telling people to contact
the Handicapped Infant Hotline if they have knowledge that a handicapped infant "is being denied food or customary medical care." Presumably whatever is "customary" cannot be "extraordinary," and so the
department is saying in its own terminology that only "ordinary" care is
required. This reference to "customary medical care" was subjected to
close questioning by Judge Gerhard Gesell, and we shall examine it after
we have looked at the more widely used distinction between ordinary and
extraordinary means.

The first question to ask about the distinction is how we are to decide
which means are ordinary and which are extraordinary. To get this
straight may seem a mere matter of terminological precision: it turns out,
however, to be a difficulty that threatens the usefulness of the distinction
itself. The problem is not merely to differentiate ordinary from extraordinary means, but to do so in a manner that is morally relevant. If we are
going to say that ordinary means of saving life must be employed, but
extraordinary means need not be, the distinction must be one in which
we can find moral significance.

The most natural understanding of the distinction is that ordinary
means are those most commonly used, whereas extraordinary means are
unusual ones. This is the sense to which the Department of Health and
Human Services appears to appeal: "customary medical care" is the care
that is commonly given. The means one is not obliged to use, then, are
the non-standard treatments, the techniques that are new and rare.

An alternative interpretation is that ordinary care is simple and
straightforward, while extraordinary means are those that involve high-
technology medicine, or are elaborate and demanding in terms of effort
and resources.

These two interpretations will agree in some cases and disagree in
others. On either interpretation, for instance, the use of antibiotics to
combat a life-threatening infection would, nowadays, be ordinary treatment. Antibiotics are very commonly used, and they are a simple form
of treatment. On the other hand, putting an infant on artificial respiration

is no longer a rare or non-standard form of treatment; it is, however, still a form of treatment that uses complex and quite expensive equipment.

Obviously, whichever interpretation we adopt, there will be border-line cases. Neither the distinction between "usual" and "unusual," nor that between "simple" and "complex" is marked by clear boundaries. The real problem, however, is not the borderline cases: it is that whether treatment is usual or unusual, simple or complex, is *in itself* totally irrelevant to morally relevant issues, such as the risk associated with the treatment. Unusual treatment may be more risky than usual treatment, but if it is, it is *this* difference that is morally relevant in deciding for or against treatment. Or again, complex treatment may be more costly than a simple one. Given limited medical resources, this may be relevant to deciding whether to use it; but again, it is the difference in cost, com-bined with the needs of other patients when we do not have the resources to treat them all, that is relevant here. The crucial point is that there is no perfect correlation between the obviously relevant features of risk and cost, and the usual/unusual or the simple/complex distinctions. To the extent that this correlation is lacking, it is clear that the distinctions themselves are not morally relevant.

Suppose that Baby *A*'s life can be prolonged by using some common means of treatment, but Baby *B* will die unless we use an unusual treat-ment. If there is *no* difference in the safety and efficacy of the two treat-ments, what is the relevance of the fact that one is more commonly used than the other? If the cases are otherwise similar, it is surely just as obligatory to treat *B* as it is to treat *A*. Or suppose that the treatment for Baby *A* is simple, but that for Baby *B* is complex and requires high tech-nology: if there are ample resources available to employ both treatments, can the difference in complexity affect the obligation to treat the babies? Those who use the ordinary/extraordinary distinction do not attempt to defend the claim that rarity or complexity are in themselves grounds for withholding a means of treatment. Instead they seek to redefine the terms "ordinary" and "extraordinary," so that they mean something quite different.

In the ethical analyses of the theologians, philosophers, and doctors who invoke the distinction, "ordinary" means neither "usual" nor "simple"; and "extraordinary" means neither "unusual" nor "complex." Consider, for example, the definitions employed in a book entitled *Médico-Moral Problems*, written by the Jesuit theologian Gerald Kelly and published by the Catholic Hospital Association. According to Father Kelly, ordinary means are all "medicines, treatments and operations, which offer a rea-sonable hope of benefit for the patient and which can be obtained and

used without excessive expense, pain or other inconvenience." Extraordinary means, on the other hand, include "all medicines, treatments
and operations which cannot be obtained without excessive expense, pain
or other inconvenience, or which, if used, would not offer a reasonable
hope of benefit."[10] Note here the reference, in both definitions, to "a
reasonable hope of benefit." In the light of our earlier discussion of the
use of the expression "medically beneficial" by the Department of Health
and Human Services, it is easy to see what is going on here: quality-of-
life judgements are again being made. Otherwise, how are we to decide
when treatment offers "a reasonable hope of benefit"? If quality of life
does not enter into it, every treatment that offers a reasonable hope of
prolonging life would be treatment that offers a reasonable hope of benefit; but this is not what those who appeal to the ordinary/extraordinary
distinction have in mind.

For a clear example of a quality-of-life judgement disguised as an
appeal to the ordinary/extraordinary distinction, let us look once more at
the testimony of Bishop Lawrence Casey in the case of Karen Quinlan.
We saw earlier that Bishop Casey testified that the artificial life support
systems thought to be keeping Karen Quinlan alive constituted extraordinary means of treatment and therefore could legitimately be discontinued. What we have not noted, up to now, is that Bishop Casey
prefaced his opinion by saying that Karen Quinlan "has no reasonable
hope of recovery from her comatose state by the use of any available
medical procedure." What is the significance of this sentence, which
immediately precedes the classification of the artificial life support system
as "extraordinary means"? Obviously, it implies that if Karen Quinlan
did have some hope of recovery from her comatose state, the use of
artificial life support systems would *not* be "extraordinary."

Why would this be so? Is it simply that the medical procedures
offered Karen Quinlan no hope of *recovery*? But there are no available
medical procedures that offer a diabetic any hope of recovery; and yet
Bishop Casey would surely not say that the administration of insulin to
a diabetic is an extraordinary means, and that it would therefore be
morally correct to request that it be discontinued. So it must be the fact
that the medical procedures offered Karen Quinlan no hope of recovery
from her comatose state that is decisive in Bishop Casey's classification
of the procedures as "extraordinary." Since the procedures could have
indefinitely prolonged Karen Quinlan's life, and since they would not
have been extraordinary if that life were the life of a person not in a
permanently comatose state, we must conclude that it is the difference in

quality of life between being in an irreversible coma and not being in an irreversible coma that is the basis for Bishop Casey's judgement.

Because the terms "ordinary means" and "extraordinary means" *appear* to mark a distinction in the nature of the means used, but *in practice* reflect judgements about the desirability of prolonging a parti-cular patient's life, the distinction has given rise to some bizarre statements. Prominent among them is a remark by Judge John Ferris, who presided over a Florida trial in which a dying seventy-six-year-old man was requesting the cessation of life-sustaining treatment, including artificial respiration. The patient's physician testified that the use of a respirator is "standard procedure" and said, "I deal with respirators every day of my life." To this the judge responded, "I understand that he deals with them every day, but in the sense of ordinary as against extraordinary, I believe it to be extraordinary."[11]

There is now increasing recognition of the fact that the distinction between ordinary and extraordinary means serves no good purpose. Robert Veatch, in *Death, Dying and the Biological Revolution*, goes through some of the confused and conflicting interpretations of the distinction and concludes that the language of ordinary and extraordinary means should "be banned from further use." The Law Reform Commis-sion of Canada, in its working paper entitled *Euthanasia, Aiding Suicide and Cessation of Treatment*, says that the distinction is "too ambiguous to serve as a solid basis for any precise description of the scope of the physician's legal duty to his patient and therefore to serve as a good basis for reform."[12]

Most damning of all, however, is the opinion of the United States President's Commission for the Study of Ethical Problems in Medicine and Biomedical and Behavioral Research. This commission, appointed by President Carter, wrote a 545-page report entitled *Deciding to Forego Life-Sustaining Treatment*. After a careful discussion of the various ways in which people have attempted to draw the distinction between ordinary and extraordinary means, the commission found that the only form of the distinction that has moral significance is when it is understood in terms of the "usefulness and burdensomeness of a particular therapy." The commission then continued:

This line of reasoning suggests that extraordinary treatment is that which, in the patient's view, entails significantly greater burdens than benefits and is therefore undesirable and not obligatory, while ordinary treatment is that which, in the patient's view, produces greater benefits than burdens and is therefore reasonably desirable and undertaken. The claim, then, that the treatment is extraordinary is more of an expression of the conclusion than a justification of it.[13]

Thus the President's Commission confirms the conclusion suggested by our examination of Bishop Casey's testimony. Even though the decision to give or withhold treatment appears at first to be based on some fact about the nature of the means of treatment, the decision is really being taken on quite different grounds: an evaluation of the kind of life the patient is expected to lead. The distinction between ordinary and extraordinary means cannot assist anyone wishing both to preserve the view that all human life is of equal value, and to explain why we are not required to keep alive a baby born without a brain. Those who invoke the distinction only explain why we are not obliged to prolong life in such a case because they covertly take account of the poor quality of such a life and the consequent uselessness, or absence of benefit, of such a treatment. In doing so, those who invoke the distinction are abandoning the view that all human life is of equal worth.

Beyond Equal Worth

We conclude that even those who claim that all human life is of equal worth do not, in practice, take this rhetoric seriously. We believe this claim cannot be defended. What then can justify our holding that the lives of some humans are of greater worth than the lives of others?

Many possible relevant differences might be suggested. Joseph Fletcher, a Protestant theologian, has listed some "indicators of humanhood." His list includes self-awareness, self-control, a sense of the future, a sense of the past, the capacity to relate to others, concern for others, communication, and curiosity.[14] Other writers have emphasized rationality, the use of language, and autonomy. Many of these characteristics are related—for instance, one could not have a sense of the past and future without at least some minimal degree of self-awareness and some capacity for rational thought. Taken as a cluster, these characteristics have undeniable moral significance. It is entirely reasonable to suggest that it is much more serious to take the life of a being possessing all or most of these characteristics than it would be to take the life of a being possessing none of them.

Various grounds could be offered for saying that these characteristics are relevant to the seriousness of killing. Some people regard it as self-evident that the life of a rational, autonomous being is of greater value than the life of a being lacking these characteristics. Others focus especially on the capacity for self-awareness, and on the sense of the future. A self-aware being with a sense of the future can have hopes and desires about what might or might not happen to it in the future. To kill it is to prevent the fulfillment of these hopes and desires. This is a wrong that we cannot possibly do to a being that does not even understand that it exists as a separate being, with a past and a future.

Michael Tooley has developed this argument more systematically than anyone else. Tooley suggests that to have a right to something, one must have an interest in it, and to have an interest in continuing to exist one must be a "continuing self"—that is, a being that has at some time had the concept of itself as existing over time.[15]

To invoke the language of "rights," as Tooley does, is not always conducive to clarity of thought. Too often there is a tendency to treat rights as somehow innate or natural or self-evident and to use claims about rights to block off any further discussion. We often make better progress in understanding moral arguments by dropping the terminology of rights, and dealing directly with the underlying moral considerations by which the claims about rights are supported. So, in the case of Tooley's argument, it might be safer not to talk of seeing oneself as a continuing self as a necessary condition for a right to life, but simply to say that when a being has this sense of itself, to kill it is to do something of much greater moral significance than to kill a being who lacks this ability. The gain in philosophical clarity thus obtained is, however, achieved at the cost of a good deal of clumsiness in expression; and since the language of rights is now so widely used in debates about the treatment of severely handicapped infants, we shall make use of it our-selves—always bearing in mind that the expression is no more than a convenient shorthand for the moral considerations on which the right is based. With this proviso, we consider Tooley's argument to be basically sound.

Tooley suggests that we reserve the term "person" for those beings who are capable of understanding that they are a separate entity with a future. In this he follows the seventeenth-century British philosopher John Locke, who defined a "person" as "a thinking intelligent being that has reason and reflection and can consider itself as itself, the same think-ing thing, in different times and places."[16] This definition makes "person" close to what Fletcher would call "human," except that it singles out self-awareness and the sense of the past and future as the core of the concept. It is clear that on Locke's and Tooley's definition, "person" is not iden-tical with "member of the species *homo sapiens*." Neither human foetus-es, nor human infants, nor humans with very severe retardation or brain damage would be persons. On the other hand chimpanzees well might be, and so might some other nonhuman animals. Thus the notion of a person, as employed by Tooley, reflects no arbitrary, species-based boundary, but characteristics of obvious relevance to the wrongness of killing.

Some will find Tooley's position more shocking than anything we have said so far. On Tooley's view, after all, an infant does not have to be severely handicapped for it to lack a right to life. *No* infant is born with self-awareness or a sense of the future. If Tooley is right, no newborn infant has a right to life. Just when normal human infants acquire some minimal degree of self-awareness is difficult to say—almost certainly not in the first month of life, perhaps not in the first three months, but quite probably within the first year. Whichever way we decide this difficult factual question, infants will be deemed not to have a right to life at birth, nor for some time afterwards.

But what of potential? A normal newborn infant has good prospects of a worthwhile, happy and fulfilling life, a life with many of the experiences that we think of as making our own lives rewarding and satisfying. Does not this potential distinguish the normal infant from the severely handicapped infant, and give the former, at least, a right to life? Tooley argues that a right to life cannot be based on potential. His argument is based on a rejection of the moral distinction between acts and omissions—a distinction we also reject. The relevance of the distinc- tion here is as follows: if one holds that it is wrong to kill a newborn infant (or foetus) because the infant (or foetus) will eventually become a person with a worthwhile life, then why is it not also wrong to omit to do an act that would have the consequence that a person with a worth- while life comes into existence? In other words, if it is wrong to kill, why is it not wrong to abstain from sexual intercourse that would lead to procreation? Both the omission and the killing have the same conse- quence: there will not be a person who might otherwise have had a worthwhile life. If the killing does not violate an actual right to life, and is said to be wrong only because of the person who will now not exist, why is it worse than abstinence?

Admittedly, when we refrain from reproducing, there is no being whose life has already begun. Intuitively, this makes a difference. We must recall, however, that when we kill a newborn infant there is no *person* whose life has begun. When I think of myself as the person I now am, I realize that I did not come into existence until some time after my birth. At birth I had no sense of the future, and no experience that I can now remember as "mine." It is the beginning of the life of the person, rather than of the physical organism, that is crucial so far as the right to life is concerned.

Rejecting the distinction between acts and omissions leads us to see that so far as the prevention of the existence of a future person is concerned, killing and not reproducing are similar. Most people hold that there is no moral obligation to reproduce. The world has enough people, and too many future persons are being created already. Even Roman Catholics, who oppose the use of artificial methods of birth control, do not disapprove of refraining from sexual intercourse during a woman's fertile periods.

All this would suggest that we should give no weight to the potential of the newborn infant. That is the conclusion we must reach if we think that there is no value in bringing extra new people into the world. There is, however, another possible view. We might hold that, other things being equal, it *is* good to bring more people into the world. We might say that the reason we do not object to people refraining from reproducing, is that other things are usually not equal. For one thing, there is the global problem of overpopulation; but let us put this issue aside, and assume we are considering bringing people into the world in a situation in which there is no population problem. A woman might still have strong personal reasons for not wishing to go through pregnancy and childbirth. Because we respect a woman's right to control her reproduction, we would leave that decision entirely to her. Once an infant is born, however, as long as there are people willing to adopt it and look after it, reasons of this kind will not apply. Hence some reasons that justify refraining from reproducing will not justify killing a newborn infant, as long as others are prepared to take responsibility for the infant's care.

This means that rejecting the distinction between acts and omissions does not, after all, necessarily lead to the conclusion that *no* weight can be given to the potential of the newborn infant. We can agree that a decision to kill a newborn infant is no more—and no less—the prevention of potential life than is a decision not to reproduce. We can add, however, that women will often have strong reasons against reproducing, much stronger reasons than anyone is likely to have in favour of killing an infant for whom others are willing to care. Unless we are prepared to hold that people ought to reproduce whenever possible, we cannot give *overriding* value to potential life; but we can give *some* value to it, so that it counts as an important factor in decisions about killing newborns. The value of potential life would then still be a factor in decisions about reproducing, but it would be much less significant, because it would usually be outweighed by reasons that point in the opposite decision.

Whether there is value in bringing new people into the world is an extremely complex philosophical issue—more complex than we have been able to show here. We will return to it in the final section and draw out further implications. What we have shown so far is that the potential of an infant can be a reason against killing it. Obviously, the greater the infant's potential for a happy and worthwhile life, the stronger this reason is. Thus there may still be good reason to protect the lives of newborn infants even if, strictly speaking, they do not have a right to life. This is a modification of Tooley's position that makes it less shocking than it at first appeared.

There are other reasons why the view we are taking is less radical than it may seem to be. A second reason is that most babies are, fortunately, much wanted and loved by their parents. Anyone who killed a wanted baby would therefore do a terrible wrong to the baby's parents, irrespective of whether the baby has a right to life.

A third reason is that even if a baby were not wanted by its parents, there might well be someone else, or another couple, who very much want to cherish that child and bring it up as their own. So once again, independently of the rights or interests of the infant itself, to kill the baby would be to harm the person or couple wanting to adopt the child.

A fourth reason is that to say that an infant has no right to life is not to say that it has no rights at all. People sometimes mistakenly assume this to be the case, reasoning that if we are dead we cannot have a right to anything. This may be so, but it does not refute the view that, as long as we are alive, we may have some rights without having a right to life. Consider how differently we think about someone who tortures stray cats, and someone who humanely kills them.

For Tooley, we can have rights only if we have the requisite interests. If newborn infants have no sense of the future, they cannot have a right to continued life; but it is plausible to suppose that newborn infants can feel pain, and prefer not to be in pain; that they can feel cold, and desire not to be cold; that they can feel hungry, and desire not to be hungry. It is therefore plausible to suppose that newborn infants have rights to have their pain relieved, and to be kept warm and fed. These rights are not absolute, but they indicate what we ought not to do to infants except for overriding reasons.

These four reasons serve to limit the cases in which killing an infant would be defensible. The fifth reason why our position is less radical than it appears is different. This fifth reason does not restrict the cases in which killing an infant would be defensible: it points out how close we already are to the kind of killing that we are suggesting might be

permitted. Recall the now-standard procedure of finding out during pregnancy whether the foetus is abnormal and allowing—even recommending—an abortion if the test should prove positive. This is not a case of
sacrificing the foetus to save the life or health of the pregnant woman.
It is, quite straightforwardly, a decision to end at an early stage a life
that does not have the usual prospects for a full human existence. The
difference between this decision and infanticide is that abortion kills the
unseen foetus in the womb, while infanticide kills the new-born infant.
In neither case, however, has the life of the *person* begun.

In accepting abortion, as so many Western nations have now done,
we have already taken a major step away from the traditional principle
of the sanctity of human life. We have, however, come to place great
weight on a boundary line—the moment of birth—that, while clear and
precise, is not really crucial from the point of view of the moral status
of the foetus or infant. The move to a less precise, but more significant,
boundary—the point at which there is self-awareness and a sense of the
future—is therefore not as big a step as one might at first think.

There is one further point about the dividing line we are proposing.
It is sometimes said if we start to kill severely handicapped infants we
will end up threatening disabled adults as well. To allow infanticide
before the onset of self-awareness, however, cannot threaten anyone who
is in a position to worry about it. Anyone able to understand what it is to
live or die must already be a person and has the same right to life as all
the rest of us. Disability that does not rule out self-awareness and a sense
of the future is totally irrelevant to the possession of the right to life.
Unlike many other forms of homicide, infanticide carried out by parents or with their consent poses no threat to anyone in the community
who is capable of grasping what is happening. This fact goes a long way
towards accounting for the equanimity with which many other cultures
have accepted it. Nor is it only in other cultures that this point has been
recognized. Jeremy Bentham criticized the severity with which infanticide
was punished in his day, and remarked that the crime is "of a nature not
to give the slightest inquietude to the most timid imagination." Infanticide
threatens none of us—for once we are aware of it, we are not infants.[17]

The Problem of Potential Life

One issue that we have so far left unresolved is the question of whether
a handicapped infant should be kept alive because of the potential it may
have, notwithstanding its handicap, for leading a happy or otherwise

KUHSE & SINGER / *The Ethical Perspective*

valuable life. This issue raises some of the most baffling ethical issues—issues discussed by Derek Parfit in his recent book *Reasons and Persons*,[18] and also by Michael Tooley in his *Abortion and Infanticide*. Parfit does not claim to have a solution to the problem. Tooley does claim to have one. His answer is that the potential of a being to become a person and have a worthwhile life does not make it obligatory to keep that being alive. Unfortunately, for reasons we cannot go into here, this is one instance in which we think that Tooley's arguments are not entirely successful. We do not think he overcomes the objections Parfit has made to those who would dismiss the value of creating extra beings who will lead worthwhile lives.

This is not the place for a full treatment of this issue. We will limit ourselves, in this final section of our paper, to showing the relevance of the issue to the question of keeping a handicapped baby alive. In this way we conclude by showing how deeply into philosophical controversies this practical question takes us.

One of the more firmly established findings about families with a disabled child is that they are less likely than other families to have further children. In one study, out of 160 mothers who could have had more children, 101 decided not to, and in 06 of these cases the decision appeared to be directly related to the presence of a retarded child.[19]

Peggy Stinson is an American woman who has published a book called *The Long Dying of Baby Andrew*. The book is based on a journal she kept during the period when doctors were, against her wishes, trying to save Andrew's life—despite the fact that he was highly unlikely to survive without very severe brain damage. Peggy Stinson's journal shows that, like most mothers in her situation, she was concerned about what Andrew's long-term survival in a damaged state might do to her plans to have another child. On February 17, when Andrew was two months old, she wrote:

I keep thinking about the other baby—the one that won't be born. The IICU [Infant Intensive Care Unit] is choosing between lives. It may already be too late for the next baby. If Andrew's life is strung out much longer, will we have the money, the emotional resources, the nerve to try again?

The journal entry for April 30, 1977 is particularly interesting because it poses the philosophical question that is at the hub of this issue:

Thirty-fifth birthday coming up next week; haven't got forever to try for another child. If we wait much longer, until our insurance runs out or we're being billed for Andrew's custodial care, we'll know we can't afford another child. Or we won't have the nerve to try again.

We want another child. I'm not going to let Pediatric Hospital [where Andrew was being kept alive against his parent's wishes] destroy our chance to have one. At this rate we'll have neither Andrew nor the next child, who, because of Andrew's extended course, will have lost the chance to exist at all.

Jeff [a junior doctor at the hospital more sympathetic to the Stinsons' views than the other senior medical staff] once said our "next child" was theoretical, abstract—its interests couldn't be considered. Strictly speaking that may be so, but that next baby seems real enough to me. To Bob too. Decision this week to change that abstraction into a real person before it's too late.[20]

Is the "next child" an abstraction whose interests cannot be considered before it is born, or even conceived? It is tempting to agree with the advice given to Peggy Stinson: after all, if she had not had any more children, no one would have been harmed by that decision. As things turned out the Stinsons did have another child, a boy whom they named Jonathan; but it would sound odd to say that if their experience with Andrew had dissuaded them from having further children, Jonathan would thereby have been harmed. He simply would not have existed. Can one harm a non-existent person?

Against this conclusion, Derek Parfit has argued that absurd consequences flow from a refusal to consider the interests of the people who will exist if we decide to conceive them. Suppose, Parfit says, that a woman is planning to stop taking contraceptive pills so that she can have a child. Before doing so she is told by her doctor that because of a temporary medical condition, any child she conceives now will be handicapped. If the woman will wait three months, the doctor says, the condition will pass and any child she conceives then will be normal.

We would all think that in these circumstances the woman ought to postpone her plans to become pregnant. We would think this, even if the handicap the child would have is not so terrible as to make that child's life one of unredeemed misery. Suppose that the handicap meant, for instance, that the child would be unable to walk without calipers, but would otherwise be normal. A life of limited mobility with no other handicaps can still be a life very definitely worth living. Yet everyone we have asked agrees that even if the handicap were of this relatively mild kind, the woman ought to wait three months before she conceives.

Behind this response may lie the thought that if the woman were to decide against waiting the three months, she would be needlessly causing her child to have a handicap, but the point to notice about Parfit's example is that if the woman waits before becoming pregnant, the child she will then conceive is a *different* child from the one she would have had if she had not postponed becoming pregnant. Each month a fertile woman produces a new egg, with different genetic material. The child who will be conceived from the egg that ripens in April cannot be the same child as the child who would have been conceived from the egg that ripened in January.

Let us assume that the handicap would have been a relatively mild one, so that the handicapped child would have had the expectation of a quality of life well above the minimal level at which life ceases to be a benefit. Then the woman could not be said to have harmed the child if she had refused to postpone her plans to become pregnant. The child conceived without delay would still have a life that would be a good one for that child; and if the woman had not become pregnant at that time, this particular child would not have existed at all. So if we claim that the woman would be harming "her child," this claim cannot be true of any particular child that the woman might have. If she does not wait, there will be no child who is harmed by her decision.

It is significant that spelling this out does not lead people to modify their judgement that the woman should wait before becoming pregnant. We are influenced by the fact that the child conceived later will have the expectation of a better life than the child conceived immediately. In saying that the woman should wait, we are clearly taking into account the interests of the "next child" who will only be born if the woman does wait.

Most of us—with the exception of right-to-life groups and their supporters—think along similar lines when we consider pre-natal testing for abnormalities. It is now routine for doctors to offer special tests to pregnant women who run an unusually high risk of having an abnormal baby. Pregnant women over thirty-five, for instance, are often tested because older women are more likely to have a child with Down's syndrome. If the test shows that the foetus does have Down's syndrome, the woman is able to have an abortion. The same thing happens with women who are known to be carriers of the gene for haemophilia; the foetus can be checked to see if it will have the disease. If it does, the woman can have an abortion, and then try again, until she has a normal baby.

Why do we regard this as a reasonable thing to do, even when the handicap is one like haemophilia, which is quite compatible with a worthwhile life? As in Parfit's example, we are offsetting the loss of one life against the creation of another life with better prospects. Richard Hare, formerly professor of moral philosophy at the University of Oxford, has defended this practice by asking us to imagine a dialogue between a defective foetus with a condition like spina bifida and its as-yet-unconceived possible brother, Andrew. (Since Hare wrote the paper to which we are referring in 1973, his choice of name can have nothing to do with the name of the Stinson's premature son; it is, however, an ironic choice, since one might have imagined Andrew Stinson having a similar dialogue with his as-yet-unconceived possible brother, Jonathan.) Hare asks us to accept that the parents of the defective foetus will not contemplate another child if the foetus survives, but if it dies they will have another child. It is therefore not possible for both the foetus and Andrew to live. The foetus and Andrew try to find a solution that chooses between them on the basis of equal consideration of both their interests in having a happy existence. The dialogue, Hare says, might go like this:

Andrew points out that if the foetus is not born there is a high probabil-ity that he, Andrew, will be born and will have a normal and reason-ably happy life . . . To this the foetus might reply, "At least I have got this far; why not give me a chance?" But a chance of what? They then do the prognosis as best they can and work out the chances of the various outcomes if the present pregnancy is not terminated. It turns out that there is a slim chance, but only a slim chance, that the foetus will, if born and operated on, turn into a normal and, let us hope, happy child; that there is a considerable chance on the other hand that it will perish in spite of the operation; and that there is a far from negligible chance of its surviving severely handicapped. In that case, I think Andrew, the later possible child, can claim that he is the best bet, because the chance of the parents dying or changing their minds about having another child before he is born is pretty small, and cer-tainly far less than the chance that the present foetus, if born, will be very seriously handicapped.[21]

Hare acknowledges that such an imaginary dialogue can be mislead-ing because it leads us to think of both the foetus and its possible brother as if they were existing beings capable of rational discussion and with desires for continued life. We must always bear in mind that neither the foetus nor the unconceived brother can feel the loss of life, or even the fear of that loss. (Hare qualifies this by admitting that a foetus might be conscious, but adding that the intensity of its feelings would presumably be low.) The essential point of the dialogue, however, is simply that when contemplating the rights and wrongs of abortion in these circum-stances, it is not only the value of the life of the foetus that should be considered. The value of the life of what Hare calls "the next child in the queue" should not be ignored.

Hare's imaginary dialogue supports the common response to the abortion of abnormal foetuses, and this in turn points in the same direction as our firm conviction that the woman in Parfit's example should wait before becoming pregnant. In each case, we are ready to allow one life to be sacrificed for the sake of the life of an unconceived possible child. We cannot defend such a judgement except by assuming that the value of the life of an unconceived possible child can properly be taken into consideration. "Theoretical," as such a child may be at the time when it is merely a "next child," if conception takes place there will soon be an actual living child. When Peggy Stinson was considering whether to bring into the world the child who became Jonathan Stinson, she was right to think that if Andrew's survival would make it impossible for her to have another child, the normal prospects for a good life of this "next child" should outweigh Andrew's much more limited chances of a minimally adequate life. The life of this "next child" may have been theoretical at that time, but Jonathan is leading a real life now.

Hare makes it clear that the moral of his dialogue applies as much to newborn infants as it does to foetuses. He suggests that the best chance the foetus has of winning the argument is to say: "All right, we'll make a bargain. We will say that I am to be born and operated on, in the hope of restoring me to normality. If the operation is successful, well and good. If it isn't, then I agree that I should be scrapped and make way for Andrew." This compromise, Hare says, gives the best possible chance of a healthy baby, and gives the foetus "all the chance it ever had of itself being that baby." The proposal assumes, of course, that infants have no automatic right to life, and therefore infanticide, either active or passive, is permissible. But Hare defends this when he concludes:

I do not think that the harm you are doing to the foetus or the unsuccessfully operated upon newborn infant by killing them is greater than that which you are doing to Andrew by stopping him from being conceived and born. In fact I think it is much less, because Andrew, unlike them, has a high prospect of a normal and happy life.

We have already argued that newborn infants do not have a right to life merely because they are human and have emerged from the womb. Their lives as persons have not yet begun. Hare is therefore right to suggest that there is no fundamental moral reason against thinking about newborn infants in the way we now think about foetuses when we allow a woman to abort a defective foetus and try again to have a normal child. The only significant difference between the foetus and the newborn infant, so far as this discussion is concerned, is that the newborn infant can be given up for adoption, whereas the foetus cannot be, unless the woman is willing to go through with the pregnancy for this purpose—an ordeal that we would not wish to see inflicted upon any woman against her will. If an infant is born handicapped, but with reasonable prospects of a life sufficiently free from suffering to be worth living, and if there is someone willing to adopt and look after that infant, then adoption is better than the pointless destruction of a potentially worthwhile life. After the adoption, the baby's natural mother can have the "next child" she would not have had if the handicapped child had remained in her care. The interests of the existing handicapped child, and of the possible future child, can then both be satisfied.

If, on the other hand, adoption is for some reason impossible, the choice then lies between the life of an existing handicapped newborn infant or an as-yet-unconceived child who will in all probability be normal. In these circumstances it would be quite wrong to ignore the fact that the survival of the handicapped infant will prevent the existence of the possible normal child.

Notes

1. For the medical history of Baby Doe, see the letter to the editor by J. E. Pless, M.D. of Bloomington Hospital, *New England Journal of Medicine* 309, no. 11 (1983): 664. The ruling of the Indiana Supreme Court was reported in the *Chicago Tribune* on April 17, 1982.

2. S. H. Kadish, "Respect for Life and Regard for Rights in the Criminal Law," in *Respect for Life in Medicine, Philosophy and the Law*, ed. S. F. Barker (Baltimore: Johns Hopkins University Press, 1977), 72.

3. Rabbi Immanuel Jakobovits is quoted by Cardinal John Heenan, Archbishop of Westminster, in "A Fascinating Story," in *The Hour of Our Death*, ed. S. Lack and R. Lamerton (a record of a conference on the care of the dying held in London, 1973) (London: Chapman, 1974), 6–7.

4. Dr. Moshe Tendler is cited by Edward H. Keyserlingk, *Sanctity of Life or Quality of Life in the Context of Ethics, Medicine and Law* (Study prepared for the Law Reform Commission of Canada (Ottawa: Supply & Services, 1979), 21.

5. P. Ramsey, *Ethics at the Edges of Life* (New Haven: Yale University Press, 1978), 191.

6. For the "Baby Doe guidelines," see Office of the Secretary, Department of Health and Human Services, *Nondiscrimination on the Basis of Handicap*, 48 Fed. Reg. 9630 (1983) Interim Final Rule modifying 45 C.F.R., par. 84.61.

7. The statements by Dr. C. Everett Koop can be found in the transcript of the proceedings before the United States District Court for the District of Columbia, *American Academy of Pediatrics et al. versus Margaret Heckler, Secretary of Department of Health and Human Services*, Washington, D.C., March 21, 1983, C.A. no. 83-0774, 44–45.

8. Bishop Lawrence Casey gave evidence before the Supreme Court of New Jersey in 1976. An abridged version of the judgement "In the Matter of Karen Quinlan, An Alleged Incompetent" is reprinted in *Killing and Letting Die*, ed. B. Steinbock (Englewood Cliffs, N.J.: Prentice-Hall, 1980). Bishop Lawrence's reference to "extraordinary means" can be found on p. 31.

9. The twelve-page *Declaration on Euthanasia* was issued by the Sacred Congregation for the Doctrine of the Faith in 1980. The American Medical Association's reference to "extraordinary means" is contained in a policy statement adopted by the House of Delegates of the American Medical Association on December 4, 1973. In its entirety the statement reads:
    "The intentional termination of the life of one human being by another—mercy killing—is contrary to that for which the medical profession stands and is contrary to the policy of the American Medical Association. The cessation of the employment of extraordinary means to prolong the life of the body when there is irrefutable evidence that biological death is imminent is the decision of the patient and/or his immediate family. The advice and judgment of the physician should be freely available to the patient and/or his immediate family."

10. Gerald Kelly, S.J., *Medico-Moral Problems* (St. Louis: Catholic Hospital Association, 1958), 129.

11. The remark by Judge John Ferris is quoted in the Report of the President's Commission for the Study of Ethical Problems in Medicine and Biomedical and Behavioral Research, *Deciding to Forego Life-Sustaining Treatment: Ethical, Medical and Legal Issues in Treatment Decisions* (Washington, D.C.: Government Printing Office, 1983), 84.

12. Robert Veatch calls for banning the words "ordinary" and "extraordinary means" from further use on p. 110 of his book *Death, Dying and the Biological Revolution* (New Haven: Yale University Press, 1976). The conclusion of the Law Reform Commission of Canada that the distinction is too ambiguous to be useful can be found on p. 36 of its working paper no. 28, *Euthanasia, Aiding Suicide and Cessation of Treatment* (Ottawa: Supply & Services, 1982).

13. The quotations are from pp. 88–89 of the American President's Commission's Report, *Deciding to Forego Life-Sustaining Treatment*.

14. Joseph Fletcher's "Indicators of Humanhood: A Tentative Profile of Man" appeared in the *Hastings Center Report*, vol. 2, no. 5 (1972).

15. M. Tooley, *Abortion and Infanticide* (Oxford: Clarendon, 1984), esp. chap. 5.

16. John Locke's definition of "person" is found in his *Essay Concerning Human Understanding*, bk. II, chap. 9, para. 29.

17. For one example of the view that the killing of severely handicapped infants will pose a threat to severely disabled adults as well, see Nat Hentoff, "The Baby Who Was Starved to Death for His Own Good," *Village Voice* (New York), December 13, 1983, 6. Jeremy Bentham's comment on infanticide is from his *Theory of Legislation* (ed. C. K. Ogden [Littleton, Colo.: Fred B. Rothman, 1987]), p. 264, and is quoted by E. Westermarck, *The Origin and Development of the Moral Ideas*, vol. 1, 2d ed. (London: Macmillan, 1912), 413n.

18. Derek Parfit, *Reasons and Persons* (Oxford: Clarendon, 1984).

19. S. Kew, *Handicap and Family Crisis* (London: Pitman, 1975), 52. Kew cites two studies: K. Holt, "The Influence of a Retarded Child Upon Family Limitation," *Journal of Mental Deficiency Research* 2 (1958); and J. Tizard and J. Grad, *The Mentally Handicapped and Their Families* (Oxford: Oxford University Press, 1961).

20. Robert Stinson and Peggy Stinson, *The Long Dying of Baby Andrew* (Boston: Little, Brown, 1983), 153, 266–67.

21. Richard M. Hare, "Survival of the Weakest," in *Moral Problems in Medicine*, ed. S. Gorovitz et al., 1st ed. (Englewood Cliffs, N.J.: Prentice-Hall, 1976), 364–69. This article was first given in lecture form to the London Medical Group.

The Days of One's Life and the Life of One's Days

BERNARD M. DICKENS

LEGAL ANALYSIS OF the obligation to sustain a sick person's life is beset by the courts' conscious refusal to allow a concept of quality of life to be a criterion of decision-making. It is recognized that what gives life quality is a personal and idiosyncratic matter uniquely determined by each individual regarding his or her own life. One person, whether a health professional or a member, for instance, of a committee or court, cannot credibly assess what affords quality to the life of another person. Accordingly, medical-treatment decisions cannot be based upon a legal concept of quality of life. Human life itself, determined negatively by clinical non-conformity with criteria of death, is the only quality the law claims to recognize, in the sense that living patients cannot be medically abandoned and simply be let die.

It does not follow, however, that all patients must be identically treated. All must be appropriately treated, of course, as an obligation of equity, appropriateness of treatment being determined by clinical factors. Appropriate care is described in law as "ordinary" care, and contrasted with "extraordinary" care.[1] Derived from moral discourse, the contrast between ordinary and extraordinary care has come to be so differently explained and understood among and between health professionals, ethicists, and lawyers, that by 1983 it was found that "the distinction between ordinary and extraordinary treatments has now become so confused that its continued use in the formulation of public policy is no longer desirable."[2] Nevertheless, the distinction is of legal significance, in that it has evolved from being a prescriptive formula to become a descriptive explanation. Before the decision in the Karen Quinlan case in 1976,[3] it was accepted that the use of particular forms of treatment was always ordinary—for instance, antibiotics and such staples of management as nutrition—and that other treatments were always extraordinary in themselves, notably

152   FUNCTIONAL ACCOUNTS OF TIME

highly invasive procedures. The moral distinction arose with the devel-opment of artificial life-supports, and extraordinary care remains other-wise known as artificial, mechanical, aggressive, or heroic care.

The *Quinlan* case took the law beyond simply labelling particular treatments either ordinary, which are legally mandatory to provide, or extraordinary, which are discretionary to offer or maintain. The law now directs central attention to the individual patient's clinical prognosis. Treatment capable of helping a patient's survival as a functioning being is considered ordinary and obligatory, whereas treatment that is unlikely so to assist the patient is extraordinary. Such treatment may be applied in a desperate or speculative attempt to improve an unfavourable progno-sis, but a decision not to make the attempt does not violate the criminal or civil legal duty of care, and the patient at the time or in advance can legally decline its use. A condition of care's being ordinary in a parti-cular case is that it is available. Under a system of provincial or national health care, the level of governmental provision of means of care may influence determination of availability, but health professionals, hospitals, and other health facilities, whether within the public or the private sector of care, are required to act according to at least minimum standards of proficiency and adequacy of resources, which the courts will determine upon the occasion of litigation.[4]

In the *Quinlan* case, the New Jersey Supreme Court observed that "the use of the same respirator or like support could be considered 'ordinary' in the context of the possibly curable patient but 'extraordinary' in the context of the forced sustaining . . . of an irreversibly doomed patient."[5] Introduction of the role of the patient's prognosis is significant to legal analysis and places health professionals, as opposed to lawyers and judges, at the centre of critical data determination. If the prognosis is favourable treatments become ordinary that would otherwise be extra-ordinary, and vice versa.

The contrast appears in consideration of the two decisions in the case of Stephen Dawson.[6] In the British Columbia provincial court, the judge found from the evidence that the hydrocephalic and severely handicapped young boy, aged about seven, "has no cognitive awareness and no means of communicating with others."[7] Citing the *Quinlan* judgement, the judge concluded that replacing a blocked shunt draining fluid from the boy's brain would involve extraordinary care, since it would not improve his condition. The judge therefore found that his parents had legal capacity to decline to consent to it, even though, as the parents clearly believed, death was likely if the surgical replacement was not done. In a trial *de novo* in the provincial Supreme Court, however, new witnesses brought in new evidence, which showed a considerably more optimistic prognosis of capacity for happiness and interactive functioning. Further, the judge found that

> there is not a simple choice here of allowing the child to live or die according to whether the shunt is implanted or not. There looms the awful possibility that without the shunt the child will endure in a state of progressing disability and pain. It is too simplistic to say that the child should be allowed to die in peace.[8]

Accordingly, it was concluded that the surgery was ordinary care by legal classification, both because it could assist the patient's functioning and because it would spare him the prospect of "disability and pain." Parental refusal of the treatment was considered unlawful, since treatment was in the child's best interests, and he was placed in charge of a provincial officer who was required to give legal consent to treatment.

The medical evidence in the *Dawson* case shows two different children, one chronically vegetative and the other happy and responsive, with the same identity. This underscores the uncertainty of medical diagnosis and prognosis, and the difficulty of making clinical assessments upon which legal distinctions and the sustaining of human life itself may depend. Health professionals are heard to deny that they can discharge the responsibility of making such predictions, since they have no prospective means to ensure that their predictions will prove correct. The disclaimer of accurate foresight misunderstands the legal requirement, however, and disregards the fact that clinical judgements as to future conditions are routinely made, and routinely result in treatment decisions. The law requires only that the clinical prognosis be responsibly made, upon the basis of relevant and contemporaneous knowledge and compatibility with the skill a competent practitioner of the given health profession's specialty would be expected to apply.[9] The law does not require that the prognosis be correct, but only that it be made with due knowledge of clinical and scientific data. Clinical judgement is accepted to bear an irreducible minimum risk of error,[10] and carries no legal sanction simply because it may be or subsequently proves to be incorrect.

Although all living patients are entitled to appropriate forms of ordinary care, the *Quinlan* court considered artificial life-supports to be extraordinary upon the facts of the case, because of a neurological test. Upon this same basis, the lower court in the *Dawson* case considered surgery to be discretionary because of the boy's perceived chronic severe intellectual impairments. In *Quinlan*, the court observed that "the focal point of decision should be the prognosis as to the reasonable possibility of return to cognitive and sapient life, as distinguished from the forced continuance of that biological vegetative existence to which Karen seems to be doomed."[11] This test of modest neurological functioning, consisting in evidence of a patient possessing a sense of self and an awareness of others, and being capable of living a life of human experience, does not include a quality-of-life component. However, it may set a minimum condition for an individual to warrant more than quite basic care requiring comfort and nursing services rather than medical services.

The English Court of Appeal applied an additional test in 1981, when it required surgical correction of an intestinal blockage in a Down's syndrome child capable of living thereafter for twenty or thirty years. In stating its decision that the surgery be done, the court noted that there "may be cases . . . of severe proved damage where the future is so certain and where the life of the child is so bound to be full of pain and suffering that the court might be driven to a different conclusion."[12]

Accordingly, it appears that no more than basic sustenance is legally required for patients incapable of maintaining or of being restored to cognitive and sapient life,[13] or for conscious, sentient patients clearly shown to face an existence of only pain and suffering. Further, nutrition and hydration may lawfully be denied or withdrawn when appropriate consent is given. For the patient they can assist to reach a life of consciousness and comfort, mechanical or surgical means of sustaining life, however invasive, may be ordinary care, legally mandatory for health professionals and facilities to provide.[14] For the patient incapable of achieving consciousness, or facing a life only of conscious suffering, routine antibiotics are extraordinary and so discretionary. The patient affected by a terminal malignancy, for instance, who contracts treatable pneumonia, may be left to die in the comfort of that condition if its cure would lead to death shortly later in acute distress. A newborn child with multiple mental and physical handicaps requiring surgery to remove intestinal blockage may remain untreated, and be given only sedatives, appetite suppressants, and conservative measures of comfort until death.[15] For such a child born dying, nutrition may be extraordinary care.[16]

This legally drawn contrast may appear too stark for practical comfort, since it marks only the extremes and fails to address the wide middle ground where prognostic uncertainty exists. The law's response to this challenge is not substantive, but procedural. An attending physician for an individual patient bears responsibility to make the clinical prognosis. If made with proper knowledge and as a conscientious exercise of clinical judgement, that prognosis provides the necessary and

DICKENS / *The Legal Perspective*

a sufficient basis for legal decision-making. The fact that the prognosis is uncertain to prove correct and that professional peers or superiors may have arrived at a different conclusion is of no legal consequence.[17] Provided that it falls within the range of reasonable prognosis that competent practitioners may reach, and is based upon adequately skilled interpretation of available data[18] not influenced by non-medical ideology, the prognosis will satisfy legal requirements of professional judgement. Upon the basis of such assessment, for instance, it would be legally appropriate to write a Do Not Resuscitate or No-Code order, provided that it was accompanied by a protocol requiring periodic reassessment, for instance every seventy-two hours, and that it was open to review upon evidence of an improved prognosis.[19]

While the law requires that all patients be appropriately treated, it relates treatment required in particular cases to patients' potential for achieving or maintaining consciousness, insight, and comfort. Quality-of-life criteria are rejected in that even the chronically vegetative patient must be cared for and the patient in enduring agony must be afforded every available means of care. Lives of such patients may not be prematurely ended, under criminal homicide provisions[30] and civil liability for causing wrongful death. As against this, however, only conservative care and comfort measures are legally indicated for patients with an unfavourable prognosis measured by the criteria of consciousness and liability to pain and suffering outlined above. In that the law may thereby appear reluctantly to accommodate quality-of-life considerations, it does so by setting satisfaction of a low neurological criterion as a condition of eligibility for care, and by acknowledging that a patient may legitimately wish a natural ending to a life afflicted by unmitigated pain and suffering.[21]

Judicial unwillingness to recognize quality-of-life considerations may be yielding in the face of claims for so-called wrongful life. This is the negligence claim brought by a child against a doctor, health facility, or, for instance, clinical laboratory, for having been born with severe congenital anomalies that competent foresight could have predicted and prevented, for instance by proper genetic diagnosis of parents or prenatal diagnosis of the unborn child itself. Plaintiffs' claims that they should not have been allowed to be conceived, or should have been aborted before birth, were at first rejected by courts with scorn. Compensation is designed, as far as money can, to put plaintiffs in the positions in which they would have been had alleged wrongs not occurred. In a wrongful-life claim in 1967 the New Jersey Supreme Court refused to consider compensation, however, observing that

156   FUNCTIONAL ACCOUNTS OF TIME

the infant plaintiff would have us measure the difference between his life with defects against the utter void of nonexistence, but it is impossible to make such a determination. This Court cannot weigh the value of life with impairments against the nonexistence of life itself.[22]

This attitude regularly prevailed in the courts until 1980, when the California Court of Appeal held that the claim was admissible and, if successful, could be compensated.[23] The decision was subsequently followed in California,[24] Washington state,[25] and, perhaps significantly in light of the history of rejection of the claim, in New Jersey.[26] English courts adhere to the traditional practice of rejecting such claims, however,[27] a Lord Justice of Appeal observing that, having heard counsel's argument on the question of the claims, he had come "to the same answer as [he] felt inclined to give the question before [he] heard argument, namely that plainly and obviously the claims disclose no reasonable cause of action."[28] In contrast, when a judge of the Supreme Court of British Columbia addressed the issue in a fully reasoned judgment in 1991, he found that a child's claim for wrongful life could be upheld.[29] Judicial favour of the wrongful-life action in the United States is resisted by legislation in some states, inspired by fear that the successful claim provides an incentive for physicians to advise and perform abortions, in order to reduce legal liability upon birth of handicapped children.[30]

Some American jurisdictions' willingness to consider painful impaired life to constitute compensable injury indicates that life itself is not necessarily a benefit compared to no life. This may suggest that, at the other end of human existence, sustaining of a life of pain and suffering when the alternative is to allow death may similarly justify a wrongful-life claim. If a court can in fact "weigh the value of life with impairments against the nonexistence of life itself,"[31] and assess that quality of life to be a deficit capable of compensation, it may appear that the same weighting can be made of life sustained with impairments against the nonexistence of life itself following natural death. The focal point of permitted wrongful-life claims has come to centre upon compensation for special medical costs incurred due to handicap and disability, rather than for the experience of being alive.[32]

Nevertheless, it must be observed that judicial recognition of the wrongful-life claim remains anomalous. The general tendency of jurisdictions in the common law tradition has been to reject these claims. This conforms to the general disposition to consider an individual's life a quality and benefit in itself that always outweighs the absence of life. This absolutist contrast between impaired life and no life may fail to

DICKENS / *The Legal Perspective* 157

address different qualities of lives, but the contrast may indicate legal outcome of the conflict between a shorter life of good days and a longer life of poor quality. It suggests that imposition of more days of poor quality may not be actionable by or on behalf of the patient subjected to such unwanted additional time of life.[33] This raises the issue, however, of the patient's right to natural death.

Natural Death: The Terminal Patient

Consistent with the conclusion reached above that sustaining of life of an unwilling but viable patient is not legally actionable through a wrongful-life action, it appears that there is no legal right to experience avoidable death. To describe death as avoidable is relative, of course, since death itself can only be postponed. To recognize this reality in doctrine, a distinction is drawn between patients in terminal conditions and patients not in such conditions. Non-terminal patients generally have no right to die, even in jurisdictions that have decriminalized attempted suicide.

The law respects a life-affirming ethic, and encourages rescue of those who are capable of being saved by protecting would-be rescuers. Section 45 of the *Criminal Code* of Canada provides, for instance, that:

Every one is protected from criminal responsibility for performing a surgical operation upon any person for the benefit of that person if:

(a) the operation is performed with reasonable care and skill, and

(b) it is reasonable to perform the operation, having regard to the state of health of the person at the time the operation is performed and to all the circumstances of the case.

The provision leaves something to be desired as a definitive guide to permitted conduct. It makes no reference, for instance, to the role of the rescued person's wishes, or to the effect of that person's refusal of intervention. It may accordingly be contended that rescue over objection cannot be "reasonable . . . having regard to . . . the circumstances of the case."[34] As against this, however, a person unreasonably refusing rescue may offend against section 262, which provides that:

Every one who . . .

(b) without reasonable cause prevents or impedes or attempts to prevent or impede any person who is attempting to save the life of another person,[35]

is guilty of an indictable offence. . . .

Again, it is not self-evident that this covers life-sustaining medical care,[36] but it reinforces rescuers' rights when resisting them would be objectively unreasonable.

A defence may be made of a rescuer's conduct alleged to offend criminal law or rights protected by civil law, on the ground that the conduct was necessary to save human life. Common law courts remain uncomfortable with the necessity defence,[37] since it invokes principles of higher and lower levels of law reflecting natural law thinking unsympathetic to positivist perceptions, and provides grounds to subvert the general and legislatively enacted legal order. Nineteenth-century cases in which defendants invoked necessity to save their own lives by deliberately taking others' lives rejected the defence,[38] but it has been recognized in the twentieth century, particularly in cases defending abortion.[39] In this context, it has been recognized that preservation of life is not limited to achieving the bare fact of survival, but includes preservation of the quality of life, meaning good health, which has physiological and mental health dimensions.[40] In this sense, the law further recognizes the priority of protecting quality of life.

Preservation of the fact of life may be inimical to protection of an individual's preferred quality of life. This is the basis of permitting terminal patients to succumb to natural death rather than have their lives sustained by aggressive or mechanical means. In the sometimes unhelpful language used in contesting the sanctity of life and the quality of life, this may constitute "death with dignity." At times, it is urged in doctrine and indeed accepted by courts that non-terminal persons may be allowed the dignity of risking their lives for causes which are important to them. Modern American and Canadian case law and doctrine are ambivalent on whether hunger-striking prisoners should be force-fed,[41] and political protesters and similar activists may undertake motivated campaigns of refusing nutrition in which public authorities decide not to intervene. Equally, adventurers, thrill-seekers, and professional stunt practitioners are afforded autonomy to place their lives at risk. While they may be allowed the privilege of risking their lives, however, they cannot necessarily claim a right, since intervention to protect and prolong their lives may be legally defensible, and judicially mandated.

Until recently, religious freedom did not prevail over preservation of life, but the Ontario Court of Appeal's unanimous decision in *Malette v. Shulman*[42] is likely to change this for the future. Courts have ordered blood transfusion of Jehovah's Witnesses when they were pregnant or had small dependent children,[43] although when they owed no duties of care to others, and when duties could be discharged by another, such as a surviving parent, their autonomy of choice has been allowed.[44] Religious adherents refusing blood transfusion do not wish to die, of course, but hope to survive by divine intervention. They may be contrasted with the suicidal, who intend to die.[45] The classic proposition, echoed throughout the common law world, that "every human being of adult years and sound mind has a right to determine what shall be done with his own body,"[46] may be hard to apply to suicide. Emphasis may be given to its limitation to those "of . . . sound mind," and suicidal tendencies may be taken to be symptomatic of unsound mind. This is reflected in coroners' juries' almost invariable verdicts in such cases, of "suicide while the balance of the mind was disturbed."[47] Rejection of a wish to die as unnatural has its most common expression in a physician's refusal to permit a patient's death when the patient wishes to die a death that is in fact medically avoidable.[48] When a patient exists in mental or spiritual anguish and wishes to die, the despairing condition will be considered a relievable pathological symptom to be aggressively treated rather than passively accepted or tolerated. The physician becomes the would-be sustainer of life the law has been inclined to protect.[49]

Premature, self-willed avoidable death may appear unnatural death. Natural death may be artificially postponed, but when death becomes imminent in the course of nature, the patient is considered to have entered a terminal condition, in which aggressive care is legally extra-ordinary and discretionary. In this condition, the quality of life of the patient is expected to experience may enter into the medical decision to offer aggressive care, and into the patient's decision on accepting it. Since the patient may legally decline such care, it may be said that a terminal patient has a right to a natural death.

The expression "terminal condition" may seem to require definition or at least description, but in practice the most that may be achievable is a procedure to assess upon clinical grounds whether an individual's condition is terminal.[50] The Natural Death Act of California,[51] which was a pioneering enactment in this area, provides that:

"Terminal condition" means an incurable condition caused by injury, disease, or illness, which, regardless of the application of life-sustaining procedures, would, within reasonable medical judgement, produce death, and where the application of life-sustaining procedures serve [sic] only to postpone the moment of death of the patient.[52]

The establishment of the condition so defined is dependent upon "reasonable medical judgement," so that the patient's achievement of autonomy is conditional upon a physician's prognosis. This is reinforced in the act's provision that:

"Life-sustaining procedure" means any medical procedure or intervention which utilizes mechanical or other artificial means to sustain, restore, or supplant function, which . . . would serve only to artificially prolong the moment of death and where, in the judgment of the attending physician, death is imminent whether or not such procedures are utilized. "Life-sustaining procedure" shall not include the administration of medication or the performance of any medical procedure deemed necessary to alleviate pain.[53]

Language and its applications in the area of terminal care have proven to be a source of difficulty.[54] Individual decisions can be shown to be inconsistent with others, for instance, on the expected duration of life and the likely effects of treatment. A reconciliation may exist, however, in recognizing that the clinical opinion of the attending physician prevails on the issue of whether a patient is terminal. Consistent consequences follow from those opinions, regarding required treatment and discretions to yield to patients' preferences, even though opinions may differ upon comparable cases. Attending physicians are gate-keepers of their patients' autonomy in that they diagnose patients to be outside or within a terminal condition.

Patients who are dead appear to be beyond a terminal condition. Whether a patient is dead depends, however, upon the criteria of death. Increasing recognition is being afforded to neurological criteria of death, often described as brain death. Distinctions are drawn between brain-stem death and whole-brain death, including death of both the brain-stem and the outer brain, and refinements of measurement have been elaborated.[55] It may be recalled that Karen Quinlan had not been considered dead, although she suffered from permanent loss of consciousness owing to destruction of her outer brain. The contrast is that the dead, including those assessed to be brain-dead, may be buried, cremated, or with appropriate consent have tissue removed for transplantation or, for instance, for scientific research or medical education, whereas the permanently unconscious must be given ordinary care. Depending upon their conditions, ordinary care may be only nursing care and comfort measures, rather than active medical care. They may be allowed to die in the course of nature by the withholding of aggressive measures.

While permanently unconscious patients are not necessarily terminal, since their brain-stem activity may preserve spontaneous organic functioning for an immeasurable time, they do not have to be offered advanced

DICKENS / *The Legal Perspective*

resources of medical technology. This suggests that more sophisticated medical care serves achievable preservation or restoration of a life of human experience, described in the *Quinlan* case as "cognitive and sapient life."[56] It may therefore be concluded that, although the law does not make a patient's achievement of a given quality of life a condition of others rendering appropriate care, a quality-of-life standard may be influential in distinguishing the intensity or sophistication of care that is appropriate. Days incapable of being spent in a condition of human perception, which is a minimum condition of a human quality of life, and days that can be lived only in pain and suffering, do not have to be forcefully pursued.

Principles of Decision-making

The paternalism that once was taken to characterize physician-patient relations is now in decline and discredit.[57] The doctrines of free consent and particularly of informed consent, based upon ethical values of individual autonomy but given a critical cutting-edge through judicial decisions, are having the effect of limiting medical paternalism by placing patients in charge of the goals of their treatment, and often in charge of the individual means of treatments that affect them. The doctrine of informed consent, based upon such leading cases as *Natanson v. Kline*,[58] *Canterbury v. Spence*,[59] and *Cobbs v. Grant*,[60] has been incorporated in Canadian law through the Supreme Court decision in *Reibl v. Hughes*,[61] although older doctrine influenced by medical professional preferences seems to persist in England.[62] In the Supreme Court of Canada, the expression "informed choice" was used,[63] which is preferable to "informed consent" since the decision may be not to consent.[64]

This is particularly so regarding extraordinary care, which may be offered to a terminal patient or to one facing a life of unrelievable distress. It has been seen that patient autonomy implicit in the health professional's duty to act only upon the patient's free and informed choice may be compromised when the patient is not in a terminal condition. A wish to die may then be considered evidence of pathology rather than of autonomy. Where the issue to be addressed is resolution of conflicts between pursuit of the terminal or comparable patient's length of days and of the patient's perception of quality of life, however, the patient's wishes should prevail regarding treatment beyond comfort measures.

Legal concern with the patient's wishes may be contrasted with medical concern with the patient's interests.[65] Health professionals have traditionally been trained to identify and pursue patients' best interests, measured by therapeutic and health-oriented criteria. A patient's wish to follow a dysfunctional lifestyle seems perverse, and while health professionals recognize a need to tolerate patients' idiosyncrasies, they do not easily suffer their patients to make poor treatment choices. Indeed, they regard their function of informing patients to be directed to offering not just neutral data, but to orienting patients towards good decisions addressed by the informants' perspectives. This approach is interpreted as being consistent with ethical imperatives to do no harm, and to place above all the well-being of the patient.

This conscientious professional approach has lacked appreciation that harm is not limited to physical harm but can include harm to dignity and respect for personality, and that well-being is similarly not only physiological but also concerns a sense of psychological and spiritual well-being.[66] Assessment of a patient's well-being has come to be governed less by the health professional's objective determination of best interests and more by the particular patient's subjective determination of what he or she wishes. Wishes and interests are not necessarily incompatible, of course, since most patients wish that their best interests be served. They seek information from health professionals on such matters as their prognosis if they remain untreated, available goals of treatment and means of pursuing those goals, and associated risks, discomforts, and potential benefits, in order to identify their interests. The doctrine of informed consent requires health professionals to provide adequate and requested scientific and medical information to serve patients' informational needs and assist their choices. The so-called therapeutic privilege of non-disclosure of countertherapeutic or dysfunctional information is accordingly quite narrow.[67] The evolving role of the health professional is to facilitate the patient's choice, rather than to direct or limit choice to what the professional approves.

Properly informed patients may have perceptions of their own interests that health professionals do not share, and indeed that they fear, deplore, and oppose because of concern for their vision of patients' best interests. The paternalistic view encourages patients to make "right" decisions and not "wrong" decisions, but the more modern libertarian view encourages patients to be governed by their own free and adequately informed choices, even if their outcomes may be less than the best achievable. Competent patients are not to be subjected to others' possibly wiser choices: wisdom is not a condition of autonomy. The challenge of this latter view to health professionals is that it obliges them to suffer their patients to make poor choices, and to serve those choices conscientiously, unless they feel compelled to withdraw from professional relationships (consistently, of course, with legal provisions against abandonment). Further, if some patients' potential preferences are conscientiously unacceptable to health professionals, they are ethically and often legally required to so inform patients, lest patients remain unaware of treatment options, or falsely believe the professionals' disfavour to have a scientific or medical basis.[68]

Legal emphasis upon terminal and comparable patients' autonomy, notably regarding use of extraordinary means of sustaining their lives, supposes them to have achieved legal competence to exercise autonomy. Once a patient has been competent, however, the right to be governed by his or her independent wishes is not forfeited simply because the patient ceases to be competent. It may fall to others, such as relatives, to iden-tify and apply the wishes of a patient who is no longer competent, but the governing criterion remains the subjective wish of the patient. A once-competent person whose competence fails is not thereby cast under the subjective preference of a related or other decision-maker, nor under the objective assessment of a health professional. The function of a sub-stitute or surrogate decision-maker is not to decide what he or she wishes to do regarding the patient, but to determine what the patient would wish to have done. Accordingly, the identity of the particular decision-maker is of minor significance, provided that the individual expressing the patient's wish can do so with fidelity to the patient's most recently demonstrated authentic personality.

Legal means are increasingly available to permit competent persons to state their wishes on medical management if, when in the future they enter a terminal condition, they are not competent to express themselves. Executed under authority of legislation such as a Natural Death Act,[69] declarations often called "living wills" or advance "medical directives" declare that the maker will not consent to administration of extra-ordinary care, but wishes only for comfort measures and natural death. A number of legal problems surround these declarations, not least because they are more easily revoked than made, since revocation may be desired by feeble or incompetent patients,[70] and, unlike true wills made by competent testators, family members may in fact be able to veto them because they disagree with them. Such declarations may justify withholding extraordinary care, but do not necessarily prohibit and sanction use of such means unless the legislation under which they are made so provides. It must be remembered, furthermore, that an effective declaration becomes operative only when the patient enters a terminal condition, and it has been seen that whether or not the patient is terminal is determined by the attending physician's clinical judgement.

An alternative device may be created under a "durable power of attorney" statute. This does not attempt to predetermine a particular treatment decision that will have to be made when the maker becomes terminal and incompetent, but identifies the person who will have legal authority to make the decision. The effect is to give the individual maker a legal means to displace near relatives and others who may become influential decision-makers, in favour of a person chosen in advance, perhaps because of known sympathies with the individual. Traditional powers of attorney lapse if the maker becomes incompetent, but durable powers are executed in anticipation of that very event, and afford the maker control over the identity of the person under whose authority he or she then falls. The alternative may be that, upon incompetency, a court order may be sought by an interested person, usually a relative, to gain power over the incompetent's property and/or person. It is clearly preferable that an individual should be able to anticipate and make provision for that circumstance, rather than leave it to the court to resolve *ex post facto*.

Although living wills can be effective under provisions of Natural Death Acts, they were developed before emergence of such enactments, and were binding in honour only; indeed, Natural Death Acts were developed in order to add legal effect to these declarations. In their earlier form, their contents were notified to attending physicians, and were added to the patients' medical records. A modern equivalent is a patient's request not to be resuscitated in the event of cardiopulmonary arrest, and not to be given comparable extraordinary care upon the occurrence of other terminal events. The patient's request will be recorded in the course of routine care, and will have the credibility the law gives to contemporaneous records made in the normal course of conduct. Canadian courts are likely to give effect to advance directives that particular forms of medical care should not be administered, as they would to Jehovah's Witness cards that decline blood transfusions and blood products.[71] Family members' requests and opinions may also be noted on the patient's chart, although the patient's request should not be communicated to family members without the patient's prior consent, under usual principles of confidentiality. If there is doubt or ambiguity as to the patient's wishes, they may be clarified with others the patient permits to discuss them with him or her, such as another physician, a nurse, or a hospital chaplain.

Means therefore exist by which terminal competent patients may decline medical care with legal effect, and by which competent patients anticipating a terminal or chronically vegetative condition can be treated under a regime over which they have exercised control. It must be observed, however, that while such means may be used to decline medical care, they may not have the effect of requiring that such care be used to the fullest possible extent. Extraordinary means remain discretionary, and physicians and health facilities may consider it inappropriate to employ them, notwithstanding patients' requests that they be available. Patients cannot command the devotion to their cases of extraordinary, disproportionate resources. The *Quinlan* court noted that the same support might be ordinary and therefore mandatory for one patient but extraordinary and discretionary for another.[72] Accordingly, health professionals must exercise judgement regarding the discretionary means of care of a terminal or chronically vegetative patient would accept, but are bound by a refusal of such care that has been adequately communicated.

Quite often, no wishes of a competent or formerly competent patient have been communicated or can be discerned through reliable witnesses, and many patients have never achieved competence. This may be because of mental retardation, or lack of natural development. The handicapped newborn is an obvious case of a patient who has never achieved competence to express wishes. Decision-making clearly cannot be based upon the patient's subjective preference, but it must be asked whether the patient is then at the disposal of the subjective preference of a substitute or surrogate, such as a parent. Anglo-Canadian jurisprudence suggests that parents and others making decisions in these cases must be governed by an objective assessment of the child's interests.[73] The *Dawson* case in Canada,[74] following the English Court of Appeal decision in the case *In re B.*,[75] reflects the thrust of the so-called Baby Doe regulations in the United States,[76] to the effect that parents' subjective preferences are superseded by more objectively based decisions directed to children's interests. In the English case *In re B.*, parental refusal of surgery to correct intestinal blockage was judicially displaced in order to give the child the prospect of two or three decades of life, which she would live affected by Down's syndrome. In *Dawson*, parental refusal of surgical replacement of a blocked shunt was displaced in order to give the boy the prospect of interactive life affected by severe retardation, and in order to save him from a perhaps shorter life of acute distress. Protection of interests does not necessarily always result, however, in life-prolonging decisions. In the case *In re B.*, the court recognized that upon clear demonstration that the life of a severely damaged child would be "bound to be full of

pain and suffering,"[77] a decision to decline surgery and allow death, in this case from starvation, could be appropriate.[78] In the *Saikewicz* case,[79] the Massachusetts Supreme Judicial Court considered the future of a sixty-six-year-old profoundly retarded permanent institutional resident with the mental age of an immature child.[80] He suffered from leukemia, and was eligible for chemotherapy. The court determined that it should not be applied if it was not in his best interests. It might have prolonged his life, but it was assessed that he could not comprehend the prospect of survival. He would understand the experience of chemotherapy, however, and would find it an infliction of pain, discomfort, and distress for an incomprehensible reason.

The approach in principle of distinguishing competent and formerly competent terminal or chronically vegetative patients from the never-competent, treating the former according to their wishes insofar as they are reliably shown, and treating those whose wishes are not discernable along with the never-competent according to their objectively shown best interests, may accord to an ethical ideal.[81] The approach may prove diffi-cult in practice, of course, since identification of an alleged wish may be contested between equally caring relatives, and relatives bound to pursue objective interests may be influenced in fact by their own subjective preferences. Further, health professionals determining evidence of formerly competent patients' wishes or of patients' best interests may be particularly receptive to information leading to conclusions that coincide with their own preferences. This raises the issue of how the principles of decision-making may be applied through different decision-participants, and what such participants' appropriate roles may be.

Decision-Participants

(a) Patients

The central role of patients in life-sustaining decisions that affect them has been explored above. In principle, competent patients should be in charge of the commanding heights of therapeutic decisions. In terminal conditions they may decline medical care that is offered, but may not be legally able to compel application of such care that their health attendants refuse, fail, or lack the means to make available. Formerly competent patients in terminal or permanently vegetative conditions are equally entitled to prevalence of their wishes to decline medical care, if their wishes can be shown to have been directed to that decision. Expressions of preference may be made through living wills, whether or not reinforced by legislation, and by statements to physicians, for instance, regarding orders not to resuscitate, documented on medical records. Alternatively, they may execute powers of attorney to place their treatment under the charge of persons of their own choosing.

The aim of affording maximum legal effect to autonomous choices of terminal and chronically vegetative patients is to give their lives quality through respect for dignity and self-determination. Further, autonomy permits such patients to opt for fewer days of their lives with a tolerable quality of such days, and to escape others' imposition upon them of post-poned death through days of pain and suffering, or of enduring unconsciousness. Competent persons are accordingly afforded legal means to regulate the quality and duration of their lives.

(b) Family Members and Friends

The primary function of family members and close friends in treatment decisions affecting terminal or chronically vegetative, formerly competent patients is to assist in identification of their wishes, where these have not been expressed in, for instance, living wills or instructions given to physicians. The function is displaced, however, by durable powers of attorney appointing, for instance, friends to act instead of family members. Health professionals may try to find patients' wishes by questioning appropriate surrogates such as family members and friends about patients' dispositions, philosophies, and lifestyles, and such acquaintances have to distill and interpret patients' personalities, and project them onto treatment options. Health professionals must seek authentic expression of patients' preferences, and may have to give more significance to views of those who know the patients and respect them than to views of relatives, including close relatives and spouses, who have lost contact with the patients and are tied to them only by blood or marriage rather than by affinity.[82] When such patients' wishes are incapable of determination in good faith, family members may participate in decisions by seeking patients' objectively assessed best interests. It has been seen that decisions by parents affecting severely handicapped newborns have to be governed by this principle. Where clear criteria of interests exist and are agreed among parents and health professionals, decisions may be implemented without more. Fears that such private decisions may prejudice children's rights have led to development in the United States of the Baby Doe Regulations,[83] however, and in a number of cases have caused third parties to seek judicial or other review of decisions unfavourable to sustaining of life. A dysfunction of crude intervention is that it may

168   FUNCTIONAL ACCOUNTS OF TIME

cause courts to react against strangers' attempts to use instance for furtherance of their own purposes, and to afford parents unduly protected rights of decision-making. The Baby Jane Doe case,[84] for instance, arose when a stranger chose to involve himself in a parental decision to decline treatment of their severely impaired newborn child, by seeking court review. The court considered this repugnant, and condemned his attempt to enter "the very heart of a family circle, there to challenge the most private and most precious responsibility vested in the parents for the care and nurture of their children."[85] This opens up the wider issue of an impaired child's survival and the effect upon the quality of life of other members of its family.

(c) Health Professionals

In the *Quinlan* case,[86] the court recognized that the attending physician has some role in treatment decisions. The physician may be considered not as an individual, but as a representative or spokesperson for the entire health team giving care to the patient in question. In this capacity, the physician may legally decide that it is inappropriate to offer extra-ordinary care to a particular terminal or chronically vegetative patient. A no-resuscitation order may accordingly be written. If the physician considers that the treatment offers a reasonable prospect of improving the patient's condition, by restoring cognitive or sapient life or by affording relief from pain and suffering, the treatment will be medically indicated and, as ordinary care, it should be rendered. Where a given treatment does not offer that prospect, however, a health professional has a discre-tion to decline to apply it, and in any event will be bound by a compe-tently made refusal of such care. Where no expression of the patient's preference is available, and the issue arises of the patient's best interests, the health professional may take a treatment initiative under the protec-tion available to rescuers; withhold treatment in agreement with appropri-ate surrogates acting on the patient's behalf, subject to judicial challenge; or have recourse to another agency for a second opinion, such as a hospital or other ethics committee. Further, as professionals with responsibilities for patients, they have *locus standi* before courts to challenge others' decisions and seek ratification of their own.

(d) Ethics Committees

There is growing interest in North America in the creation of hospital ethics committees, composed of members drawn from different disciplines and designed to be available to assist in the reaching of difficult decisions required to be made upon objective grounds.[87] Such committees were part of the tripartite process recommended in the *Quinlan* case, although subsequent practice in the United States, where such committees have been created, has been to describe them as "prognosis committees."[88] The effect of this, although not necessarily the purpose, is to give physicians dominant if not exclusive influence. Such committees cannot in themselves make legally effective decisions, but they can reinforce others' decisions, notably upon patients' best interests, with the effect of showing them to be objectively appropriate. The function of confirming the attending physician's diagnosis and prognosis may afford him or her protection against allegations of negligence and indifference in management of patients. Committees may also or alternatively review general policy on protocols governing non-resuscitation orders, and may introduce macro-ethical perceptions upon allocation of scarce resources, which may affect clinical decisions on offering or withholding extraordinary care. The most helpful role for hospital ethics committees has still to be determined. Insofar as they may comfort troubled hospital personnel they may be welcomed, but if they adopt a proactive posture and trouble comfortable or complacent personnel, objection to them may arise.[89]

(e) Strangers

It has been seen that in the **Baby Jane Doe** case,[90] the intervention of a stranger to the decision was strongly criticized by the court. In the *Dawson* case, however, the Supreme Court of British Columbia allowed the provincial Association for the Mentally Retarded to address the court. The cases are distinguishable, in that the pro-life activist in the former initiated the case, whereas the association in the latter was allowed to intervene in a case already commenced by an authorized agency, in order to reinforce arguments proposed by that agency. It is questionable whether the intervenors would have been allowed to introduce novel issues. Nevertheless, they were in court, and their arguments and evidence may well have contributed to the decision they preferred. A complete stranger moved by a philosophy may be distinguished from a person who is not a blood relative but who has an affinity for the very patient whose life or other interests may be at stake. Courts have allowed strangers personally familiar with potential patients to initiate successful proceedings to bar improper sterilizations upon which parents and physicians have privately agreed,[91] and may be similarly moved to hear such strangers' complaints about irreversible treatment—decisions regarding

dependent patients that are required to be determined by objective criteria. Although strangers may be more credible when they urge that life-
sustaining treatment is ordinary in a given case and should therefore be
legally mandated, those urging permission of natural death may be no
less compelling in acting to protect a dependent individual's personal and
bodily integrity.

(f) (Quasi-) Public Agencies

A number of public and quasi-public agencies have statutory authority to
intervene in treatment decisions, mainly by taking them to courts for
review.[92] In the *Dawson* case, the provincial superintendent of Family and
Child Service took the initiative to go to court, and in other provinces
such as Ontario initiative may be taken by a Children's Aid Society. This
is a quasi-public agency in that its board is elected by persons in the
community who have become society members, although agency funds
come almost entirely from governmental sources. These societies are
mandated by legislation to prevent and redress child abuse, which may be
defined to include parental failure or refusal to provide or obtain proper
medical, surgical, or other recognized remedial care or treatment necessary for the child's health, and refusal to permit such care or treatment
to be supplied to a child when it is recommended by a physician.[93]

Social welfare literature indicates that victims of abuse or neglect are
not limited to the young. Grandparents may be victimized by their families, for instance, and may be denied appropriate medical care. Public
responses through agencies and otherwise appear to focus, however, upon
the dependent young. Ontario has no universally available aid societies
for the elderly, although some Children's Aid Societies claim to be
concerned with family and children's services, reflecting the title of British Columbia's provincial superintendent. Similarly, the United States'
regulations are the *Baby* Doe rather than *Grandparent* Doe regulations.
This may have been conditioned by the popular name of the case from
which the regulations arose, but the governmental focus upon babies
appears insensitive under a constitutional order proscribing discrimination
based on age. The elderly are no less liable to non-treatment decisions
than the handicapped young, and are no less exposed to invasive, painful,
and futile care resisting natural death.

Other public officers such as an official guardian or patient advocate
may take initiatives to challenge surrogates' decisions, and the attorney-
general of the jurisdiction has standing before the courts to seek judicial
monitoring of decisions affecting dependent patients. The role of these

officers is not to make their own decisions, but to bring before courts the decisions of others. Because of the adversarial nature of legal process, they may have to adopt a contentious posture, but their purpose is not to have the court accept their arguments but to obtain judicial review of the options for their charges that authentic decision-makers have selected, and to have such selections assessed in light of the patients' objectively determined best interests.

(8) Courts

Lawyers consider the courts to be the natural repository of decision-making authority.[94] Decisions of individuals affecting the legal rights and interests and the legitimate expectations of others may be presented there for judicial inspection, which is directed both to the substance of decisions reached and to the process of reaching them. In the *Saikewicz* case,[95] indeed, the Massachusetts Supreme Judicial Court, considering withholding possibly life-sustaining chemotherapy from an elderly, chronically incompetent patient, observed that

such questions of life and death seem to us to require the process of detached but passionate investigation and decision that forms the ideal on which the judicial branch of government was created. Achieving this ideal is our responsibility and that of the lower court, and is not to be entrusted to any other group purporting to represent the "morality and conscience of our society," no matter how highly motivated or impressively constituted.[96]

This approach may appear to require judicial review of all decisions affecting terminal and chronically vegetative patients, and to reject the role the *Quinlan* court considered that ethics committees had to play. Commentators tend to limit the *Saikewicz* observation to analogies of the facts of that case, however, involving a profoundly retarded patient facing life-sustaining but incomprehensible pain. They find numerous instances of critical decision-making in less contentious areas, for instance where patients when competent clearly expressed a wish to be spared extraordinary care, which do not require reference to the courts.[97] The *Saikewicz* court itself addressed the issue about three years later,[98] and reflected generally that "our opinions should not be taken to establish any requirement of prior judicial approval that would not otherwise exist."[99] By way of illustration is the *Dinnerstein* case,[100] in which the Massachusetts Court drew a contrast with *Saikewicz*. This case concerned a sixty-seven-year-old patient with Alzheimer's disease who was considered to be in a terminal condition when her life expectancy was no more than one year, and she was liable to suffer a cardiac or respiratory arrest at any time. The court noted that:

This case does not offer a life-saving or life-prolonging treatment alternative within the meaning of the *Saikewicz* case. It presents a question peculiarly within the competence of the medical profession of what measures are appropriate to ease the imminent passing of an irreversibly, terminally ill patient in light of the patient's history and condition and the wishes of her family.[101]

It may therefore appear that when a decision concerns withholding possibly life-sustaining care from an incompetent patient, the courts are properly engaged in determining that patient's best interests by objective criteria. On the other hand, when a decision concerns means of managing the non-postponable death of a once-competent terminal patient, the answer is suitable for medical determination; the reference in *Dinnerstein* to the wishes of the patient's family may mean their interpretation of her wishes rather than their expression of their own, although due account should be taken of these.

The courts, unlike strangers, agencies, and public officers who may seek judicial review of others' decisions, may state and apply their own decisions on treatment and non-treatment of patients. Beyond deciding individual cases, however, courts may also set guidelines that others may then observe in decision-making without necessary recourse to the courts for ratification.[102] Once legally relevant criteria are determined, and consequences of key facts are laid down, the criteria may be applied and facts be determined with regard to an individual patient according to clinical circumstances and judgement. This is not to say, however, that once the courts have clearly spoken, the path of legally approved conduct is set for all time. The occasion of litigation gives courts opportunities to develop legal principles in accordance with evolving perceptions and sensitivities. The courts must therefore be periodically monitored in order to see how they balance the conflicting needs of certainty and development in legal principles.

Conclusion

When a patient is not competent to express wishes on terminal care, or has not taken the opportunity while competent to arrange for decisions to be applied following onset of incompetence, the question of who decides upon the patient's care can be difficult to resolve. Underlying the conventional form of the question is the belief that different results for the patient will follow from determinations of different decision-makers. Once principles of decision-making have been clarified, however, it may be seen that the identity of the person or body serving the application of those principles may be of reduced significance. If the patient's wishes prevail, they may be comparably found by seeking evidence from a number of different sources and persons. If the patient's best interests must be found, they may be pursued by courts and, for instance, ethics committees to much the same effect, under the guidance of judicial reasoning in earlier cases. Even where particular decision-makers may differ among themselves as to what the proper outcome should be, they may nevertheless afford the patient the equitable advantage of their seeking the same goal of his or her wishes or best interests, as appropriate to the circumstances. This may at least spare patients at the end of their days the indignity of being treated according to others' whims, obsessions, or needs, and according to institutions' impersonal presumptions or doctrines. To be treated at the end of life as an individual whose personality or interests should govern others' responses may preserve a final quality of uniqueness in one's life.

Notes

1. See generally B. M. Dickens, "The Right to Natural Death," *McGill Law Journal* 26 (1981): 847.

2. Report of the President's Commission for the Study of Ethical Problems in Medicine and Biomedical and Behavioral Research, *Deciding to Forego Life-Sustaining Treatment: Ethical, Medical, and Legal Issues in Treatment Decisions* (Washington, D.C.: Government Printing Office, 1983), 88. A brief review of the report appears in B. M. Dickens, "The Final Freedom: Deciding to Forego Life-Sustaining Treatment," *Public Law* (1984): 34.

3. *In the Matter of Karen Quinlan* (1976), 335 A.2d 647 (N.J.S.C.).

4. See D. Kretzmer, "The Malpractice Suit: Is It Needed?" *Osgoode Hall Law Journal* 11 (1973): 55.

5. *In the Matter of Karen Quinlan* (1976), 335 A.2d 647 (N.J.S.C.), at 668.

6. See B. M. Dickens, "Medicine and the Law: Withholding Paediatric Medical Care," *Canadian Bar Review* 62 (1984): 196.

7. *Re S. D.* [1983] 3 W.W.R. 597, at 611.

8. *Re Superintendent of Family and Child Service and Dawson et al.* (1983), 145 D.L.R. (3d) 610, at 623.

9. See *Wilson v. Swanson* (1956), 5 D.L.R. (2d) 113 (S.C.C.).

10. See *Whitehouse v. Jordan* [1981] 1 W.L.R. 246 (H.L.).

11. *In the Matter of Karen Quinlan* (1976), 335 A.2d 647 (N.J.S.C.), at 669.

12. *Re B. (A Minor) (Wardship: Medical Treatment)* [1981] 1 W.L.R. 1421, at 1424. This was adopted in *Re Superintendent of Family and Child Service and Dawson et al.* (1983), 145 D.L.R. (3d) 610, at 623.

13. See the discussion of "relational-potential" in G. P. Smith II, "Quality of Life, Sanctity of Creation: Palliative or Apotheosis?" *Nebraska Law Review* 63 (1984): 732ff.

14. See the surgery eventually required in *Re Superintendent of Family and Child Service and Dawson et al.* (1983), 145 D.L.R. (3d) 610, at 623.

15. See the November 1981 acquittal for (attempted) murder in *R. v. Arthur*, *The Times* (London), November 6, 1981, discussed in B. M. Dickens, "Medicine and the Law."

16. This is recognized in the United States, where the amended "Baby Doe" regulations accommodate nontreatment where this would be proper without regard to a child's mental or other handicap; see generally note 83 below.

17. See *Whitehouse v. Jordan* [1981] 1 W.L.R. 246 (H.L.).

18. If others are negligent in giving data to the attending physician, with the result that the patient's condition is misdiagnosed and inappropriate treatment is prescribed, the negligent parties will bear legal liability for injury the patient suffers due, for instance, to the withholding of care which, upon correct diagnosis, would have been ordinary; see A. R. Holder, *Medical Malpractice Law*, 2d ed. (New York: Wiley, 1978), 87.

19. See the April 1984 Joint Statement on Terminal Illness of the Canadian Nurses Association, the Canadian Medical Association, and the Canadian Hospital Association, regarding "no-resuscitation" orders.

20. The *Criminal Code*, R.S.C. 1970, c. C-34, provides in s. 209 on homicide that "where a person causes bodily injury to a human being that results in death, he causes the death of that human being notwithstanding that the effect of the bodily injury is only to accelerate his death from a disease or disorder arising from some other cause."

21. On the contrast between pain and suffering, see Margaret A. Somerville, "Pain and Suffering at Interfaces of Medicine and Law," *University of Toronto Law Journal* 36 (1986): 286.

22. *Gleitman v. Cosgrove* (1967), 227 A.2d 689, at 692.

23. *Curlender v. Bio-Science Laboratories* (1980), 165 Cal. Rptr. 477 (Cal. C.A.).

24. *Turpin v. Sortini* (1981), 174 Cal. Rptr. 128 (Cal.C.A.).

25. *Harbeson v. Parke-Davis, Inc.* (1983), 656 P.2d 483 (Wash.S.C.).

26. *Procanik v. Cillo* (1984), 478 A.2d 755 (N.J.S.C.).

DICKENS / *The Legal Perspective*

27. *McKay v. Essex Area Health Authority* [1982] 2 W.L.R. 890 (C.A.).

28. Stephenson, L.J., ibid., at 899.

29. *Cherry v. Borsman* (1991), 75 D.L.R. (4th) 668 (S.C.B.C.).

30. See P. Donovan, "Wrongful Birth and Wrongful Conception: The Legal and Moral Issues," *Family Planning Perspectives* 16 (1984): 64, and B. M. Dickens, "Abortion and Distortion of Justice in the Law," *Law, Medicine & Health Care* 17 (1989): 395.

31. See *Gleitman v. Cosgrove* (1967), 227 A.2d 689, at 692.

32. See *Harbeson v. Parke-Davis, Inc.* (1983), 656 P.2d 483 (Wash.S.C.).

33. It is interesting to observe that, despite growing emphasis in the United States upon death with dignity, no case appears to have been decided against a health facility that sustained a patient's terminal condition over the patient's objection. On the contrary, patients have had to initiate litigation in order to have life supports removed, which was the origin of the Karen Quinlan case; see *In the Matter of Karen Quinlan* (1976), 335 A.2d 647 (N.J.S.C.).

34. See B. Starkman, "A Defence to Criminal Responsibility for Performing Surgical Operations: Section 45 of the Criminal Code," *McGill Law Journal* 26 (1981): 1048.

35. S. 262(a) concerns a person "attempting to save his own life," suggesting that the reference in s. 262(b) to "another person" means a second person, including the person attempted to be rescued, rather than a third person.

36. S. 249 of the *Criminal Code* addresses dangerous navigation, and s. 263 imposes duties to safeguard openings in ice and excavations on land.

37. See the Supreme Court of Canada's restrictive approach in *Perka v. The Queen* (1984), 14 C.C.C. (3d) 385, including a useful review of the history and case law on the defence, and an elaboration of the distinction between necessity as a justification and as an excuse.

38. Leading cases were *United States v. Holmes* (1842), 26 Fed. Cas. 360 (Cir.Ct., E.D.Pa.) and *R. v. Dudley and Stephens* (1884), 14 Q.B.D. 273.

39. See *R. v. Bourne* [1939] 1 K.B. 687 and *Morgentaler v. The Queen* (1975), 53 D.L.R. (3d) 161. The *Bourne* case has been widely followed in the Commonwealth, including in the West African Court of Appeal, Australia (Victoria, Queensland), New Zealand, Zambia, and, for instance, Fiji; see R. J. Cook and B. M. Dickens, *Abortion Laws in Commonwealth Countries* (Geneva: World Health Organization, 1979), 13–14.

40. The successful defence in *R. v. Bourne* [1939] 1 K.B. 687 was necessity to prevent a person from becoming "a mental wreck."

41. See B. K. Tagawa, "Prisoner Hunger Strikes: Constitutional Protection for a Fundamental Right," *American Criminal Law Review* 21 (1983): 569, and R. Ansbacher, "Force-Feeding Hunger-Striking Prisoners: A Framework for

Analysis," *University of Florida Law Review* 35 (1983): 99; compare G. Zellick, "The Forcible Feeding of Prisoners: An Examination of the Legality of Enforced Therapy," *Public Law* (1976): 153. In Canada, see *Re Att.-Gen. of British Columbia and Astaforoff* (1983), 6 C.C. (3d) 498 (C.A.B.C.).

42. *Malette v. Shulman* (1990), 67 D.L.R. (4th) 321 (C.A. Ont.).

43. See respectively *Raleigh Fitkin—Paul Morgan Memorial Hospital v. Anderson* (1964), 201 A.2d 537 (N.J.S.C.), and *Application of President and Directors of Georgetown College* (1964), 331 F.2d 1000 (D.C.Cir.), and generally *John F. Kennedy Hospital v. Heston* (1971), 279 A.2d 670 (N.J. S.C.), denying a constitutional "right to die."

44. See *In re Brooks' Estate* (1965), 205 N.E. 2d 435 (Ill.S.C.) and *Fosmire v. Nicoleau* (1989), 536 N.Y.S. 2d 492 (N.Y.App.).

45. Genuine suicide, based upon an express wish for death, may be contrasted with attempted suicide or parasuicide, which uses a suicide attempt as a gesture of despair or condemnation, but which is a symbolic call for help to live. An act of attempted suicide may be clumsily undertaken, and may inadvertently result in death. See E. Stengel, *Suicide and Attempted Suicide* (London: Penguin, 1964).

46. Cardozo J. in *Schloendorff v. Society of New York Hospital* (1914), 105 N.E. 92 (N.Y.C.A.).

47. This form of verdict may relieve survivors' guilt and family stigma, and may permit burial in consecrated ground.

48. See *Bouvia v. County of Riverside*, No. 159780, Sup.Ct., Riverside Co., Cal., Dec. 16, 1983, Tr. 1238-50, unreported but critically discussed in G. J. Annas, "When Suicide Prevention Becomes Brutality: The Case of Elizabeth Bouvia," *Hastings Center Report* 14, no. 2 (1984). See subsequently *Bouvia v. Superior Court* (1986), 225 Cal. Rptr. 297, 305 (Cal.App.).

49. In contrast, the medical profession in the Netherlands has developed a protocol for inducement of death on competent terminal patients' request; see M. de Wachter, "Active Euthanasia in the Netherlands," *Journal of the American Medical Association* 262 (1989): 3316.

50. The Report of the President's Commission, *Deciding to Forego Life-Sustaining Treatment*, used expressions such as "terminally ill" in an explicitly colloquial sense, without attempting to be precise; see the explanation on p. 26.

51. Cal. Stats. 1976, c. 1439, constituting c. 3.9 of the *Health and Safety Code*.

52. Ibid., 7187(f).

53. Ibid., 7187(c).

54. See generally B. M. Dickens, "The Right to Natural Death," 862-66.

55. See the Law Reform Commission of Canada's two publications entitled *Criteria for the Determination of Death:* working paper no. 23 (1979) and report no. 15 (1981) (Ottawa: Supply & Services).

56. See *In the Matter of Karen Quinlan* (1976), 335 A.2d 647 (N.J.S.C.).

57. On the distinction between ethically justified and unjustified paternalism, see B. Gert and C. Culver, *Philosophy in Medicine* (New York: Oxford University Press, 1982), 126, 143.

58. *Natansan v. Kline* (1960), 350 P.2d 1093 (Kan.S.C.), clarified at 354 P.2d 670.

59. *Canterbury v. Spence* (1972), 464 F.2d 772 (U.S.C.A., D.C.).

60. *Cobbs v. Grant* (1972), 502 P.2d 1 (Ca.S.C.).

61. *Reibl v. Hughes* (1980), 114 D.L.R. (3d) 1.

62. See *Sidaway v. Bethlem Royal Hospital Governors* [1985] 1 All E.R. 643 (H.L.).

63. Per Laskin C.J.C., *Reibl v. Hughes* (1980), 114 D.L.R. (3d) 1, at 11.

64. Care must be exercised in projecting principles of U.S. judgements onto other jurisdictions, because of the special role of the constitutional fundamental right of privacy recognized in U.S. courts; see *Roe v. Wade* (1973), 410 U.S. 113 (U.S.S.C.).

65. See B. M. Dickens, "Patients' Interests and Clients' Wishes: Physicians and Lawyers in Discord," *Law, Medicine & Health Care* 15 (1987): 110.

66. It may be remembered that the World Health Organization's charter provides, in its preamble, that health is "a state of complete physical, mental and social well-being and not merely the absence of disease or infirmity."

67. In *Canterbury v. Spence* (1972), 464 F.2d 772 (U.S.C.A., D.C.), at 789, it was observed that "the physician's privilege to withhold information for therapeutic reasons must be carefully circumscribed, however, for otherwise it might devour the disclosure rule itself."

68. The Canadian Medical Association's Code of Ethics dealing with responsibilities to the patient provides in para. 16 that an ethical physician, "when his morality or religious conscience alone prevents him from recommending some form of therapy, . . . will so acquaint the patient."

69. Many of which reflect California's original act; see Cal. Stats. 1976, c. 1439, constituting c. 3.9 of the *Health and Safety Code*.

70. See the Report of the President's Commission, *Deciding to Forego Life-Sustaining Treatment*, 139-45.

71. *Malette v. Shulman* (1990), 670 D.L.R. (4th) 321 (C.A.Ont.).

72. See text at note 5 above.

73. See generally B. M. Dickens, "The Modern Function and Limits of Parental Rights," *Law Quarterly Review* 97 (1981): 462.

178 FUNCTIONAL ACCOUNTS OF TIME

74. *See Re Superintendent of Family and Child Service and Dawson et al.*
(1983), 145 D.L.R. (3d) 610, at 623.

75. *See In re B. (A Minor) (Wardship: Medical Treatment)* [1981] 1 W.L.R.
1421, at 1424.

76. *See*, for instance, D. Krez, "Comment. Withholding Treatment from Seriously Ill and Handicapped Infants: Who Should Make the Decision and
How?—An Analysis of the Government's Response," *De Paul Law Review*
33 (1984): 495.

77. *Re B. (A Minor) (Wardship: Medical Treatment)* [1981] 1 W.L.R. 1421,
at 1424.

78. Shortly after this decision, a jury in *R. v. Arthur* acquitted a physician who
conservatively treated a severely handicapped child until death from starvation. See the November 1981 acquittal for (attempted) murder in *R. v.
Arthur, The Times* (London), November 6, 1981, discussed in B. M.
Dickens, "Medicine and the Law."

79. *Superintendent of Belchertown State School v. Saikewicz* (1977), 370 N.E.
2d 417.

80. The patient was inarticulate, with an I.Q. of ten and a mental age of about
two years and eight months.

81. *See* the proposal and discussion of R. M. Veatch, "Limits of Guardian
Treatment Refusal: A Reasonableness Standard," *American Journal of Law
and Medicine* 9 (1984): 427.

82. R. M. Veatch has distinguished between "bonded guardians" and "non-
bonded-guardians," suggesting that those bonded to a patient by friendship
and close knowledge should have more influence in decisions than others;
see ibid.

83. The original Baby Doe regulations were judicially held unconstitutional, in
part upon procedural grounds. New regulations were issued to take effect
early in 1984, see 49 Fed. Reg. 1622 (1984), but their effect was doubted
in *United States v. University Hospital at Stony Brook* (1984), 729 F.2d
144 (2d Cir.). *See generally* A. E. Winner, "Baby Doe Decisions: Modern
Society's Sins of Omission," *Nebraska Law Review* 63 (1984): 888.

84. *Weber v. Stony Brook Hospital* (1983), 456 N.E. 2d 1186 (N.Y.C.A.),
unsuccessfully appealed in *United States v. University Hospital at Stony
Brook* (1984), 729 F.2d 144 (2d Cir.).

85. *Ibid.*, at 1188.

86. *See In the Matter of Karen Quinlan* (1976), 335 A.2d 647 (N.J.S.C.).

87. *See* R. E. Cranford and A. E. Doudera, "The Emergence of Institutional
Ethics Committees," *Law, Medicine & Health Care* 12 (1984): 13, and C.
Levine, "Questions and (Some Very Tentative) Answers About Hospital
Ethics Committees," *Hastings Center Report* 14, no. 3 (1984): 9.

88. See W. J. Curran, "Law-Medicine Notes: The Saikewicz Decision," *New England Journal of Medicine* 298 (1978): 499.

89. See R. A. McCormick, "Ethics Committees: Promise or Peril?" *Law, Medicine & Health Care* 12 (1984): 150.

90. See *United States v. University Hospital at Stony Brook* (1984), 729 F.2d 144 (2d Cir.).

91. See *In re D. (A minor)* [1976] 1 All E.R. 326 (Fam.D.).

92. These agencies may be regarded as "non-bonded-guardians" according to R. M. Veatch; see note 82 above.

93. See B. M. Dickens, "Legal Responses to Child Abuse," *Family Law Quarterly* 12 (1978): 1, and "Legal Responses to Child Abuse in Canada," *Canadian Journal of Family Law* 1 (1978): 87.

94. For a concurring view of a leading ethicist, see R. M. Veatch, "Limits of Guardian Treatment Refusal," 463.

95. See *Superintendent of Belchertown State School v. Saikewicz* (1977), 370 N.E. 2d 417.

96. Ibid., at 435.

97. See for instance G. J. Annas, "Reconciling *Quinlan* and *Saikewicz*: Decision Making for the Terminally Ill Incompetent," *American Journal of Law and Medicine* 4 (1979): 367.

98. *In the Matter of Earle Spring* (1980), 405 N.E. 2d 115.

99. Ibid., at 120.

100. *In the Matter of Shirley Dinnerstein* (1978), 380 N.E. 2d 134.

101. Ibid., at 139.

102. See K. M. Whitlock, "Court Establishes Guidelines for Removal of Life Support Systems From Incompetents in a Persistent Vegetative State," *Gonzaga Law Review* 19 (1983/84): 417, a case comment on *In re Colyer* (1983), 660 P.2d 738 (Wash.S.C.).

III

THE TIME OF ONE'S LIFE

Special Issues in Society

Indian World View and Time

CECIL KING

I WAS BORN on the Wikwemikong Indian reserve in Ontario. I was raised by Native people and am fluent in my Native tongue, Odawa. It is from this background that this paper is written. I will attempt to relate how the topic and concept of time does an implied under-standing as well as an implied law that we, Native and non-Native alike, follow. We are all governed by it. For we all believe that if we exist without the strictures of time, we invite complete and total chaos. Time is our life. Even as we read this text we are conscious of time. I'm sure those of you that still wear wristwatches look at your wristwatch to find out, not so much what time it is now, but rather what time it isn't yet. That should tell us something of how we are governed by time today.

In the Native perception or in the scheme of things, there is a thing we'll call the Indian world view. Everyone, however, has a world view, because, as human beings with intellects, we don't just bump along through life without some thought of why we are; there is some reason to be. For some of us it may be somewhere deep in our subconscious and may be very difficult to dig up, but nevertheless it is there. The fact that you are here indicates that perhaps you have some gnawing need to fulfill a perception—a world view. For Native people it is no different. The Native people view their world in their own way—a Native way, if we can use that term. You no doubt have heard the saying that "Indians live in harmony with nature," perhaps a quaint expression but certainly true. In the natural world around them the Indians see all the manifesta-tions of an ever-present benevolent power who has created a world to sustain the natural children of creation, the plants, and our brothers and sisters, the animals, all in their own place, and then last in the order of things, human beings. Out of this has grown the Indian world view, a philosophy of life.

The philosophy of the Indian is built on the perception that in the order of the universe ("the order of things") human beings are last. They are entirely subject to the moods of the universe and graciously accept their subservient coexistence with the more animate creations of the plant and animal kingdoms. The Indians know their lives are dependent upon the life of others in the scheme of things and yet the others' lives are not dependent upon the Indians'. The recognition of their own family makes the Indians feel the sacredness of all life, animate and more animate. They feel humble when they recognize that all things are interdependent, but that they are the most dependent. All other things within the universe can exist without them and remain in harmony. They alone cannot exist without the others. In the Indian world, plants are closest to the Maker of all things, followed by the animals. Plants and animals are more animistic than humankind. For example, a bear is more animistic than a person, for a bear can assume anthropomorphic traits while a person can never assume ursine characteristics. In Indian mythology, one basic theme is evident and repeated in legend after legend: human powerlessness without magical intervention. Every weakness and frailty of humanity is painted against a background of the natural superiority of the plant and animal kingdom. Even intermediaries, like Waysakayjak, use their super-natural powers to assume an animal or plant form in order to achieve their goal. The Indian concept of animism is the central tenet of the Indian "thinking" that evolves from this concept. The concept of ani-mism is without parameters. It is as large as the universe and limitless as time. Anything can at some time be animistic. It is the mood that determines this. A valley has one mood in the morning, another at noon, and again another in eventide.

Animism to the Indian means life. However, the definition of life is not established on its converse, death, but rather from its extension into further life. Animism transcends death. Animism encompasses the past and the future simultaneously in the present and unites all things into one. This contradicts Western thought that animism is established on the restricted dichotomy of animate/inanimate which linguists apply to the Indian dichotomous perception, which is in fact animate/more animate. All things in the universe are at times animate, but circumstances of the moment can make them more animate or less animate. Two trees growing side by side may appear identical, and yet one tree appeals to the observer in a different way. The mood of what one sees affects how one thinks about it, and this in turn affects the way one speaks of it. If one chops the tree down, it obviously becomes less animate; but alter its mood by anthropomorphizing the remains—that is to say, for an inner personal reason you carve it into a form of a living creature—and what was once a tree becomes more animate than it was originally. Unlike the Western person, who imposes a mood on the surroundings, the Indian is imbued by the mood of the surroundings.

The concept of animism is implicit in the Indian language, but Indians are not consciously aware of it, nor do they attempt to explain the function of their language. They are secure in the knowledge that their language is right, for it is a gift from the Maker of all languages and, therefore, unquestioningly, they use it. When Indian children enter the world of their languages, the reality of the world is implicit and they become one with their world. They are completely enveloped within its order, logic, and harmony. But when Indian-speaking children enter school they are met by a chaotic world, a world inconsistent with the logic of "their" reality. The teacher, usually an English-speaker, is totally unfamiliar with the child's reality. The school reflects the teacher's reality. The contradictions are many and immediate. For, not only do the children learn a new language but, as well, they have to master all the nuances, behaviour clues, emotional clues, and philosophy in order to be "in" with the new reality.

The school system, from its classification of subject matter to its classroom-management procedures, is ruled by Western language presuppositions. Western intellectual tradition maintains that to be educated is to be literate. Subservience to the ideal of literacy has made Western man stress the analytical structure which literacy suggests is a step-by-step, deductive, linear progression. An example of the Indian's way of view-ing time contradicts this reasoning. This difference can be attributed to a totally different world view, one which isn't linear. The Western mind took time (that rush of eternity that passes by us) and structured it—broke it into units; then it broke the units into other units, then each unit was named and became distinct. For example, Monday, Tuesday, Wednesday, Thursday, Friday, Saturday, Sunday; what makes one day different from another day? The Western mind functions on the artificial structure which makes Monday different from Tuesday.

The Native person runs on a cyclical system. In congruence with the moods of the environment, there is a word for day and one for night; the seasons are distinguished by their distinguishing character, for there is no need to describe a season if it is the same as all other seasons. A distinction is made only when a change occurs. You experience each day and each day is the same day over again.

The perception of intermediaries is common to Indian people. Because human beings are last in the order of things, there is a gulf between the Maker and them. To bridge this gulf, human beings have the perception of an intermediary—a between-spirit, all powerful but also possessing all the weaknesses of human beings. The intermediary of the Cree people is Waysakayjak. They would invoke Waysakayjak to intercede for them—to ask the Maker for aid. In legends, Waysakayjak is accounted of great wisdom yet is countered by depictions of lack of wisdom. He is depicted as kind in some instances, only to be totally selfish in others. He can be generous, then stingy, honourable yet promiscuous, fair to niggardly. Waysakayjak seemed afflicted with every weakness of man—starvation, cold, misery, laziness, stubbornness, sickness, jealousy, greed, and so on. Therein lie the paradoxes, for while humans may be endowed with intellect and wisdom and be capable of noble things, they are also afflicted with weaknesses that at times needed intercession. Waysakayjak, possessing the powers of the Maker, would intercede by beseeching the indulgences of the plants or animals and thereby acknowledging their natural superiority. Legends contain many messages; they are lessons for humanity that convey a code of values by which to live together, humans with plants, humans with each other, and humans with time.

Out of this philosophy evolves the Indian's values, such values as the importance of time, the importance of the present, of patience, of silence, age, sharing, respect for nature, of not showing fear, of living one's vision and honouring self by respecting one's body as a gift to keep, pride, the will to achieve, placing the common good of the group above self. Out of this grew the society that was cooperative, communistic, with its foundation rooted in the construct of the extended family, where from the elders to the youngest each was individually a person. Living in harmony with nature, the Indian enjoyed the Maker's providence. With prudence, it was there to be used, and would continue to sustain all the Indians' needs, physical and spiritual. The Indian viewed the world as a total, a whole, a world made up of more than the sum of its parts. Nonstructured, the cyclic world of the Indian contrasted with the linear, structured, time-oriented world of the Western individual.

Schooling as it was brought to Native communities reflected the philosophy of the West, which is established on the belief that human beings are created in the image and likeness of "God" and therefore are next to the Creator. The person is seen as "Homo sapiens," the most intelligent of the animals and the most capable of controlling the environment. The reach of human beings is limited only by imagination; anything is possible. Human beings are infinitely able to control their own destiny through applying their intellect to any problem. To apply the

KING / *Time and the Native Community* 187

products of intellect—science and technology—to any problem will render the solution. Human beings' only dependence is upon God or science. Nothing in the rest of the universe is beyond their control. Out of this philosophy evolves Western values. Such values as the importance of time, of routine, of competition, of conformity, of punctuality, self-discipline, submission to authority, acceptance, become the catchwords for a society that exalts "talking," a society that is literate, scientific, urban, multicultural, industrialized, commercialized, complex, and inter-dependent; that is, the "we," and "they" syndrome for survival. The inex-orable march of Western values established the legitimacy of disciplines, certain core subjects like mathematics and science. The English language became established as the first language and therefore the language of instruction. Language became objectified to give a permanence establish-ing reading and writing as imperative skills for learning.

Western thinking is linear, and legitimizes a scientific format for learning, where everything must be dissected, segmented, measured, anal-yzed, deduced, and recorded. Out of this, knowledge becomes separated into classes, elements, and stages. The ever-increasing content and the complexity of today's knowledge paradoxically present the need for a Western intellect to become a specialist in the limiting constructs of segments of knowledge. The knowledge perception of Western intellects, grounded on the scientific theory of cause and effect, seeks to answer solely the "whys" and the "hows." As a Western value, schooling is established as a good thing and necessary for a positive future. Learning for tomorrow and the implied emphasis on the value of education for humanity's survival epitomize the invisible culture brought by teachers from the Western intel-lectual tradition into the educational environment of the Indian child.

However, the march of time goes on. Father Sun punctuates each day with light and darkness, and each day is the same day over again. The Moon, our grandmother, punctuates the months into their seasonal distinc-tions, as the budding moon, the falling-leaves moon, the exploding-frost moon, the crusty-snow moon, each in their turn return as before. In this way the Indians were never late for anything. They knew when it was right to pick medicines, when the birch tree would release its bark, when to fish, hunt, trap; the rhythm of life was governed. In the perception termed "the Four Hills of Life," we view infancy, youth, adulthood, and old age. We know the responsibility of each of the Hills of Life, and we are governed by that knowledge. Each must be lived, and only in that way is the quality of life kept in balance. Life is basically a circle, and in it the past, the present, and the future are one. We are the grandchildren of past generations just as we will be the grandparents of the generations to come.

Gender and the Value of Time

MARGRIT EICHLER

WHEN I WAS first invited to provide a paper on women and time, I panicked, for two reasons: for one, I did not have much time to reflect on time, which made reading about scarcity of time unexpectedly interesting and even joyful; for the other, I was not familiar with the existing literature. Apparently, this is not an uncommon problem. Bergmann, in his extensive review article on "the problem of time in sociology,"[1] complains that many authors who deal with this topic tend to begin from scratch without paying attention to the existing literature. This results in sometimes interesting but essentially theoretically marginal studies that do not build upon each other in a cumulative manner.

In order to avoid writing one more piece of this nature, I shall use the work of Barry Schwartz[2] as a jumping-off point, even though he does not address the specific topic that I wish to explore in my paper. Nevertheless, his general approach is useful and can be adapted and extended.

In this paper, then, I shall start from Schwartz's basic proposition that there is an intimate connection between power and the value of a person's time. I will look at the value of time both in terms of time itself, as Schwartz does, as well as in terms of money, arguing that the same mechanisms apply to the one as to the other. Finally, I will apply the general propositions to the relationship of the sexes, in order to look specifically at the question of the potentially different value of time of women and men.

I would like to thank Linda Williams, who served as a research assistant for this paper. An abbreviated version of the paper appeared in James E. Curtis and Lorne Tepperman, *Images of Canada: The Sociological Tradition* (Scarborough, Ont.: Prentice-Hall, 1990).

The Exchange Theory of Waiting

Starting generally from within the framework of exchange theory, Schwartz begins with the proposition that "[w]aiting is patterned by the distribution of power in a social system."[3] Looking at patterns of delay and waiting and asking himself who can keep whom waiting, he suggests that

the relationship between servers' and clients' power in waiting is asymmetrical. On the one hand, servers' holding power is contingent on clients' inability to frequent more distant and/or more expensive servers; on the other, client autonomy requires the presence of alter-native services. Despite their covariation, though, resources and alter-natives seem to affect waiting time independently of one another. The resourceful wait less within both monopolistic and competitive organi-zations; regardless of clients' resources, however, waiting time tends to be longer in monopolistic settings.[4]

Schwartz concludes that power is "the ultimate determinant of delay, the main assertion being that the distribution of waiting time coincides with the distribution of power. This proposition turns on the assumption that power is related to the scarcity of the goods and skills that an indi-vidual server possesses."[5] He identifies, following Stinchcombe, the rela-tionship between servers and clients in respect to waiting as an instance of an "organized dependency relationship." He argues that "[d]elay is therefore longest when the client is more dependent on the relationship than the server; it is minimized, however, when the server is the over-committed member of an asymmetrical relationship."[6]

Schwartz has therefore postulated a relationship between waiting time, power of server and served, and the social system within which a client relationship exists, whether monopolistic or competitive. Schwartz's postulate can be put into a propositional format as follows:

PROPOSITION 1:

Within a relationship, the more powerful a person, the more control this person has over his or her own time as well as that of others. This results in minimal waiting on the part of the powerful person, and maximal waiting on the part of the least powerful person.

In this approach, time itself is seen as the resource that is being wasted or gained. This analysis can be extended in at least two ways: it can be extended to the prime measure of value in our society, namely money, and it can be applied to specific groups with differential access to power, such as the sexes. Considering the first issue first, we find that although a monetary parallel is drawn by Schwartz, the connection be-tween the value of the time of a person, his or her position in the social structure, and the value of time in monetary terms is not made. Schwartz suggests that "[t]ime, like money, is valuable because it is necessary for the achievement of productive purposes; ends cannot be reached unless an appropriate amount of it is 'spent' or 'invested' on their behalf."[7]

> Just as money possesses no substantive value independent of its use as a means of exchange, time can only be of value if put to substantive use in an exchange relationship. Both time and money may be regarded as generalized means because of the infinity of possibilities for their utilization: both are possessed in finite quantities; both may be counted, saved, spent, lost, wasted, or invested.[8]

Others have made the relationship explicit, but in cursory form. Balla argues that economic success depends largely on the optimization of econo-mic processes, that is, it is premised on economizing with scarce goods with-in a social system that is characterized by scarcity of time.[9] And Zerubavel suggests that the capitalist orientation to time "as a scarce resource (implying both linearity and convertibility into monetary terms) is among the basic cultural constituents of modern social organization of time."[10]

The intimate connection between the value of time and money is per-haps best expressed in the popular saying that "time is money." If Schwartz is right in postulating that the value of time is socially patterned, and that the value differs systematically with one's power position, then we should also find that the value of time measured in money is socially patterned, and that its value as measured in money differs systematically by one's power position, with the person with the most power being able to com-mand most money for his or her time, and the person with least power being able to command least money. In the following, we shall therefore address the question of under what circumstances time is money, whose time is money, and how much money time is worth.

Under What Circumstances is Time Money?

The question contains within itself its opposite, namely: Under what cir-cumstances is time *not* money? If time was money under all circumstances, we would all be rich, and the longer we lived, the more so. In a sense this is true, when we regard life itself—that is, our personal time—as a value in and of itself. But we are here not concerned with the intrinsic value of time, but only with its socially constructed value that can be expressed in terms of money, that is, an economic value. All other values are disregarded here. Looking at the issue in this way, we note that elderly people in Canada are disproportionately poor, especially if they are female. The value of time is therefore certainly not determined by the sheer quantity available to a person as measured through his or her lifespan.

Nor is *all* time money. When we sleep, barring a few exceptions, time is not worth money. When we are "killing time," in whatever manner, it is not worth money. When we spend time with family or friends, generally our time is not worth any money (although the way we spend it may cost us money). Our time *is* worth money when we work for pay.

It seems, then, that time is money only when an economic transaction is involved. Therefore, time spent with a prostitute is worth money, while time spent in sexual activity with one's lover is not worth money. The activity may be the same, but one is an economic transaction, the other is not. Similarly, talking with one's friend about personal problems is not worth money, while talking with one's psychiatrist about these same problems is worth money. Eating dinner with one's family is not worth money, while taking a client to dinner and maybe eating exactly the same dish is worth money. It is therefore not the activity itself that determines whether time spent in its pursuit is worth money, but the social context that determines whether the time so spent is worth money or not.

We have therefore answered our first question: time is worth money within the context of economic relationships, otherwise it is not worth any money. Economic relationships are relationships that produce a product that can be sold or bought for money. The potential money value is not inherent in the product or directly related to the time needed to produce it, but depends on the value it has been attributed by people. A giant jigsaw puzzle may take a long time to complete, but generally the time spent on this activity is not worth any money, since the product of the time invested is not saleable. Likewise, trees have a value that inheres in them, but it is non-economic, and the time needed for them to grow makes no difference in terms of money, unless they can be sold for money. For Christmas tree operators, by contrast, the time required by trees to grow does indeed become economically valuable. If it can be reduced, profits can be increased (assuming that there is a market for increased production, of course). The statement that economic relationships are relationships that produce a product that can be sold or bought for money is therefore not tautological, but indicates the essential arbitrariness of whether time spent producing something is worth money or not.

Having come up with a preliminary answer to the first question, we can now address the second question:

Whose Time is Money?

If we go back to the examples of transactions mentioned above and consider their participants—the prostitute/client, the psychiatrist/patient, the client/host—it becomes apparent that it is only the time of *one* of the parties involved that is worth money, not that of both. The client pays the psychiatrist for his or her time—but the psychiatrist does not pay the client for her or his time, the expense of which was probably greater than for the psychiatrist, since it was probably the client who needed to add travel time and possibly waiting time to the total time expense, and not the psychiatrist. Likewise for other client-practitioner relationships in the broadest sense possible. For instance, if we consider the student-professor relationship, students not only engage in activities similar to those of the professors—reading materials, observing and reflecting on natural, cultural, and social phenomena—but they may even produce similar outputs, such as papers, which may or may not get published. In the one case, this is seen as part of the professorial role for which the university pays money, namely a salary, whereas in the other case, while it is also seen as part of the student role, there is the important difference that the student pays rather than is paid for this privilege. This becomes interestingly muddled when a student has a scholarship. In that case, he or she is in effect paid for doing the same work that another student must pay for.

In general, then, it is the "expert" or server whose time is considered worth money, while that of the client (1) is worth none, and (2) she or he has to pay, directly, as in the case of paying an electrician who does your wiring, or indirectly, through taxes, the garbage collector, professor, psychiatrist,[11] or police officer.

While this statement seems clear enough—the service provider's time is worth money, the service recipient's time is not—upon closer inspection the issue becomes less clear. Sometimes, it is difficult to determine just who is receiving a service if we look at the transaction from the outside without further knowledge about the context. In the case of the client dinner, client and host are eating the same meal. In the case of the student-professor, both of them discuss the same topic, and they may even publish a paper together. It is only upon knowing the *roles* that people play that we will be able to predict who will be paid for the activity engaged in and who will pay.

194 SPECIAL ISSUES IN SOCIETY

Nor can we say that it is always the *service* that is being paid for. In some situations, it is indeed the product (output) that is being paid for, as is the case when employers pay for piecework, such as in the garment industry. In other cases, however, it is the time spent (input) that is paid for, as is generally the case with professionals and salaried employees such as doctors, lawyers, teachers, or nurses as well as clerks, reception-ists, or bank tellers. In cases in which time spent (input) is paid for, rather than the product, the service or product may or may not be re-ceived: the students may not have learned, the patient may not be healed, the clerk may have misfiled the letter.

With respect to the question, Whose time is money? we also find an essential arbitrariness: it is the time of someone *presumed* to provide a service because of his or her role within the context of an economic rela-tionship that is worth money, rather than an activity or product itself. In other words, it is the social context that determines whose time has mone-tary value, rather than the value being an inherent characteristic of a person or activity. This leads us to the question:

How Much Money is Time Worth?

We have seen that it is not an activity that is worth money, nor a person whose time is always money; the role a person plays within the context of an economic relationship and the way this relationship is organized that determines whether his or her time is worth money. There is there-fore an essential element of arbitrariness in the way value is assigned to time. We find the same phenomenon with respect to the amount of money that is assigned to time. It is by no means the case that the same amount of time is considered worth the same amount of money. In fact, our soci-ety is premised on the assumption that the time spent in the performance of some roles is more valuable than the time spent performing others. This is exemplified most dramatically by the fact that we have differential salary scales for different types of work.

For instance, in 1980, according to the Economic Council of Cana-da,[12] men in the five highest paid occupations had the following average annual earnings:

Directors general	$ 59,131
Physicians and surgeons	57,273
Dentists	54,312
Judges and magistrates	50,791
Lawyers and notaries	38,380

EICHLER / *Gender and the Value of Time*

By comparison, men in the five lowest paid occupations in that same year had the following average annual earnings:

Inspecting and sampling, fabri-cation of textile products	$ 12,311
Guides, hosts, stewards, et al.	8,346
Other farm, horticulture, and animal husbandry	7,399
Waiters, hosts, and stewards	*6,677*
Babysitters	4,311

These figures are based on combining a large set of categories of occupations into a smaller set. Had the analysis focused on the five high-est and lowest paid occupations in the larger set, the earnings differential would have certainly been considerably higher, since some chairmen of boards and directors general command salaries in the hundreds of thou-sands of dollars.

We have therefore seen that time *per se* has no objective money val-ue, but that it has a monetary value only within an economic relationship for a person presumed to perform a service for another person, and that the amount will vary systematically by the role performed. If Schwartz's thesis on the relationship between the value of time and power is also applicable to the monetary value of time, the time should be worth more money the more powerful the incumbent of a role is. We are therefore now ready to formulate a second general proposition:

PROPOSITION 2

The more powerful the incumbent of a role, the more money his or her time will be worth within the context of economic relationships; the less powerful the incumbent of a role, the less money his or her time will be worth.

So far, we have considered only situations in which the time of one party to a client relationship (which includes, of course, the employer-employee relationship) was worth money—in which, in other words, there was an exchange of time against money. In such situations, one person renders a service ("works") while the other person receives the product of the service. The time of the service-producer is worth money, that of the service-recipient has no monetary value within the parameters of that relationship. There are, however, some situations in which the time of one of the participants in a relationship may have a negative monetary

195

value, that is, it carries costs for another person who is *not* receiving a service in return.

When Does Time Cost Money?

If the most powerful can command most money for their time, one would expect that it would be the least powerful who might not just carry a zero-value on their time, but possibly even a negative value. Searching for cases in which people's time costs money rather than earns them money, we find that this is the case, for example, with small children who need adult supervision. Small children constitute a cost for their parents or guardians for the time spent supervising them, without producing monetary value in return (other values, as noted above, are not being considered here). The same is true for people in institutions such as prison, mental hospitals, treatment centres, and the like.

In such a situation, then, time has no money value for the person who spends it under supervision,[13] but nevertheless the time so spent costs somebody money: often the taxpayer, who has to pay for the time of the staff and the other expenses associated with running an institution. In the case of small children, their supervision costs money if done within the framework of an institution (e.g., a daycare centre or a nursery school) or by a non-family member, such as a neighbourhood sitter. If done by a family member, such as the mother, it costs time that could otherwise be employed earning money. The case of small children (or disabled adults living at home but needing constant assistance) indicates that the phenomenon under discussion goes beyond people who are inmates in institutions and includes people who are defined as dependents.

If we see dependency as a form of powerlessness,[14] this permits us to look at the time expenditure of dependent people in relation to the economic value they derive (or fail to derive) from it. The extreme form of dependency is surely slavery. Although slaves typically engaged in activities that gained money for their owners, nevertheless the slaves themselves were not entitled to any recompense for their time expenditure, while the money needed to minimally feed and house them (and to buy them in the first place) was seen as a cost to their owner.

Just as we have seen that it is a social convention that fixes the value of a particular role at a particular monetary level, so we find that when people are defined as dependents, the products of their time expenditure are seen as valueless in money terms, irrespective of whether a valuable product or service has been produced or performed, while their upkeep and/or supervision is seen as a cost.

We can now formulate our third general proposition:

PROPOSITION 3:

To the degree that people are perceived as dependent (whether on an institution, a person, or a set of persons), their time will carry a negative economic connotation, irrespective of their actual activity.

We have formulated three general propositions that, if true, should be applicable to all populations. If so, they should also shed light on the relationship of the sexes. In the following, the three general propositions will therefore be reformulated, taking sex as a stratifying variable into account.

Gender and the Value of Time

Overall, women as a group are less powerful than men as a group. This statement has received sufficient attention in the recent past to need no elaborate defence, and the literature supporting it is quite voluminous.[15]

The three general propositions concerning the value of time stated above should therefore be applicable to women and men as a group. This implies a double modification: for one, the propositions need to be changed from the general to the specific by identifying two particular parties that are in a differential power relationship. For the other, they need to be made applicable to groups rather than people within a given relationship; that is, on this score, the proposition changes from the specific to the general. As a consequence, the propositions would apply only *in general*, or with respect to average patterns, rather than with respect to all female-male situations.

The three propositions can, with these considerations in mind, be reformulated as follows:

PROPOSITION 1a:

To the degree that men as a group are more powerful than women as a group, women will wait longer than men.

PROPOSITION 2a:

To the degree that men are more powerful than women, women's time will be worth less money than men's time.

198   SPECIAL ISSUES IN SOCIETY

PROPOSITION 3a:

To the degree that women are dependent on men, their time will carry a negative economic connotation.

In the following, we will briefly examine the three modified propositions.

Do Women Wait Longer Than Men?

In order to answer this question properly, we would have to be able to draw on some comprehensive studies of the sex composition of line-ups, as well as have empirical information on the amount of time waited, by sex, in other contexts such as waiting rooms, at home, and so forth. Such information is, to my knowledge, not available for Canada.

However, there are two other indicators that are useful in this context. Waiting *on* is a form of waiting *for*. "To wait on others and to be kept waiting exhibit the common element of subordination."[16] It is therefore useful to look at the occupational structure and ask ourselves: What are the occupations in which people wait on others? Are women more likely to be in such occupations than men? We can also examine what happens within the home and ask ourselves: Who waits upon whom in the home?

Looking at the occupational structure first, we can consider the sex composition of major occupations in Canada. Using the data in the Report of the Commission on Equality in Employment[17] and computing the female/male ratio,[18] we find five occupations in which in 1981 women exceeded men as incumbents: those in the social sciences and related fields (1.1), teaching and related occupations (1.47), occupations in medicine and health (3.46), clerical and related occupations (3.48), and service occupations (1.1).

These ratios tell us something about the sex composition of an occupation, but they do not tell us anything about the importance of such an occupation for each sex. This is found in another set of figures. In 1981 the highest participation of women in the labour force was in clerical and related occupations, with 35.1 percent of all women in this set of occupations, while the second highest percentage was in service occupations, with 15.4 percent of all women in this field. That is, more than 50 percent of all women in the labour force were in only two types of occupations. (The next highest female participation was in occupations in medicine and health, with 8.3 percent of all women in this field.[19]

Clerical and related occupations and service occupations by definition involve waiting upon other people. By contrast, only 6.8 percent of all men in the labour force were in clerical and related positions in 1981, and 9.5 percent were in service occupations.[20]

While this is a rather crude analysis, it nevertheless does suggest that within the occupational structure women are more likely to wait upon other people than are men.

Considering the second possible indicator of the amount of waiting by sex, we can turn towards time-budget studies. Here the evidence is very clear that in general, and irrespective of labour-force participation of women or presence of children in the home, women do more of the housework than do men, who tend to have more leisure time.[21] On both indicators, of occupational distribution and housework, it turns out that women do more waiting on other people than do men. Nevertheless, it would be a better test of the proposition if it could be supported by empirical data on direct waiting behaviours, rather than by using indirect indicators as has been done here. We can therefore consider the proposition as having been supported by the analysis, but not proven. In other words, the answer to the question whether women wait more than men is only a qualified yes.

Turning now to the second modified proposition, we can ask:

Is Women's Time Worth Less Money Than Men's Time?

This question is, unfortunately, very simple to answer. There is abundant information available that documents that women and men *within the same occupations* are being paid differentially, with women receiving substantially less pay for the same amount of time worked within the same occupation. This pattern is, unfortunately, consistent over time and across different occupations, whether these are receiving high pay or low pay.[22] Looking at the average income of women and men in the six occupations with the highest male average employment income in 1981 in which we find enough females to make the comparison,[23] we find that women earn substantially less, as seen in Table 1.

The answer to the question posed above is therefore unambiguous: Yes, on average, women's time is worth less than men's time.

This leads us to our third modified proposition, which results in the question: Does women's time carry a negative economic connotation when they are defined as dependent on men?

TABLE 1. AVERAGE INCOME, CANADIAN MALES VS. FEMALES

	Male	Female
Physicians and surgeons	$ 59,834	$ 36,115
Dentists	58,128	40,510
Salesmen and traders, securities	46,718	18,375
General managers and other senior officials	46,160	24,915
Lawyers and notaries	40,978	23,935
Other managers (mines and oil wells)	40,506	19,303

Source: Adapted from Economic Council of Canada, *On the Mend: Twentieth Annual Review 1983* (Ottawa: Supply & Services, 1983), 74.

Does Women's Time Carry a Negative Economic Connotation When They are Defined as Dependent on Men?

The major form of female dependence on men takes place within the framework of marriage, in which wives who do not have an independent income (housewives) are conceptualized as dependents of their husbands. While by now more than half of all Canadian wives are in the labour force, this is a very recent change (it occurred in the 1980s) and one that embodies a significant departure from previous patterns. It is therefore not particularly astonishing if we find definitions in flux.

Until about 1978, it would be appropriate to state that in general a patriarchal model of the family underlay Canadian policies. A patriarchal model of the family has been defined by eight characteristics:

1. Household and family are treated as congruent.
2. The family is treated as the administrative unit.
3. The father/husband is seen as responsible for the economic well-being of the family.
4. The wife/mother is seen as responsible for the household and personal care of family members, especially child care.
5. Conversely, the father/husband is *not* seen as responsible for the household and personal care of family members, especially child care, and
6. The wife/mother is *not* responsible for the economic well-being of the family.
7. Society may give some support to the man who supports his dependents (wife and/or children), but is not responsible for the economic

well-being of the family where there is a husband present, and is not responsible for the household and personal care of family members, especially child care, when there is a wife present.

8. As a derivative of 1 and 7, a husband is equated with a father, and a wife is equated with a mother.[24]

What is most important in this model in our context is that the wife is defined as her husband's dependent, independent of the value of the services she renders within the household. It is only since women have started in large numbers to withdraw from unpaid household work as the *sole* occupation (housework continues to be an important secondary occupation for the majority of women), that the economic value of their services has become somewhat more visible than before. With the majority of Canadian wives and mothers in the paid labour force, it becomes evident that some of the work that women have done and still do within the home has been economically valuable all along. Today, some of the services previously rendered ostensibly for free within the household have to be purchased or, if the wife becomes a full-time household worker, it has now become more obvious—simply through greatly increased participation rates of women in the labour force—that she forgoes a salary if she spends her entire time in unpaid household work.

For as long as wives were defined as their husbands' dependents, their unpaid work was, by definition, valueless, and they were seen as an expense to their husbands rather than an asset—hence the spousal tax deduction, which still applies. Family law, however, has changed considerably since 1978, and the wife's potential contribution through her *unpaid* work to her husband's assets is now to some degree recognized in all provinces.[25]

We can, then, answer our third question: Yes, to the degree that women are defined as men's dependents, the value of their work will not only go unrecognized, but they will be seen as an economic expense rather than as an economic asset, irrespective of the real value of the work that is being performed by them.

Conclusion

In this paper, I have looked at the value of time in terms of time itself as well as in terms of money. Starting from the premise that the value of a person's time varies systematically with the power of that person—the more power, the more valuable one's time—I asked specifically whether women's time is worth less than men's time. The answer to this latter

question is a qualified yes. Looking at the value of time in terms of time
itself, there is some limited evidence that women as a group wait more
on men than as a group, although the indicators are indirect rather
than direct. Looking at the value of time in terms of money, there is no
question that women's time is worth less money than men's time within
the paid work world as well as in the household.

This led to the question of a negative value attached to a person's
time, and it was postulated that people who are defined as dependents
carry a negative economic value on their time. In the past, wives were
conceptualized as their husbands' dependents. This completely obscured
wives' economic contributions to a marriage, while at present this contribution is slowly emerging into the public view, concomitant with reduced
(but not eliminated) female dependency.

What is particularly interesting is the realization that the monetary
value of a person's time in no way inheres in particular activities or
persons, but depends on the power of the role incumbents who engage
in various activities. Since the value of time assigned to a person or
activity is merely a social convention, it follows that we can alter the
value by creating another social convention.

This approach presents a rather different view of the value of time
than we would obtain if we follow the logic of market economics. Market economics assumes that there is an internal logic and dynamic in the
market that fixes the monetary value of a person's time according to the
inherent quality of a product, which equals its value as a commodity.
However, we have seen that in the case of slaves or housewives the
product of their time expended is not worth any money to them, even
though its replacement would cost money, owing to their lack of power,
which expresses itself in their being defined as dependents. It also
follows that when we cease to define people as dependents, or when the
power position of a group of people changes, the value of their time will
change, even though in some cases the use to which this time is being
put may not have changed.

Notes

1. Werner Bergmann, "Das Problem der Zeit in der Soziologie. Ein Literatur-
    überblick zum Stand der 'zeitsoziologischen' Theorie und Forschung,"
    Kölner Zeitschrift für Soziologie und Sozialpsychologie 79 (1983): 462–504.

2. Barry Schwartz, "Waiting, Exchange, and Power: The Distribution of Time in
    Social Systems," *American Journal of Sociology* 79 (1974): 841–70.

3. Ibid., 843.

4. Ibid., 855.

5. Ibid., 867.

6. Ibid., 867-68.

7. Ibid., 868.

8. Ibid.

9. Bálint Balla, *Soziologie der Knappheit. Zum Verständnis individueller und gesellschaftlicher Mangelzustände* (Stuttgart: Ferdinand Enke, 1978), 28.

10. E. Y. Zerubavel, "Timetables and Scheduling: On the Social Organization of Time," *Sociological Inquiry* 4, no. 2 (1976): 87-94.

11. If the psychiatrist or medical doctor has opted out of the provincial health plan, the client pays both directly and indirectly, of course.

12. Economic Council of Canada, *On the Mend: Twentieth Annual Review 1983* (Ottawa: Supply & Services, 1983), 88-89.

13. Nor has the time much intrinsic value for the person who is being supervised. Kathy Calkins, "Time: Perspectives, Marking and Styles of Usage," *Social Problems* 17 (1970): 487-501, has identified six ways in which patients in a rehabilitation institution used their time, which she classified as "passing time, waiting, doing time, making time, filling time, and killing time." While the institution she studied was certainly not a prison, nevertheless all of the modes of time usage noted are a reaction to being an inmate in an institution and constituted attempts to spend time so that it did not become an irritating void.

14. Margrit Eichler, "Women as Personal Dependents: A Critique of Theories of the Stratification of the Sexes and an Alternative Approach," in *Women in Canada*, ed. Marylee Stephenson (Toronto: New Press, 1973), 38-55; idem, "Power, Dependency, Love and the Sexual Division of Labour. A Critique of the Decision-Making Approach to Family Power and an Alternative Approach with an Appendix: On Washing My Dirty Linen in Public," *Women's Studies International Quarterly* 4 (1981): 201-19.

15. For a few Canadian examples, see the Royal Commission on the Status of Women in Canada, *Report* (Ottawa: Information Canada, 1970); Royal Commission on Equality in Employment, *Equality in Employment*, vol. 1 (Ottawa: Supply & Services, 1984); Committee on Sexual Offenses Against Children and Youths, *Sexual Offenses Against Children*, 2 vols. (Ottawa: Supply & Services, 1984); Angela Miles and Geraldine Finn, eds., *Feminism in Canada: From Pressure to Politics* (Montreal: Black Rose Books, 1982); Maureen Fitzgerald, Connie Guberman, and Margie Wolfe, eds., *Still Ain't Satisfied! Canadian Feminism Today* (Toronto: Women's Press, 1982); Janine M. Brodie and Jill McCalla Vickers, *Canadian Women in Politics: An Overview*, CRIAW paper no. 2 (Ottawa: Canadian Research Institute for the Advancement of Women, 1982); and Micheline Dumont,

Michèle Jean, Marie Lavigne, and Jennifer Stoddart, *L'Histoire des femmes au Québec depuis quatre siècles* (Montréal: Les Quinze, 1982).

16. Schwartz, "Waiting, Exchange, and Power," 858.

17. Royal Commission on Equality in Employment, *Equality in Employment*, 63, t. 5.

18. There are a total of twenty-three major occupations listed. For each, the female percentage was divided by the male percentage. Since there are more men than women in the labour force (in 1981 there were 7,152,205 men and 4,853,120 women—see report, ibid., 64–65—that is, a female/male ratio of 0.68), the representation of women and men within a given occupation would be proportionate if the female/male ratio was 0.68. This is approximately the case for sales occupations, with a ratio of 0.69, which translates into 9.5 percent of all men and 9.6 percent of all women in the labour force being in this occupation. When the female/male ratio exceeds 1, the discrepancy is, therefore, very considerable. Since the sex segregation of occupations in Canada is quite high, all ratios (with the exception of sales occupations) were either quite low or above 1.

19. Royal Commission on Equality in Employment, *Equality in Employment*, 65.

20. Ibid., 64.

21. Martin Meissner et al., "No Exit for Wives: Sexual Division of Labour and the Cumulation of Household Demands," *Canadian Review of Sociology and Anthropology* 12, pt. 1 (1975): 424–39; Susan Clark and Andrew S. Harvey, "The Sexual Division of Labour: The Use of Time," *Atlantis* 2, no. 1 (1976): 46–66.

22. Cf. Economic Council of Canada, *On the Mend*.

23. Two occupations, judges and magistrates as well as optometrists, were eliminated from the table because no female salary figures were provided owing to the low number of female incumbents.

24. See Margrit Eichler, "The Connection between Paid and Unpaid Labour and Its Implication for Creating Equality for Women in Employment" (Paper prepared for the Royal Commission on Equality in Employment, 1984, forthcoming in vol. 2 of Royal Commission on Equality in Employment, *Equality in Employment*, 2–3).

25. Cf. Margrit Eichler, *Families in Canada Today: Recent Changes and Their Policy Consequences* (Toronto: Gage, 1983).

Women, Time and Societal Values: Lessons from the Farm

SEENA B. KOHL

The Issues: Women, Time, Societal Values

THE CONCERN OF this paper is to answer the call to "examine some of the particular ways in which the roles of women as individuals and as members of families are affected by societal values." These ways include the worth attributed to the time women work inside and outside of the home; the value conflicts experienced by women, families, and communities associated with women's use of time; and the economic and legal implications of women's choices in their use of time. Additionally, the goal of the paper is to do more than report about issues of specific concern to women, but to respond to a second conference call to explore use-of-time as a potentially powerful avenue for designing and conducting research. These two calls pose formidable tasks indeed!

In this paper I make use of past research that addressed the issues of time, values, and women's roles. The research was a longitudinal study of family life and agricultural enterprises in southwestern Saskatchewan.[1] It looked at the fusion of the economic and work demands of family agricultural enterprises with the social and personal dynamics of family and household members, and in particular examined the strategic position of women and the role they played in the small, family-owned and -run agricultural enterprise—the North American family farm.

The concept of time was crucial to understand both developmental processes of enterprise development and those of the individual life cycle. The interpenetration of economic enterprise needs and family household demands also required recognition of time use by individuals, since both systems compete for allocation of labour from the same members. It was necessary to look at the multiplicity of activities of women in the household, enterprise, and community in terms of the larger cultural meanings assigned to women and women's roles, and in particular their unpaid and unrecognized work as "housewife." Ann Oakley writes:

A housewife is a woman: a housewife does housework. In the social structure of industrialized societies, these two statements offer an interesting and important contradiction. The synthesis of "house" and "wife" in a single term establishes the connections between woman-hood, marriage and the dwelling place of family groups. The role of housewife is a family role: it is a feminine role. Yet it is also a work role. . . . [2]

The characteristic features of the housewife role in modern industrialized society are (1) its *exclusive allocation to women*, rather than to adults of both sexes; (2) its association with economic dependence, that is, with the dependent role of the woman in modern marriage; (3) its *status as non-work*—or its opposition to "real," that is, economically productive, work; and (4) its *primacy* to women, that is, its priority over other roles. The research spanned the same years that saw numerous challenges to the accepted social views about women and to the national political and economic structures that maintained unequal remuneration and recognition. This paper will review the past research and then consider the continuity and changes at both national and local levels—the impact of time as process.

The Field Setting: The Jasper Region

The locale of the study is the southwestern portion of Saskatchewan, to which we have given the pseudonym "Jasper," after the principal town. The livelihood of these agriculturists is based upon small-scale grain farming and cattle ranching.

Settlement of the Jasper region was relatively recent; the earliest settlers, cattlemen, arrived in the 1880s, and the year 1906 witnessed the end of the open range. Districts were established for homesteading around 1900, with the majority of farm homesteaders arriving during the years 1912 through 1916. A majority of the contemporary agricultural families in the region are the children and grandchildren of the original homestead population. The struggles of the pioneer generation on the frontier and during the drought and depression were both recent enough and sufficiently vivid to influence the behaviour and aspirations of the contemporary Jasper population.[3]

The region is sparsely populated (1.7 persons per square mile). Often one must drive from one to seven miles from the main road to reach a ranch house. The topography is varied. There are rolling hills intersected by small streams, where ranchers settled, and flat plains north and south of the range of forested hills, which constitute the region's most prominent natural feature, where the farmers homesteaded.

The town of Jasper, population 2,400, is a few miles off the major east–west Trans-Canada highway and is the chief service centre for the region. Since 1952 school children have been bussed from the surrounding area (in some cases up to thirty miles) to the central school in Jasper. In 1964 accepted conveniences such as plumbing, electricity, telephones, and passable roads were still not available in some districts. Consequently, where they were available, the occupants made special note of them. By 1970 virtually all urban amenities were available and expected.

The Fusion of Work and Family

Many aspects of Jasper family life are familiar ones. Jasper men and women share with the larger North American society similar expectations of gender and marital roles. They share with others in North American society the prevailing view that expects women to consider marriage and the raising of a family as their primary life goal, and expects men to consider an occupation as their primary life goal. However, the fact that it is not possible to separate the domestic and private sphere of the household from the public-productive sphere of the enterprise imposes a unique set of structural constraints upon the enterprise family members.[4] These constraints can be clearly seen when we consider the life choices available for farm sons and farm daughters in contrast with those in the urban sector and when we examine the role of the farm woman as "housewife."

Continuity of family enterprises is a major goal around which most families organize their expectations. This remains as true in 1984 as in 1964. Sons are brought up to consider succession to the family enterprise and farming their major objective. A relatively high proportion of sons remain within the family occupation: 68 percent of all sons who came of age during the decade of research succeeded to the family enterprise by 1972. (This continues to be true in 1984.) However, without economic aid and support from one's family, a young man cannot hope to acquire the capital necessary for entrance into agricultural production. The most common route for a young man is to serve an "apprentice-ship" under his father by which he earns "shares" in the enterprise for his work. He works under the direction of the father, who retains control of the enterprise, and the relationship between father and son has many of the features of the relationship between boss and hired hand.

Entrance into agriculture requires the young man to "get along" with his father/boss; to accede to his father's demands and defer to his father's priorities. As one informant put it: "A man is stuck with his father. . . . He knows he is with him for life, and the only way to get along is not to complain or argue too much."

The young man who desires to farm is, by virtue of situational demands and cultural precedents, encouraged to remain within the family. This is in sharp contrast with the position of the urban middle-class male child, who is pushed out and away from the family, his occupational choices outside family ownership and control, mediated for the most part by educational and bureaucratic institutions.

Since daughters are not considered successors, they are expected to leave the family enterprise. Girls learn early in childhood that women do not become ranchers or farmers. The rationale made is rarely justified in terms that suggest women are not *competent* to assume control of the enterprise. Rather, it is taken as a given that women have other life choice priorities—marriage and children—whereas although men may marry and father children, their primary life choice is outside the family—as rancher or farmer. The terms *farmer* and *rancher* remain linked to the male gender, just as the terms *housewife* and *homemaker* are linked to the female gender. Hill notes: "Men are farmers simply because they are males living on farms. Women, however, are told that they must prove their labour contributions before they presume to claim either the title of 'farmer' or the right to their property."[5]

Where there are no male successors, and where the daughters married men with agricultural backgrounds, enterprises were likely to be transferred to the daughter's husband's control. This pattern has continued for the most part, although there were two exceptions in 1982-84. (These exceptions will be discussed in a later section.)

For both time periods, young women not married upon completion of high school (approximately 60 percent of those girls who completed high school between 1962-1972) leave for training in one of the service skills—teaching, nursing, or secretarial work—retaining the eventual goal of marriage.

Mothers see no contradiction in desiring the emigration of their daughters and the retention of their sons. Thus, one stated:

Our son thought he wanted to live in the city, and took a job in Winnipeg for two years. But he's back on the farm now, helping us and working his own land. The job paid too poorly, and in the city a job is everything. The farm is more secure than packing that lunch kit every day. . . . Fathers should encourage their sons to come back to the farm . . . my daughter married a farmer, but I'd rather have seen her marry a teacher. Teaching is her whole life, and now she's had to give it up.

Since expectations for the daughter's maturity are rarely tied to the development or continuity of the family enterprise, as are sons', her emigration from the region is virtually a given, unless she marries a local son either before graduation from high school or upon graduation. In contrast with sons who are tied to the family enterprise, daughters have wider alternatives despite cultural pressures upon them to marry—pressures that in an urban context we view as diminishing or restricting a woman's alternatives. While the young woman's wider alternatives are a consequence of exclusion from succession to enterprise management, exclusion has its own costs. These costs are variable, depending upon the individual woman's view of urban life and urban work alternatives.

Leaving the region is recognized as part of maturation. For the most part, leaving is not perceived as a hardship, but rather is seen as a novelty or opportunity for change. Most young women viewed this period as one phase of their lives. The subsequent phase involved the rearing of children, and for that period they preferred to return to a rural setting, sharing with other Jasperites a preference for rural life over urban settings.[6] As one young woman wrote:

I . . . would like to continue my education. I am going to take my hairdressing course in Winnipeg. Then I would like to travel across Canada, South America, England, and especially to Australia. . . . When I return to Jasper, if he still wants to marry me I would accept. There is no other place in Canada as nice. I wish to settle here and raise my family as my parents raised my sisters, brothers and me. . . .[7]

One consequence of the expectations for migration held for young women was that educational expectations were higher for daughters than for sons, and there are differential rates in fulfillment of these expectations. Daughters do better in school than do sons: between 1960 and 1970, 66 percent of the girls (out of a total of 117) finished twelfth grade, the minimal education needed for entrance to further vocational training, in comparison with 45 percent of the boys (out of a total of 121).[8] Similar female-male differentials in educational achievement were present in the parental generation.

Women's Contribution to the Enterprise

The merged character of farm family and economic enterprise is fully recognized by Jasper women. They do not clearly separate the household from the enterprise and are acutely aware of the interplay between the two. In contrast, men do make a distinction between enterprise and "house." They firmly locate the household and its associated members and their needs in the woman's sphere of action and responsibility. Nevertheless, when discussing enterprise development virtually all men use "we," as illustrated by the following quotation from a young farmer: "We did everything here ourselves . . . we didn't get much help from anyone . . . we plan to add some land as soon as we can manage it. . . ."

In most cases in Jasper, the enterprise takes precedence and house-hold members and needs defer to enterprise needs—something that all household members learn to accept. As one woman said: "The farm comes first after the house—but it's from the farm that everything comes—so it has to be first." It is a rare situation where a woman will state that the "house" comes first; and it is a rare housewife who is unwilling to defer household consumption in favour of investment in the enterprise. As another woman remarked: "When it comes to spending a dollar I always ask myself, what is it going to make? . . . If you buy a rug, well, you have a rug, but if you use the same money and buy a cow, the cow has calves and with the calves you can get the rug but you still have the cow!"

Similarly, work on the enterprise is usually given priority over work in the house. However, the work of the household still remains; meals to be fixed, children cared for, household cleaned—these are women's responsibilities, but not priorities in terms of the allocation of shared labour resources. The fact that household tasks are taken for granted as women's responsibilities alone, means that any other tasks that the woman may assume are added to her basic work load in the household. Women share a common means for controlling the expectations regarding their participation in enterprise activities. They simply do not *learn* how to do certain tasks. For example, one woman never learned how to drive: as she said, "If I did, it would always be 'mother get this, mother get that.' I have enough to do." Another woman never learned how to milk: "If I did, then it would be my job forever . . . this way Joe [her husband] does it." Men also refrain from learning certain tasks, but when they deny knowing how to cook, bathe a child, or wash clothes, they phrase their lack of learning in terms of gender-linked appropriate tasks: "It's the wife's job—she's in the house and I'm in the fields."

Throughout all phases of household and enterprise development there is a constant juggling of family and enterprise needs. The family agricultural enterprise is based (with few exceptions) upon the availability of labour within the residential group, the domestic household; and the labour resources that the enterprise are limited and depend upon the phase in the household domestic cycle. Availability of labour in the family enterprise is dependent upon the ages and number of children, the physical health of the household members, as well as the kinds of linkages the household has to other agricultural households. The last factor involves the wider kinship and friendship (quasi-kin) network of relationships.

Availability of labour also depends on psycho-social factors that establish how the "need" for help is viewed and the way in which household members preferentially allocate their time and labour. These involve shared agreements as to priorities in decisions of expenditure of time and labour.

The technological constraints of the enterprise affect definitions of "need" for household labour. Where the enterprise can substitute machine labour for human labour, as in grain-farm operations, the "need" for household participation is less and family members have fewer demands on their time: they are freer to organize their time according to their own lights. Where the technological demands of the enterprise are labour-dependent, as in cattle ranching, the organization of the household's time and labour will be more relevant to the success of the enterprise.

The particular phase of the development of the enterprise also sets constraints upon the household and its members. In its initial stages, an enterprise requires deferment of consumption as well as important labour contributions from the household members. Moreover, during any expansion process, resources must be devoted to the enterprise and consequently away from the household.

Along with the dependence on family labour, the enterprise relies on the shared agreements of the household members as to the definition of consumption "needs." Where consumption demands on the part of household members are low, a greater proportion of capital can be reinvested in the enterprise. Jasper agrarians are subject to consumption pressures similar to those of members of an industrial society. What is considered "acceptable" has changed; what one generation perceives as luxuries is seen as the next generation's needs. Further, consumption "needs" do not remain stable. Both the household and its members are subject to developmental changes.

These temporal rhythms are diagrammed in Figure 1. By reading down, one can gain some idea of the ways the individual life course and

COMPONENTS AND FUNCTIONS	CYCLES	PROCESS
Decisions & Tasks-Accomplishment		
Enterprise Manager	Bachelor "starters" → Establishes → Develops → Retires → "develops down"; "Slows"; New operator	Aging
Economic & Technical		
Enterprise	Establishment phase → Development phase → Maintaining phase → Redevelopment phase	Developing
Reproduction & Socialization		
Nuclear Family Household	Courtship → Marriage → Birth → Transmission of headship → Courtship, marriage & training of children	Expanding & Contracting
Reciprocal Exchange		
Instrumental Network	Wife's family added (Various events will influence) Offspring's family added	Ramifying & Attenuating

FIGURE 1. TEMPORAL RHYTHMS OF LOCAL COMPONENTS
OF A TYPICAL JASPER AGRIFAMILY SYSTEM

Source: John W. Bennett and Seena B. Kohl, "The Agrifamily System," chapter 5 in *Of Time and the Enterprise*, ed. John W. Bennett (Minneapolis: University of Minnesota Press, 1979), 142.

agrifamily enterprise intersect with concomitant areas of tension. These intersections are common to all agricultural families, although the strategies of family households will differ.[9]

Women are of critical importance in both generating and resolving the conflicts or the potential conflicts between the demands placed upon shared resources of family household and enterprise. The degree to which women are able to control household expenditures, to free income for reinvestment in the enterprise while maintaining shared commitment on the part of the household members who supply the labour for the enterprise, affects the success or failure of the enterprise. Women who see their primary role in the enterprise as one of household activities nevertheless participate in important ways in the economic health of the enterprise simply by virtue of household budgeting and consumption control, and by serving as chef and quartermaster. The control the wife is able to exercise over the allocation of family members' time is important in the degree to which labour is available for the enterprise. She makes decisions that encourage or prevent the child's activities outside the enterprise; for example, whether children go to 4H camp or help on the enterprise; whether they play on school teams or return home for chores.

Women organize the social relationships between the household, the kin group, and the community. They establish reciprocal ties with the larger community: a vital instrumentality for the exchange of labour. A farm wife with little aptitude for these social relational skills puts the enterprise at a disadvantage, since the exchange of labour in Jasper is deeply embedded in social relationships.[10] (Hired labour is difficult to find and decidedly not preferred.)

There is wide latitude in the role in the enterprise that the farm or ranch wife can play. The image of the ideal woman is that of the frontier woman who "does what has to be done," but, aside from this vague prescription, which takes for granted the woman's household tasks, participation in the enterprise will vary according to the desires and values of the women, the needs of the enterprise, and the expectations of her husband and other members of the enterprise.

Women's participation spans virtually the entire range of enterprise activities. Women are the hired hands; they feed animals, are truck drivers, get supplies, participate in the continual task of fencing, and so on. They are also owner/managers: they provide cash and land, function as accountants, help in business decisions, and serve as labour brokers and personnel counselors.

While averages are deceptive, in Jasper the time women spend in enterprise activities ranges from about ten hours a week to more than fifty hours, depending upon the seasonal demands of enterprise production. This is similar to other analyses of the contribution of women to the family enterprise, which note averages ranging from "half-time" to over forty hours a week.[11] Table 1 indicates the ways women contribute to the enterprise.

The relatively high proportion of women who function as book-keepers, bankers, investment advisers, business managers, and information gatherers is based on differences in education of men and women and the wider literacy, book-keeping, and clerical experience of women prior to marriage.

Fifty percent of the farm and ranch wives worked as teachers, in secretarial positions, and in nursing before their marriage. In contrast, the jobs men held before farming (60 percent had work experience outside the region) were, for the most part, in areas that made use of their agricultural skills. These jobs included farm work, construction, factory work, carpentry, and mechanical work. Only 8 percent held jobs that were based upon literacy or organizational skills, such as in business, sales, and service occupations. These literacy and book-keeping skills are crucial for enterprise decision-making. Jasper women maintain breeding

214   SPECIAL ISSUES IN SOCIETY

TABLE 1. MAJOR TYPE OF WOMEN'S CONTRIBUTION (1970)

	Number	Percentage
Household organization*	6	8.2
Control of consumption	15	20.5
Book-keeping/literary skills	9	12.3
Agricultural labour	5	6.8
Social relational skills	6	8.2
Women who contribute in all fields	21	28.7
Cash input	9	12.3
Operating head	2	2.7
Total number of women	73	99.7

*These women see their primary work as the routine work in the household, in contrast with women who see their important activity in the control of consumption along with the routine household tasks. *Source:* This table was compiled from interviews with a smaller subpopulation within the regional sample.

records and financial accounts of the enterprise. They are important for the necessary letter writing to national agencies that control the agriculturists' access to resources of land, water, and credit, and although male agents of the various bureaucracies that control vital resources stated in interviews that they prefer to deal with men on enterprise matters. There are numerous anecdotes illustrating the common experience of women who attempted to transact business for the enterprise, but were put off with explanations implying that the agent would prefer to talk with the husband. At the same time, it is recognized as necessary for the man to check with his wife for an accurate accounting of the enterprise.

Logically, it is possible to conceptualize household and enterprise as complementary systems: each composed of the same personnel but with different directors and tasks. In reality, there are dual expectations for women. Women are responsible for the household through the default of men—for example, it is "women's work." Women also share in the directorship and tasks of the economic enterprise.

Men do not experience dual expectations. In Saskatchewan as elsewhere they have no formal or informal responsibility in the household.

They are freed from dual sets of expectations and dual work loads. Their freedom from dual sets of responsibilities is commonly regarded as an attribute of supremacy. However, what has been only recently appreciated in industrial settings is that men in their "freedom" from household and family tasks are rigidly locked into male work roles, and particularly in Jasper, men are locked into a specific work role of agricultural operator. However, while we commonly think of flexibility in role prescriptions as a "good," and role specificity as a failure of the social system to take into account individual differences, it is important to remember that the flexibility of roles for women has a double-edged character. The sharp side of the blade emerges in the analysis of women's work with its dual work load, a situation that has grave consequences for women where they are unable to control the dual sets of expectations.[12]

The duality of expectations for women is one aspect of the broader topic concerned with the relative status of women. Analyses of women's position have linked their relative status with their economic contributions, noting that where women control land, seed, or distribution of production, their status and associated power have been found to be greater than in those settings where they only contribute labour.[13] While Jasper women are subject to heavy work demands, at the same time they exercise important control over their lives and the lives of their family members. They are active participants in production decisions and are important for capital formation, although social remuneration and public recognition have been only partially forthcoming.

Women—The Hidden Producers

In the analyses of the women's tasks for both farm and non-farm women, the economic contribution of housework has been ignored. This is a reflection of the larger society's view of housework as "non-work"—that is, housewives, who are not paid, do not produce commodities of value to the economy, and are dependents of men. It also reflects the lack of value accorded to women's time. The fact that the non-farm household, in contrast to the farm household, is isolated from the work sphere and lives are most often distinctly divided into work and non-work segments, gives some basis for understanding the ignoring of women's economic contributions—what Rowbotham[14] and Oakley's[15] among others call the "hidden factors" of production.

Even where farm women perform important enterprise tasks, they are not usually taken into account as economic contributions since the activities of women, outside the wage market, are considered "personal services" donated to husbands and children. Although both rural sociologists and agricultural economists have recognized the merged character of the farm family and economic enterprise, with few exceptions until recently, they have failed to pay attention to the economic contribution of the farm women in both spheres: household and enterprise.[16]

It has been recognized that the maintenance of the family agricultural enterprise involves a set of shared agreements among the household members. Among other issues, these agreements include acceptance of the importance of continuity of the enterprise, acceptance of generational authority, and acceptance of deferred consumption agreements that affect allocations of labour, time, and expenditures. In essence, these agreements fall within the domestic sphere—the arena of the wife and mother. These contributions towards the maintenance of the smooth operation of the enterprise fall within the interpersonal sphere, and most of the research and advice in North America concerned with women on farms has emphasized this aspect of women's participation.[17] Other research that has looked at the role of farm women has been concerned for the most part with her role in innovation, adoption of new farming techniques, and decision-making. Most of this research has related value attitude data of the wife to the profitable operation of the enterprise, recognizing that interpersonal relationships and managerial functions of farm women have an "economic" or productive outcome in terms of profit maximization.[18]

Thus, as one reviews the farm-management literature written from the 1950s through to the mid-1970s, one notes that, although there has been recognition of the role of women in affecting management decisions of men, there is no systematic method of calculating the value of women's contributions or even the inclusion of women's labour in the traditional agricultural research model of the family farm.[19] Even when there was recognition of her economic contribution to the enterprise, there was no call to change public policy. For example, in 1956, although the Royal Commission on Agriculture and Rural Life discussed the unrecognized status of the farm wife as an economic partner,[20] in the subsequent recommendations there was no proposal for change in her status, and she was not ensured any right in the property accumulated during the marriage.

Public Recognition of Women's Work

Not until the mid-1970s did agricultural research begin to take into account women's economic activity.[21] This change was part of the general

Kohl / *Women, Time and Societal Values* 217

re-evaluation of the work of women and its hidden non-cash character, changes that have come about as concomitants of strenuous political activity by women for social and economic parity. What farm women have always known has now been given public or state recognition. Thus, the 1976 Canadian census changed the definition of "employed" to include anyone who has "helped without pay in a family business or farm" providing they have contributed a minimum of twenty hours per week. This change makes clear the involvement of farm women in the labour force, whereas previous counting ignored their participation.

In a similar way, there has been a call for farm family research that recognizes the farm wife.[22] In general, the widespread interest in and use of the Farming Systems Model for research[23] as well as the recent surveys directly concerned with women's work on and off farms in both the U.S. and Canada are indicative of the recognition of women's work, and reflect reassessment within the research community as to what are considered relevant areas of study.[24]

With emerging public recognition that women are farmers, other changes in legal codes regulating farm women's property rights to the family enterprise have evolved. In particular, the May 1976 Saskatchewan Matrimonial Property Act goes a long way in taking into account non-monetary contributions in determining a fair division of property on dissolution of marriage; however, the burden of proof of contribution remains with the claiming spouse and the court determines the value of this contribution.[25] There is no guarantee under law that a woman will be entitled to half of the assets of the enterprise upon divorce or death of her spouse. As wife she is, however, guaranteed the right to veto any dealings with the matrimonial home and as widow she is ensured the use of the matrimonial home.[26]

The Saskatchewan Labour Women's Division newsletter notes:

Although human rights codes protect against discrimination in credit, a farm wife may have trouble borrowing money unless she has legal title to land or is receiving wages. If she does not have a source of income, the creditor may require her husband's signature as guarantor. Loan officers discourage farm wives from participating in farm credit by seeking only the man's signature on contracts. Even if they allow the wife to co-sign the loan some banks only life insure the husband.[27]

The newsletter goes on to indicate that a number of provincial and federal assistance programs, such as Farm Credit Corporation, Farm Cost Reduction Program, and Western Grain Stabilization Act, have criteria that do not recognize the contribution or partnership of farm

218   SPECIAL ISSUES IN SOCIETY

wives in the family operation. With the best of intentions, its advice to women is to "be prepared to deal with the traditional attitudes of family and lending institutions, and to build up both their credit and their agricultural experience."[28]

In keeping with the public view of women's household work as non-productive and, by extension, her enterprise work as "personal service" to spouse, Brown writes:

Federal income tax legislation does not allow wages paid to a farm wife as a legitimate farm expense, although a farmer can deduct wages paid to hired help or to his children. . . . The wife cannot pay into or earn benefits from Canada Pension Plan and unemployment. . . . One way the wife can claim farm income as her own is to incorporate the farm unit with the corporation paying her wages. However, incorporation costs of $500 in legal fees, a $75 registration fee, a $20 to $30 annual filing fee, plus accountant's fees for preparing the financial report may not make this an alternative for the marginal farm . . . if a wife is not receiving a wage, the Workers' Compensation Board could refuse coverage on the grounds that she cannot be defined as a "worker.". . .[29]

Reform of these statutes as well as social pressure to rethink women's position as dependent have been part of the continuing political pressure for women to minimally have equal access to the existing opportunity structure. For the most part, these activities have occurred outside of the Jasper region. However, these struggles have been carefully watched. Local women (and men) have been connected to them through farm and political organizations as well as through the media, and change has occurred at the local level; important changes have begun.

Change at the Local Level

In 1962-64, the first field sessions, there was little discussion of women's lives distinct from the traditional pattern of marriage and children. When the work of women in the enterprise was discussed, the general position was that, similar to the frontier period, "women do what has to be done"; that "it was all right for women to work like a man (or do the same jobs that men do if she had to) but she should look and act like a woman," and "if she runs the enterprise she shouldn't let on." Twenty years later, 1982,[30] common topics for discussion were the women's movement and the change in aspirations of young women. Equality of opportunity for women was an accepted topic of conversation, if not an equally shared belief between men and women, Jasperites and myself. Men did agree women should be given recognition for their work in the enterprise, a change from an earlier view. They were not sure about the degree of remuneration, holding that most men contributed more to the enterprise. They failed to give value to the contribution women make as the mediators of household relationships. What was agreed upon was equal pay for equal work even among those who felt women should not have to "work like a man."

The 1980s saw increased participation of farm women in the paid labour force. Between the mid-1960s and mid-1970s, the period of the longitudinal study, the percentage of farm women who worked off the farm increased from 5 percent to 9 percent. In 1982 this increase in off-farm work continued, as it has throughout Canada as well as the U.S.[31] Further change in Jasper can be seen in (1) the entrance of young women into paid farm work for non-kin within the region; (2) farm daughters being considered as potential successors to the family enterprise, and (3) married women operating an agricultural enterprise independent from their spouses' enterprise.

Jasper women have continuously, since the frontier period, been actively engaged in farm and ranch work. In an earlier period, during the 1920s when there was less mechanization, women did hire out to help in the fields during harvest. However, most of the "hiring out" was in the domestic sphere: cooking, housekeeping, and child care. Daughters (as well as wives) did work within their own family enterprises, and daughters along with sons were paid for their work in the enterprises. However, unlike their brothers, daughters were not considered as potential hired hands for their neighbours. (It is neighbours or kin that provide the labour pool.) In 1982 there were four cases of young women working as full-time paid agricultural workers: as hired hands for non-kin and in the cattle auction ring. It is not that four cases is such a large number, for it is not; what is relevant is the change in what is considered possible for young women to do.

Throughout the history of the Jasper region there have always been women who operated an economic enterprise independently. They consisted of two types: first were women who were viewed as running the enterprise by default through either illness or death of their husbands. These women (four cases between 1962 and 1972) saw themselves "holding things together until their sons were grown." The second type of women represented a major departure from the traditional concept that women must marry and leave the family enterprise. These women (two cases between 1962 and 1972) either rejected the goal of marriage and remained with their father, assuming control of the enterprise after his retirement, or (two cases between 1962 and 1972) married and with termination of their marriage returned to the family enterprise, eventually succeeding their father.

In 1963-64 and in 1970-72, despite the presence of women as enterprise heads without male associates, neither Jasper agriculturalists nor their daughters saw direct succession for women as a viable occupational choice. This position was held even in those situations where the families had no sons and the enterprise labour of both daughter and wife was economically important.

In those cases without successors, and where the daughters married men with agricultural backgrounds, enterprises were likely to be transferred to the daughter's husband's control. These women did participate in the development and management of an agricultural enterprise; however, it was through the assumption of enterprise control by their husband. Women noted that in this way they entered agriculture "through the back door" via the bedroom.

In 1982 there were specific examples of young women who had both married and retained control over their parental enterprise (two cases). Both these women retained clear separation in their enterprise from the enterprises of their husbands. Again, these are small numbers, but they do indicate change in the association of gender with occupation and local expectations for women.

These changes are not isolated acts, but have been occurring elsewhere throughout North America, as reflected in the increase of women in agricultural programs,[32] in the appearance of advice addressed to women by public agencies such as the Saskatchewan Labour Women's Division, and in the increase in research concerned with the contributions of women.

Lessons from the Farm

In 1979 John Bennett and I noted the structural difficulties women faced in gaining economic remuneration and social recognition for their work on family-held and -run enterprises. We wrote the following: "The roles of man and wife and the general informality of the women's relationship to the enterprise in Jasper are simply reflections of larger institutional forms, and the situation is an example of how national institutions shape local customs." Examining this statement in 1985, we would not summarize women's relationship to the enterprise in the same way. Without doubt, national institutions shape local responses and there is comple-mentarity between local and national structures. Women's "informal" or non-wage relationship to the enterprise is a reflection of women's unpaid nurturance/dependant role in a wage-earning marketplace economy. No economic value has been accorded to her time. However, there are con-tradictions as well as complementarities in the relationship between local and national structures, and it would be a mistake to see women (and men) as merely victims of national forces. Through our daily lives we respond to and proceed to change (or reinforce) the social system of expectations in which we find ourselves. The continued activities of Jas-per women working towards continuity of the agricultural enterprise in spite of the lack of acknowledgement contributes to change in expecta-tions of selves as women and family members as well as to the more ephemeral generalized ideas about women.

Women and men in Jasper, as elsewhere, respond to the local histor-ical situation using previous patterns of action and evolving new ones. The phrase "Doing what has to be done" was a continual refrain in look-ing back to experiences in establishing a homestead, in coping with drought and depression, and in managing the vagaries of economic and climatic circumstances common to all agriculturists.

Much of what is "doing what has to be done" is not "doing what one would like" or "doing what someone thinks women should do" or "doing what one had hoped to do." In a previous paper we characterize Jasper agriculturalists as "survivors,"[33] by that we emphasize their ability to cope with social and economic hardships through a wide variety of beha-vioural strategies concerned with continuity and maintenance of the family enterprise. The emphasis and the constraints placed upon the family household by the economic enterprise established what we term an "instrumental tilt" to the family household.[34] This cultural emphasis or cultural guide has, I feel, served Jasper women (and, I would suggest, farm women in general[35]) well. Despite difficult times, farm women are not isolated in the house, separated from work activities. As Elbert writes:

[They have a] real stake in passing a family business and the necessary operator skills on to their children. . . From their own perspective, one of their crucial responsibilities and rights is the facilitation of inter-generational transfer. The facilitation involves both productive and repro-ductive work in an integrated setting.[36]

In the family agricultural enterprise the merger of household and enterprise does not permit isolation of women from production. The contradiction between the reality of women's work and the ideology of what is proper for women was resolved in Jasper, as elsewhere, through "cultural amnesia"—women's contributions were invisible, ignored, hidden, or considered in terms of special circumstances.

The emerging recognition of women's contribution to production represents a lifting of the amnesiac veil. It does not mean, however, that numerous social justice problems do not remain. Of course they do. It does mean that the basis exists for discussion of equal remuneration and recognition for women.

Notes

1. The primary source of data comes from the Saskatchewan Cultural Ecological Research Project's longitudinal study, which began in 1962 and formally ended in the mid-1970s, with continued short field trips to the present. The adult members of 139 agricultural households constitute the population on which this discussion is based. This is called the regional sample. A generalized account of the region and its populations can be found in John W. Bennett, *Northern Plainsmen: Adaptive Strategy and Agrarian Life* (Chicago: Aldine, 1969) and in Seena B. Kohl, *Working Together: Women and Family in Southwestern Saskatchewan* (Toronto: Holt, Rinehart & Winston, 1976). A historical account of the project can be found in John W. Bennett and Seena B. Kohl, "A Longitudinal Cultural Ecology Study in Rural North America: The Saskatchewan Cultural Ecology Research Program," in *Anthropologists at Home: Towards an Anthropology of Issues in America*, ed. D. Messerschmitt (Cambridge: Cambridge University Press, 1981), 91–105.

2. Ann Oakley, *Women's Work: A History of the Housewife* (New York: Pantheon, 1974), 1.

3. John W. Bennett and Seena B. Kohl, "Characterological, Institutional, and Strategic Interpretations of Prairie Settlement," in *Western Canada Past and Present*, ed. A. W. Rasporich (Calgary: The University of Calgary and McClelland & Stewart West, 1975).

4. While this type of merged role behaviour is routine for agricultural societies throughout the world, in North America, where lives are most often distinctly divided into work and non-work segments, with the exception of small family business such fusion is virtually unique and requires recognition by researchers of the "interpenetration of kinship and capitalism." Frances Hill, "Farm Women: A Challenge to Scholarship," *The Rural Sociologist* 1 (1981): 371.

5. Ibid., 373.

6. Most Jasperites viewed social life in cities as impersonal and distasteful. While they talked about the shortcomings of the region—the weather, the lack of urban amenities, few recreational facilities for young people, and the lack of occupational and educational alternatives—all agreed that country living compared favourably with living in urban or town centres. In answer to one of the attitudinal questions we asked, 52 percent never wanted to leave the region; 20 percent did leave but returned; 10 percent thought about leaving but never did. Similar views of rural life have been noted in a longitudinal study of rural women in Ontario conducted by H. C. Abell: "The Rural Women's Perception of Urban and Rural Life" (School of Urban and Regional Planning, University of Waterloo, 1970, mimeo); and by Norma Taylor, "'All This for Three and a Half a Day': The Farm Wife," in *Women in the Canadian Mosaic*, ed. G. Matheson (Toronto: Peter Martin Associates, 1976), 151-64.

7. This quotation comes from a series of essays written in 1971 by Jasper high school students who were asked to compare life in rural and urban settings and to discuss their plans for the future. Essays written by high school students in 1984 were similar.

8. At this writing, data for 1982-84 are not available.

9. John W. Bennett and Seena B. Kohl, "The Agrifamily System," chap. 5 in *Of Time and the Enterprise: North American Family Farm Management in a Context of Resource Marginality*, ed. John W. Bennett (Minneapolis: University of Minnesota Press, 1979).

10. John W. Bennett, "Reciprocal Economic Exchanges Among North American Agricultural Operators," *Southwest Journal of Anthropology* 24 (1968): 276-309.

11. Similar averages are reported by the Saskatchewan Department of Labour, *Farm Women* (Regina: Saskatchewan Women's Division, Department of Labour, 1977). See also W. E. Huffman, "The Value of the Productive Time of Farm Wives: Iowa, North Carolina, and Oklahoma," *American Journal of Agricultural Economics* 58 (1976): 836-41.

12. Gelia T. Castillo, *The Changing Role of Women in Rural Societies: A Summary of Trends and Issues*, seminar report no. 12 (New York: Agricultural Development Council, 1977) reviews the position of women in rural societies, citing several instances of the particularly heavy work burden of rural women.

13. E. Friedl, *Men and Women: An Anthropological View* (New York: Holt, Rinehart & Winston, 1975); P. R. Sanday, "Towards a Theory of the Status of Women," *American Anthropologist* 75 (1973): 1682-1700.

14. Sheila Rowbotham, *Hidden From History* (New York: Pantheon, 1975).

15. Oakley, *Women's Work*.

16. Hill, "Farm Women"; Elizabeth Maret and James Cobb, "Some Recent Findings on the Economic Contribution of Farm Women," *The Rural Sociologist* 2 (1982): 112-15.

17. For example, see Carl C. Malone and Lucile Holaday Malone, *Decision Making and Management for Farm and Home* (Ames, Iowa: Iowa State College Press, 1958).

18. Cornelia Butler Flora, "Farming Systems Research and Farm Management Research: What is the Difference?" *The Rural Sociologist* 3 (1983): 292-7; Barbara J. Sawer, "Predictors of the Farm Wife's Involvement in General Management and Adoption Decisions," *Rural Sociology* 38 (1973): 412-26; Eugene A. Wilkening, Lakshmi K. Bharadwaj and Sylvia Guerrero, "Consensus in Aspirations for Farm Improvement and Adoptions of Farm Practice," *Rural Sociology* 34 (1969): 183-96; Eugene A. Wilkening and Lakshmi K. Bharadwaj, "Aspirations and Task Achievement as Related to Decision-Making Among Farm Husbands and Wifes," *Rural Sociology* 33 (1968): 30-44.

19. H. C. Abell, "The Women's Touch in Canadian Farm Work," *The Economic Annalist* 24 (1954): 37-38, represents one of the few exceptions in research prior to 1980 where women's labour in enterprise activities, such as care of poultry and cleaning of milk equipment, is not taken for granted.

20. Saskatchewan Royal Commission on Agricultural and Rural Life, *The Home and Family in Rural Saskatchewan*, report no. 10 (Regina: Queen's Printer, 1956).

21. Hill, "Farm Women"; Huffman, "The Value of the Productive Time of Farm Wives"; Carolyn E. Sachs, *The Invisible Farmers* (Totowa, N.J.: Rowman & Allanheld, 1983).

22. Hill, "Farm Women"; Jessica Pearson, "Note on Female Farmers," *The Rural Sociologist* 44 (1979): 189-200.

23. Flora, "Farming Systems Research and Farm Management Research."

24. Frederick H. Buttel and Gilbert W. Gillespie, Jr., "The Sexual Division of Farm Household Labor: An Exploratory Study of the Structure of On-Farm and Off-Farm Labor Allocation Among Farm Men and Women," *Rural Sociology* 49 (1984): 183-209; Susan E. Koski, *The Employment Practices of Farm Women* (Saskatoon: National Farmers Union, 1983); Kathleen K. Scholl, "Farm Women's Triad of Roles," *Family Economic Review* 1 (1983): 10-15.

25. Saskatchewan Department of Labour, *This is the Law* (Regina: Saskatchewan Women's Division, Department of Labour, 1981), 22-23.

26. Ibid., 12-13.

27. Saskatchewan Department of Labour, Women's Division, *About Women 5*, no. 2 (March/April 1981): 7.

28. Ibid., 7.

29. Rosemarie Geoffrion Brown, "Farm Women," *Briarpatch* 9, no. 8 (1980): 10. Prevalent attitudes and feelings about the importance of sentiment in organizing a family enterprise rather than adopting the use of formal bureaucratic regulations are also factors in avoiding incorporation.

30. The data for this section were collected during two field trips in 1982 and 1984.

31. Buttel and Gillespie, "The Sexual Division of Farm Household Labor"; Koski, *The Employment Practices of Farm Women*; Mary R. McCarthy, Priscilla Salant, and William E. Saupe, "Off-Farm Labor Allocation by Married Farm Women: Research Review and New Evidence from Wisconsin," in *Women and Farming*, ed. Wava G. Haney and Jane B. Knowles (Boulder, Colo.: Westview, 1988), 135–51.

32. Sachs, *The Invisible Farmers*.

33. Bennett and Kohl, "Characterological, Institutional, and Strategic Interpretations of Prairie Settlement."

34. Kohl and Bennett, "The Agrifamily Household," in *Of Time and the Enterprise*, ed. John W. Bennett (Minneapolis: University of Minnesota Press, 1979), 148–71.

35. Surveys of farm women indicate that they desire recognition and equal remuneration—not that they want to leave agricultural production. Koski, *The Employment Practices of Farm Women*; Scholl, "Farm Women's Triad of Roles."

36. Sarah Elbert, "The Challenge of Research on Farm Women," *The Rural Sociologist* 1 (1981): 389.

Spending Time

ANDREW S. HARVEY

TIME, LIKE MONEY, can be spent, and it goes whether we wish it to or not. Today, more than ever before, the task is not getting time, but properly using it. Time is spent in many and varied domains, reflecting not only what is being done but also where and with whom; when, both in relation to other activities and to the clock and calendar; and in what frame of mind, happy or sad, rushed or leisurely, planned, by necessity or on the spur of the moment. Continually, our understanding of how time is spent is expanding and is being used to shed light on a myriad of social concerns. However, both the expansion and application of the knowledge of time use have been carried out virtually independently of relevant theory. The purpose here is to explore, in a very summary way, something of how knowledge of time use has been gained, something of what has been learned about the way time is spent, how it has been used, and the directions in which thinking and research must go if they are to provide a useful theoretical base on which to expand our knowledge of the manner and meaning of how time is spent.

How time is spent has been measured in many ways, including observation, standard questionnaires, activity lists, activity diaries, and time diaries or budgets. It is through the use of time budgets that we have come to gain our greatest understanding. Time budgets, collected by means of an ongoing or retrospective diary, typically for a twenty-four-hour period, provide a systematic recording of individual time use in a wide array of domains that can include what is being done, what else is being done, where, with whom, and a number of other objective and subjective dimensions. Typically, however, subjective dimensions receive little attention in time use studies, although there are exceptions, including the work of Cullen and Godson, Partushev, and Shaw.[1] Such studies show clearly the need to incorporate subjective data into any analysis of how time is spent.

The earliest published time-budget study appears to have been Bevans's *How Working Men Spend Their Spare Time*,[2] while the earliest known large-scale measurement of time use is attributed to Strumilin, a Russian economist, who—in the early 1920s—used the approach in a study of industrial workers in Moscow. Since these origins, the measurement of how time is spent has grown at an accelerating rate. In the last five years, national time use studies have been carried out in a number of countries, including Norway, Finland, the U.K., Japan, and Sweden, while a number of other countries, including France, Italy, Japan, and the Netherlands, are in the planning stages for such studies. In 1981 a pilot time-use study in Canada, which has provided considerable insight into the time use of Canadians, was conducted.

The lessons regarding how time is spent differed little from study to study, with the greatest variation in time use occurring among peoples in different circumstances with regard to basic demographic, social, and economic constraints, within given countries rather than among similar groups across countries. Thus, an examination of the time use of persons in any given country provides a fairly clear statement of the condition of similar persons in any other country with respect to the use of time, assuming the countries have a roughly equivalent level of social and economic development.

The most frequent use of time-budget information has been to study the behaviour of relevant subgroups in society. The plight of dual-earner families, particularly of the working mother, is a favourite object of scrutiny, being addressed in such works as "On Being Up Against the Wall," "No Exit for Wives," and *From Sun to Sun*.[3] These studies chronicle the shortfall of leisure time owing to the excessive time allocation of employed women to paid work, housework, and child care, and typically also examine the husband's contribution to such activities. Other work, such as Walker's "How Much Help for Working Mothers?",[4] seeks to quantify the contribution of children to home and family care when their mother works.

Children also have been the subject of time-use studies. Medrich et al.[5] found that most children when away from their parents engaged in a rather narrow set of activities that was shaped in fairly predictable ways by sex and ethnicity, while there was clear evidence that the things families did together reflected cultural, educational, and material differences. Almost all of the children in their sample did weekly chores, which took little time around the house and subjectively meant little to the children, while organized activities, which also took little time, were clearly important. Television was the time use most fully integrated into the children's daily life, and there was little evidence of simple displace-ment of other activities by television.

Teenage activity patterns, or use of time, have also been the subject of study.[6] Chapin and Foerster found that watching TV, recreation and other diversions, and socializing took up about 75 percent of a teenager's free time, and that variations due to household income or the occupation or education of the household head led to no significant differences.

The elderly, too, have been studied by means of time budgets. For example, one study comparing time use of the elderly in four different living arrangements suggested a remarkable similarity of daily patterns of the four groups, although the differences actually observed clearly demonstrated how environmental and personal characteristics bring about shifts in time use.[7]

Nissel, on the other hand, has used time budgets to measure the time costs of caring for the handicapped elderly.[8] She points out that the tim-ing of care determines most substantially the carer's freedom to pursue other activities.

In *Labor and Leisure at Home*,[9] Berk and Berk went beyond a simple totalling of minutes and hours to examine the sequential aspects of house-hold activities. In doing so, they concluded that perhaps a third of the daily household activities were constrained by a sort of necessary order. Additionally, they found that the contributions of husbands tend to be sensitive to the particular hours when employment occurs. For example, men pick up chores after they get home, and particularly if the wife leaves for work after supper.

These findings match well the findings of Cullen and Phelps[10] regard-ing subjective evaluations of premeditation with respect to the use of time. Examining the extent to which activities were planned, routine, or time filling, they found a picture of a dominant and relatively inflexible pattern of routine activities, typically related to household and paid work, both of which are relatively inflexible.

Time budgets also facilitate the study of specific activities such as lei-sure,[11] commuting,[12] mass-media use,[13] shopping,[14] housework[15] and child care,[16] and specific situations such as social interaction[17] and marital cohesion.[18]

In general, however, specific activities and situations have been examined primarily in terms of who does them and for how long, rather than in terms of how they themselves can be characterized and under-stood in terms of duration, timing, sequencing, context, and other relevant dimensions. Thus, we know relatively little about the essence of activities themselves, having only an *a priori* understanding of their nature. Further work along the lines of papers by Stone and Nicolson and Harvey, Elliott, and Macdonald[19] is necessary if we are fully to understand the nature or essence of activities.

Another important use of time-budget information has been to examine the temporal arrangement of society. In this vein, Grønmo[20] has used such data to examine the implications of eliminating Saturday shopping in Norway, and Patrushev[21] and Petkov[22] have examined the implications of five- versus six-day work weeks. In his work, Grønmo found, among other things, that Saturday shopping gave rise to participation and social interaction that was more comprehensive and of a different kind than on other days of the week. In essence, Saturday shopping was of a genre different from weekday shopping.

Time-budget information is also useful in the area of urban planning[23] Work integrating both time and space has begun to shed considerable light on the use of the city. As Goodchild and Janelle have pointed out,[24] when time and space are taken into consideration in terms of traditional models of urban social structure rooted in standard census data, it is clear that significant diurnal aspects of such structure have been neglected.

The Canadian Time Use Pilot Study[25] provides some insight into the time use of Canadians. The study collected 2,685 time diaries, in the fall of 1981, from a random selection of Canadians in fourteen centres selected to provide information on Canadians in both rural and urban settings. Here it is only possible to present a cursory glance at what was learned, and yet even that glance tells much about the time use of Canadians and, indeed, the time use of men and women in the developed world.

Canadians 15 years of age and over devote on average 28 hours per week to paid work and education, 21 hours to home and family maintenance, and 78 hours to personal maintenance (Table 1). This leaves 41 hours free for all other activities. In essence, nearly half the week, 46.4 percent, is required for personal maintenance; nearly 30 percent is required for market work and for home and family maintenance, 16.7 plus 12.5 percent respectively; and about one-quarter of the week is free for other activities. These findings essentially hold for both men and women (Table 1). The equivalence of overall workloads, including education, for men and women observed here reconfirms earlier findings of Clark and Harvey.[26] The essential difference between the sexes is reflected in the mix of work time, not in its quantity. The male's time is primarily devoted to market work, while the female's time is primarily allocated to home and family maintenance. In essence, the male's time split is 70/30

TABLE 1. TIME ALLOCATION OF CANADIANS, 1981

	MALES		FEMALES		AVERAGE	
	Hrs/wk	%	Hrs/wk	%	Hrs/wk	%
Work and education	35	21.8	21	12.5	28	16.7
Home and family	14	8.3	27	16.1	21	12.5
Meals, sleep, personal	77	45.8	79	47.0	78	46.4
Free time	42	25.0	41	24.4	41	24.4
TOTAL	168	100.0	168	100.0	168	100.0

Source: Canadian Time Use Pilot Study, reported in Brian L. Kinsley and T. O'Donnell, *Marking Time*, vol. 1 of the *Explorations in Time Use* series, ed. Brian L. Kinsley and M. Catherine Casserly (Ottawa: Employment & Immigration Canada, 1983).

in favour of paid work and education, while the female's time split is 60/40 in favour of home and family work.

An examination of relevant subpopulations based on main economic role provides considerably greater insight into the realities of time use for individuals in particular circumstances. Examining first the allocations of employed males and females, it is evident that during the employment phase of one's life, there is a bias away from the rough overall societal balance between work time and leisure, towards work and away from leisure. Males spend 32.7 percent of their time working (25.0 + 7.7) and only 22.0 percent in free-time activities (Table 2). This split is slightly more pronounced for employed females, who devote one-third of the week to all work activities and only approximately one-fifth to free time activities. The overall balance must thus be achieved by imbalances in favour of free-time activities during periods of non-employment; such periods are reflected in the time allocations of homemakers (Table 2), and the time allocations of students, unemployed members of the labour force, and retirees and others not in the labour force (Table 3). Home-makers find the scales tipped slightly in favour of free-time activities, with 46 hours a week going to such activities in comparison with 44 hours devoted to paid and unpaid work (Table 2). While employed women spend a considerable amount of time on home and family activities, it amounts to only one-half the amount spent by homemakers (Table 2). This finding is consistent with the findings of others regarding the effects of employment on the time allocation to housework and child care.[27]

Table 2. Allocation of Time by Selected Subpopulations, Canada, 1981

	Employed Males		Employed Females		Homemakers	
	Hrs/wk	%	Hrs/wk	%	Hrs/wk	%
Work and education	42	25.0	36	21.4	2	1.2
Home and family	13	7.7	21	12.5	42	25.0
Meals, sleep, personal	76	45.3	78	46.5	78	46.4
Free time	37	22.0	33	19.6	46	27.4
Total	168	100.0	168	100.0	168	100.0

Source: Canadian Time Use Pilot Study.

The scales are clearly tipped in favour of free-time activities for the unemployed, retirees, and others. Males in these subpopulations allocate on average 61 hours per week to free time activities (Table 3). Retired and unemployed females devote somewhat less, but still considerable, time to free-time activities (Table 3).

The effects of unemployment are most evident in the time allocations of the unemployed to necessary and free-time activities. Unemployed males devote 7 hours a week more than the overall male average time allocation to necessary activity, and unemployed females 3 hours a week more than the overall female average. In terms of free time, unemployed males spend 15 hours and unemployed females 6 hours more than the respective overall allocations to free time by males and females (Table 1). Thus, for the unemployed the combined increase to necessary and free-time activities is 22 hours for men and 9 hours for women. If we relate the unemployed to the employed rather than to the overall average, we get a combined increase of time in necessary and free-time activities of 30 hours for men and 20 hours for women.

Students represent a special case of non-employed persons. They devote little time to paid work or home and family activities. However, if study is considered part of the work time of students, their time allocation to work is comparable to that of employed workers (Table 3). A distinguishing feature of the time-use pattern of students is their low allocation of time to home and family activities. This undoubtedly reflects the fact that they live at home or are otherwise housed in a

TABLE 3. TIME ALLOCATION OF STUDENTS, UNEMPLOYED, RETIREES, AND OTHERS

| | STUDENTS | | | | UNEMPLOYED | | | | RETIRED/OTHER | | | |
| | Male | | Female | | Male | | Female | | Male | | Female | |
	Hrs/wk	%	Hrs/wk	%	Hrs/wk	%	Hrs/w	%	Hrs/wk	%	Hrs/wk	%
Paid work	4	2.4	6	3.6	5	3.0	2	1.2	3	1.8	1	.6
Home and Family	7	4.2	11	5.5	18	10.7	31	18.5	22	13.2	28	16.7
Meals, sleep, personal	78	46.4	78	46.4	84	50.0	82	48.8	82	48.8	85	50.6
Education	34	20.2	36	21.4	1	.6	2	1.2	0	0	0	0
Free time	44	26.2	37	22.0	61	36.3	51	30.4	61	36.3	55	32.7
TOTAL	168	100.0	168	100.0	168	100.0	168	100.0	168	100.0	168	100.0

Source: Canadian Time Use Pilot Study.

TABLE 4. ALLOCATION OF TIME BY LOCATION OF ACTIVITY, CANADA, 1981

	MALE		FEMALE		AVERAGE	
	Hrs/wk	%	Hrs/wk	%	Hrs/wk	%
Home	106	63.9	120	71.3	113	67.2
Workplace	25	14.9	16	9.5	20	11.9
Car	8	4.8	6	3.6	7	4.2
Other transit	4	2.4	4	2.4	4	2.4
Homes of others	9	5.4	8	4.8	8	4.8
Places of business	7	4.2	8	4.8	8	4.8
Bars, restaurants	3	1.8	2	1.2	2	1.2
Other places	6	3.6	4	2.4	6	3.6
TOTAL	168	100.0	168	100.0	168	100.0

Source: Canadian Time Use Pilot Study.

manner that demands relatively little from them in terms of home or family care. Also, as in the case of employed workers, female students have somewhat less free time than do males (Tables 2 and 3).

Time is spent not only doing but also being. It can be spent in different places, with different people, in different frames of mind. Time-use studies can reflect such states as well. The Canadian pilot study captured not only what people were doing, but where and with whom they were doing it.

The majority of time, 113 of 168 hours a week, is spent at home (Table 4). Time at home is slightly higher for females, at 120 hours, than it is for males, who average 106 hours a week there. The other major activity setting is the workplace, at which men average 25 hours per week and females 16 hours per week (Table 4). Across all other settings the differences between men and women are small. Only in the case of time spent in cars is there as much as a two-hour-a-week difference (Table 4). Time can also be spent alone or with various other people. Roughly one-third of one's waking hours are spent alone, and approximately one-fifth are spent with one's partner (Table 5). In short, one spends approximately one-half of one's waking hours primarily alone or with one's

TABLE 5. ALLOCATION OF TIME BY PRIMARY SOCIAL CONTACT, CANADA, 1981

	MALE		FEMALE		AVERAGE	
	Hrs/wk	%	Hrs/wk	%	Hrs/wk	%
Alone or awake	38	30.6	40	32.0	39	31.2
Partner	26	21.0	24	19.2	25	20.0
Children	11	8.9	18	14.4	15	12.0
Other adults	4	3.2	4	3.2	4	3.2
Relatives, friends, neighbours	19	15.3	20	16.0	20	16.0
Co-workers, fellow students	21	16.9	14	11.2	17	13.6
Other	5	4.0	5	4.0	5	4.0
TOTAL	124	100.0	125	100.0	125	100.0

Source: Canadian Time Use Pilot Study.

partner, and the other half is allocated across a number of different groups of individuals. The differences between the sexes in terms of social contact revolve around time spent with children and time spent with co-workers and fellow students. Both men and women spend 32 hours a week on the two combined. However, females, relative to males, spend on average an hour a day more being primarily with children, while males, relative to females, average an hour a day more being with co-workers and fellow students (Table 5).

While examination of the separate contextual elements is instructive, it can be more useful to examine behaviour in the context of activity settings that incorporate several contextual elements.[28] Aside from a setting dominated by sleep, "paid work engaged in out of home with others" in the morning and in the afternoon is the most dominant setting over a life-time.[29] One spends over 10 percent of one's life in these settings. According to another study,[30] the dominant setting for spending free or discretionary time was "home in the evening with family," and it was itself dominated by television viewing, which occupied over 70 percent of the time spent in it. Indeed, TV viewing in this time slot accounted for nearly half of all

236   SPECIAL ISSUES IN SOCIETY

TV viewing. The next major setting, "home in the evening alone," was much less dominated by TV viewing and more likely to be spent reading or studying. The major out-of-home setting, "away in the evening with friends," was dominated by social visiting, which accounted for over half the time allocated to it.[31] An examination of study in relation to settings shows that it is somewhat incompatible with family involvement, being undertaken alone or with others.[32]

In short, examining how time is spent in terms of activity settings provides a richness of context that yields far greater insight into the nature of how time is spent than does a univariate examination of time use. A key lesson from examining time use in terms of settings is the extent to which time spent on certain activities is spent in specific settings, especially work, study, and civic-service activities. It is possible, even likely, that the setting fixity of these activities does much to shape the pattern of spending time.

In a cross-national comparative study of Canada and Norway examining social contact and the use of time, it was found that, on average, time spent in various activity settings was a better discriminant between the countries than either socio-demographic variables or social contact patterns.[33]

Additionally, there tends to be a daily pattern to the way time is spent, which unfolds from the time one arises until one retires, with certain time slots in the day tending to provide homes for specific activities. According to the Canadian pilot study, on both weekdays and weekends paid work activity peaks at 10:15 a.m. and 2:15 p.m. and is heavily concentrated between 8:15 a.m. and 4:15 p.m.[34] However, the pattern of involvement varies somewhat by sex, with the relative involvement in paid work by males 15-64 years peaking at 6:15 a.m. when men account for 72 percent of all paid work activity, and that of women 15-64 years peaking at 2:15 p.m., when women account for 39 percent of all paid work activity.[35]

A recent time-use study in Bogota, Colombia, registers a working schedule for men similar to that found in Canada, only running about one hour later, with peaks coming around 11:10 a.m. and 3:10 p.m.[36] The same study examined the way various economic strata spent time, and showed that while nearly half of working-class men were engaged in paid work at 5:10 p.m. on weekdays, about one-third of upper-class men were so engaged; the difference between the two was made up primarily by a different time allocation to domestic work, with 19 percent of upper-class men and 8 percent of working-class men so engaged at 5:10 p.m.[37] Japanese studies have shown that over the period 1965-75, the rising and retiring time of the population became later by about half an hour; however, little change was recorded between 1975 and 1980,[38] suggesting a levelling off of the trend towards later rising and retiring.

Research suggests that such temporal patterns may play an extremely important role in how time is spent. According to Cullen and Godson,[39] activity choice for particular time slots in the day is the primary factor that establishes the "pegs" about which the day is structured.

Sequencing of activities is also a major element in the spending of time, and yet it has received virtually no attention. Exceptions are the work of Cullen and Godson and of Elliott.[40] Cullen and Godson found for a university-based sample that cyclical patterns of eating and sleeping overlaid each other and dominated the daily structure. They found that while the day started out with a variety of personal, domestic, and other routine chores, beyond mid-morning it started to break into a more social-ly arranged and gregarious pattern of activities. They believe that the pattern of regular oscillation of behaviour they observed is the result of more than gaps in well-defined time tables and that it might be a feature of more regularized behaviour. Elliott has addressed theoretical and methodological aspects of activity sequencing, identifying some of the complexities involved.

Time budgets provide considerable insight into how people spend their time, as outlined above; however, it is clear that that insight is somewhat cryptic and anecdotal, having been grounded on a rather weak and disparate theoretical base. If time-use studies are to be optimally useful, they must be grounded on a considerably firmer theoretical base than has heretofore existed. Although time is spent in many settings, as has been observed above, virtually all theoretical frameworks attempting to address its allocation have focused on what was being done, to the exclusion of context or setting characteristics, and on duration rather than timing, sequencing, and other temporal dimensions. Primarily, it is not that the theoretical constructs proposed and examined in the literature cannot or do not apply across most or all settings, but rather that they have only been applied to explaining unidimensionally what is being done, in terms of the duration of primary-activity content. A much firmer theoretical base needs to be established to guide the structuring and analysis of time-use data, and more venturesome approaches to its analy-sis need to be adopted.

Research to date suggests that temporal behaviour is shaped by, among other forces, preferences,[41] constraints,[42] opportunity,[43] percep-tion,[44] routine,[45] and the interaction of a variety of social-psychological factors.[46] In reality, behaviour must be viewed as the intersection of several such forces.[47]

While at one moment behaviour may be freely chosen when one is alone, in the next moment it may be shaped by the presence of another person. While one can watch TV at home, it is generally unacceptable behaviour at the workplace. While one can go to concerts in the evening, it is typically not possible to do so in the morning. While one typically retires at night and arises in the morning, social visiting or attendance at cultural events is much less routine. At any given moment the *raison d'être* of behaviour may be any of a wide range of forces past, present, or even future, and it may change virtually from moment to moment. The task of theory is to isolate and explain the meaningful aspects of spending time and show how they interrelate.

The relevant questions with regard to spending time may well be "What is done, who does it, and when?" rather than "How long does one spend doing something?" Research into spending time needs to proceed along two avenues. One must consider activities and contextual settings, examining their nature, duration, time sequencing, and relevance to other activities. The other must attempt to explain who does what in various relevant contexts. Work in this area will need to define the relevant and measurable contexts before proceeding to the second phase of relating the contexts or settings to individuals.

The understanding of how time is spent is still very much in its infancy, being based on constructs that are few and inadequate. The major task ahead is to identify and define a more complete and integrated set of constructs that can be measured, evaluated, and used to help individuals and society spend time more wisely.

Notes

1. Ian Cullen and V. Godson, *Urban Networks: The Structure of Activity Patterns* (Oxford: Pergamon, 1975); V. D. Patrushev, "Satisfaction with Free Time as a Social Category and an Indicator of Way of Life," in *It's About Time: Proceedings of the International Research Group of Time Budgets and Social Activities*, ed. Zahari Staikov (Sofia, Bulgaria: Institute of Sociology at the Bulgarian Academy of Sciences and Bulgarian Sociological Association, 1982), 259-67; Susan M. Shaw, "The Sexual Division of Leisure: Meanings, Perceptions and the Distribution of Free Time" (Ph.D. diss., Carleton University, 1982).

2. G. Bevans, *How Working Men Spend their Time* (New York: Columbia University Press, 1913).

3. Philip J. Stone, "On Being Up Against the Wall: Women's Time Patterns in Eleven Countries" (Department of Psychology and Social Relations, Harvard University, Cambridge, n.d.); Martin Meissner et al., "No Exit for Wives: Sexual Division of Labour and the Cumulation of Household Demands," *Canadian Review of Sociology and Anthropology* 12, pt. 1 (1975): 424–39; William Michelson, *From Sun to Sun: Daily Obligations and Community Structure in the Lives of Employed Women and their Families* (Totawa, N.J.: Roaman & Allan, 1985).

4. Kathryn E. Walker, "How Much Help for Working Mothers? The Children's Role," *Human Ecology Forum* 1, no. 2 (1970).

5. Elliot Medrich et al., *The Serious Business of Growing Up: A Study of Children's Lives Outside School* (Berkeley and Los Angeles: University of California Press, 1982).

6. F. Stuart Chapin and James F. Foerster, "Teenager Activity Patterns in Low-Income Communities," in *Time-Budgets and Social Activity*, vol. 1 (Toronto: Centre for Urban and Community Studies, 1975).

7. Miriam S. Moss and M. Powell Lawton, "Time Budgets of Older People: A Window on Four Lifestyles," *Journal of Gerontology* 37 (1982): 115–23.

8. Muriel Nissel, *The Use of Time Budgets in Measuring the Cost of Family Care of the Handicapped Elderly* (London: Policy Studies Institute, 1980).

9. Richard A. Berk and Sarah Fenstermaker Berk, *Labor and Leisure at Home* (Beverly Hills: Sage, 1979).

10. Ian Cullen and Elizabeth Phelps, *Diary Techniques and the Problems of Everyday Life* (Final report to the Social Science Research Council Grant no. HR2336, London, 1975).

11. Susan Ferge, "Social Differentiation in Leisure Choices," in *The Use of Time*, ed. Alexander Szalai (The Hague: Mouton, 1972); Zigmut Skorgyn-ski, "The Use of Free Time in Torun, Maribour, and Jackson," in *The Use of Time*, ed. Szalai; Johan Arndt, Sigmund Gronmo, and Douglas K. Hawes, "Allocation of Time to Leisure Activities: Norwegian and Ameri-can Patterns," *Journal of CrossCultural Psychology* 11 (1980): 498–511; Shaw, "The Sexual Division of Leisure."

12. Claude Javeau, "The Trip to Work," in *The Use of Time*, ed. Szalai, 415–27.

13. J. P. Robinson and P. E. Converse, "The Impact of Television on Mass Media Usage: A Cross-National Comparison," in *The Use of Time*, ed. Szalai; Naomichi Nakanishi, *Changes in Mass Media Contact Times* (Tokyo: Public Opinion Research Institute, Japan Broadcasting Corporation [NHK], 1982); idem., "A Report on the 'How Do People Spend Their Time Survey' in 1980," *Studies in Broadcasting* 18 (1982): 93–113.

14. Sigmund Grønmo, *Lørdag Som Handledag* (Oslo: Fondet for markeds-og distribusjonsforskning, 1983).

15. Kathryn E. Walker and Margaret E. Woods, *Time Use: A Measure of Household Production of Family Goods and Services* (Washington, D.C.: American Home Economics Association, 1976); Chiyono Matsushima, "Time-Input and Household Work-Output Studies in Japan—Present State and Future Prospects," *Journal of Consumer Studies and Home Economics* 5 (1981): 199-217.

16. Philip J. Stone, "Childcare in Twelve Countries," in *The Use of Time*, ed. Szalai.

17. Annerose Schneider, "Patterns of Social Interaction," in *The Use of Time*, ed. Szalai; Susan Clark and David H. Elliott, "Social Involvement and Social Diversity: An Examination of Social Contact and Location Sequences" (Paper presented at the World Congress of Sociology, Uppsala, Sweden, August 1978).

18. Karoly Varga, "Marital Cohesion as Reflected in Time-Budgets," in *The Use of Time*, ed. Szalai.

19. Philip J. Stone and Nancy Nicolson, "Behaviour and Behaviour Settings" (Paper presented at the Tenth World Congress of Sociology, Mexico City, 1982); Andrew S. Harvey, David H. Elliott, and W. Stephen Macdonald, *The Work of Canadians*, vol. 3 of *Explorations in Time Use*, ed. M. Catherine Casserly and Brian L. Kinsley (Ottawa: Employment & Immigration Canada, 1983).

20. Sigmund Grønmo, "The Issue of Saturday Retail Closing in Norway: Some Consumer Welfare Aspects" (Paper presented at Corporate Social Concerns and Public Policy Conference, Bergen, Norway, April 1978).

21. V. D. Patrushev, "Time Budget Utilization by Working People at Industrial Enterprises with Five and Six-Day Working Weeks and Tendencies for it to Change" (Paper prepared for meeting of the International Research Group on Time Budgets and Social Activities, Mexico City, August 1982).

22. K. Petkov, "The Five-Day Working Week and the Time-Budget," in *It's About Time*, ed. Staikov, 118-22.

23. F. Stuart Chapin, *Urban Land Use Planning* (Urbana, Ill.: University of Illinois Press, 1965); W. Michelson, "Discretionary and Nondiscretionary Aspects of Activity and Social Contact in Residential Selection," *Society and Leisure* 3 (1973): 29-53; Dimitri Procos and Andrew S. Harvey, "Modelling for Local Planning Decisions," *Ekistics* 264 (1977): 257-66.

24. M. F. Goodchild and D. G. Janelle, "The City Around the Clock: Space-Time Patterns of Urban Ecological Structure," *Environment and Planning A* 16 (1984): 807-20.

25. Brian L. Kinsley and Terry O'Donnell, *Marking Time*, vol. 1 of *Explorations in Time Use*, ed. Brian L. Kinsley and M. Catherine Casserly; Brian L. Kinsley and Frank Graves, *The Time of Our Lives*, vol. 2 of

26. Susan Clark and Andrew S. Harvey, "The Sexual Division of Labour: The Use of Time," *Atlantis* 2, no. 1 (1976).

27. Joann Vanek, "Time Spent in Housework," *Scientific American* 231 (November 1974): 116–20; Sharon Nickols, "Work and Housework: Family Roles in Productive Activity" (Paper presented at annual meeting of the National Council of Family Relations, New York, October 1976).

28. Andrew S. Harvey, *Discretionary Time Activities in Context*, occasional paper no. 3 (Halifax: Institute of Public Affairs, Regional and Urban Studies Centre, Dalhousie University, 1978).

29. Harvey, Elliot, and Macdonald, *Activities and Settings*.

30. Andrew S. Harvey, "The Context of Discretionary Activities," in *Management of Work and Personal Life: Problems and Opportunities*, ed. M. D. Lee and R. N. Kanungo (New York: Praeger, 1984), 112–32.

31. Ibid.

32. Harvey, *Discretionary Time Activities in Context*.

33. Andrew S. Harvey and Sigmund Gronmo, "Social Contact and Use of Time: Canada and Norway," in *Time Use Studies: Dimensions and Applications*, ed. D. Aas, Andrew S. Harvey, E. Wnuk-Lipinski, and I. Niemi (Helsinki: Central Statistical Office of Finland, 1986), 108–32.

34. Harvey, Elliot, and Macdonald, *Activities and Settings*.

35. Ibid.

36. Juan Camilo Rodriguez-Gomez, "Use of Time and Attitudes Towards Time From the People of Bogata, Colombia" (Paper presented at meeting of the International Working Group on Time Budgets and Social Activities, Helsinki, August 1984), 6.

37. Ibid., 8.

38. Nakanishi, *Changes in Mass Media Contact Times*.

39. Cullen and Godson, *Urban Networks*.

40. Ibid.; David H. Elliott, "Constraints and Sequences: Elements of Formal Models of Activity Patterns" (Paper prepared for Ad Hoc Group 10, "Time Budgets and Social Activities," at the Ninth World Congress of Sociology, Uppsala, Sweden, August 1978).

41. Chapin, *Urban Land Use Planning*.

42. Torsten Hagerstrand, "What About People in Regional Science?" *Regional Science Association Papers* 24 (1970): 7–21; G. S. Becker, "A Theory of

the Allocation of Time," *Economic Journal* 75 (1965): 493-517; A. C. DeSerpa, "A Theory of the Economics of Time," *Economic Journal* 81 (1971): 838-46; S. B. Linder, *The Harried Leisure Class* (New York: Columbia University Press, 1970).

43. F. Stuart Chapin, Jr., *Human Activity Patterns in the City* (Toronto: Wiley, 1974).

44. Cullen and Phelps, *Diary Techniques*.

45. Ian Cullen and Elizabeth Phelps, "Patterns of Behaviour and Responses to the Urban Environment," in *Public Policy in Temporal Perspective: Report on the Workshop on the Application of Time-Budget Research to Policy Questions in Urban and Regional Settings*, ed. William Michelson (The Hague: Mouton, 1978), 165-81.

46. J. P. Robinson, *How Americans Use Their Time: A Social-Psychological Analysis of Everyday Behaviour* (New York: Praeger, 1977).

47. Andrew S. Harvey, "Urban Modelling and Time Budgets: A Behavioural Framework" (Paper presented at annual conference of the North American Regional Science Association, Toronto, 1976).

Time-Budget Research: Methodological Problems and Perspectives

JIRI ZUZANEK

PROFESSOR A. HARVEY in the previous paper outlined major uses and contributions of time-budget research to the understanding of human behaviour, and summarized most of the interesting time-budget research conducted in recent years. I will address a somewhat different set of questions, namely, some methodological problems connected with time-budget research.

As G. Gutenschwager[1] observed, time budgets provide solid behavioural and quantifiable evidence on an individual's lifestyle preferences. According to J. Robinson and P. Converse, we may visualize the twenty-four hours of a day as the available input of lifestyle resources to all members of the population, with the output represented by the choice of activities and the time allocated to each one of them. In the words of these authors, time budgets offer "a unique view of the intersection between the imperatives of the human condition and the range of individual behavioural choice."[2]

Time budgets have a number of advantages as a social indicator.

1. Unlike money, time expenditures need not be converted into "constant" dollars or pounds. They represent a *universal* and bias-free measurement of human behaviour.

2. Time budgets provide us with a measurement that represents a true "ratio scale." The amount of time spent in one activity always affects and is affected by the amount of time spent in other activities. In this sense, time budgets are uniquely suited for a "holistic" analysis of the trade-offs in human behaviour.

3. Compared to studies of participation, which use as a measurement the rates of participation in preselected activities (the so-called activity list studies), time-budget studies are less susceptible to the

so-called normative biases in reporting behaviour. By focusing on behaviour during the day of the survey or the day preceding the sur-vey, and by covering the whole range of human activities rather than singling out one particular type (leisure, cultural activities, etc.), time budgets reduce possible biases towards inflating participation in socially desirable or normatively approved activities.

For these and other reasons time-budget data lend themselves particu-larly well to three types of analysis: the analysis of social differences in the uses of time by various socio-demographic and socio-occupational groups (stratification analysis); the analysis of social change as reflected in changing allocations of time through a given period of time (trend analysis); and, finally, comparative analyses of similarities and differ-ences in allocations of time for various activities in different countries and cultures (comparative or cross-cultural analysis).

However, some researchers point out that time-budget research has some important deficiencies as well. Charges against time-budget research can be summarized in three major points.

1. The failure of recall typical of the "activity list" studies also affects time-budget studies. Presumably, respondents fail to recall details of their present or past-day behaviour. It is said, for example, that they typically forget to report activities such as being on the telephone, as well as other "in between" or "filler" activities.

2. The second criticism concerns lack of qualitative information, that is, information about the meanings and motivations of human behaviour, in most time-budget studies. Allegedly, while time-budget research tells us what people do in their time, it does not tell us why they do it and what meaning they attach to what they are doing. As a result, much time-budget research is descriptive rather than interpretative.

3. Finally, some critics point to the lack of consensus and a certain arbi-trariness in the classifications of activities used by time-budget researchers. It is said that respondents vary considerably in how they label essentially the same activities, and leave researchers who code their behaviour at a loss as to how to define this behaviour or how to group various activities into universally acceptable larger categories.

How valid are these criticisms?

It appears that some criticism aimed at time-budget research is misdirected. It attacks deficiencies typical of the earlier and less sophisticated time-budget studies while overlooking new developments in time-budget research.

It is, for example, somewhat unfair to accuse time-budget research of descriptive quantophrenia and lack of interest in qualitative aspects of human behaviour. Most large-scale time-budget surveys conducted recently in different countries contain, apart from traditional time-diary questions, numerous questions eliciting information about respondents' attitudinal predispositions, as well as relationships between human behaviour and selected attitudes, such as satisfaction with participation in various activities.

Nor does the alleged "failure of recall" prevent relatively accurate reporting of respondents' involvement in major activities. Detailed observation studies as well as the so-called beeper research, of which we will speak later, indicate that, in general, time-diaries provide a reasonably objective picture of the sequence and duration of human behaviour.

However, at least two major issues remain open to debate and represent serious methodological challenges to time-budget research.

The first of these issues concerns the classification of daily activities in time-budget studies. How comprehensive and functional are the categories of activities we use in time-budget studies, and what rationale except for tradition and convenience is there for classifying various activities the way we do?

The second issue concerns the ability of time-budget research to examine daily activities as a sequence of structured and purposeful experiences rather than as an aggregation of time spent in various activities.

To put it somewhat differently, questions which may not yet have been answered by time-budget researchers are: How do we define the principal unit of the time-budget analysis, namely the activity? And how do we reconstruct the patterns of daily life as a structured sequence of meaningful and purposeful behaviour? I will address each one of these issues in somewhat greater detail.

The question of why we classify daily activities the way we do was raised some time ago by F. S. Chapin in his book *Human Activity Patterns in the City*. Chapin says in this book, among other things:

An activity has a number of properties. It has a duration, a position in time, a place in a sequence of events, and fixed location or a path in space. The activity may involve only the subject whose actions are being reported, or the activity may be shared with others. An activity has a *purpose or character* [emphasis added] which can be used in establishing the taxonomy of activities in the classification system being used.[3]

Having said this, Chapin recognizes, however, the ambiguity of most definitions and classifications of activities in the actual research practice.

An activity class, he suggests, might be simply shopping. It might, however, also be (1) driving from home to the shopping centre, (2) buying groceries, and (3) driving home again. Further on, the same activity may be classified in an even more detailed way, as (1) driving from one's home to the shopping centre, (2) hunting for a parking space, (3) parking the car, (4) walking from the parking lot to the supermarket, (5) picking up a cart, walking the aisles, and selecting grocery items, (6) going through the check-out and paying the cashier, (7) carrying the groceries to the parking lot, (8) driving home, (9) carrying the grocery bags into the kitchen, and (10) putting the groceries away.

Chapin states correctly that the choice of one of the three classifica-tions of activities depends largely on the purpose of the investigation. A concern with shopping as a phenomenon of our *culture* may be well served by the first and broadest definition. A concern with *public trans-portation planning* may benefit from the second classification. Finally, a concern with the *organization and efficiency of the supermarket opera-tion* can make use of the third, most detailed classification.

The questions that most researchers have to address when they at-tempt to classify daily behaviour are essentially twofold. First, what are the specific goals that the researcher is setting and, accordingly, what classification of activities will be optimal for the chosen purpose? Second, activities are defined by a number of important structural and contextual factors, such as personal, bio-physiological, and socio-cultural function; social "morphology" or structure of the activity (i.e., patterns, rules, norms, and regulations typical of the activity); place or location; social context (i.e., with whom the activity is typically performed); instrumentation (i.e., what tools or equipment are used in connection with the activity); and attitudinal context. While all of these factors have to be considered in defining the activity, it is the first two, function and structure (morphology), that are probably most important for any univer-sally acceptable classification.

Methodologically, there are two major avenues open to researchers in arriving at a classification of activities suited to a given research project. The first of these involves a *conceptual* classification of activities based on their functional, structural, and other attributes within a given cultural context, as well as the operational goal of the researcher. The second uses *statistical* analyses, such as factor analysis or cluster analysis, to cluster various activities that have some common properties. Although some researchers view these two approaches as contradictory or mutually exclusive, for all practical purposes they may be complementary. Briefly stated, it appears that some general conceptual or functional classification of daily activities is both needed and practical. In fact, many of the existing time-budget classifications of daily activities impli- citly recognize functional distinctions between economically motivated behaviour (work for pay), biologically or physiologically determined behaviour (sleep, eating, personal hygiene), and family-role-oriented and household-maintenance activities (child care, house chores).

The issue becomes, however, more complex when we examine that part of daily human behaviour which is traditionally defined as leisure or discretionary time.

It is not easy to single out *one* particular function or need underlying all leisure activities. The principal criterion for defining leisure is often a "negative" one, that is, that part of the day which is *not* occupied by gainful employment or physiological or other needs. Most researchers agree that leisure activities serve a number of personal and social func- tions, such as self-actualization, rest/respite, spiritual renewal, social lubricant/entertainment, and social integration.[4]

Since a universally acceptable functional grouping of leisure activities seems to be rather difficult to arrive at, it may be advisable to make use of statistical analyses, such as factor, cluster, or discriminant analyses, to establish some preliminary groupings of leisure activities based on their behavioural clustering or substitutability.

The study of human behaviour as a structured sequence of experi- ences rather than a proportionate distribution of time between activities, can benefit from the so-called beeper technique recently introduced into the studies of daily life by Professor M. Csikszentmihalyi of the Univer- sity of Chicago. The experiential sampling method, as it is officially called, uses pagers (similar to the ones used by doctors) randomly activa- ted by a central transmitter, to collect detailed information about what members of a surveyed population are doing at a given moment of the day, with whom, and how they feel about this activity (moods, attitudes). The ESM has vastly increased the amount of information available to researchers for the analysis of changing behaviour, moods, feelings, and attitudes of the surveyed population. It allows, among other things, to assess the role of *immediate and circumstantial* meanings of and motiva- tions for human actions.[5]

As opposed to traditional time-budget studies, which reconstruct pat- terns of daily behaviour post factum, and use attitudinal measures inde- pendent of the immediate behavioural context, the ESM studies focus on the *process* of daily behaviour as a set of experiences. The ESM studies have documented, among other things, that much of human behaviour, including leisure behaviour, is highly patterned and, perhaps, less free than we would expect it to be. These studies have also shown that moods associated with different types of activities may vary considerably across different population groups. Thus, perhaps somewhat surprisingly, a study of a group of senior citizens in the Kitchener–Waterloo area established that older male adults experience a considerably greater affective affinity with household duties than female respondents in the same age group. The same study has shown that there is significant difference in experiences of identical activities at different times of the day or or during different days of the week.

To summarize, I suggest that complementing traditional time-budget research with new survey techniques may broaden the scope and increase the analytical penetration of the studies of the uses of time and daily behaviour, by bringing more forcefully into the forefront of this research questions about the functions, the structure, and the meanings of everyday life.

Notes

1. Gerald Gutenschwager, "The Time-Budget-Activity Systems Perspective in Urban Planning and Research," *Journal of the American Institute of Planners* 39 (1973): 378–87.

2. J. P. Robinson and P. E. Converse, "Social Change as Reflected in the Uses of Time," in *The Human Meaning of Social Change*, ed. A. E. Campbell and P. E. Converse (New York: Russell Sage Foundation, 1972), 19.

3. F. Stuart Chapin, Jr., *Human Activity Patterns in the City: Things People Do in Time and Space* (New York: Wiley, 1974), 37.

4. See R. J. Havighurst and K. Feigenbaum, "Leisure and Life-Style," *American Journal of Sociology* 64 (1959): 396–404; R. Meyersohn, "Leisure," in *The Human Meaning of Social Change*, ed. Campbell and Converse; and M. Csikszentmihalyi, *The Value of Leisure: Towards a Systemic Analysis of Leisure Activities* (Waterloo: Otium Publications, 1979).

5. See R. Larson and M. Csikszentmihalyi, "The Experience Sampling Method," in *Naturalistic Approaches to Studying Social Interaction*, ed. H. T. Reis (San Francisco: Jossey-Bass, 1983).

TIME IN ART AND MUSIC

IV

Time and the Drama

RONALD MAVOR

SHAKESPEARE CALLED IT "this bloody tyrant time," and Chekhov regarded it as the one hope for mankind. But those concerned with the drama live in a particular relationship with time. Their art, like music, lives in time. Like music, it has to be recreated by artists in a different age or place, artists with different backgrounds, different experience, different attitudes. This is both its tyranny and its hope.

It is the art of the dramatist to reveal progressively to an audience "what they need to know." The ideal listener—it was a remark of Tovey's about music—should forget nothing that has happened, but know nothing of what is to come. I wonder if conductors live to great ages because of their ability to use time, when they are at work, to the full. The conductor has to live more fully, and more precisely, for the hour-long symphony, than most of us can conceive of. It was, of course, Shaw's dream that some day everyone would live with that intensity through a lifetime. Shakespeare from the sonnets through to *A Winter's Tale* was obsessed with time, to be conquered only by progenity or "this timeless verse." And the plays are saturated with the consciousness of time's tyranny and its brevity. His remarkable contemporary, Raleigh, wrote that

> Even such is Time, that takes in trust
> Our youth, our joys, our all we have,
> And pays us but with earth and dust.[1]

and he lived a full life. The modern Beckett says, "They give birth astride of a grave, the light gleams an instant, then it's night once more."[2]

It is in time that we live, like fish in water and birds in the air. So plays, which are imitations of our actions, are bounded by time. But, because they are art, or artefact, and not real, they can play with time as they play with life.

The neo-classicists believed, wrongly, that play-time and real-time should be the same, and that Aristotle had said so. Happily, Shakespeare knew, or cared for, no such nonsense and bended time, as he bended space and character and history, to his own ends.

And time is not a regular metronome beat.

Brecht has a potent tale of Mr. K. who expected his friend at seven one evening. He waited until eight, then nine, then ten. He thought he might come the next day, but he didn't. A week or two later he called his friend again and arranged another meeting. Weeks, months passed. Whether or not the friend eventually arrived, Mr. K.'s conclusion was that he could easily have coped with the months, and even the weeks. It was the days and the hours that had tortured him.

It's interesting to practise on the piano, say, a Mozart sonata. Once you've got it under your fingers, play it against a metronome. The rhythm of the piece as you have learnt it is in your head, regular, appropriate, moving in a formal pattern. But what, you ask, has happened to the metronome? In the exciting but easy bits it suddenly begins to go slower and slower. In the difficult bits, which seemed to you perfectly in time, it is rushing like a student late for a bus. That clockwork pyramid is watching you. And it is right, and you are wrong. You have been twisting time for your own ends, to disguise your own deficiencies. A little more practice and you can play your sonata in measurable time. Then, but not before, you can twist time for a proper artistic purpose. So Shakespeare.

Harley Granville-Barker, in his Preface to *Hamlet*, gives an example:

[Shakespeare] turns time to dramatic use also, ignores or remarks its passing, and uses clock or calendar or falsifies or neglects them just as it suits him.

The play opens upon the stroke of midnight, an ominous and "dramatic" hour. The first scene is measured out to dawn and gains importance by that. In the second Hamlet's "not two months dead" and "within a month" give past events convincing definition, and his "tonight . . . tonight . . . upon the platform 'twixt eleven and twelve" a specific imminence to what is to come. The second scene upon the platform is also definitely measured out from midnight to near dawn. This framing of the exordium to the tragedy within a precise two nights and a day gives a convincing likeness to the action, and sets its pulse beating rhythmically and arrestingly.

But now the conduct of the action changes, and with this the treatment of time. Hamlet's resolution—we shall soon gather—has paled, his purpose has slackened. He passes hour upon hour pacing the lobbies, reading or lost in thought, oblivious apparently to time's passing, lapsed—he himself supplies the phrase later—"lapsed in time." So Shakespeare also for a while tacitly ignores the calendar. . . .

It is not until later that Shakespeare, by a cunning little stroke, puts himself right—so to speak—with the past. *The Murder of Gonzago* is about to begin when Hamlet says to Ophelia: "look you, how cheerfully my mother looks, and my father died within's two hours," to be answered: "Nay, 'tis twice two months, my lord."

There is the calendar reestablished, unostentatiously, and therefore with no forfeiting of illusion. Yet at that moment we are expectantly attentive, so every word will tell. And it is a stroke of character too. For here is Hamlet, himself so lately roused from his obliviousness, gibing at his mother for hers. But the use of time for current effect has begun again. . . .[3]

Time, Shakespeare seems to imply, is where we live, where we do things. But, between times, we are out of time, "lapsed in time." I cannot resist quoting Philip Larkin, whose poem "Days" expresses, I believe, the same thought:

What are days for?
Days are where we live.
They come, they wake us
Time and time over.
They are to be happy in:
Where can we live but days?

Ah, solving that question
Brings the priest and the doctor
In their long coats
Running over the fields.[4]

But if all we have are days, segments of time, to be happy in, and they are, how is it that the drama seems to offer us something else?

The drama—perhaps all art, but drama more than the others—offers us a perpetual present. Pirandello, in a famous phrase, describes how, no matter how often we open the *Divina Commedia*, "we shall find Francesca alive and confessing to Dante her sweet sin, and if we turn to the passage a hundred thousand times in succession, a hundred thousand times in succession Francesca will speak her words, never repeating them mechanically, but saying them as though each time were the first time, with such living and sudden passion that Dante every time will turn faint. . . ."

And, in the theatre, everything is always happening, "quick now, here, now, always," and as if for the first time. In our long afterwards we can brood on the events, the emotions, lapsed from time, but they have been born of the immediacy of something lived. They have not been reported, or commented upon. The emotions—and the theatre is the theatre of emotions—attach themselves to the incidents, and they do not vanish from the memory. What we remember of those emotion-charged events enriches us. Sure, "Where can we live but days?" but not all our days lay up in store such rich recollections.

The drama strove, from Beaumarchais and Diderot towards the end of the eighteenth century until Ibsen towards the end of the nineteenth, for what was called "realism." The objective portrayal of life as it was really lived by ordinary people like you and me, as free as possible from the manipulation of the writer, was called for, and to some extent achieved. But not, to be honest, by Ibsen and Chekhov. To a really great mind life is too interesting and too complex to be reduced to the daily data of time, place, social context, even psychology. And Ibsen and Chekhov transcended "realism" as a Concorde passes through the sound barrier.

They had to, because we do not, any of us, live within the sociologically quantifiable parameters of the realists. "Where can we live but days?" is a marvellous and potent question, but we do not live only by living. Inert, in a cork-lined room, we can still recreate time past and contemplate time future. And if we do, we find ourselves "lapsed in time" and guided by what Proust called "the only reality that exists for each of us, our own sensitiveness to impressions." And he continues:

Yes, in that sense and that sense only, but it is even more extensive, something we looked at long ago, if we see it again, brings back to us, along with the look we cast upon it, all the images it conveyed to us at that time. This is because things—a book in its red binding, like so many others—as soon as we take conscious notice of them, become something immaterial within us of the same character as all our sensations and preoccupations of that moment and combine indissolubly with them. Some name we read in a book in bygone years, for example, contains among its syllables the strong breeze and brilliant sunshine of the day when we came across it. In the slightest sensation conveyed to us by the most ordinary food—the fragrance of a cup of coffee, for instance—we recapture that vague hope of fair weather which beguiled us so often in the uncertainty of the morning sky when the day was still intact and full. An hour is a vase filled with perfumes, with sounds, with moments, with changing moods and climates. Consequently, that literature which is satisfied to "describe objects," to give merely a miserable listing of lines and surfaces, is the very one which, while styling itself "realist," is the farthest removed from reality, the one that impoverishes and saddens us the most, for it sharply cuts off all communication of our present self with the past, the essence of which was preserved in those objects, or with the future, in which they stimulate us to enjoy the past anew. It is that essence which art worthy of the name must express . . ."[5]

So when Henry Woolf and I read Eliot's "Burnt Norton" on the first evening of the "Time as a Human Resource" conference, we were making a pitch for the art that we have both practised and now attempt to teach. The drama is an art that lives in time. It cannot but be conscious of time, its passing, its transience. But, in its eternal present, it can get a little bit of its own back.

Notes

1. Sir Walter Raleigh, "Even such is Time," in *A Book of English Poetry*, comp. G. B. Harrison (Harmondsworth: Penguin, 1937), 48.
2. Thomas Beckett, *Waiting for Godot* (London: Faber & Faber, 1960), 89.
3. Harley Granville-Barker, *Prefaces to Shakespeare*, vol. 1 (Princeton: Princeton University Press, 1974), 39–41.
4. Philip Larkin, "Days," in *The Whitsun Weddings* (London: Faber & Faber, 1964), 27.
5. Marcel Proust, *Remembrance of Things Past*, vol. 2, *The Past Recaptured*, trans. Frederick A. Blossom (New York: Random House, 1932), 1005.

Of Time in Art and Nature

ELI BORNSTEIN

The illimitable, silent, never-resting thing called time, rolling,
rushing on, swift, silent, like an all-embracing ocean tide, on
which we and all the universe swim like exhalations, like
apparitions which are, and then are not: this is forever very
literally a miracle; a thing to strike us dumb.

Thomas Carlyle

COMPARE A MAN'S life of seventy years to the age of the earth,
estimated at four and one half billion years. Civilization hardly
occupies a minute fraction of the earth's history. Time, its running out,
plagues all mortals, but perhaps none more keenly than the artist. Will
he "reach the promised land," as Cézanne expressed this anxiety? Artists
work at tasks they often know will never be completed and work as if
they will live forever, despite their knowledge to the contrary. While
seeming to ignore or refusing to be hopelessly driven by time's relentless
passing, their only means of not being completely overwhelmed by time
is their art, which demands its own full time for realization. For time
remains the greatest force with which the artist must cope. In a very real
sense, *time is the ultimate medium of all the arts.* It is with time itself
that all art struggles to shape its images, its forms and structures, its
songs and poems. Art in turn gives shape to time.

It has often been suggested that art is a human means of defying
death, and it is not difficult to sustain this comforting belief, however

---

This article is partly excerpted from "Art Towards Nature," originally published
in *The Structurist* 15/16 (1975-76), 142-55, which dealt with space as well as
time. It has been revised and adapted by the author.

exaggerated it may prove. Artists strive for the strength and time within a lifespan to pursue their creative intentions to a significant level of accomplishment; they strive at the same time for any measure of genuine sympathy or recognition of their work within, and they hope beyond, their lifetime. These pursuits, as we shall see, are often in conflict. The endless sea of time in which the artist, along with all other living creatures, floats momentarily promises little beyond eventual oblivion. Nevertheless, the creative drive persists and endures in human nature as a counterpart to that same larger force in nature—in every seed germ—for endless creation.

The perception of time, our consciousness of time's passing—which is the most inexplicable, elusive, and awesome phenomenon of our existence—the awareness of our own aging, the aging of culture and of the entire universe, is a capacity unique to man alone. The preeminent consciousness of the texture of time covers our lives like a mantle from birth to death, and we do not know whether we pass through time or time passes through us, taking with it finally our lives. But we do know that time is the ultimate processor in art as well as life. Time alone sifts, selects and discards, modifies, confirms or perpetuates all values, be they of flesh or paint. All is subject to the grinding wheels of time's never-ending mill of creation/destruction/creation.

One of the primary temporal concerns of artists is their mortality—how much time they have to work and how they use it. A second concern is the timeliness of their work and vision—their relationship to present and future time. Timeliness in art refers to new creations being ready for their time, or, perhaps more correctly, the time being ready for their appearance. The readiness or coincidence of temporal events that welcome certain developments, an art whose "time has come," or events that block or postpone or circumvent others, an art "ahead of its time," are notions commonly linked to "fate," "chance," or "destiny." Such references are to the time-lags in a culture—the more complex the culture, the more complex and varied levels of what we call culture or cultural synchronous are rarely synchronous or concurrent at all levels. Where culture is concerned, time is often out of joint. Life-span and art-span seldom coincide.

An important aspect of time in art is the fact that most genuinely new art comes into existence without a pre-existing art of seeing prepared for it. "Seeing, of course, is also an art," said Lissitzky, and the cultivation of this art of seeing requires considerable time. Learning to see can be a slow process, and the full seeing of new art has often taken generations, if not centuries. The cultivation of the large audiences that great art is said to require is contrary to Cézanne's statement that "art only addresses itself to an excessively small number of individuals." Certain kinds of art cannot be recognized instantaneously because of culture-lag; looking without seeing, unbelievable in retrospect, can prevail. Through the passage of time all human perceptions are modified—maturing or enlarging through reflection or experience—so that encounters with the same art at different times result in different reactions. Such changes in perception are sometimes mistakenly attributed to the work, whereas time itself continually alters our vision.

Certain times can be cruel to certain artists. The cruelty is in the neglect. During such artists' lifetimes, the value of their work may be ignored while the most incredible banalities imaginable are celebrated. Such "ill-fated" artists, whose work or vision finds little or no contemporary interest, are "unlucky" enough to find their work and themselves "ill timed" or "out of step." Although this occurs repeatedly, it is still something of a romantic myth to believe that eventually such neglect will always be acknowledged and posthumously corrected. Alternatively, there are artists who achieve acceptance and celebrity for the wrong reasons, and others who are consumed by idolatry and suffer the cruelty of over-exposure. Théophile Gautier observed in the nineteenth century, "To be of one's own time—nothing seems easier and nothing is more difficult. One can go straight through one's age without seeing it, and this is what has happened to many eminent minds." This is no less—and perhaps more—true in our own century. Fashion is the enemy of art. Its currency colours our senses and obscures the perception of our own age.

Is our own time conducive to the growth and development of art? Or are we living in a time whose complexity and turbulent character is such that, while seeming to be open and accepting to every and all art acti-vities, it is actually indifferent to the significance—values or lack of values—of all art? Never before has art changed so rapidly in so short a period of time. This acceleration of change has left all current activity tentative in its appearance and momentary in its impact.

Hasty anticipations of the future are at best conjectures and involve considerable unverifiable speculation. We require a levelling-off period, a stabilization of culture, and of art in particular. We need time to fully absorb and understand our recent past, to evaluate the influence of all the significant changes that have taken place. Without this necessary time, all the varieties of directions in art become almost indistinguishable from each other through their sheer volume and are quickly displaced by more of the same kinds of changes. Perhaps our time really requires, more than anything, a moratorium on art—a suspension of all art, and a time to fully acknowledge and harvest the seeds of modern art first planted by the pioneer movements of the nineteenth and twentieth centuries. Such voluntary suspension—or the consensus required for it—is of course impossible to imagine. We are thrown back upon the mill wheels of time itself to eventually resolve and silence time's current clamour.

Timeliness inevitably raises the entire subject of history, its epochs, cycles, or periods. The question of how and why art changes involves problems of distinguishing origins, movements, styles, and fashions. For our purpose here a sampling of some of the more influential preoccupa-tions with time in art in the recent past will serve to indicate something of their different involvements with time. Impressionism, Cubism, and photography are ready examples of how the element of time has func-tioned in art.

Monet's pursuit of instantaneity, the total colour-light image of the instant, and his concern with the changing moments of time or seasons upon the same subject, introduced the element of time into painting in a more concerted manner than ever before. Although impressions of momentary landscape phenomena occurred long before in numerous other painters' work, time had never taken on such deliberate importance. The subjects of Monet's painting were not only colour and light but time. His various series, such as the *Haystacks*, *Poplars*, *Rouen Cathedral*, and *Waterlilies*, demonstrate this. The importance that he himself attached to each series being seen all together—and which was largely, and shock-ingly, ignored, even to our present day—verifies the time-centred orienta-tion that dominated so much of his work. The numerous series do not simply represent the same subject at different times, but a greater grasp on the reality of time than any single painting could possibly convey. His *Nymphéas*, along with the over 230 paintings of the same subject, were painted from 1899 until his death in 1926, and represent his most ambi-tious statement of this concern with the continuum of time. Georges Clemenceau, Monet's close friend, described this work well:

With twenty pictures . . . the painter has given us the feeling that he could have . . . made fifty, one hundred, one thousand, as many as the seconds in his life. . . As long as the sun shall shine . . . there will be as many ways of being . . . as man can make divisions of time. . . . Monet's eye, the eye of a precursor, is ahead of ours, and guides us in the visual evolution which renders more penetrating and more subtle our perception of the universe.

Cubism, especially in its early days, was yet another phenomenon in art preoccupied with aspects of time. The concepts of multiple fragmented

This obviously refers to the fragmentation, speed, simultaneity, com-pression, mosaic, and disjointed character of modern times.

The displacement of the single, static, Renaissance point of view by the multiple, simultaneous, and relativistic viewpoint, which nineteenth- and twentieth-century science and technology bestowed upon us, has affected all the arts as well as life itself. The disintegration of the solidly rendered object was already operative in the earliest Impressionist paint-ings of Boudin, and the dynamic shifting viewpoint in the later paintings of Cézanne preceded Cubism. The emergence of Cubism was the result of a multiplicity of simultaneous influences, not least of which was the age itself and its new perceptions of time. (It is interesting to note that Cubism's earlier and more vital contributions took place about fifteen years before Monet's *Nymphéas* series was completed.) Analytical Cubist paintings and Cubist collages tried to represent multi-dimensional objects from multiple viewpoints, or movement itself in multiple moments of time on a two-dimensional surface. The contradiction and conflict of media between painting and sculpture notwithstanding, its influence was wide-spread, including Italian Futurism, Russian Cubo-Futurism, and beyond.

Photography, our third sample, although some hundred and fifty years old, is of special interest in its relationship to Cubism and its far-reaching involvements with time. It is not difficult to see the obvious influence on a variety of Cubist painters in Jules Étienne Marey's chrono-photographs or multiple exposures in a single photograph of men in action (1880s). The early cinema or silent motion pictures preceded and were contemporaneous with Cubism, and their influence upon Cubism is also considerable. The appearance of Charlie Chaplin's image in the work of several Cubist painters is indicative, if not symbolic, of the close relationship between Cubism and the film media. The camera has often been referred to as our "time machine" because of its incredible capacity to capture time, to stop time's moving image and preserve it. Through photography images of the past are recorded forever as visual history. The past is recaptured and we are provided with the "miraculous" means of travelling, almost instantaneously, across time as well as space. Snapshots of our dead grandparents or parents, or of when we were young, astonish us with the impact of a leap through time. In the movie theatre or on the television screen, past and present images of all things visible to man in endless flow in successive movements through time.

While the affairs of men and art may wax and wane with erratic uncertainty, the seasons and cycles in nature occur and recur with eternal regularity long before and long after each person's brief lifespan. Our own living bodies share something of this process with all of nature in the functions of our heartbeats, breathing, blood and air circulation, and so forth. Time in nature as process is ever changing and eternal. All of nature's rhythms, from the migration of birds and insects to the life cycles of mammals and the periodic movements of our solar system, are functions of time. Time is the essence of evolution and the fundamental ingredient of all maturation, growth, and development in nature. All organic forms and processes in nature seem connected to a biological or cosmic clock that strikes its hours or light-years of duration and signals the changes that all forms undergo. Regard the bare earnestness of a tree in fall and its nascent leaf bud. Having lost its leaf close-by, it is already formed to wait out the long cold winter in its hard shell before it stirs again. In the spring it will break open its streamlined shelter and come forth as a fresh new leaf. It is inconceivable that art is entirely unrelated to time in nature. Although not easily discernible, especially during any single lifespan, art involves its own periods of maturation, of growth and decline and renewal.

Time in art has only barely begun to approach the character or magnitude of time in nature. From the earliest mimetic descriptions to the more sophisticated re-creations of aspects of nature's time (and space), art gradually moved from representation to transformation to translation and then to abstraction-creation-invention. Photography and the entire film media replaced the mimetic functions and involvements with which art preoccupied itself for centuries. Photography, cinema, and television in light, colour, sound, and motion could perform these functions far beyond the limited capacities of the traditional visual arts media, and hastened the liberation of these media towards the discovery of their own unique potentials. Monet, Cézanne, and all the pioneers of modern art formed the foundation of the new explorations that were launched. Abstraction was the inevitable result of pursuing each medium's own inherent capacities and appeared as the simultaneous and independent discovery of numerous, often widely dispersed, artists. To some, abstraction and its immediate implications seemed like the end of art; by others, it was recognized as a new beginning.

Since the turn of this century art has struggled with the difficult problems and implications first raised by the appearance of abstract art.

The conflicts over abstract art persist and are not yet fully resolved. Abstract Cubism, as exemplified by Russian Suprematism and Dutch de Stijl, carried the explorations of time and space in art further, with the Suprematists/Constructivists transforming the very medium of painting from the Cubist-collage construction into the abstract constructed relief. Tatlin's abstract relief-constructions and those of his colleagues were the most significant step leading abstract painting from pictorial space out into real space involving time. Real time, as well as real space/colour/structure, now became the elements with which artists could create in a manner not mimetically descriptive or representative, but paralleling the use of these same elements in nature.

Can an abstract art serve to express and communicate visually the fullest dimensions of the human spirit? Can it avoid mere pattern making or mere decoration? Can the abstract-real elements of light/colour/space/structure transcend their generalness, their pureness, their neutralness to become tangible creations of human concern that speak to and stir us as creatures of time? The human spirit reflects nature as an integral part of itself. "The landscape thinks itself in me, and I am its consciousness," said Cézanne. Abstract art cannot communicate and express all aspects of human concern. Over the last half-century, abstract constructed spatial art has undoubtedly moved precariously out onto narrower and perhaps heightened levels of creation and expression as a valiant affirmation and pursuit of new affinities between man and nature. Can the abstract constructed relief eventually evolve towards a use of more fluid, flowing forms, more fluxive, supple structures and processes, towards the organic mobility of nature? This fluid and flowing quality of nature is best approached in the media of music and the cinema. As time-arts, music in an aural sense, and cinema in both a visual and aural sense, are closest to the time-flowing qualities of nature. Some artists believe in, and are committed to, the continued exploration and development of vision—how we see nature and how we see art. They work towards the creation of a tangible art that can envelope one with the same emotion visually and spatially that music—most abstract of all the arts—evokes aurally and temporally.

Time in art, the actual parallel movement of art towards fuller involvement with this element in nature, remains only a direction towards which art aspires and slowly moves. This unique affinity is more percep-tible in larger spans of human history. It is a journey forever half-way as our awareness of nature itself expands and deepens, yet it is the only foothold that art has on the future in its pursuit of real time.

Michael Praetorius on Time and Tempo

ROBERT SOLEM

TIME IS TRULY a human resource for the musician who uses it in special ways to produce sound in time. Two of the published works of Michael Praetorius (1569/73–1621)—the *Syntagma musicum*, Volume 3, and a collection of compositions called *Polyhymnia caduceatrix et panegyrica*—provide an opportunity to compare our own perceptions of musical time with those of a gifted seventeenth-century theorist and composer.

The *Syntagma musicum* (1619) is a rich source of information about the music and the musical practices of that day. At the end of a chapter devoted to a description of his method of numbering the voice parts in the *Polyhymnia* (Chapter X, Part II), Praetorius adds this intriguing note[1] about a scheme he has devised to enable a musician to calculate quickly how long each of these compositions would last if performed at a moderate tempo:

At this point I should also like to recall that I have indicated at the end of each *Generalbass* part how many *tempora* each *song*, or each part of a song, contains. For it is necessary to know how many *tempora* can be performed in a quarter hour, when one holds to a moderate *Tact*: namely:

$$
\left.\begin{array}{l}
80 \\
160 \\
320 \\
640
\end{array}\right\}
\text{*tempora* in}
\left.
\begin{array}{l}
\text{a}
\end{array}\right\}
\begin{array}{l}
\left.\begin{array}{l}\text{half}\\ \text{whole}\end{array}\right\}\text{quarter hour} \\[1em]
\left.\begin{array}{l}\text{half}\\ \text{whole}\end{array}\right\}\text{hour}
\end{array}
$$

He goes on to explain that he devised this scheme to make it easier to determine the duration of each piece so that it might be fitted into a church service without delaying the start of the sermon or other parts of the service.

Praetorius's tempora-scheme deals with duration (a practical matter of timing) rather than tempo (a musical matter of pacing). Because of this, he can express the time as parts of an hour. Assuming that Praetorius's hour was not significantly different from our own, we are able to calculate the durations intended by the composer for each of his *Polyhymnia* by using the ratio of

80 tempora : 7.5 minutes : : n tempora : x minutes

where *n* equals the number of tempora given for the piece in question and *x* equals the duration of the piece if taken at Praetorius's "moderate" (*mittelmässigen*) pace. For example, we find the following note at the end of the bass part of *Nun freut euch lieben Christen gemein*—"*32 Tempora sind 64 Tact*," that is, 32 tempora are 64 tact. Using the value of 32 for *n* results in the value of *x* being three minutes. Apparently Praetorius intended that this composition should take three minutes if performed at his moderate tempo.

When one looks at this piece as it appears in Wilibald Gurlitt's modern edition (Volume 17 of the *Gesamtausgabe*), one sees the sign "C" followed by 32 "measures," each containing modern note-forms equivalent to a breve, that is, 2 whole notes = 4 half notes = 8 quarter notes, and so on. Praetorius evidently considered each of the "tempora" to equal the value of one breve. The reference to "tact" need not detain us, except to recall that "tactus" referred to the motions used to indicate the pace of specified note-forms and to note that Praetorius calls for two tactus to be used for each of the tempora, a matter of interest to conductors.

If one merely looks at the music it seems quite straightforward; however, if one sets out to perform the music at what we would consider a moderate tempo, we discover that our performance takes significantly less time than the three minutes required for 32 tempora at a moderate tempo. Our performances of other *Polyhymnia* produce a similar result. All are significantly shorter than the tempora scheme calculations would indicate.

In order to perform these compositions at such a tempo that they last as long as Praetorius indicated they should, we arrive at the very problem his tempora-scheme was designed to solve. We have discovered that our "moderate" tempo is faster than Praetorius's; we know we have to use a slower tempo. But how much slower? We might answer this question by repeatedly performing the piece until we found a tempo that would yield the prescribed duration, or we might turn the tempora-scheme about so that it would indicate how many breves would be

SOLEM / Time in Music   267

performed in one minute. We could then set our metronome to that number and proceed.

Using Praetorius's values of 80 tempora (breves) = 7.5 minutes, we calculate the number of breves per minute by dividing 80 by 7.5. We go on to calculate the number of semibreves, minims, semiminims, and fusas (assuming for the moment that one breve equals two semibreves, one semibreve equals two minims, and so on) with the following results:

10 2/3 breves per minute,	i.e., M.M. [𝅜]	=	10.67
or 21 1/3 semibreves per minute,	i.e., M.M. [𝅝]	=	21.33
or 42 2/3 minims per minute,	i.e., M.M. [𝅗𝅥]	=	42.67
or 85 1/3 semiminims per minute,	i.e., M.M. [𝅘𝅥]	=	85.33
or 170 2/3 fusas per minute,	i.e., M.M. [𝅘𝅥𝅮]	=	170.67

Of these values, only M.M. 85.33 would be considered a "moderate" tempo in our day. M.M. 42.67 would be considered "slow" and M.M. 170.67 would be considered "fast."

We have not considered Praetorius's use of proportions (*tripla* and *sesquialtera*) or his use of the Italian terms *lento* and *presto* in some of the *Polyhymnia*. Nor have we made reference to statements dealing with tempo that can be found at other places and in different contexts in his *Syntagma musicum*, Volume 3. We have not considered these because Praetorius himself did not. He does not qualify his scheme in any way except to state that it applies specifically to his *Polyhymnia*.

The tempora totals he gives in the *Polyhymnia* do not appear to be affected by his use of proportions, various metric signs, or even by the appearance of the Italian tempo words *lento* and *presto*. Since the tempora-scheme refers to duration rather than to tempo, it is reasonable to assume that if one portion of a song were taken faster, another portion would have to be taken proportionately slower to compensate for the change of tempo.

There is another problem to be considered, arising out of Praetorius's statement that 32 tempora equal 64 tact. If we accept M.M. 85 as our moderate tempo, it would have applied to Praetorius's semiminim [𝅘𝅥], which looks like our modern quarter-note, resulting in M.M. [𝅘𝅥] or [𝅘𝅥] = 85. If conducting quarter-notes, the conductor would be obliged to indicate 8 beats per measure, resulting in a total of 256 beats. But Praetorius indicates that these 32 measures would equal 64 tact, which would total a maximum of 128 movements (64 down and 64 up). If the conductor tries to solve that problem by conducting Praetorius's minim [𝅗𝅥], which looks like our modern half-note, he would indicate

128 beats (4 half-notes × 32 measures), but the piece would either take half as long as Praetorius intended, or the conductor would have to adopt a tempo of M.M. 42, in which case the duration would be correct but the tempo would seem "slow" rather than "moderate."

The problem will not go away. It seems that Praetorius's "moderate" pace has become our "slow" tempo.

Having discovered that our choice of tempi for Praetorius's *Poly-hymnia* was invariably too fast, we extended our inquiry to colleagues who are experienced in conducting early music. We asked them to exa-mine the score of *Nun freut euch* and to conduct it using what they con-sidered a moderate tempo. The durations of these informal performances varied somewhat, but all were significantly shorter.

It was decided to extend our inquiry further to some of the available recorded performances of the *Polyhymnia*. It should be noted that the sole criterion for inclusion was local availability; no attempt was made to include or exclude any particular recording. Fortunately, the recorded performances available for this study are directed by the distinguished conductors Wilhelm Ehmann and David Munrow, both of whom are well known for their expertise with early music performance. A third record-ing is to be found in *The History of Music in Sound* series (Vol. 4).

Our procedure was simple. It involved a calculation of duration using Praetorius's tempora-scheme, a timing of the recorded performance, and a comparison of the difference between these two values. The results giv-en below include the title of the piece, the number of tempora according to Praetorius, the duration calculated from that number, the name of the conductor, the timing of the recorded performance, and the difference between calculated duration and record timing expressed both in minutes and seconds and as a percentage of the calculated duration.[2]

1. *Puer Natus*, Part I

Praetorius	59 Tempora =	5' 32"	
Ehmann	Timing	4' 34"	
Difference		0' 58" shorter	17.5% shorter

2. *Puer Natus*, Part II

Praetorius	38 Tempora =	3' 34"	
Ehmann	Timing	2' 56"	
Difference		0' 38" shorter	17.7% shorter

3. *Vom Himmel hoch*, Part I

Praetorius	65 Tempora =	6' 06"	
Ehmann	Timing	4' 36"	
Difference		1' 30" shorter	24.6% shorter

4. Omnis mundus

Praetorius	92 Tempora =	8' 38"
Ehmann	Timing	6' 21"
Difference	2' 17" shorter	26.5% shorter

5. Als der gütige Gott, Part I

Praetorius	69 Tempora =	6' 28"
Ehmann	Timing	4' 47"
Difference	1' 41" shorter	26.0% shorter

6. Als der gütige Gott, Part II

Praetorius	43 Tempora =	4' 02"
Ehmann	Timing	3' 17"
Difference	0' 45" shorter	18.6% shorter

7. Als der gütige Gott, Part III

Praetorius	40 Tempora	3' 45"
Ehmann	Timing	2' 54"
Difference	0' 51" shorter	22.7% shorter

8. Als der gütige Gott, Part IV (A)

Praetorius	55 Tempora =	5' 09"
Ehmann	Timing	4' 05"
Difference	1' 04" shorter	20.7% shorter

9. Als der gütige Gott, Part IV (B)

Praetorius	26 Tempora =	2' 26"
Ehmann	Timing	1' 58"
Difference	0' 28" shorter	19.2% shorter

10. Erhalt uns Herr, Part I

Praetorius	98 Tempora =	9' 11"
Munrow	Timing	4' 07"
Difference	5' 04" shorter	55.2% shorter

11. Erhalt uns Herr, Part II

Praetorius	75 Tempora =	7' 02"
Munrow	Timing	3' 56"
Difference	3' 06" shorter	55.9% shorter

12. Wie schön leuchtet

Praetorius	79 Tempora =	7' 24"
HMS, Vol. 4	Timing	4' 23"
Difference	3' 01" shorter	59.2% shorter

Praetorius's tempora-scheme provides quite precise values to enable us to calculate his intended performance times for each of the *Polyhymnia*. Twentieth-century performance times of the *Polyhymnia* are all significantly shorter than intended by the composer and, therefore, the tempi selected must also be significantly faster than he intended. Conductors wishing to perform Praetorius's *Polyhymnia* at the composer's recommended "moderate" pace would have to consider the quarter note (assuming no reduction of note-values) to represent the beat and adopt a tempo of M.M. 85 for that note-value. Since our own performance times tend to be too short, it seems that our instinct for, and ideas about, tempi do not accurately reflect those of the composer. Praetorius's "moderate" tempo has clearly become our "slow" tempo. Presumably our "moderate" tempo would have seemed "fast" to Praetorius.

Further studies might determine whether this difference in perception is limited to Praetorius, his *Polyhymnia*, and the recordings used for this study, or whether it is part of a more general and fundamental shift in time-perception between the seventeenth century and our own.

Notes

1. Michael Praetorius, *Syntagma musicum*, vol. 3 of *Termini musici* (Wolfenbüttel, 1619). Facsimile edition edited by Wilibald Gurlitt, *Documenta Musicologica* (Cassel, Germany: Baerenreiter, 1958), 87–88; and as translated by Hans Lampl, "A Translation of Syntagma Musicum III by Michael Praetorius," Ph.D. diss., University of Southern California, 1957, 149.

2. Michael Praetorius, *Polyhymnia caduceatrix et panegyrica (1619)*, in *Gesamtausgabe der Musikalischen Werke von Michael Praetorius*, ed. Wilibald Gurlitt, vol. 17 (Wolfenbüttel: Möseler Verlag, n.d.). The timings are based upon the following recordings: Wilhelm Ehmann, "Polyhymnia caduceatrix et panegyrica: Christmas Music," Westphalian Ensemble, Nonesuch 71242; David Munrow, "Music of Praetorius," Early Music Consort, Angel S-37091; and *The History of Music in Sound*, Vol. 4, E.M.I. Records.

FOCUS ON THE FUTURE

Emergent Research

Issues

V

Time and the Power of Law

DONNA GRESCHNER

T HIS MULTI-DISCIPLINARY VOLUME has been most stimulating, pointing out many directions for thought and research in my discipline, law. I will mention only two general research areas very briefly and in broad terms.

Lawyers are very powerful. They rarely acknowledge their power; indeed, most would likely deny it. Maybe it disturbs the spirit late at night to face up to one's power over the lives of other individuals. But this plain truth is undeniable. Dr. Bernard Dickens directly referred to one instance of this power in his paper. As he told us, judges—who are just a group of lawyers—decide in many situations who is to live or die: an awesome power, one that clearly requires strong justification and careful application. Moreover, besides being occasionally God-like, the power of the law is pervasive. Virtually every human activity discussed during the conference on time takes place within a framework of legal rules.

When I was asked to participate in this volume, I asked myself what demarcated law from other disciplines. Given that legal rules permeate all facets of life, is there any area in which the law, and its practitioners, lawyers, have made a special contribution or may claim to have unique expertise? One answer many legal thinkers would likely give is "procedure." Over the centuries, lawyers have developed sets of procedures that people use in settling disputes. These procedures are the steps that must be followed to resolve types of disagreements. They are designed ideally to protect persons from the exercise of abusive power by others, and to arrive at fair substantive results.

The concern of the law for procedure is perhaps best encapsulated in the ringing pair of words, "natural justice." If you asked a person on the street what "natural justice" means, you likely would receive, I believe, an answer that involved substantive moral or political principles. Perhaps

274 EMERGENT RESEARCH ISSUES

some people would equate natural justice with *a priori* ethical standards or religious tenets. Others might reply that the phrase delineates the minimum substantive criterion of a just society. In law, however, "natural justice" means fair procedure. Its requirements, binding on most legal decision-makers, involve only the process of arriving at a result, not the substance.

A concern for procedure is not wrong-headed. To the contrary, due process is often of the utmost value in protecting people from coercion and arbitrary action. As Justice Frankfurter of the American Supreme Court once said, "The history of freedom is, in no small measure, the history of procedure." No one can denigrate, for example, the importance of criminal procedure in checking the possible abuse of the state's police powers. Persons accused of crimes require fair procedures.

But procedures take *time*. By definition, a process requires time's passage. It is not the time of lawyers that interests me today. For one thing, to apply Dr. Margrit Eichler's dictum, a lawyer's time is money. Indeed, lawyers are usually paid in terms of time spent on a case. Rather, it is the time of the people that lawyers deal with, the clients, that demands close attention. People come to lawyers for assistance when they are in stressful, disruptive situations that they want resolved. Often, the law is the *only* method of resolution. The lengthy time it takes to deal with the problems frequently exacerbates the stress and lessens these people's enjoyment of their lives. As Dr. Eichler told us, the longer you can make people wait for you, the more power you have. With cases taking years to complete, the law, we see, is an extremely powerful master. It is not uncommon, though fortunately still not typical, for some disputes to grind through legal processes for over ten years before they are finally resolved. The ghosts of Dickens's *Bleak House* rattle again their chains. Lawyers recognize that time is of the essence. One very old legal maxim reflects this concern: Justice delayed is justice denied. Our new Charter of Rights and Freedoms also speaks to the importance of speediness in one area, by prohibiting unreasonable delay in bringing accused persons to trial.

I do think, however, that lawyers must constantly evaluate the procedures implanted throughout the legal system. We must be convinced that the procedures are truly valuable. The reassessment of procedures is a research direction indicated by the conference. We should not fritter away the precious time of others by pointless or marginally useful procedures. The second research direction I will mention stems from the provocative paper given by Dr. Taylor at the beginning of this conference and the other papers presented by eminent philosophers such as Dr. Singer.

GRESCHNER / *Time and Law's Power*

If creativity gives life fulfillment and time its meaning, or if we accept some other definition of fulfillment, then we as lawyers should ensure that opportunities for fulfillment are available to all people. I think it impossible, or at least very onerous, for someone burdened with poverty to devote time to creative endeavours. The time of too many persons is spent on survival, not fulfillment. Lawyers are overly concerned with *natural* justice at the expense of *distributive* justice. Surely the allocation of benefits and burdens within our society is of fundamental importance. It should be of especial concern to lawyers for two reasons.

First, the distribution is implied or supported by laws, and it is lawyers who maintain and operate that legal system. Our maintenance lawyers who maintain and operate that legal system should not be unreflective. Second, lawyers do not merely apply laws and work with them, they also help create laws. Politicians are often lawyers; lawyers influence laws through drafting, lobbying, and argument; and judges have law-making as well as law-applying power.

Here again we see the power of lawyers. We as lawyers need to think about, firstly, the *quantity* of time that the *legal process* eats up, and secondly, the *quality* of time and hence life reflected or permitted in the *substance of the laws.*

The Creative Imagination

R. L. CALDER

NEARLY ALL OF the papers presented at the conference on time and
most of those presented in this volume explore the problems of
time in a practical sense. They examine the ethical questions posed by
profound changes to the average lifespan and by growing awareness of
the quality and value of time for various segments of society—especially
women and Native Canadians. Clearly, the recent surge of research activity in these areas will continue as medical and social scientists respond
to technical and physical alterations to the human condition. Much of the
research, moreover, will itself create further changes, perhaps at an
accelerating rate.

Any attempt to understand the implications of our evolving use of
time or our developing perceptions of it, however, will be insufficient
without the special insight offered by art. One of the major functions of
the artist has always been to interpret in human terms the effects of new
knowledge and advancing technology. Thus, while it is essential to produce the studies, the papers, and the projections of the scientists, it is the
creative imagination that will make the average person *feel* their impact.
Time has always fascinated artists, from the earliest classical poets
and dramatists to the most contemporary writers, painters, and musicians, and their representation of it naturally reflects its impact on the
human life of their times. Since for most of human existence the human
lifespan has been precarious and short in the face of disease, the natural
elements, and human conflict, the most common treatment of time has
developed the *carpe diem* theme. The Roman poet Catullus, who himself
died at thirty, wrote in the century before Christ of the brevity of life
and the permanence of death:

> The sun that sets may rise again,
> But when our light has once set
> Our night will be unbroken.[1]

Many seventeenth-century English poets—notably Robert Herrick, Edmund Waller, Richard Lovelace, and Andrew Marvell—urged their lovers to seize the day because, in Marvell's words,

At my back I always hear
Time's winged chariot hurrying near;
And yonder all before us lie
Deserts of vast eternity.

In the twentieth century, however, the average lifespan has doubled, and within several decades a great many people will expect to live vigor-ously into their nineties. The contemporary Marvells will therefore have more difficulty in persuading their young ladies to hop into bed with them on the grounds that their beauty and life is so transitory. The result may be a new genre of "grey passion" verse addressing the romantic lives of an expanding population of septagenarians and octogenarians.

More seriously, though the extension of the human lifespan will never really kill the *carpe diem* impulse—after all, what is even ninety years measured against eternity?—the shifting of the centre of population to the aged will elicit artistic responses to its newly created problems. In particular, the elderly perception of the expanded time, so different from the consciousness of the breathless teenager or the achieving forty-year-old, will be dramatized with the power inherent only in great art. For example, in his marvellous little book *The View From Eighty*, Malcolm Cowley captured in a poem more vivid than any essay the poignant evan-escence of life:

For his birthday they gave him a red express wagon
with a driver's high seat and a handle that steered.
His mother pulled him around the yard.
"Giddyap," he said, but she laughed and went off
to wash the breakfast dishes.
"I wanta ride too," his sister said,
and he pulled her to the edge of a hill.
"Now, sister, go home and wait for me,
but first give a push to the wagon."
He climbed again to the high seat,
this time grasping the handle-that-steered.
The red wagon rolled slowly down the slope,
then faster as it passed the schoolhouse
and faster as it passed the store,

the road still dropping away.
Oh, it was fun.

But would it ever stop?
Would the road always go downhill?

The red wagon rolled faster.
Now it was in strange country.
It passed a white house he must have dreamed about,
deep woods he had never seen,
a graveyard where, something told him, his sister was buried.

Far below
the sun was sinking into a broad plain.

The red wagon rolled faster.
Now he was clutching the seat, not even trying to steer.
Sweat clouded his heavy spectacles.
His white hair streamed in the wind.[3]

Nowhere, surely, is the view from ninety more dramatically illustrated than in Margaret Laurence's novel *The Stone Angel*. Though Laurence, ironically, died of cancer at the age of sixty, her creative sensibility allowed her to imagine life as seen through the eyes of a ninety-year-old woman "rampant with memory." Though there are two stories simultaneously being told—that of the self-induced diminution of the woman's past life and that of the struggle of a defiant nonagenarian to preserve her dignity—the portrait of the ravages of aging is graphic. No reader can fail to be moved by pity and fear when the still emotionally energetic Hagar is forced to recognize that her body is betraying her, rendering her dependent on the goodwill of others, many of whom she despises.

In this and many other areas of twentieth-century life, our attitudes towards time, and its changing effect on us, need to be defined and communicated emotionally and intuitively through art. Whether via Salvador Dali's limp clocks draped like melted cheese over a bleak landscape, Tom Stoppard's clever play about schedules and measurement of time, *If You're Glad, I'll Be Frank*, or John Cleese's comically frenzied film, *Clockwise*, it will be through the creative imagination that we truly understand the nature of humanity's bondage to time.

Notes

1. Catullus, *Carmina*, v, 15.
2. Andrew Marvell, "To his Coy Mistress," in *A Book of English Poetry*, comp. G. B. Harrison (Harmondsworth: Penguin, 1937), 164.
3. M. Cowley, "The Red Wagon," in *The View From Eighty* (New York: Viking, 1980), 6–7.

Concluding Comments

E. J. McCULLOUGH

THE CONCEPT OF TIME is the focal concept not only of our confer-ence but also of current scientific and ethical thinking. In a recent popular book, *Order out of Chaos*, Ilya Prigogine says that in the current conceptual revolution in science, "Science is rediscovering time."[1] Science has discovered the centrality of the concept for its own work and for its relations with the social and ethical world around us. The concept of time and of eternity and their relationship is, in Prigogine's words, "at the origin of human symbolic activity"[2] and yet, as a by-product of the skepticism and cynicism of our era, time is seen to have no clear mean-ing; agreement in social and ethical matters seems beyond hope. Two brief stories might bring this home.

Some years ago Ludwig Wittgenstein, the brilliant analyst of modern thought, was reportedly asked by a colleague, "What is the meaning of time?" Wittgenstein replied, "It is 11:15."

This reply did not satisfy his questioner. "No," he said, "I do not mean *that* time. I mean what does time mean in itself?"

Again Wittgenstein answered, "11:15."

The questioner persisted. "I do not mean that common-sense meaning of time. I mean time in its true and absolute meaning."

Again, Wittgenstein said "11:15! And if you persist in this line of questioning, I shall be unable to continue our conversation." It is reported that the questioner did persist and Wittgenstein did close the conversation and refused to discuss the matter further. Wittgenstein's reluctance to consider absolute "meanings" of this kind arose out of his concern to avoid the shocking errors of idealists such as Bradley who, in Wittgenstein's view, left the real and the discernible for the order of free-floating abstract truths.

The second story relates to the meaning of a particular event in time, the Holocaust. In conversation with Richard Taylor, one of the contributors to this volume, I described the historical events of Auschwitz as grossly immoral and wrong. Taylor responded that he did not know what I meant by this claim since, in his view, there is no absolute right or wrong. I responded that in a straightforward way I meant that the historical acts of Hitler's regime—murdering millions of innocent people—were vicious and wrong. Again, Taylor responded that he did not know what it could mean to describe a particular act or an act of a government as vicious or wrong. We were at an impasse and the question was never resolved.

The two stories illustrate fundamental disagreement on the most primitive of concepts dealt with in the conference: the meaning of time and the interpretation of history. The conference brought one quickly to these fundamental questions. In a positive way, it was the best of conferences, realizing all the hopes of University of Saskatchewan president Krisjanson and his committee. A collection of eminent scholars from a variety of disciplines was assembled to deal with fundamental questions arising for all humanity. In another way it was the worst of conferences, since individual perspectives were maintained but community interests were neglected. Even among our fellow scholars at the University of Saskatchewan, the conference passed largely unnoticed and unattended. It was a sign of a community close to death as a community while very alive in its individual parts.

I propose to briefly address the successes and failures of the conference: first, the success in gathering the many participants who represented the scholarly assemblage that could realize the president's vision; and second, the failure of the conference in drawing the attention of the local community. The latter illustrates the plight of three human communities that are close to moribund: the university, Western civilization, and the human community.

Positive Accomplishments

The aims of the president and of the committee were threefold. The first was to provide a general perspective from which key issues regarding time could be examined. Richard Taylor, a philosopher, and Robert Banks, a theologian, provided this setting in a controversial and challenging first session. The second concern was to consider time from the perspective of special human physical and ethical life. Duncan Robertson and Byron Spencer dealt with aging functionally and economically, as a facet of the human experience of time. Economic questions about time were the concern of Joseph Tindale. Peter Singer, an internationally renowned ethicist, and Bernard Dickens, a Canadian legal expert, looked at ethical, legal, and medical problems. The third concern was to identify specific issues related to time in a variety of areas: native questions were dealt with in an exciting way by Cecil King. Women and societal values formed the subject for Margaret Eichler and Seena Kohl. Time use was studied by Andrew Harvey and Jiri Zuzanek. Finally, our panel—Donna Greschner, Robert Calder, and I—attempted an overview of the confer- ence, each from his or her own perspective. Aside from these events, we had a dramatic treat at our banquet with Henry Woolf and Ron Mavor, and a beautiful musical evening with Robert Solem's Greystone Singers and Daniel Swift's symphony artists in the Prairie Arts Ensemble. Mavor and Solem contributed to the volume with articles on drama and music. As well, we had a colourful art exhibit from the Fine Arts Department. Eli Bornstein's article is the result of a painter's reflections on time in the visual arts. Vincent Matthews, Hilliard McNab, Chief Richard Redman, Tony Cote, Steen Esbenson, John Jackson, Doug Ray, Theresa MacNeil, Karl Strange, Margaret Hughes, and Kathleen Storrie contributed in an variety of submissions. It was an impressive exhibition of the variety of talents and the wealth of scholarship available at our university and brought to Saskatoon the reputation that our university enjoys. This was the exciting and positive result of our conference, which must have come close to or surpassed the president's hopes.

What were its negative sides?

Future Research Problems

The president hoped that identifiable research projects would be set out that would stimulate future inquiry; the areas were identified in general and specific ways. I will focus on one aspect of this, the research into the future of three communities: the university, Western civilization, and the human community.

First, the university as a community is faced with an enormous prob- lem in rendering a logical service. It is a task of great complexity to render the meaning of such terms as "time" accessible to people from different disciplines and to the general population. If Ludwig Wittgenstein and his questioner, or Richard Taylor and I, are unable to bridge that logical gap between disciplines—or even between members of the same discipline—then the university itself may find that it cannot survive save as a collection of individual disciplines in isolation from each other: in other words, not as a *university*.

Second, the community of Western civilization is built on the principle of the equal worth of its citizens. From the earliest moment of the establishment of city states to the present, notions of justice and fairness have survived within the context of a concept of equal worth. Dr. Taylor's argument for functional superiority and Dr. Singer's argument for the usefulness of the members of a species and his identification of that utility in self-awareness threaten the bedrock foundations of Western civilization.

Third, the general notion of a human community functioning in time can be seen cyclically, as the Natives see it, or linearly, as many modern scientists see it. The two models result in vastly different notions of human community: the first subject to rhythms and characterized by being in metaphysical relation; the second a collection of individuals, each with his or her own acts of doing.

There are three controversial propositions that emerge from these considerations of logical, ethical, and metaphysical matters surrounding time, history, and being:

PROPOSITION 1

Since we create time, time is a pluralistic concept with no common meaning.

PROPOSITION 2

The notion of the equal worth of the members of the species is indefensible.

PROPOSITION 3

There is no important distinction between being and doing.

These three propositions, which I would argue are false, should raise crucial research questions. Proposition 1 was a serious historical question for the Greeks. The difference between the Greek notion of *kyros* (decision time) and *chronos* (clock time) was a problem in antiquity. Modern conflicting notions of objective time in science and "subjective" history are equally puzzling for our contemporaries. Some logical escape from this impasse is needed through study by logicians, literary figures, and common folk. If the first proposition holds, there can be no university community.

Proposition 2 reverses the distillation of Greek, mediaeval, and enlightenment views about the nature of humanity. The equal-worth principle superseded all earlier principles, which involved the acceptance of elementary forces of blood as the determining criteria of worth. True brotherhood and sisterhood were not seen as determined by utility, force, or function. Two contrasting propositions cancel proposition 2: the equal- ity of being and the hierarchy of function. Political scientists, citizens, and common folk must deal with these questions, but much depends on the response to proposition 3.

The claim of proposition 3 is that we are defined according to func- tion; this claim is disputed by Native people, by women, by children, and by all oppressed minorities. Their successful defence depends on our ability to defend the distinction between being and doing, and then to establish the relationship. Philosophers, theologians, and common folk all need to face this proposition together.

Let me sum up. The positive results of the conference are visible in the participants' contributions. The success or failure of the civilized community depends on clarification and support of the concept of equal worth. The success or failure of the human community depends on a clear understanding of the difference between being and doing. The concept of time brings these three questions into clear focus.

My differences with Dr. Taylor and Dr. Singer are profound. In my view Taylor's extreme individualism threatens all communities and ig- nores the creative role that communities play in maintaining civilization. The democracy of the past gives communities—past, present, and future— an essential role. Singer identifies being and function, and hence under- mines the real community and civilization itself. The identified research questions, for which we are grateful to Dr. Taylor and Dr. Singer, are for all scholars to address.

It is my own hope that these identified research questions will lead us to the proper sense of three communities functioning over time: the university, the civilized community, and the human community.

Individuals and communities proceed over time, yet they live in the present of individual and collective memory. Time is united in the histor- ical consciousness in individual and collective memory. Poets capture intuitively this unity of time, as Eliot does in "Burnt Norton" when he places time in the eternal present.

Augustine also puts time in the story of the present in the *Confes- sions*, XI, 28, when he says that as one reads a text such as a psalm, the past reading is remembered, and the future is expected, but the "atten- tion" is in the present. So also, in human lives, both past and future have a presence. The past exists in the memory, and the future exists in an

286   EMERGENT RESEARCH ISSUES

expectation, both included in a narrative that embraces the story of individuals and society. This complete narrative is the life of individual men
and women, with actions as parts. This narrative sense of time provides
a comprehensive unity, a common meaning.

If we believe time has no common meaning, if we deny the notion of
equal worth won through long temporal struggle, if we see no distinction
between our being what we are and our functions in special time, then
we shall certainly die in the next twenty years, possibly not individually
or collectively but certainly as communities, as university, as civilized,
and as human. We are not individuals alone. We are not small isolated
groups, but a community that flows over history. Focusing on time brings
us to recognize our temporal dependence on each community. We must
be grateful to our university and to President Krisjanson for providing
the opportunity for these reflections. Much depends on them.

Notes

1. I. Prigogine, *Order Out of Chaos* (New York: Bantam, 1984), xxviii.
2. Ibid., 312.

EPILOGUE

Narrative and Time

E. J. McCULLOUGH

> For instance, now, there's the King's Messenger. He's in prison now,
> being punished: and the trial doesn't even begin till next Wednesday:
> and of course the crime comes last of all.
>
> *Lewis Carroll, Through The Looking Glass*

QUESTIONS CONCERNING TIME as a reality are central to human experience. If, in Shelley's words, it is time on whose last steps we climb, then we are puzzled by the ascent and its meaning. The questions are unsettling and obscure, the answers dizzying and long. As with seemingly pretentious questions on "The Nature of Being," they threaten the sense of balance or they nauseate in their generality. The foundational section of the conference on time as a human resource sought meaning in the temporal experience. In the functional, social, and artistic sections, two distinct types of time consciousness emerged: felt time and quantitative time. The paradoxes inherent in relating these two are present in *Through the Looking Glass*.

The White Queen's claim that she remembers best "things that happened the week after next"[1] points to a problem with time-consciousness recognized by Lewis Carroll in the nineteenth century: a growing confusion about commonsense meanings of time and time sequence. The twentieth century has presented an even more complex picture. We can speak much more obscurely from the twin perspectives of relativity and quantum theory. In our century, studies about time "tend to destroy rather than enhance reputations, so the worldly wise fight shy of it:" research institutes abandon the field to "cranky private groups, gurus, or religions."[2] Despite these warnings, some of the most popular and insightful

290   EPILOGUE

work written in this century is on the topic of time, enhancing the reputations of scientists such as physicist Stephen Hawking and geologist Stephen Jay Gould. The phenomenon of an abstruse book by an astrophysicist reaching the top of the non-fiction best seller lists attests to the pervasive curiosity about time and its meaning in the modern mind.

It is the purpose of this epilogue to escape Alice's vertigo and impatience and find a meaning of time that is accessible to common sense, a meaning implicit and explicit in the conference and in this volume. First, by reflecting on the two commonsense notions of time in the papers in this collection, we arrive at a sense of narrative. Narrative is present in all the papers. Second, two complex alternative modes of expressing time, logical and scientific, are examined briefly, with narrative in biology as a model for science. In the third section, narrative is advanced as the central temporal concept that brings meaning and unity to this volume and to the research programs that could emerge from it.

There is more at stake in this enterprise than in any previous historical examination of time. The paradoxical claims of the White Queen are now a commonplace in modern science, in modern fiction, and in modern film. What appeared absurd to Lewis Carroll and appears absurd to our own commonsense notions of the irreplaceable past, simultaneity in the present, and reflections on a non-existent future, are now taken for granted. The reality of time is the greatest single puzzle in contemporary philosophy, cosmology, art, and, indeed, in our own personal lives.

Unity in Narrative:
Meaning and Research Between Disciplines

Narrative gives time studies a sense of unity, which is necessary in interdisciplinary research. Here, in the words of one commentator, we have "a prototype of the difficulties in interdisciplinary analysis of a single topic." The notion of narrative is the key to a solution of these difficulties. It is a special sense of history as narrative that provides the best opportunity for achieving unity of theme and meaning. A primitive sense of "narrative" arises out of the origins of the term: the verb *noscere*, "to know" (old form *gnoscere*) and the Greek word for knowledge. In this etymological sense, the gnostic tradition is one of arcane knowledge. In common English usage, the notion of narrative is one of a story, a historical account of events. More precisely, it is a story set in a cultural context with a personal and temporal foundation. It has become a common feature of recent scholarship to point to a narrative account of history, and even of explanation, within different traditions. In other words, time-consciousness has a contextual element.

Each of the five sections of this interdisciplinary volume—Foundational, functional, social, artistic, and summary—provides a narrative model. In the first section, theologian Robert Banks provides a theistic interpretation of time and history and a linear account of creation. In this model, there are traceable connections to a divine source who plays a significant role in human history. Richard Taylor, a non-theistic philosopher, argues for the significance of personal and social cultural history as the grounds for meaning and for the human understanding of time. David Skelton, a physician, researcher, and Anglican clergyman, puts science and human history, divine and existential, into relationship. The accounts are comple-mentary and relatable if historical consciousness, or narrative, is accepted as a common matrix.

The research potential of this section is apparent in the concern to deal with theological and philosophical insights in a contemporary con-text. Faith is no longer the overarching reality that it was in mediaeval times. The research possibilities lie in a renewed search for the reconcili-ation of faith and reason in a world of evolutionary biology and relativity in science. At the personal level, there is a need to see how aging and death can be given both sacred and secular meaning.

In the second functional section, lifespan, economic, and social fac-tors, and the ethical dilemmas surrounding the beginning and the end of life, are seen at a more specific personal level. The narrative is not cosmic, but local and specific to each person. It is contained within the parameters of statistical, social, and ethical consciousness of the individ-ual's and the community's life.

Research possibilities include examining the transformations to be expected in an growing yet aging population. Projections by Spencer and Denton that health costs will increase and education costs will diminish as reproduction falls below the replacement level are not realized in such locations as Saskatchewan, where a high proportion of adults continue with formal education as an enriching source of personal growth. These reflections on the personal and social effects of demographic change are challenging, but not less so than the challenges in ethical research concerning the beginning and end of life. Reproductive technologies are the most contro-versial areas of contemporary ethics. Singer and Dickens are at the lead-ing edge of that research. Ethical, legal, and social approaches to death and dying are vital areas for future research.

In the special areas of Native culture, woman's studies, and time management, narrative is central. The Native community provides a dynamic story of its relationship to nature and of its history, which follows the natural rhythms of the seasons rather than the chronological order of Western society. Seena Kohl puts the sociological account of women in a farm economy in the form of a mythical prairie community. Even the statistical accounts of Harvey and Zuzanek depend on the summary account of individual and community narratives.

Research in the areas of special groups can be anecdotal or statistical. Some concern with the relation between anecdotal accounts and rigorous statistical evidence, the personal and the sociological, is crucial. Theorists such as Bellah and Habermas lead the way in such research, which is not restricted to one discipline.

The artist's approach to time is even more in the felt perspective. Dramatists, painters, and musicians give a profound personal dimension to time-consciousness. The personal stories of Eliot or Shakespeare, of Monet or van Gogh, of Beethoven or Elgar, are all part of the narrative source of the creative impulse. Research in this area can provide the background for the artist's intuitions. Eliot's indebtedness to Bradley's philosophic intuitions about time, for example, are everywhere in the *Four Quarters*. The story of Michelangelo's work on the Sistine Chapel, or of Rodin's relationship with Claudel, is crucial to a deeper understanding of the works. The relationship between the thought of Nietzsche and the music of Wagner is an essential research topic. The article by Solem shows the possibilities in the analysis of musical tempo, and invites sociological and philosophical reflection.

The concluding summary comments on law, literature, and philosophy contribute to the sense of narrative. The focus in procedural law is on the account of procedures followed, as the sense of narrative is clear in the poetry of Malcolm Cowley, or in the novels of Margaret Laurence. Research in these areas cries out for some cross-disciplinary sense involving time. For example, in the conflict between judicial conservatism, which focuses on seemingly timeless constitutional issues, and judicial activism, which focuses on contextual and changing social values, theorists such as Hart and Dworkin provide a deeper analysis of the issues at stake. The logical and scientific candidates for root meanings for time, such as contemporary thermodynamics, would not appear to favour a seemingly messy and contextually located notion of time.

Time: Logical and Scientific

First the question is asked "What is time?" This question makes it appear that what we want is a definition. We mistakenly think that a definition is what will remove the trouble (as in certain cases of indigestion we feel a kind of hunger which cannot be removed by eating).

Wittgenstein, The Blue and Brown Books

Lewis Carroll lived as two persons: the storyteller revelling in paradox, and the logician rejecting paradox. He saw the collapse of Euclidean geometry, with all the logical problems that would entail. Alice's experiences pointed to the problems. His defence of Euclid provided a solution. Logic would seem to provide a sense of meaning for time and space that could escape the paradoxes.

It was a concern of logicians from the beginnings of Greek philosophy to place time within some classification or order. For Aristotle, logic provided categories that derived from grammatical usage. Categories represented answers to simple questions such as what, how, when, where, and how much. These questions were placed in the general context of substance and being. Time, for Aristotle, was one of ten categories; he recognized, however, that time involves a human element, since in some sense time is the measure of change.

Philosophers through the Greek and mediaeval periods speculated on time, but always against the Aristotelian or Neo-Platonic background. In Augustine, the background was in the Plotinian reflections that brought Plato and Aristotle into a kind of harmony. With the Enlightenment, scientific figures such as Newton provided a mathematical sense of time, but coupled it with some sense of its mystical quality in the divine. Kant put the Newtonian intuitions into a fourfold empirical sense: quantitative, qualitative, relational, and modal. Time became the form of inner intuition. Hegel and Marx expanded this notion with a concept of history. Heidegger and Wittgenstein reacted to the history of this concept in ways reminiscent of Alice's problem: Heidegger with a dizzying account of time and its relation to being; Wittgenstein with an impatience.

Wittgenstein argued that there was no exact or pure concept of time; terms such as "time" and "knowledge" have no agreed meaning.[3] There are several acceptable uses of the term in different contexts. It is, in Gilbert Ryle's phrase, a polymorphous term, or one that functions in different formal ways in distinct contexts. The reason that we seek a single, pure concept, as Wittgenstein saw it, is that we are dazzled by the success of mathematics and science, and want to apply the same sort of exactness in these orders.[4] But it is the analogies drawn from science that mislead us into thinking that we can provide an exact definition of time. Temporal experiences of the past, of the future, and of the moment share this quality of contextual determination. Remembering, for example, can apply equally to memory images, past expectations, and past experiences; there are three distinctive uses.[5] Similarly, there can be uses of the term dependent on and independent of a clock;[6] neither is less "pure" or less "real" than the other. Time is thus experienced in a variety of equally acceptable ways. For Wittgenstein there was no single category that expressed the meaning of time in a pure sense, and he was notoriously impatient with metaphysical speculations about it.

It was in Martin Heidegger's *Being and Time* that time as present and presence were brought together. Not only was time seen as somehow co-equal with being, but time and being were united against the horizon of human experience. Time assumed a personal character:

> But we have so far omitted showing more clearly what the present in the sense of presence means. Presence determines Being in a unified way as presencing and allowing-to-presence, that is in unconcealing.[7]

Heidegger pointed to a forgetfulness of being in philosophy perhaps best realized in the Kantian intuition that time is the form of all inner experience. The subjectivity of this insight was brought to the objective world through art in Kant's Third Critique, through historical consciousness in Hegel, and brought back to unity in being in Heidegger.

Once again, the pre-Socratic problem of the divisions of being and the place of time within being became a problem with Heidegger, and with the revolutions in modern physics. The Greek way to a partial solution was in the formulation of logical categories in which time could be located. Could this be the way to find meaning and unity for time in being? At least three fundamental options remain open: the Greek option, with a limited number of categories; the Kantian categories, which are related to sensible intuitions; and the contextual placement of concepts in orders of usage (or the Rylean polymorphous concept). The first two can be characterized as foundational, the third as operational or functional.

The search for a single meaning and a unifying theme is not satisfied by logic. There are two categorial candidates, Aristotle's and Kant's, both of which have strengths and weaknesses. Neither is the search satisfied by a polymorphous or contextual approach, which does not establish relationships. Is a scientific solution using scientific methodologies and doctrines more acceptable in leading to thematic unity? It seems that science could answer the call for an unambiguous concept of time, or at least a primitive and primary sense.

Science

It is hard to avoid the impression that the distinction between what exists in time, what is irreversible, and, on the other hand, what is outside of time, what is eternal, is at the origin of human symbolic activity.

Ilya Prigogine, *Order Out of Chaos*

Time, Prigogine maintains, is central to human symbolic activity. In the rediscovery of time as central, science has entered into close relation to the social and ethical domains. But the hope that we might find a unified notion of time and a thematic unity is undermined to some extent by Einstein's recognition that, from the perspective of the physical sciences, the "now," the "present," and the "moment" are of almost no interest.[8] From the perspective of the humanist scholar or of the lived experience of individuals and of narrative, the now, the present, and the moment are of the utmost significance. There is thus a puzzling conflict between the chronometric and reversible approach to time with no present followed in science, and the non-metric and non-reversible temporal approach in which there is room for the present as both a lived moment and as a limit to past and future.

Dramatic advances in the physical measurement of time have made previously unimaginable feats of measurement commonplace. The advances in navigation in the seventeenth and eighteenth centuries owed much to similar advances in the clocks of the time.[9] We have moved far beyond water clocks and Huygen's pendulum, which was accurate up to one second an hour, or Harrison's marine chronometers, which could be accurate up to a second a day. The quartz clock extended accuracy to one second in several years. Atomic clocks now achieve an accuracy of one second in hundreds of years. Clocks of the future might lose one second in thirty million years. Accompanying this has been a notable change in notions of time.

The debates between Adolph Grünbaum, chronometrician and mathematician, and George Whitrow, scientist and natural philosopher, provide a useful insight into scientific attitudes to time. Grünbaum argues for the chronometric approach rooted in the special theory of relativity.[10] In his account, the qualitative notion of time as transient lacks material content and, hence, must be disregarded. He argues for an empirical, mathematical account of space and time based in the notion of congruence. Space is given mathematical congruence or harmony by a mathematical formula. The harmony lies in the metric aspect of space and time. The methods applied to space and time must be mathematical, but rooted, as in Poincaré's account, in a theory of knowledge.[11] Poincaré's theory assumes that the congruence is conventional, but not trivially so. Grünbaum's approach is to claim a priority for metric and mathematical accounts of time and analysis based on a mathematical function.

Whitrow's is an entirely different approach. Both a mathematician and natural philosopher, he does not assume for methodological purposes that the primary elucidation of time comes from mathematics. He looks to different dimensions of time experience: mathematical, biological, astronomical, psychological, and in everyday experience. The contemporary notion of time, he maintains, is based, as in Grünbaum, on the geometric idea of a line.[12] In contrast to Grünbaum, however, for Whitrow the very essence of time is its transience. There is no more fundamental account of time, whether mathematical or geometric, than as a mode of activity: "Without activity there can be no time."[13] From the practical point of view, time involves counting.[14] This does not mean, however, that time is comparable to a mathematical instant; it means that time is divided into physical instants, or "chronons," of uncertain magnitude.[15]

Grünbaum and Whitrow disagree fundamentally on the methodic approaches to time. Grünbaum regards the elucidation of time as a geometric and arithmetic task. Whitrow regards it in its various physical contexts. For Grünbaum, the metric and the psychophysical ideas of time are in accord.[16] In Grünbaum's view, "The metric of psychological time is tied causally to those physical cycles which serve to define time congruence in physics."[17] For Whitrow, there are two interpretations of time at the cosmic level, that of Archimedes and that of Aristotle. Temporal concepts were neglected by Archimedes but considered central by Aristotle. In Aristotle, time was related fundamentally to motion and to change. In Archimedes, in contrast, time is isomorphic with space. Whitrow sees modern approaches to time divided into biological, mathematical, relativistic, space-time, and cosmic time; the foundation for time lies in *activity* and in *change*. Grünbaum maintains that the "disavowal" of becoming as an attribute of elementary physical events is a necessary condition for the meaningful affirmation of the denseness of physical time."[18] Events do not come into being in any way; "they merely occur tenselessly in a network of time like separation . . ."[19]

Different sciences have different temporal notions. Theoretical physicist Thomas Morris points to a simple arrow and cyclical model;[20] the astrophysicist and cosmologist Stephen Hawking suggests a threefold model: thermodynamic, psychological, and cosmological. At first glance, the simple linear/arrow model seems to accord with common sense. The scientific realist keeps us in his camp by agreeing with either of arrow or circle models initially, but tells us in the end that the concept changes with the observer. Paradoxes in time emerge as *we choose* which is the more useful notion. Hawking provides us thus with a polymorphous model but one which does not admit any logical resolution of the puzzle as to the true nature of time.

Hawking dispenses with the logical problem experienced in common-sense concerns about whether time has a beginning or an end; it is sense-less to ask what the real nature of time is. The question, rather, is which notion of time is more useful.[21] The thermodynamic concept is prior to the psychological and may or may not be in harmony with the cosmological. In the thermodynamic approach, there is an increase in entropy; in the cosmological approach, entropy may increase or decrease, but the increase would be limited to the experience of the human race. Hawking does not provide a final solution to problems of meaning, other than to hint that the answers come from thermodynamics and not from psychology or cosmology. Still, time is relative to the observer, and it is space dependent.

Geologists and biologists provide quite a different perspective. Geologist Stephen Gould points to the role of dichotomy in advancing scholarship: the linear notion of time as a sequence of unrepeatable events is contrasted with the idea that "fundamental states are immanent in time, always present and never changing."[22] Apparent motions are parts of repeating cycles, and differences of the past will be the realities of the future. Time has no direction. Gould presents historical representations from the history of science to point to the fruitfulness of the dichotomy in leading to a deeper understanding of the nature of time. Referring to Goethe, he argues that some dichotomies must interpenetrate and "not struggle to the death of one side, because each of their opposite poles captures an essential property of any intelligible world."[23] History and the immanence of time are vital to geological science.[24] Gould argues that history is essential to understanding the processes of science; the theory of punctuated equilibrium resulted from the sort of historical reflections scientists so often disdain.[25]

It is in biology, however, that the historical dimension becomes central to the rational process itself. Ernst Mayr takes a position that is fundamentally opposed to the non-historical accounts of physicists and their philosophic interpreters. He gives new status to the history of a scientific discipline in his magisterial work *The Growth of Biological Thought*. Philosophers, inspired by physics, he argues, make a fundamental mistake in applying the same model for classifying inanimate objects to biological phenomena. The unitary model for method and classification used in physics does not fit biology, basically because biology deals with origins as well as separated items. The physicist's reductionist approach to the study of life has not proven helpful in the life sciences.[26] The notion of origin in time and history is central to the biological enterprise. Mayr thus looks at time historically and narratively.

In order to understand Mayr's narrative approach, it should be contrasted with the non-narrative approach seen most clearly in the physical sciences. In physics, as Mayr sees it, "processes can be explained as the consequence of specific laws with prediction symmetrical to causation."[27] Biology, as rooted in history, does not fit into this mold. In biology, the unique event is the outstanding feature of evolution, while in physics a covering-law hypothesis looks plausible. Mayr presents the notion of narrative explanation using the work of Thomas Goudge to illustrate the model. No general laws are mentioned. The development of a historical narrative proceeds in a continuum through time. Cosmogony, geology, paleontology, and biogeography all share this characteristic of historical focus:

Philosophers trained in the axioms of essentialist logic seem to have great difficulty in understanding the peculiar nature of uniqueness and of historical sequences of events. Their attempts to deny the importance of historical narrative or to axiomatize them in terms of covering laws fail to convince.[28]

Biology thus needs to combine the "cybernetic-functional-organizational" ideas of functional biology with the populational historical program-uniqueness–adaptedness concepts of evolutionary biology."[29] Biologists uniformly reject a whole generation of philosophers of science, including Popper, Russell, Bloch, Bunge, Hempel, and Nagel. Part of the reason is their extreme focus on notions of consciousness[30] and their uncritical

McCULLOUGH / Epilogue

use of the hypothetico-deductive model.[31] It has become clear that the explanatory models that worked in the physical sciences do not work in the life sciences.[32] There is no way to understand or explain in biology without combining proximate and evolutionary causes, which introduces us to a historical enterprise.[33]

The several notions of time—logical, physical, geological, and biological—recognize that time has many meanings and that it is in principle contextual. Narrative satisfies the need for an intelligible, unifying notion that is contextual. In the narrative account, science is seen, at least in part, as a likely story, not simply a rigorously coherent mathematical story.

Time and Narrative

Although our awareness of time is based on psychological factors and on physiological processes below the level of consciousness, we have seen that it is also dependent on social and cultural influence. Because of these, there is a reciprocal relation between time and history. For just as our idea of history is based in that of time, so time as we conceive it is a consequence of our history.

Whitrow, *Time in History*

Thus far, the conference papers have been seen to be narrative in nature. The alternative logical and scientific approaches to time have been seen to be polymorphous and contextual. In this section three approaches—from natural philosophy, from biology, and from philosophy—illustrate the sense of narrative that satisfies the cross-disciplinary demands for connection.

The failure to find a unified meaning of time either in logic or in science leads us to the possibility that history itself forms the ground from which some understanding of time can be achieved. It is the sense of history rooted in the foundational, functional, and artistic understanding of time, that brings unity to this volume. It is, however, a special sense of history—history as narrative—that provides the best opportunity for achieving unity of theme. We have seen that narrative is concerned with stories and the recounting of events. It has become a common feature of recent scholarship to point to a narrative account of history and even of explanation, within different traditions. Time is given a personal, social—and even an ideological—meaning. Recent studies of time have reflected this interest in history, narrative, and ideology as fruitful standpoints from which ideas and themes can achieve unity.

300 EPILOGUE

Whitrow's *Time in History* focuses on two aspects of time-consciousness: the general intellectual history of time and its influence on different civilizations, and the development of modes of measuring time, from primitive sundials to atomic clocks. Whitrow sees in current computer technology an advance equal in scale to that of the development of the clock. The rapidity of change accomplished with these technological developments led to revolutionary scientific and social change. Innovations in thinking led to conflicting ideas concerning the instant and duration, and contrasting notions of relativized time and cosmic time.

The shift away from mathematically oriented instant to process notions of time was anticipated in Bergson and Whitehead, and developed further in modern studies in biology, particularly in evolutionary theory. Relativity in time, associated with Einstein's account of simultaneity, was said to be observer dependent. Astronomers pointed to cosmic time associated with receding galaxies. These insights, as Whitrow sees it, have radically changed the contemporary understanding of time.

Whitrow concludes his survey of time in history by pointing to the focus on temporal process in evolutionary theory: "The continuing momentum of scientific, medical and technological progress makes it impossible for our civilization to be regarded as either static or cyclic."[34] Thus, two primitive models for temporal change are left behind. Modern civilization needs to see its place in a historical continuum as well as in the present; we cannot understand the present without understanding the past.[35] Whitrow sees three major traditions of time understanding: the Greek, in which time played a judicial role; the Enlightenment, in which mechanical clocks led to a view of universal mechanism; and the contemporary view, which originated in the eighteenth century and in which both the universe and society are regarded as evolving in time. The dominant model is a temporal one that demands understanding of both astronomical and biological notions of time.

The biological model is presented best by Ernst Mayr, who sees history as the best way of gaining entrance to a science, particularly biology:

The study of the history of a field is a best way of acquiring an understanding of its concepts. Only by going over the hard way by which these concepts were worked out—by learning all the early wrong assumptions that had to be refuted one by one, in other words by learning all past mistakes—can one hope to acquire a really thorough and sound understanding. In science one learns not only by one's own mistakes, but [also] by the history of the mistakes of others.[36]

For Mayr, three things follow from his position: (1) there is a logical connection between history and explanation in biology and in all sciences;[37] (2) there is a vital role for the expression of contrasting positions, or for a non-ideological but dialectical approach to science;[38] and (3) there is a need for a narrative or story-like approach to the development of a science, since the "earlier events in the historical sequence usually make a causal contribution." In other words, earlier events are vital to explanation and understanding.[39] It is this aspect of historical explanation that renders biology accessible to the lay person, and allows a writer to leave out the mathematical and technical aspects of the science.[40]

But precisely how does history play a vital role in scientific explanation? We might see history as a useful pedagogical tool,[41] but does this mean that history has an essential explanatory function in biology? The answer to this question for Mayr derives from the place of teleology in biological explanations.

We have been used to the story of the history of science in which one of the dramatic events was the withdrawal of final causes from the scientific order. Aristotle is usually blamed (perhaps unjustly) for the insertion of final causes in an objectionable way into everything. How does Mayr explain the reinsertion of final causes into biology?

For some time, evolutionary biologists have placed finality in the account of evolution. As Mayr expresses it, "By far the most important departure in Darwin's methodology was that he demonstrated the legitimacy of why questions."[42] In deference to the almost universal repugnance of final causes, evolutionary biologists have avoided describing these causes as final. Mayr has no such reticence, but he qualifies his notions of teleology. There are four types: teleonomic activities, such as genetic programs, which are goal directed; teleomatic processes, in which an end is reached as a result of physical laws, such as in gravitational fall; adapted systems, such as the functional systems of elimination developed by the kidneys; and cosmic teleology, which Mayr sees as a result of Aristotle's recognition of ends combined with Christian notions of finality. It is only this last position that science rejects.[43] The reintroduction of teleology into the scientific order places history at the heart of science. There is thus continuity and goal directedness at the very heart of biology.

Teleology is not, therefore, a merely contingent part of the explanation of biological phenomena. Teleology and history are necessary

302   EPILOGUE

conditions for the explanations themselves. The kind of history that Mayr sees himself involved in is not chronological, not lexicographical, not biographical or anecdotal, and not cultural or sociological; it is a problematic historical approach in which many of the problems persist throughout the history of thought. Biology is thus irretrievably dialec-tical. Mayr thinks that this is a good thing; it puts biology in the closest contact with the other sciences and the humanities. Given the breach with the law-like character of all explanations—one of the most revered logical and scientific principles—it is not a difficult step to move to a narrative account of biology that is neither anecdotal nor subjective.[44]

What does Mayr mean by a "narrative account" of history? He takes Thomas Goudge's account as an adequate description.

Narrative explanations enter into evolutionary theory at points where singular events of major importance for the history of life are being discussed . . . Narrative explanations are constructed without mention-ing any general laws . . . Whenever a narrative explanation of an event in evolution is called for, the event is not an instance of a kind (class), but is a singular occurrence, something which has happened just once and which cannot recur [in the same way]. Historical explanations form an essential part of evolutionary theory.[45]

As Mayr puts it, "Any phyletic line, any fauna (in zoogeography) or any higher taxon is a central subject in terms of the historical narrative theory and has continuity through time."[46] Historical events have a causal role within the historical narrative. The attempts of people like Hempel to axiomatize events under covering laws is unconvincing, since they fail to see the uniqueness of the events in question.

The question "why" can be asked in biology, and it has both heuris-tic and explanatory value. The latter value comes in describing fertiliz-ation, for example. Fertilization, in a functional account, can describe the event as the beginning of growth, but it is not necessary for partheno-genic species or for developing the egg without fertilization. The evolu-tionary biologist can point to fertilization as the "achievement of a recombination of paternal and maternal genes."[47]

One of the major difficulties with narrative accounts is that they are not open to the same kind of test that is available to the hypothetico-deductive account. Mayr has already stated his dissatisfaction with the various reductive accounts that are characteristic of positivist science. In Darwin's case, the narrative account can be the object of speculation and can be tested by observations.[48]

We have seen three essential features of Mayr's account of biological thought: historical, dialectical, and narrative. Physical scientists and philosophers of science have promoted the hypothetico-deductive model as the only model for science. Biology provides another.

The claim by Whitrow and Mayr that history plays an explanatory role in physics and biology is challenged most forcefully by the French philosopher Michel Foucault. Foucault claims that history is at root ideological and discontinuous. In response to this claim, Paul Ricoeur argues, as do Whitrow and Mayr, that the notion that there is not continuity in history is a result of the breakdown of the covering-law model. Ricoeur maintains that the rediscovery of the explanatory role of narrative is crucial to a proper grasp of the role of time concepts in both science and philosophy.

There are, in Ricoeur's view, two great contributions that narrative makes to understanding: first, it is explanatory in a foundational way, which takes us back to the neglected insights of Greek philosophy;[49] second, it provides a sense of meaning that is lacking in contemporary accounts of history and time.[50] Narrative relates historical understanding and human activity in a combination of teleological significance and law-like segments within a composite model.[51] The result is what Ricoeur calls explanations involving "quasi character" and "quasi events."

Ricoeur relates the physical notions of time present in Aristotle's *Physics* with the notion of time implicit in Aristotle's *Poetics*. In this way, time becomes known through its articulation in a narrative mode. Narrative provides meaning when it becomes a condition of temporal events. Ricoeur moves the focus away from a mathematical and purely physical notion of time to a sense of time rooted in agency. He joins Whitrow and Mayr in placing history at the centre of explanation, and goes even farther in placing agency at the heart of all temporal accounts. This puts us close to the central themes of the conference on which this volume is based: the conjunction of time concepts and human resources. The central role of human agency, either personal or social, in understanding time is relatively new. There have been epistemological notions of time (such as those of Kant), and historically rooted notions of time (such as those of Hegel), which anticipate the movement towards understanding time through human actions, personal or social. Heidegger gives this a personal grounding in human presence or in the dramatic now. The understanding of time as a correlative of agency describable in narrative terms is characteristic of all the papers in this volume. It is this quality of personal or social agency and the intersection of agency with the physical phenomenon that gives this volume its core meaning.

Conclusion

The lapse of time and rivers is the same,
Both speed their journey with a restless stream;
The silent pace, with which they steal away,
No wealth can bribe, no prayers persuade to stay;
Alike irrevocable both when past,
And a wide ocean swallows both at last.
Though each resemble each in every part,
A difference strikes at length the musing heart;
Streams never flow in vain; where streams abound,
How laughs the land with various plenty crown'd!
But time, that should enrich the nobler mind,
Neglected leaves a dreary waste behind.

William Cowper, "A Comparison"

The central themes of the early foundational papers in this volume focus on divine and human agency. The social sciences and ethics are presented in the context of individual and social activities, and the final section deals with the artistic activities that are revelatory of meaning. The focus has been on agency in intellectual, personal, social, and artistic experience. Central to this unity is the explanatory role that history and time play, and that anticipates the future in a common narrative: foundational, functional, and artistic.

In general, the foundational and historical perspective provided background for the more specific applications in human life and in reflective understanding through art. The first section provides an ontological perspective from which the remaining sections can be judged. Banks provided a theological view, Taylor an existential. The second and third sections can be combined in the lived experience of time as an individual and as a social phenomenon. Here ethical, economic, and social factors play a narrative role in placing time in the lived context of the present. The final section, on time-consciousness in art, provides an overall thematic unity through intuitive acts of the artist. It is through the dramatic narrative that an overall unity is recognized.

The foundational section on time focuses on the connection of time to human theological and philosophical experience of it. The physical consideration of time in modern physics was not a part of the conference agenda. The reason for this was that the focus was on the more human applications of temporality to human life. The physical sciences can be excluded from consideration initially but cannot be ignored in an over-arching synthesis of the proceedings. The epilogue brings in these scientific considerations. References to the Newtonian and the Einsteinian approaches to time form part of this epilogue.

The functional aspects of human life begin with the elementary facts about human lifespan and human decisions regarding lifespan. This pro-vides the context from which reflections on social applications of time are provided. Native perceptions, women's perceptions, and perceptions of specialized occupations such as farming place the operational considera-tions in the social context. It becomes clear in that context that there is a narrative element in time-consciousness that might be regarded as "sub-jective." It is not, however, "subjective," in any negative sense, because agency is a central theme in narrative.

The artistic synthesis of the concepts of time provides us with an essential reintegration of the objective and the subjective through artistic agency and narrative. Art synthesizes the objective and the subjective in intuitions, which can be considered theoretically but cannot be limited to the theoretical. The artistic intuitions provide the emotional matrix from which one can escape the dualism of object and subject and effect a uni-fied vision. There remains the task for philosopher, theologian, and those who would bring unity to the university, to reflect on the grounds for the ultimate synthesis of time consciousness. Narrative and the concepts of agency provide us with resources to achieve that end. This leads us to the final section.

Time must be seen as both an objective fact about the relational world that we live in and as a subjective experience that finds its ultimate realization in human life and death. It is in the actions of agents and the narrative of observers that this unity is achieved. The scientific discourse forms a more formal aspect of this narrative account.

The invitation of the conference is to go one step beyond the intuitive understanding of the present time-consciousness to a broader grasp of time without the preconception of current fashion, which is largely mathe-matical. The research challenge that remains is the invitation for all disciplines to cooperate in reflections on time.

If the notion of narrative relieves some of the dizziness associated with reflections on time or the impatience associated with ponderous accounts, then, as Eliot sees it, with age time ceases to be sequential or even developmental. Time becomes an essential part of a journey, a story, a human life, the life of a community. Time becomes a narrative.

Notes

1. Lewis Carroll, *Alice's Adventures in Wonderland and Through the Looking Glass*, 5th ed. (New York: Signet, 1962), 172.

2. D. King-Hele, "Making Us Tick," *Times Literary Supplement*, July 21–27, 1989, 793.

3. Ibid., 27.

4. Ibid., 25.

5. Ibid., 183.

6. Ibid., 106.

7. Martin Heidegger, *On Time and Being* (New York: Harper & Row, 1972), 373–75 (H326–27).

8. P. A. Schilpp, ed., *The Philosophy of Rudolph Carnap* (Lasalle, Ill.: Open Court, 1963), 37.

9. D. S. Landes, *Revolution in Time* (Cambridge, Mass.: Belknap, 1983).

10. A. Grünbaum, *Philosophical Problems of Space and Time*, 2d ed. (Boston: Reidel, 1973), 341–43.

11. Ibid., 24–27, 64–65.

12. G. J. Whitrow, *The Natural Philosophy of Time*, 2d ed. (Oxford: Clarendon, 1980), 373.

13. Ibid., 372.

14. Ibid., 373.

15. Ibid.

16. A. Grünbaum, "Geometry, Chronometry, and Empiricism," in *Scientific Explanation, Space, and Time*, ed. Herbert Feigl and Grover Maxwell, vol. 3 of *Minnesota Studies in the Philosophy of Science* (Minneapolis: University of Minnesota Press, 1962), 479.

17. Ibid., 481.

18. A. Grünbaum, *Modern Science and Zeno's Paradoxes* (London: George Allen & Unwin, 1968), 51.

19. A. Grünbaum, "Zeno's Paradoxes of Motion," in *The Philosophy of Time*, ed. R. M. Gale (Garden City, N.Y.: Anchor, 1967), 442–43. "The mere fact that becoming is a feature of perceived time does not at all warrant its incorporation in the time of physics."

20. R. Morris, *Time's Arrow* (New York: Simon & Schuster Touchstone, 1985).

21. Ibid., 139.

McCULLOUGH / Epilogue

22. Stephen Jay Gould, *Time's Arrow, Time's Cycle: Myth and Metaphor in the Discovery of Geological Time* (Cambridge: Harvard University Press, 1987), 10-11.

23. Ibid., 19. This is reminiscent of Bohr's statement that the opposite of a profound truth is another profound truth and not a contradiction.

24. Ibid., 200.

25. Ibid., 178-79.

26. Ibid., 34-35, 39-43, 112-14.

27. Ibid., 71.

28. Ibid., 72.

29. Ibid., 74.

30. Ibid. Mayr goes so far as to assign consciousness to invertebrates and even protozoans and magnetic bacteria.

31. Ibid., 35-36.

32. Ibid., 2.

33. Fertilization is given as an example. It might be considered as the begin- ning of a process of development by functional biologists. Evolutionary biologists maintain that the true object of fertilization is the recombination of genes, which results in genetic variability; ibid., 73.

34. G. J. Whitrow, *Time in History: Views of Time from Prehistory to the Present Day* (New York: Oxford University Press, 1988), 181.

35. Ibid., 183.

36. Ernst Mayr, *The Growth of Biological Thought* (Cambridge, Mass.: Belknap, 1982), 20.

37. Ibid., 71.

38. Ibid., 9.

39. Ibid., 71.

40. "Let me assure the prospective reader of this volume that he will hardly find any mathematics in its pages and that it is not technical to the extent that a layperson would have difficulty with the exposition . . . . Many of these concepts (and the terms that go with them) have now also been incor- porated into many branches of the humanities, and it has simply become a matter of education to be acquainted with them." Ibid., 19.

41. Ibid. The historical demonstration of the gradual replacement of these pre- scientific or early scientific beliefs by better based scientific theories and concepts greatly assists in explaining the current framework of scientific theories.

42. Ibid., 521.

43. Ibid., 48-51.

308   EPILOGUE

44.   Ibid., 9. I agree with Passmore, "Comments on Historical Assumptions of
the History of Science," in *Scientific Change: Historical Studies in the
Intellectual, Social and Technical Conditions for Scientific Discovery and
Technical Invention, From Antiquity to the Present*, ed. A.C. Crombie
(London: Heinemann, 1965), 853-61, that histories should even be polemi-
cal. Such histories will arouse contradiction and will challenge the reader
to come up with a refutation. By a dialectical process, this will speed up
a synthesis of perspective. The unambiguous adoption of a definite viewpoint should not be confused with subjectivity.

45.   Mayr, *The Growth of Biological Thought*, 71.

46.   Ibid.

47.   Ibid., 73.

48.   Ibid., 521.

49.   P. Ricoeur, *Time and Narrative* (Chicago: University of Chicago Press,
1984), 178-79.

50.   Ibid., 180.

51.   Ibid., 230.

Select Bibliography

The editors are grateful to the contributors to this volume for their additional bibliographical information, to Professor Howard McConnell of the Faculty of Law of the University of Saskatchewan for selected references on euthanasia, and to Dr. Steven Snyder of North Dakota State University, who provided a selected group of sources from the mediaeval period. The bibliography is not meant to be exhaustive but to point to some critical studies in the areas covered by this volume.

I Foundational: Theological, Philosophical, Historical

Theological

Biblical references: *Old Testament:* Gen. 1:1–5, 14–18; Neh. 9:6; Job 38:1–13; Pss. passim; Prov. passim; Eccles. 1:2, 18:10, 23:19–20; Wis. 7:17–25; Isa. 45:12, 18, 48:13, 65:17–25; Jer. 51:15; *New Testament:* Matt. 13: 24–30, 36–43, 49–50, 24:3–35; Mark 13:3–33; Luke 21:5–33; John 1:1–3; Col. 1:16–17; Heb. 1:10–12; 2 Pet. 3:3–13; Apo. 10:5–6. Biblical references locate time in the context of eternity and in relationship to creation. Citations drawn from the *Synopticon*, vol. 3, infra under "Philosophical" sources, 905–14, and *The Jerome Biblical Commentary* (edited by R. E. Brown, J. A. Fitzmyer, and R. E. Murphy [Englewood Cliffs, N.J.: Prentice-Hall, 1968]).

Barr, J. *Semantics of Biblical Language.* Oxford: Oxford University Press, 1961. A useful reflection and critical view needed to approach the work of Cullmann.

——. *Biblical Words for Time.* London: SCM, 1962. A corrective to the purely qualitative approach to time in the Bible presented by Marsh.

Berkhof, H. *Christ and the Powers.* Translated by J. H. Yoder. Scottdale, Pa.: Herald, 1962.

Cullmann, O. *Christ and Time: The Primitive Christian Conception of Time and History.* London: SCM, 1951. The nearest approach to the work by de Vries on the Old Testament, but it needs the critical reflections of J. Barr.

Dawn, M. J. *Keeping the Sabbath Wholly: Ceasing, Resting, Embracing, Feasting.* Grand Rapids, Mich.: Eerdmans, 1989.

de Vries, S. *Yesterday, Today and Tomorrow: Time and History in the Old Testament.* London: SPCK, 1975. A magisterial volume on the topic of time in the Old Testament.

Ellul, J. *Hope in a Time of Abandonment.* New York: Seabury, 1972.

Heschel, A. *The Sabbath: Its Meaning for Modern Man.* New York: Farrar, Strauss, 1951. On time as a gift, and on the importance of celebrating time.

Lewis, C. S. "The Weight of Glory." In *Screwtape Proposes a Toast.* London: Collins, 1965.

Marsh, J. *The Fulness of Time.* London: Nisbet, 1952. A purely qualitative notion of time in biblical texts.

Moltmann, J. *Theology and Joy.* London: SCM, 1970, 69.

Stiemotte, Alfred P. *God and Space-Time: Deity in the Philosophy of Samuel Alexander.* New York: Philosophical Library, 1954.

Wolff, H. *Anthropology of the Old Testament.* London: SCM, 1974, 119ff.

Philosophical

Adler, Mortimer J., and William Gorman, eds. *The Great Ideas: A Syntopicon of the Great Books of the Western World.* Vol. 2. Chicago: Encyclopedia Britannica, 1952, esp. 896-914. This work provides many of the foundational philosophic sources for the treatment of time as duration; its relation to eternity, infinity, and creation; its existence; the instant; its measurement, relationships, succession, and simultaneity; knowledge and perception of time; grammatical uses of time; the past and future; the passions and time; and historical time. It contains references to theology, philosophy, literature, history, and science. This is an invaluable starting point for the study of time in the classical tradition. Its limitations lie in the amount of research done after the date of publication.

Aristotle. *Categories* 1, 6, 7; *Generation of Animals* II, 6; *On Interpretation* 9; *Metaphysics* III, 5; V, 2; *Physics* IV; *Politics* III, 1; *Posterior Analytics* I,

2; II, 12 (citations from R. McKeon, ed., *The Basic Works of Aristotle* [New York: Random House, 1941]). Bonitz's *Index Aristotelicus* (Graz: Akademische Druck U. Verlagsanstalt, 1955), 855-56, provides a sample of the term *chronos* used throughout Aristotle's works. These texts and others in the corpus are the classical locations for philosophical reflections on the origins of notions of time.

Plato. *Alcibiades* I, 106; *Laws* III, 680A, 698C; IV, 711; V, 738D; VI, 758B, 769C; VII, 797A-B, 891A; VIII, 850B; IX, 872E, 891A; *Parmenides* 141D, 146E; *Phaedrus* 228A, 233A-C; *Philebus* 36B, 38E, 60E, 65C; *Protagoras* 339, 345B, 353D; *Republic* II, 363D; III, 409D; VI, 486, 493B; VIII, 566; IX, 576B; *Sophist* 265; *Symposium* 217B, 219A; *Theaetetus* 172B, 177D, 186C; *Timaeus* 21D-22D, 26A-B, 36E, 37D. These are some of the crucial texts in the Platonic corpus that illustrate various aspects of time. They are drawn from the *Syntopicon*, vol. 7 (supra, this section), and from the *Lexicon Platonicum* by D. F. Astius (Bonn: Rudolf Habelt, 1956).

Solmsen, F. *Aristotle's System of the Physical World*. Ithaca: Cornell University Press, 1960. An invaluable historical study showing the relationship of the Platonic works to the doctrines of Aristotle. Chapter 7, pp. 144-59, on time is a most important section of the work.

Greek and Mediaeval Commentators

The *locus classicus* for the Middle Ages is Aristotle, *Physics* IV.10-14 (217b30-224a15). Numerous mediaeval commentaries were written on this text, the most important being Averroes', Saint Albert's, Saint Thomas Aquinas's, and William of Ockham's. Commentaries on Lombard's *Sentences* usually discussed time when discussing *aevum* in Book II, distinction 2.

The Platonic notion of time as the moving likeness of eternity (*Timaeus* 29A-42E) had little impact on mediaeval philosophy, but see Plotinus. *Enneads* III, tract 7.

Augustine. *Confessions*, Book XI (London: J. M. Dent, 1949), gives a psychology of our perception of time as an answer to the question of what time is. The analysis has been interpreted as subjective by Anneliese Maier, who suggests that the Augustinian doctrine was rejected by scholastics particularly after 1277. ("Die Lösung, die Augustin selbst gegeben hat, besteht in einer völligen Subjektivierung . . . . Aber trotz der grossen und unbestrittenen Autorität, die Augustin für die Scholastik besass, ist diese radikale Subjektivierung durchweg abgelehnt worden, insbesondere seit 1277 . . . ." Maier, infra, 51).

Another Aristotelian view of time, which takes a position like that which Averroes will later take—that if there were no minds to number numerable events, time would only exist potentially, not actually—is to be found in Alexander of Aphrodisias, *Opusculum de tempore Alexandri*, in *Autour du décret de 1210: II—Alexandre d'Aphrodise aperçu sur l'influence de sa noetique*, édited by G. Théry (Paris, 1926). The *Opusculum de tempore* is on pp. 92-97 and is translated in R. W. Sharples, "Alexander of Aphrodisias, *On Time*," *Phronesis* 27 (1982): 58-81. The Greek original is lost; Théry gives a Latin translation from the Arabic.

The indispensible introduction to philosophical analyses of time in the Middle Ages is Anneliese Maier, *Metaphysische Hintergrunde der spätschol-astichen Naturphilosophie* (Rome, 1955), 47-137. Similarly authoritative but less broad in scope, concentrating on Averroes, Albert the Great, and Thomas, is A. Mansion, "La théorie aristotelicienne du temps chez les peripateticiens medie-vaux," *Revue neoscolastique de philosophie* 36 (1934): 275-307. Other secondary works of interest include:

Annas, J. "Aristotle, Number and Time." *Philosophical Quarterly* 25 (1975): 97-113. Arguing that Aristotle's definition of time is an anti-Platonic one, the author, after discussing time as number, gives what amounts to an Averroistic interpretation of the extra-mental reality of time (motion as "stuff temporally numerable" exists extra-mentally, but only a mind can number, i.e., count or time, the duration of motion).

Ariotti, Piero. "Celestial Reductionism of Time: On the Scholastic Conception of Time from Albert the Great and Thomas Aquinas to the End of the 16th Century." *Studi Internazionali di Filosofia* 4 (1972): 91-120. Concentrating on Averroes, Albert, Thomas, and William of Ockham, the article shows the interrelation of two questions: the question of time's extra-mental reality and the question of what the material principle of time is.

Bostock, David. "Aristotle's Account of Time." *Phronesis* 25 (1980): 148-69. The article offers a refutation of Aristotle's understanding of time, especially that it is to be defined as an attribute of motion.

Callahan, John F. *Four Views of Time in Ancient Philosophy*. Cambridge: Harvard University Press, 1948. Callahan gives a textual and comparative analysis of Plato, Aristotle, Plotinus, and Aristotle on time.

Corish, Denis. "Aristotle's Attempted Derivation of Temporal Order from that of Movement and Space." *Phronesis* 21 (1976): 241-51. Corish argues that Aristotle's use of "before and after" in his definition of time—as "the number of motion according to prior and posterior (or 'before and after')"—renders the definition either circular or meaningless.

Miller, Fred D. "Aristotle on the Reality of Time." *Archiv für Geschichte der Philosophie* 56 (1974): 132-55. Miller offers a correction of Aristotle on time by examining the relation of the instant to the temporal flux. He considers what Albert called the problem of time as having successive being rather than enduring being (*esse successivum* rather than *esse permanens*); his analysis on Albertian and Thomistic grounds is inadequate.

Owen, G. E. L. "Aristotle on Time." In *Motion and Time, Space and Matter,* edited by Peter K. Machamer and Robert G. Turnbull. Columbus, Ohio: Ohio State University Press, 1976. (Reprinted in Barnes, J., M. Schofield, and R. Sorabji, eds. *Articles on Aristotle.* Vol. 3, *Metaphysics.* London: Duckworth, 1979.) The essay questions the assertion, fundamental to Aristotle's understanding of time, that spatial priority is conceptually basic to the order of movement and the order of time.

Quinn, John Michael. "The Concept of Time in Albert the Great." *Southwestern Journal of Philosophy* 10 (1979): 21–47. (Reprinted in Kovach, K. J., and R. W. Shahan, eds. *Albert the Great: Commemorative Essays.* Norman, Okla.: University of Oklahoma Press, 1980.) Quinn argues that Albert formulated "a quasi-mathematical time, essentially formal number applied to motion" (p. 44).

Snyder, Steven C. "Albert the Great's Analysis of Time in its Historical and Doctrinal Setting." Ph.D. diss., University of Toronto, 1984. Snyder contradicts Quinn's position.

Sorabji, Richard. *Time, Creation, and the Continuum: Theories in Antiquity and the Middle Ages.* Ithaca: Cornell University Press, 1983. A historical and critical analysis of problems of time's reality and of metaphysical problems concerned with God, eternity, and creation that arise from a natural philosophy of time.

Wallace, William A. "Aquinas on the Temporal Relation between Cause and Effect." *The Review of Metaphysics* 27 (1974): 569–84. Wallace argues that Aquinas's understanding of physical process and scientific methodology provides a reasonable middle ground that maintains the insights, and corrects the errors and omissions, of Aristotle and Hume on the temporal relation between cause and effect.

Two excellent presentations of the Thomistic understanding of time, especially time's extra-mental reality, are:

Fuente, P., and G. Alberto. *Caracter cosmologico de la nocion de tiempo en Santo Tomas.* Santander: Las Caladas de Besaya, 1955.

Jocelyn, M. "Time, The Measure of Movement." *The Thomist* 24 (1961): 431–40. (Reprinted in Weisheipl, J. A., ed. *The Dignity of Science: Studies Presented to William Humbert Kane, O.P.* n.p.: Thomist Press, 1961.)

Time as Experienced

On mediaeval *computus,* i.e., computation of calendar dates, especially Easter, see Jones's introduction and Bede's texts in Charles W. Jones, ed., *Bedae Opera de temporibus* (Cambridge: The Mediaeval Academy of America, 1943).

Bibliography

On differing cultural understandings of time in the High Middle Ages:

Chenu, M.-D. "Conscience de l'histoire et théologie." *Archives d'histoire doc-trinale et littéraire du moyen âge* (1954): 107–33. (Reprinted in Chenu, M.-D. *La théologie au douzième siècle*. Paris: J. Vrin, 1957. Translated by Jerome Taylor and Lester K. Little as "Theology and the New Aware-ness of History." In *Nature, Man, and Society in the Twelfth Century: Essays on New Theological Perspectives in the Latin West*. Chicago: University of Chicago Press, 1968.) A study of the theological and psycho-logical background of Christendom's becoming "aware of its historical evolution in the twelfth century."

Gilson, Étienne. "Le moyen âge et l'histoire." Chap. 19 in *L'Esprit de la philo-sophie médiévale*. 2d ed. Paris: J. Vrin, 1948. (Translated by A. H. C. Downes as *The Spirit of Mediaeval Philosophy*. New York: Charles Scrib-ner's Sons, 1940.) A discussion of mediaeval reflections on human pro-gress through history and on the enduring intelligibility of a changing world.

Le Goff, Jacques. "Temps de l'église et temps du marchand." *Annales econo-mies, sociétés, civilisations* 15 (1960): 417–33. (Reprinted in Le Goff, Jacques. *Pour un autre moyen âge: Temps, travail, et culture en occident.* Paris: Gallimard, 1977. Translated by Arthur Goldhammer as *Time, Work, and Culture in the Middle Ages*. Chicago: University of Chicago Press, 1980.) Le Goff presents a sociological study of different ways of thinking about time, as natural time, professional time, and supernatural time, in the twelfth to fourteenth centuries.

———. "Le temps du travail dans la 'crise' du XIVe siècle: Du temps médiéval au temps moderne." *Le moyen âge* 69 (1963): 597–613. (Reprinted in Le Goff, Jacques. *Pour un autre moyen âge: Temps, travail, et culture en occident*. Paris: Gallimard, 1977. Translated by Arthur Goldhammer as *Time, Work, and Culture in the Middle Ages*. Chicago: University of Chi-cago Press, 1980.) The article presents evidence that the conditions of urban labour and profit provided some impetus for a shift from a mediaeval to a modern cultural concept of time.

General Philosophical

Aguessy, H., M. Ashish, Y. F. Askin, Boubou Hama, H.-G. Gadamer, L. Gardet, A. Hasnaoui, T. Honderich, A. Jeannière, S. Karsz, S. Ohe, P. Ricoeur, A. J. Toynbee, and J. Witt-Hansen. *Time and the Philosophies.* Paris: UNESCO, 1977.

Banks, R. *The Tyranny of Time.* Downer's Grove: IVF, 1983.

Bibliography

Basri, Saul A. *A Deduction Theory of Space and Time.* Amsterdam: North Holland, 1966.

Bell, Thelma H., and Corydon Bell. *The Riddle of Time.* New York: Viking, 1963.

Bergson, Henri. *Time and Free Will: An Essay on the Immediate Data of Consciousness.* New York: Macmillan, 1913.

Braine, David. *The Reality of Time and the Existence of God.* Oxford: Clarendon, 1988. A contemporary project in the model of the project of Augustine to show the relation of time to metaphysical realities. Presented as the Gifford Lectures of 1983-84. A most useful bibliography is provided (pp. 365-70).

Brohm, J. M. *Sport—A Prison of Measured Time.* London: Ink Links, 1978.

Callahan, John F. *Four Views of Time in Ancient Philosophy.* Cambridge: Harvard University Press, 1948.

Carlsteen, Tommy, Don Parkes, and Nigel Thrift. *Making Sense of Time.* Vol. 1 of *Timing Space and Spacing Time.* London: E. Arnold, 1978.

Chapman, T. *Time: A Philosophical Analysis.* Boston: Reidel, 1982.

Cleugh, Mary Frances. *Time and its Importance in Modern Thought.* London: Methuen, 1937.

Davies, P. C. W. *Space and Time in the Modern Universe.* Cambridge: Cambridge University Press, 1977.

Denbigh, Kenneth G. *Three Concepts of Time.* New York: Springer-Verlag, 1981.

Eiseley, L. *The Firmament of Time.* New York: Atheneum, 1975. A useful and popular introduction to the topic by anthropologist Eiseley that is the result of a lecture series at the University of Cincinnati in 1959. A short bibliography is provided on pp. 182-83.

Ellul, J. *The Technological Society.* New York: Random House, 1964.

Elton, Lewis R. B. *Time and Man.* Oxford: Pergamon, 1978.

Flood, R., and M. Lockwood. *The Nature of Time.* Oxford: Blackwell, 1986. A useful series of essays by physical scientists and philosophers on the nature of time. A brief bibliography is provided on pages 180-82.

Fraser, J. T. *Time as Conflict: A Scientific and Humanistic Study.* Basel: Birkhauser, 1978.

——, ed. *The Voices of Time: A Cooperative Survey of Man's Views of Time as Expressed by the Sciences and by the Humanities.* New York: Braziller, 1966.

Fraser, J. T., F. C. Haber, and G. H. Müller, eds. *The Study of Time: Proceedings of the First Conference of the International Society for the Study of Time*. Berlin: Springer-Verlag, 1975.

Fraser, J. T., and N. Lawrence, eds. *The Study of Time II: Proceedings of the Second Conference of the International Society for the Study of Time*. New York: Springer-Verlag, 1975.

Fromm, E. *To Have or To Be*. London: Cape, 1978.

Gale, R. M. *The Philosophy of Time*. Garden City, N.Y.: Anchor, 1967. This text provides a balanced set of readings from a variety of authors prominent in time studies in the mid-twentieth century. A useful bibliography is provided from the foundational, functional, and sociological points of view. Gale provides a helpful review of literature on the paradoxes of Zeno (pp. 506-7).

——. *The Language of Time*. London: Routledge & Kegan Paul, 1968.

Gold, Thomas, ed. *The Nature of Time*. Ithaca: Cornell University Press, 1967.

Gorman, Bernard S., and Alden E. Wessman. *The Personal Experience of Time*. New York: Plenum, 1977.

Grudin, R. *Time and the Art of Living*. San Francisco: Harper & Row, 1982.

Grünbaum, A. *Philosophical Problems of Space and Time*. Boston: Reidel, 1973.

Haber, F. C. "The Darwinian Revolution in the Concept of Time." In *The Study of Time*, edited by J. T. Fraser, F. C. Haber, and G. H. Müller. New York: Springer, 1972.

Hammerschmidt, William W. *Whitehead's Philosophy of Time*. New York: King's Crown, 1947.

Handling, Oswald. *The Quest for Meaning*. Oxford: Blackwell, 1987. Handling deals with matters such as suffering, religion, death and the value of life, self-realization, and happiness.

Heath, Louise Robinson. *The Concept of Time*. Chicago: University of Chicago Press, 1936.

Hegel, G. W. F. *The Phenomenology of Mind*. 2d ed., translated by J. B. Baillie. London: George Allen & Unwin, 1961. Preface, pp. 104-30; "Consciousness," pp. 149-60; "Absolute Knowledge," pp. 800-808. This text is an essential critical comment on the problems involved in the Kantian and empiricist notions of time. The concluding section on the Absolute provides a sense of the notion of time as the form of empty intuition, which is manifested in its fullness in history.

Heidegger, Martin. *Being and Time*. Translated by J. Macquarrie and E. Robinson. New York: Harper & Row, 1962.

——. *History of the Concept of Time*. Translated by T. Kisiel. Bloomington: Indiana University Press, 1985.

Helm, Bertrand P. *Time and Reality in American Philosophy*. Amherst: University of Massachusetts Press, 1985.

Holdheim, W. W. *The Hermeneutic Mode: Essays on Time in Literature and Literary Theory*. Ithaca: Cornell University Press, 1984.

Hood, Peter. *How Time is Measured*. Oxford: Oxford University Press, 1969.

Huizinga, T. *Homo Ludens*. London: Paladin, 1970.

Husserl, Edmund. *Ideas: General Introduction to Pure Phenomenology*. New York: Collier Macmillan, 1975. Chapter 3, section 27, pp. 91-93; Chapter 8, "General Structure of Pure Consciousness," section 81 on phenomenological time and time-consciousness, pp. 215-34, 307-9. Husserl provides the background for contemporary approaches to time in the phenomenological tradition. He develops the Kantian-Hegelian tradition and shows a constructive way of proceeding further with it.

James, William. *The Will to Believe, and Other Essays in Popular Philosophy.* New York: Dover, 1956. The founder of American pragmatism addresses himself to the problems of time and the meaning of life in a number of important essays.

Kant, Immanuel. *Critique of Pure Reason*. Translated by Norman Kemp Smith. London: Macmillan, 1963. Transcendental Aesthetic, Section 2, pp. 74-91; Table of Categories, Section 3, pp. 111-19; and the Transcendental Deduction, pp. 120-75. The Kantian aesthetic and the deduction of the categories is rooted in temporal and spatial experience. It forms the basis for the Hegelian synthesis and the resulting phenomenological enquiries. These texts are of the utmost importance.

Kerr, W. *The Decline of Pleasure*. New York: Simon & Schuster, 1965.

Kroes, Peter. *Time, its Structure and Role in Physical Theories*. Boston: Reidel, 1985.

Lakoff, G., and M. Johnson. *Metaphors We Live By*. Chicago: University of Chicago Press, 1980. On time and metaphors applied to time.

Landsberg, P. T. *The Enigma of Time*. Bristol: A. Hilger, 1982.

Lucas, John R. *A Treatise on Time and Space*. London: Methuen, 1973.

Luce, G. G. *Body Time: The Natural Rhythms of the Body*. St. Alban's: Paladin, 1973. An excellent introduction to the problems of environmental and body rhythms.

Lynch, Kevin. *What Time is This Place?* Cambridge: MIT Press, 1972.

Macey, Samuel L. *Clocks and Cosmos: Time in Western Life and Thought*. Hamden, Conn.: Archon, 1980.

Malévy, E. *The Growth of Philosophic Radicalism*. London: Faber & Faber, 1952.

Marx, Karl. *Karl Marx and Friedrich Engels: Selected Correspondence*. Translated by Peter and Betty Ross. London: Lawrence & Wishart, 1985. On time as a resource with a monetary value in his letter dated January 28, 1863, to Engels.

Mendilow, A. "The Time Obsession of the Twentieth Century." In *Aspects of Time*, edited by C. A. Patrides. Manchester: Manchester University Press, 1976.

Michon, John A., and Janet L. Jackson, eds. *Time, Mind, and Behaviour*. New York: Springer-Verlag, 1985.

Moore, Wilbert E. *Man, Time and Society*. New York: Wiley, 1963.

Mumford, L. *Technics and Civilisation*. New York: Harcourt, Brace, 1934.

Needham, Joseph. *Time and Eastern Man*. London: Royal Anthropological Institute, 1975.

Newton, Isaac. *Principia Mathematica, Definitions*. Scholium I. Berkeley and Los Angeles: University of California Press, 1962.

Newton-Smith, W. H. *The Structure of Time*. London: Routledge & Kegan Paul, 1980.

Parsons, Edward. *Time Devoured: A Materialistic Discussion of Duration*. London: Allen & Unwin, 1964.

Patrides, C. A., ed. *Aspects of Time*. Toronto: University of Toronto Press, 1976. An invaluable source of discussion on the literary and philosophical notions of time.

Pieper, J. *Leisure: The Basis of Culture*. London: Faber, 1952.

Priestley, J. B. *Man and Time*. New York: Doubleday, 1964.

Prigogine, I. *Order Out of Chaos*. New York: Bantam, 1984.

Quinones, Ricardo J. *The Renaissance Discovery of Time*. Cambridge: Harvard University Press, 1972.

Reichenbach, Hans. *The Philosophy of Space and Time*. New York: Dover, 1957. An examination of the space-time conjunction by a distinguished philosopher of science.

Ricoeur, P. *Time and Narrative*. Chicago: University of Chicago Press, 1984. Ricoeur's work is in both the current traditions of Western philosophy: the analytic and the phenomenological traditions. This particular work is a seminal one on the notions of time.

Rifkin, J. *Time Wars: The Primary Conflict in Human History*. New York: Holt, 1987

Salmon, Wesley C. *Space, Time and Motion: A Philosophical Introduction*. Ancino, Calif.: Dickenson, 1975.

Sanders, Steven, and David R. Cheney. *The Meaning of Life*. Englewood Cliffs, N.J.: Prentice-Hall, 1980. A collection of essays on the general themes of time and meaning.

Saunders, D. *An Introduction to Biological Rhythms*. Glasgow: Blackie, 1977. A good introduction to the problems of body rhythms and environmental rhythms in time.

Schlesinger, George. *Aspects of Time*. Indianapolis: Hackett, 1980.

Shallis, M. *On Time*. New York: Schocken Books, 1983. A conceptual consideration of time with a useful bibliography on pp. 200-203.

Sherover, Charles M. *The Human Experience of Time*. New York: New York University Press, 1975.

Smart, John J. C. *Problems of Space and Time*. New York: Macmillan, 1964.

Swinburne, Richard. *Space and Time*. London: St. Martin's, 1968.

Taylor, Richard. *Virtue Ethics*. Interlaken, N.Y.: Linden, 1991. Taylor defends a view of happiness based on function and argues that this is the position of Socrates and Aristotle.

Tournier, P. *Guilt and Grace: A Psychological Study*. New York: Harper & Row, 1962.

van Fraasen, Bas C. *An Introduction to the Philosophy of Time and Space*. New York: Random House, 1970.

Whitrow, G. J. *What Is Time?* London: Thames & Hudson, 1972.

——. *The Nature of Time*. New York: Holt, Rinehart & Winston, 1973.

——. *The Natural Philosophy of Time*. Oxford: Clarendon, 1980.

Wiggins, David. *Truth, Invention and the Meaning of Life*. Oxford: Oxford University Press, 1976. A reflection on Richard Taylor's *Good and Evil*

(Buffalo, N.Y.: Prometheus, 1984) and other works. An original interpretation of the problems of time and meaning.

Yaker, H. M., H. Osmond, and F. Cheek, eds. *The Future of Time: Man's Temporal Environment.* London: Hogarth, 1972. A useful recent attempt, by various authors, to present a phenomenological view of time.

Zeman, Jiri. *Time in Science and Philosophy.* New York: Elsevier, 1971.

Historical

Aikon, Paul. "Changing the Calendar." *Eighteenth Century Life,* n.s., 7, no. 2 (1982): 1-18.

Aikon, Paul K. "Historical Development of the Concept of Time." In *Bio-rhythms and Human Reproduction,* edited by M. Ferin, F. Halberg, R. M. Richart, and R. L. Vande Wiele. New York: Wiley, 1974.

Baxter, R. *A Christian Directory.* London, 1673.

Campbell, Joseph, ed. *Eranos-Jahrbücher.* Princeton: Princeton University Press, 1951.

Contents:

E. Neumann, "Art and Time"

H.-C. Peuch, "Gnosis and Time"

G. Quispel, "Time and History in Patristic Christianity"

L. Massignon, "Time in Islamic Thought"

H. Corbin, "Cyclical Time in Mazdaism and Ismailism"

M. Eleade, "Time and Eternity in Indian Thought"

L. Whyte, "Time and the Mind-Body Problem: A Changed Scientific Conception of Progress"

C. Jung, "On Synchronicity"

E. Goodenough, "The Evaluation of Symbols Recurrent in Time, as Illustrated in Judaism"

H. Wilhelm, "The Concept of Time in the Book of Changes"

H. Plessner, "On the Relation of Time to Death"

M. Knoll, "The Transformation of Science in Our Age"

A. Portmann, "Time in the Life of the Organism"

This collection, arising from meetings of world-renowned scholars, is an indispensible source of insights into religious and scientific notions of time.

Carr, Herbert Wildon. "Time" and "History" in Contemporary Philosophy. London: Oxford University Press, 1918.

Cipolla, C. *Clocks and Culture, 1300-1700.* London: Collins, 1967.

Bibliography

Franklin, B. "Poor Richard's Almanac." In *The Papers of Benjamin Franklin*, edited by L. W. Labaree and W. J. Bell. New Haven: Yale University Press, 1961.

Glasser, R. *Time in French Life and Thought*. Manchester: Manchester University Press, 1972.

Gould, Stephen Jay. *Time's Arrow, Time's Cycle: Myth and Metaphor in the Discovery of Geological Time*. Cambridge: Harvard University Press, 1987. Gould provides a most significant perspective on time from the geologist's viewpoint. This geological approach puts time in the context of geological history. The geological aspects of history and time are represented in the bibliography (pp. 211-15).

Grant, George P. *Time as History*. Toronto: CBC, 1969. Grant provides a view of time and its connection to human events that escapes the purely calculative approach to time in favour until this century.

Landes, D. S. *Revolution in Time: Clocks and the Making of the Modern World*. Cambridge, Mass.: Belknap, 1983.

Melbin, M. "The Colonisation of Time." In *Human Spacing and Human Time II: Human Activity and Time Geography*, edited by T. Carlstein, O. Parker, and N. Thrift. London: Edward Arnold, 1978.

Morris, R. *Time's Arrow*. New York: Simon & Schuster Touchstone, 1985. A valuable explanation of time by a theoretical physicist, with a broad-ranging bibliography (pp. 219-30) covering theological, mythical, philosophical, and scientific approaches to time.

Mumford, L. *Technics and Civilisation*. New York: Harcourt, Brace, 1934.

Nilsson, M. P. *Primitive Time Reckoning*. Lund: Gleerup, 1920.

Rifkin, J. *Time Wars: The Primary Conflict in Human History*. New York: Holt, 1987.

Thompson, E. P. "Time, Work-Discipline and Industrial Capitalism." In *Essays in Social History*, edited by M. W. Flinn and T. C. Smout. Oxford: Clarendon, 1974. A most valuable work, even though Thompson tends to exaggerate the Puritan preparation for later industrial attitudes.

van Leeuwen, Th. *Christianity in World History*. London: Edinburgh House, 1964.

Welch, K. *Time Measurement: An Introductory History*. Newton Abbott: David & Charles, 1972.

Wesley, John. "On Redeeming the Time." Sermon 93 in *The Works of John Wesley*, edited by Albert C. Outler. Vol. 3. Nashville: Abingdon, 1986.

Whitrow, G. J. *Time in History: Views of Time From Prehistory to the Present Day*. New York: Oxford University Press, 1988. Whitrow's book supplements his text *The Natural Philosophy of Time* (Oxford: Clarendon, 1980). It provides a survey of approaches from antiquity, the Middle Ages, and modern and contemporary life. Whitrow's ability to combine humanist and scientific approaches to time is critical to contemporary understanding. His list of references (pp. 194-206) is most useful.

II Functional: Economic, Legal, Medical, Ethical, Sociological, Psychological

Economic

Arndt, Johan, Sigmund Gronmo, and Douglas K. Hawes. "Allocation of Time to Leisure Activities: Norwegian and American Patterns." *Journal of CrossCultural Psychology* 11 (1980): 498–511.

Becker, G. S. "A Theory of the Allocation of Time." *Economic Journal* 75 (1965): 493–517.

Berk, Richard A., and Sarah Fenstermaker Berk. *Labour and Leisure at Home*. Beverly Hills: Sage, 1979.

Bevans, G. *How Working Men Spend Their Time*. New York: Columbia University Press, 1913.

Bienfeld, M. A. *Working Hours in British Industry: An Economic History*. London: Weidenfeld & Nicholson, 1979.

On the question of working hours see, for the North American situation:

Bliss, E. C. *Getting Things Done: The ABC's of Time Management*. New York: Scribner, 1976.

Chapin, F. Stuart. *Urban Land Use Planning*. Urbana, Ill.: University of Illinois Press, 1965.

Chapin, F. Stuart, and James F. Foerster. "Teenager Activity Patterns in Low Income Communities." In *Time-Budgets and Social Activity*. Vol. 1. Toronto: Centre for Urban and Community Studies, 1975.

Chapin, F. Stuart, Jr. *Human Activity Patterns in the City: Things People Do in Time and Space*. Toronto: Wiley, 1974.

Clark, J. P. "Temporal Inventories and Time Structuring in Large Organisations." In *The Study of Time III*, edited by J. T. Fraser, N. Lawrence, and D. Park. New York: Springer, 1978. Helpful in time and motion studies.

Clark, Susan, and David H. Elliott. "Social Involvement and Social Diversity: An Examination of Social Contact and Location Sequences." Paper presented at the World Congress of Sociology, Uppsala, Sweden, August 1978.

Clark, Susan, and Andrew S. Harvey. "The Sexual Division of Labour: The Use of Time." *Atlantis* 2, no. 1 (1976): 46-66.

Cullen, Ian, and V. Godson. *Urban Networks: The Structure of Activity Patterns.* Oxford: Pergamon, 1975.

Cullen, Ian, and Elizabeth Phelps. *Diary Techniques and the Problems of Everyday Life.* Final report to the Social Science Research Council, grant no. HR2336, London, 1975.

de Grazia, S. *Time, Work and Leisure.* New York: Doubleday, 1964.

For an interesting comparison of the situation today and a century ago:

Denton, Frank T., and Byron G. Spencer. "A Simulation Analysis of the Effects of Population Change on a Neoclassical Economy." *Journal of Political Economy* 81, no. 2 (1973): 356-75.

——. "Health-Care Costs When the Population Changes." *Canadian Journal of Economics* 8 (1975): 34-48.

——. "A Macroeconomic Analysis of the Effects of a Public Pension Plan." *Canadian Journal of Economics* 14 (1981): 609-34.

——. "Population Aging and Future Health Costs in Canada." *Canadian Public Policy* 9 (1983): 155-63.

Denton, Frank T., Byron G. Spencer, and Christine H. Feaver. "OASI and the U.S. Economy: A Model and Some Long-Run Projections." In *Social Security and Pensions: Programs of Equity and Security.* Joint Economic Committee of the Congress of the United States, Special Study on Economic Change. Vol. 8. Washington, D.C.: Government Printing Office, 1980.

DeSerpa, A. C. "A Theory of the Economics of Time." *Economic Journal* 81 (1971): 838-46.

Drucker, P. *The Effective Executive.* London: Pan, 1970.

Elliott, David H. "Constraints and Sequences: Elements of Formal Models of Activity Patterns." Paper prepared for Ad Hoc Group 10, "Time Budgets and Social Activities," at the Ninth World Congress of Sociology, Uppsala, Sweden, August 1978.

Evans, A. A. *Hours of Work in Industrialised Countries.* Geneva: International Labour Organisation, 1975.

Bibliography

Ferge, Susan. "Social Differentiation in Leisure Choices." In *The Use of Time*, edited by Alexander Szalai. The Hague: Mouton, 1972.

Friedman, M., and R. H. Rosenman. *Type A Behaviour and Your Heart*. New York: Knopf, 1974. A useful text on stress and time management.

Fuchs, Victor R. *How We Live*. Cambridge: Harvard University Press, 1983.

Grønmo, Sigmund. "The Issue of Saturday Retail Closing in Norway: Some Consumer Welfare Aspects." Paper presented at Corporate Social Concerns and Public Policy Conference, Bergen, Norway, April 1978.

———. *Lørdag Som Handledag*. Oslo: Fondet for markeds-og distribusjons-forskning, 1983.

Hägerstrand, Torsten. "What About People in Regional Science?" *Regional Science Association Papers* 24 (1970): 7–21.

Harvey, Andrew S. "Preference, Perception and Opportunity: The Shapers of Individual Behaviour." *Northeast Regional Science Review* 6, no. 1 (1976): 1–11.

———. *Discretionary Time Activities in Context*. Occasional paper no. 3. Halifax: Institute of Public Affairs, Regional and Urban Studies Centre, Dalhousie University, 1978.

Harvey, Andrew S., and David H. Elliott. *Time and Time Again*. Vol. 4 of *Explorations in Time Use*, edited by M. Catherine Casserly and Brian L. Kinsley. Ottawa: Employment & Immigration Canada, 1983.

Harvey, Andrew S., David H. Elliott, and W. Stephen Macdonald. *The Work of Canadians*. Vol. 3 of *Explorations in Time Use*, edited by M. Catherine Casserly and Brian L. Kinsley. Ottawa: Employment & Immigration Canada, 1983.

Harvey, Andrew S., David H. Elliott, and W. Stephen Macdonald. "Activities and Settings." Ottawa: Employment & Immigration Canada, 1984.

Harvey, Andrew S., and Sigmund Grønmo. "Social Contact and Use of Time: Canada and Norway." In *Time Use Studies: Dimensions and Applications*, edited by D. Aas, Andrew S. Harvey, E. Wnuk-Lipinski, and I. Niemi. Helsinki: Central Statistical Office of Finland, 1986.

Javeau, Claude. "The Trip to Work." In *The Use of Time*, edited by Alexander Szalai. The Hague: Mouton, 1972.

Kinsley, Brian L., and Frank Graves. *The Time of Our Lives*. Vol. 2 of *Explorations in Time Use*, edited by Brian L. Kinsley and M. Catherine Casserly. Ottawa: Employment & Immigration Canada, 1983.

Kinsley, Brian L., and Terry O'Donnell. *Marking Time.* Vol. 1 of *Explorations in Time Use,* edited by Brian L. Kinsley and M. Catherine Casserly. Ottawa: Employment & Immigration Canada, 1983.

Lebhar, G. M. *The Use of Time.* New York: Chain Store, 1958, vi, 14, 124.

Levi, L. *Stress: Sources, Management and Prediction.* New York: Liveright, 1967.

Linder, S. B. *The Harried Leisure Class.* New York: Columbia University Press, 1970.

Matsushima, Chiyono. "Time-Input and Household Work-Output Studies in Japan—Present State and Future Prospects." *Journal of Consumer Studies and Home Economics* 5 (1981): 199-217.

Medrich, Elliott A., Judith A. Roizen, Victor Rubin, and Stuart Buckley. *The Serious Business of Growing Up: A Study of Children's Lives Outside School.* Berkeley and Los Angeles: University of California Press, 1982.

Meissner, Martin, Elizabeth W. Humphreys, Scott M. Meis, and William J. Scheu. "No Exit for Wives: Sexual Division of Labour and the Cumulation of Household Demands." *Canadian Review of Sociology and Anthropology* 12, pt. 1 (1975): 424-39.

Michelson, William. *From Sun to Sun: Daily Obligations and Community Structure in the Lives of Employed Women and their Families.* Totawa, N.J.: Roaman & Allan, 1985.

Moss, Miriam S., and M. Powell Lawton. "Time Budgets of Older People: A Window on Four Lifestyles." *Journal of Gerontology* 37 (1982): 115-23.

Nakanishi, Naomichi. *Changes in Mass Media Contact Times.* Tokyo: Public Opinion Research Institute, Japan Broadcasting Corporation (NHK), 1982.

——. "A Report on the 'How Do People Spend Their Time Survey' in 1980." *Studies in Broadcasting* 18 (1982): 93-113.

Nickols, Sharon. "Work and Housework: Family Roles in Productive Activity." Paper presented at annual meeting of the National Council of Family Relations, New York, October 1976.

Nissel, Muriel. *The Use of Time Budgets in Measuring the Cost of Family Care of the Handicapped Elderly.* London: Policy Studies Institute, 1980.

Owen, J. O. *Working Hours: An Economic Analysis.* Toronto: Lexington, 1979.

Patrushev, V. D. "Time Budget Utilization by Working People at Industrial Enterprises with Five and Six-Day Working Weeks and Tendencies for it to Change." Paper prepared for meeting of the International Research Group on Time Budgets and Social Activities, Mexico City, August 1982.

Bibliography

——. "Satisfaction with Free Time as a Social Category and an Indicator of Way of Life." In It's About Time: Proceedings of the International Research Group on Time Budgets and Social Activities, edited by Zahari Staikov. Sofia, Bulgaria: Institute of Sociology at the Bulgarian Academy of Sciences and Bulgarian Sociological Association, 1982.

Procos, Dimitri, and Andrew S. Harvey. "Modelling for Local Planning Decisions." Ekistics 264 (1977): 257–66.

Robinson, J. P. How Americans Use Their Time: A Social-Psychological Analysis of Everyday Behaviour. New York: Praeger, 1977.

Robinson, J. P., and P. E. Converse. "The Impact of Television on Mass Media Usage: A Cross-National Comparison." In The Use of Time, edited by Alexander Szalai. The Hague: Mouton, 1972.

——. "Social Change as Reflected in the Use of Time." In The Human Meaning of Social Change, edited by A. E. Campbell and P. E. Converse. New York: Russell Sage Foundation, 1972.

Romaniuc, A. Fertility in Canada: From Baby-Boom to Baby-Bust. Catalogue no. 91-524E. Ottawa: Statistics Canada, 1984.

Schneider, Annerose. "Patterns of Social Interaction." In The Use of Time, edited by Alexander Szalai. The Hague: Mouton, 1972.

Selye, H. The Stress of Life. London: Longmans Green, 1956.

——. Stress Without Distress. London: Hodder & Stoughton, 1974. This work is fundamental in pointing to economic stress.

Shaw, Susan M. "The Sexual Division of Leisure: Meanings, Perceptions and the Distribution of Free Time." Ph.D. diss., Carleton University, 1983.

Siegel, Jacob S. "On the Demography of Aging." Demography 17 (1980): 345–64.

Skorgzynski, Zigmut. "The Use of Free Time in Torun, Maribour, and Jackson." In The Use of Time, edited by Alexander Szalai. The Hague: Mouton, 1972.

Stone, Philip J. "Childcare in Twelve Countries." In The Use of Time, edited by Alexander Szalai. The Hague: Mouton, 1972.

——. "On Being Up Against the Wall: Women's Time Patterns in Eleven Countries." Department of Psychology and Social Relations, Harvard University, Cambridge, n.d.

Stone, Philip J., and Nancy Nicolson. "Behaviour and Behaviour Settings." Paper presented at the Tenth World Congress of Sociology, Mexico City, 1982.

Terkel, S. *Working: People Talk About What They Do All Day & How They Feel About What They Do*. London: Wildwood House, 1975.

Tillett, A., T. Kempner, and G. Wills, eds. *Management Thinkers*. Harmondsworth: Penguin, 1970, 75-197. A helpful anthology on time and motion studies.

Vanek, Joann. "Time Spent in Housework." *Scientific American* 231 (November 1974): 116-20.

Varga, Karoly. "Marital Cohesion as Reflected in Time-Budgets." In *The Use of Time*, edited by Alexander Szalai. The Hague: Mouton, 1972.

Veblen, Th. *The Theory of the Leisure Class*. London: Unwin, 1970.

Walker, Kathryn E. "How Much Help for Working Mothers? The Children's Role." *Human Ecology Forum* 1, no. 2 (1970): 13-15.

Walker, Kathryn E., and Margaret E. Woods. *Time Use: A Measure of Household Production of Family Goods and Services*. Washington, D.C.: American Home Economics Association, 1976.

Woolfolk, R. L., and F. L. Richardson. *Stress: Sanity and Survival*. London: Futura, 1979.

Ethical/Legal

Annas, G. J. "Reconciling *Quinlan* and *Saikewicz*: Decision Making for the Terminally Ill Incompetent." *American Journal of Law and Medicine* 4 (1979): 367-96.

Ansbacher, R. "Force-Feeding Hunger-Striking Prisoners: A Framework for Analysis." *University of Florida Law Review* 35 (1983): 99-129.

Cranford, R. E., and A. E. Doudera. "The Emergence of Institutional Ethics Committees." *Law, Medicine & Health Care* 12 (1984): 13-20.

Curran, William J. "Law-Medicine Notes: The Saikewicz Decision." *New England Journal of Medicine* 298 (1978): 499-500.

Dickens, B. M. "Legal Responses to Child Abuse." *Family Law Quarterly* 12 (1978): 1-36.

——. "Legal Responses to Child Abuse in Canada." *Canadian Journal of Family Law* 1 (1978): 87-125.

——. "The Modern Function and Limits of Parental Rights." *Law Quarterly Review* 97 (1981): 462-85.

——. "The Right to Natural Death." *McGill Law Journal* 26 (1981): 847-79.

——. "Medicine and the Law: Withholding Paediatric Medical Care." *Canadian Bar Review* 62 (1984): 196-210.

Donovan, P. "Wrongful Birth and Wrongful Conception: The Legal and Moral Issues." *Family Planning Perspectives* 16 (1984): 64-69.

Kretzmer, D. "The Malpractice Suit: Is It Needed?" *Osgoode Hall Law Journal* 11 (1973): 55-79.

Krez, D. "Comment. Withholding Treatment from Seriously Ill and Handicapped Infants: Who Should Make the Decision and How?—An Analysis of the Government's Response." *De Paul Law Review* 33 (1984): 495-543.

Law Reform Commission of Canada. Two publications both entitled *Criteria for the Determination of Death*. Working paper no. 23 (1979) and report no. 15 (1981). Ottawa: Supply & Services.

Levine, C. "Questions and (Some Very Tentative) Answers About Hospital Ethics Committees." *Hastings Center Report* 14, no. 3 (1984): 9-12.

McCormick, R. A. "Ethics Committees: Promise or Peril?" *Law, Medicine & Health Care* 12 (1984): 150-55.

President's Commission for the Study of Ethical Problems in Medicine and Biomedical and Behavioral Research. *Deciding to Forego Life-Sustaining Treatment: Ethical, Medical, and Legal Issues in Treatment Decisions.* Washington, D.C.: Government Printing Office, 1983. A brief review of the report appears in B. M. Dickens, "The Final Freedom: Deciding to Forego Life-Sustaining Treatment," *Public Law* (1984): 34-43.

Somerville, Margaret A. "Pain and Suffering at Interfaces of Medicine and Law." *University of Toronto Law Journal* 36 (1986): 286-317. On the contrast between pain and suffering.

Starkman, B. "A Defence to Criminal Responsibility for Performing Surgical Operations: Section 45 of the Criminal Code." *McGill Law Journal* 26 (1981): 1048-55.

Tagawa, B. K. "Prisoner Hunger Strikes: Constitutional Protection for a Fundamental Right." *American Criminal Law Review* 21 (1983): 569-98.

Veatch, R. M. "Limits of Guardian Treatment Refusal: A Reasonableness Standard." *American Journal of Law and Medicine* 9 (1984): 427-68.

Winner, A. E. "Baby Doe Decisions: Modern Society's Sins of Omission." *Nebraska Law Review* 63 (1984): 888-940.

Whitlock, K. M. "Court Establishes Guidelines for Removal of Life Support Systems From Incompetents in a Persistent Vegetative State." *Gonzaga*

Law Review 19 (1983/84): 417-35, a case comment on *In re Colyer* (1983), 600 P.2d 738 (Wash.S.C.).

Zellick, G. "The Forcible Feeding of Prisoners: An Examination of the Legality of Enforced Therapy," *Public Law* (1976): 153-87.

Key judgments, in order of appearance:

United States v. Holmes (1842), 26. Fed. Cas. 360 (Cir.Ct., E.D.Pa.).

R. v. Dudley and Stephens (1884), 14 Q.B.D. 273.

Cardozo J. in *Schloendorff v. Society of New York Hospital* (1914), 105 N.E. 92 (N.Y.C.A.).

R. v. Bourne [1939] 1 K.B. 687.

Wilson v. Swanson (1956), 5 D.L.R. (2d) 113 (S.C.C.).

Application of President and Directors of Georgetown College (1964), 331 F.2d 1000 (D.C.Cir.).

Raleigh Fitkin—Paul Morgan Memorial Hospital v. Anderson (1964), 201 A.2d 537 (N.J.S.C.).

In re Brooks' Estate (1965), 205 N.E. 2d 435 (Ill.S.C.).

Gleitman v. Cosgrove (1967), 227 A.2d 689, at 692.

John F. Kennedy Hospital v. Heston (1971), 279 A.2d 670 (N.J.S.C.), denying a constitutional "right to die."

Roe v. Wade (1973), 410 U.S. 113 (U.S.S.C.). Important in establishing right to privacy.

Morgentaler v. The Queen (1975), 53 D.L.R. (3d) 161.

Cal. Stats. 1976, c. 1439, constituting c. 3.9 of the *Health and Safety Code*.

In the Matter of Karen Quinlan (1976), 335 A.2d 647 (N.J.S.C.).

Superintendent of Belchertown State School v. Saikewicz (1977), 370 N.E. 2d 417.

In the Matter of Shirley Dinnerstein (1978), 380 N.E. 2d 134.

Curlender v. Bio-Science Laboratories (1980), 165 Cal. Rptr. 477 (Cal.C.A.).

In the Matter of Earle Spring (1980), 405 N.E. 2d 115.

Per Laskin C.J.C., *Reibl v. Hughes* (1980), 114 D.L.R. (3d) 1, at 11.

Bibliography

R. v. Arthur, reported in *The Times* (London), November 6, 1981. Acquittal for (attempted) murder.

Turpin v. Sortini (1981), 174 Cal. Rptr. 128 (Cal.C.A.).

Whitehouse v. Jordan [1981] 1 W.L.R. 246 (H.L.).

McKay v. Essex Area Health Authority [1982] 2 W.L.R. 890 (C.A.).

Stephenson, L.J., in *McKay v. Essex Area Health Authority* [1982] 2 W.L.R. 890 (C.A.), at 899.

Bouvia v. County of Riverside, No. 159780, Sup.Ct., Riverside Co., Cal., Dec. 16, 1983, Tr. 1238-1250. Unreported to date but critically discussed in G. J. Annas, "When Suicide Prevention Becomes Brutality: The Case of Elizabeth Bouvia," *Hastings Center Report* 14, no. 2 (1984).

Harbeson v. Parke-Davis, Inc. (1983), 656 P.2d 483 (Wash.S.C.).

Re Superintendent of Family and Child Service and Dawson et al. (1983), 145 D.L.R. (3d) 610, at 623.

Weber v. Stony Brook Hospital (1983), 456 N.E. 2d 1186 (N.Y.C.A.), unsuccessfully appealed in *United States v. University Hospital at Stony Brook* (1984), 729 F.2d 144 (2d Cir.).

Perka v. The Queen (1984), 14 C.C.C. (3d) 385. Review of the history and case law on the defence of necessity, and an elaboration of the distinction between necessity as a justification and as an excuse.

Procanik v. Cillo (1984), 478 A.2d 755 (N.J.S.C.).

Sidaway v. Bethlem Royal Hospital Governors [1984] 1 All E.R. 643 (H.L.).

Ethical/Medical

Arras, J. D. "Quality of Life in Neonatal Ethics: Beyond Denial and Evasion." In *Ethical Issues at the Outset of Life*, edited by W. Weil and M. Benjamin. Oxford: Blackwell Scientific Publications, 1987.

Battin, Margaret P. "Age Rationing and the Just Distribution of Health Care: Is There a Duty to Die?" *Ethics* 97 (1987): 317-40.

Brown, A. "Assisted Suicide and Active Voluntary Euthanasia." *Canadian Journal of Jurisprudence* 2 (1989): 35-56.

Callahan, Daniel. *Setting Limits: Medical Goals in an Aging Society*. New York: Simon & Schuster, 1987. By one of the directors of the Hasting Institute, a biomedical-ethical institute.

Cantor, Norman. "The Permanently Unconscious Patient, Non-Feeding and Euthanasia." *American Journal of Law and Medicine* 15 (1989): 381-437.

Carmeie, Fran. "Euthanasia and Self-Determinism: Is There a *Charter* Right to Die in Canada?" *McGill Law Journal* 32 (1987): 299-335.

Ferguson, G. "The Canadian Charter of Rights and Individual Choice in Treatment." *Health Law in Canada* 8 (1988): 63-70.

Fletcher, Joseph. "Indicators of Humanhood: A Tentative Profile of Man." *Hastings Center Report* 2, no. 5 (1972): 1-4.

Grindes, D. "Judicial Postponement of Death Recognition: The Tragic Case of Mary O'Connor." *American Journal of Law and Medicine* 15 (1989): 301-31. A consideration of nutrition and hydration in the permanently unconscious.

Hare, Richard M. "Survival of the Weakest." In *Moral Problems in Medicine*, edited by S. Gorovitz, R. Macklin, J. M. O'Connor, E. V. Perrin, B. Page St. Clair, and S. Sherwin. 1st ed. Englewood Cliffs, N.J.: Prentice-Hall, 1976.

Heenan, John, Cardinal. "A Fascinating Story." In *The Hour of Our Death*, edited by S. Lack and R. Lamerton. London: Chapman, 1974. Rabbi Immanuel Jakobovits is quoted (pp. 6-7) by Cardinal Heenan, Archbishop of Westminster, in a record of a conference on the care of the dying held in London, 1973.

Kadish, S. H. "Respect for Life and Regard for Rights in the Criminal Law." In *Respect for Life in Medicine, Philosophy and the Law*, edited by S. F. Barker. Baltimore: Johns Hopkins University Press, 1977.

Kelly, Gerald, S.J. *Medico-Moral Problems*. St. Louis: Catholic Hospital Association, 1958.

Kew, S. *Handicap and Family Crisis*. London: Pitman, 1975. Stephen Kew cites two studies: K. Holt, "The Influence of a Retarded Child Upon Family Limitation." *Journal of Mental Deficiency Research* 2 (1958): 28-36; and J. Tizard and J. Grad, *The Mentally Handicapped and Their Families* (Oxford: Oxford University Press, 1961).

Keyserlingk, E. *Sanctity of Life or Quality of Life in the Context of Ethics, Medicine and Law* (Study prepared for the Law Reform Commission of Canada. Ottawa: Supply & Services, 1979. An argument for a moderate approach to euthanasia with concern for the sanctity of human life.

——. "Nontreatment in the Best Interests of the Child." *McGill Law Journal* 32 (1987): 413-36.

King, N. "Federal and State Regulation of Neonatal Decision-Making." In *Euthanasia and the Newborn: Conflicts Regarding Saving Lives*, edited by

Bibliography

Richard C. McMillan, H. Tristram Engelhardt, and Stuart F. Spicker. Boston: Reidel, 1987.

Kirby, M. D. "The Rights of the Living and the Rights of the Dying." *Legal Medical Quarterly* 7 (1983): 192–205.

Kluge, E. *The Practice of Death.* New Haven: Yale University Press, 1975. An interesting series of arguments from the medical advisor to the Canadian Medical Association and an advocate of active euthanasia.

Kuhse, Helga. "'Letting Die' is not in the Patient's Best Interests: A Case for Active Euthanasia." *The Medical Journal of Australia* 142 (1985): 610–13. An argument that since passive euthanasia will often involve more suffering and pain than active euthanasia, it cannot be justified. The patient has a right to terminate her own life if it is in her interest.

———. *The Sanctity of Life Doctrine in Medicine: A Critique.* Oxford: Clarendon, 1987. An attack on the sanctity-of-life principle as inconsistent. She argues that refraining from preventing death is an instance of the intentional termination of life, and hence arguments prohibiting taking life are inconsistent with life preservation. The final arguments are based on interest and "quality of life."

Judgements—Ontario Court of Appeals—*Malette v. Shulman* (1990), 670 *Dominion Law Reports* (4th ser.) 321.

Law Reform Commission of Canada. *Euthanasia, Aiding Suicide and Cessation of Treatment.* Working paper no. 28. Ottawa: Supply & Services, 1982. This document provides a good summary of the legal-medical state of affairs in the early 1980s, with the proposed reform of the laws limited to clarification of cessation of treatment and palliative care. The document provides a very useful bibliography (pp. 75–78) that contrasts with many of the items in this section.

———. *Euthanasia, Aiding Suicide and Cessation of Treatment.* Report no. 20. Ottawa: Supply & Services, 1983. The result of the study of the Law Reform Commission of Canada. The concern is to provide for protection of life and at the same time make room for compassionate care through palliative care facilities.

Locke, John. *Essay Concerning Human Understanding,* bk. II, chap. 9, para. 29. Oxford: Clarendon, 1960. Notable for the definition of a person.

Lucyk, S. R. "Theological Reflections on Euthanasia." *Provincial Judges Journal* 11, no. 1 (1987): 22–25.

MacKinnon, P. "Euthanasia and Homicide." *Criminal Law Quarterly* 26 (1984): 483–508.

———. "Two Views of Murder." *Canadian Bar Review* 63 (1985): 130–47.

McMillan, Richard C., H. Tristram Engelhardt, and Stuart F. Spicker, eds. *Euthanasia and the Newborn: Conflicts Regarding Saving Lives.* Boston: Reidel, 1987. An account of the influence of Christian culture on attitudes to infanticide. Consideration of the Baby Doe regulations in the United States, which regulate attitudes to defective newborns. Final assessment is based on interest, and harms and benefits to society and the newborn.

Office of the Secretary, Department of Health and Human Services. *Nondiscrimination on the Basis of Handicap.* 48 Fed. Reg. 9630 (1983) Interim Final Rule modifying 45 C.F.R., par. 84.61.

U.S. Supreme Court—*Cruzan by Cruzan v. Director, Missouri Department of Health* (1990) 110 S.Ct. 2841.

For the "Baby Doe guidelines":

Gillon, Raanan. *Philosophical Medical Ethics.* Chichester, West Sussex: Wiley, 1986. A discussion based on a series of articles in the *British Medical Journal* that deal with the *Arthur* case and a variety of utilitarian and deontological arguments.

——. "Conclusion: The Arthur Case Revisited." *British Medical Journal* 292 (1986): 543-45.

Pless, J. E. (M.D., Bloomington Hospital). Letter to the Editor. *New England Journal of Medicine* 309, no. 11 (1983): 664. Dr. Pless discusses the medical history of Baby Doe. The ruling of the Indiana Supreme Court was reported in the *Chicago Tribune* on April 17, 1982.

President's Commission for the Study of Ethical Problems in Medicine and Biomedical and Behavioral Research. *Deciding to Forego Life-Sustaining Treatment: Ethical, Medical and Legal Issues in Treatment Decisions.* Washington, D.C.: Government Printing Office, 1983.

Proceedings before the United States District Court for the District of Columbia. *American Academy of Pediatrics et al. versus Margaret Heckler. Secretary of Department of Health and Human Services,* Washington, D.C., March 21, 1983, C.A. no. 83-0774.

Rachels, J. *The End of Life: Euthanasia and Morality.* Oxford: Oxford University Press, 1986. An argument that the distinction between the intentional and non-intentional termination of life has no moral relevance. Also argues that "mercy killing is not reducible to homicide," and provides a historical examination of the basis for this claim.

——. "Euthanasia." In *New Introductory Essays in Moral Philosophy,* edited by T. Regan. New York: Random House, 1986. A series of cases to support the practice of active euthanasia.

Bibliography

Ramsey, P. *The Patient as Person.* New Haven: Yale University Press, 1976. Arguments against active euthanasia and for a compassionate approach to death and dying by a prominent Episcopal theologian and philosopher.

———. *Ethics at the Edges of Life.* New Haven: Yale University Press, 1978.

Raphael, D. D. "Handicapped Infants: Medical Ethics and the Law." *Journal of Medical Ethics* 14 (1988): 5–10.

Samek, R. "Euthanasia and Law Reform." *Ottawa Law Review* 17 (1985): 86–115.

Schiffer, Laura. "Euthanasia and the Criminal Law." *University of Toronto Faculty of Law Review* 42 (1984): 93–113. A good review of the arguments and their relation to criminal law.

Shelp, E. *Born to Die?* New York: Free Press, 1986.

Steinbock, B. "In the Matter of Karen Quinlan, An Alleged Incompetent." In *Killing and Letk Keting Die,* edited by B. Steinbock. Englewood Cliffs, N.J.: Prentice-Hall, 1980. Interesting references to extraordinary means.

Stinson, Robert, and Peggy Stinson. *The Long Dying of Baby Andrew.* Boston: Little, Brown, 1983.

Tooley, M. *Abortion and Infanticide.* Oxford: Clarendon, 1984.

Veatch, Robert M. *Death, Dying and the Biological Revolution.* New Haven: Yale University Press, 1976. A variety of distinctions are discussed, with support for the principle of self-determination and guidelines for application of the principle.

———. "Ethics and the Dying." In *Contemporary Issues in Health Care,* edited by D. J. Schnall and C. L. Figliola. New York: Praeger, 1984.

Weir, Robert F. *Ethical Issues in Death and Dying.* 2d ed. New York: Columbia University Press, 1986. A summary of the various positions by the author with a number of cases to illustrate the problems.

———. *Treatment with Critically Ill Patients: Ethical and Legal Limits to the Medical Prolongation of Life.* Oxford: Oxford University Press, 1989.

Westermarck, E. *The Origin and Development of the Moral Ideas.* Vol. 1. 2d ed. London: Macmillan, 1912. Notable for the account of Jeremy Bentham (p. 413n.) and his comment on infanticide from his *Theory of Legislation.*

Social Sciences: Sociology, Psychology

Achenbaum, W. Andrew. *Old Age in the New Land.* Baltimore: Johns Hopkins University Press, 1978.

Bibliography

Bengston, V. L., and J. Treas. "The Changing Family Context of Mental Health and Aging." In *Handbook of Mental Health and Aging*, edited by J. E. Birren and R. B. Sloane. Englewood Cliffs, N.J.: Prentice-Hall, 1980.

Cain, L. D., Jr. "Life Course and Social Structure." In *Handbook of Modern Sociology*, edited by R. E. L. Faris. Chicago: Rand McNally, 1964.

———. "Age, Status and Generational Phenomena: The New Old People in Contemporary America." *The Gerontologist* 7 (1967): 83-92.

Carroll, J. *Sceptical Sociology*. London: Routledge & Kegan Paul, 1980.

Chudacoff, Howard P., and Tamara K. Hareven. "From the Empty Nest to Family Dissolution: Life Course Transitions Into Old Age." *Journal of Family History* 4 (1979): 69-83.

Cohen, Ronald. "Age and Culture as Theory." In *Age and Anthropological Theory*, edited by D. Kertzer and J. Keith. Ithaca: Cornell University Press, 1984.

Cowgill, D. O. "Aging and Modernization: A Revision of the Theory." In *Late Life: Communities and Environmental Policy*, edited by J. F. Gubrium. Springfield, Ill.: Thomas, 1974.

Cowgill, D. O., and L. D. Holmes. *Aging and Modernization*. New York: Appleton-Century-Crofts, 1972.

Fischer, D. H. *Growing Old in America*. New York: Oxford University Press, 1978.

Foner, Nancy. "Age and Social Change." In *Age and Anthropological Theory*, edited by D. Kertzer and J. Keith. Ithaca: Cornell University Press, 1984.

Goffman, E. *Stigma*. Englewood Cliffs, N.J.: Prentice-Hall, 1963.

Government of Canada. *Fact Book on Aging in Canada*. Ottawa: Supply & Services, 1983.

Hareven, Tamara K. "Historical Changes in the Timing of Family Transitions: Their Impact on Generational Relations." In *Aging: Stability and Change in the Family*, edited by Robert W. Fogel, Elaine Hatfield, Sara B. Kiesler, and Ethel Shanas. New York: Academic Press, 1981.

———. "The Life Course and Aging in Historical Perspective." In *Aging and Life Course Transitions: An Interdisciplinary Perspective*, edited by Tamara K. Hareven and K. J. Adams. New York: Guilford, 1982.

Hirsch, F. *The Social Limits to Growth*. London: Routledge & Kegan Paul, 1976.

Bibliography

Holt, J. *Escape from Childhood: The Needs and Rights of Children.* New York: Dutton, 1974.

Hughes, E. *The Sociological Eye: Selected Papers.* Chicago: Aldine, Atherton, 1971.

Laslett, P. *The World We Have Lost.* London: Methuen, 1971.

——. "Societal Development and Aging." In *Handbook of Aging and the Social Sciences,* edited by R. Binstock and E. Shanas. New York: Van Nostrand Reinhold, 1976.

Marshall, Victor W. "No Exit: An Interpretive Perspective on Aging." In *Aging in Canada: Social Perspectives,* edited by V. W. Marshall. Toronto: Fitzhenry & Whiteside, 1980.

Marshall, Victor W., and Joseph A. Tindale. "Notes for a Radical Gerontology." *International Journal on Aging and Human Development* 9 (1978-79): 163-75.

McPherson, B. "The Meaning and Use of Time Across the Life-Cycle: The Influence of Work, Family and Leisure." Keynote address presented to annual meeting of the Canadian Association on Gerontology, Vancouver, November 3, 1984.

Quadagno, Jill. *Aging in Early Industrial Society: Work, Family and Social Policy in Nineteenth Century England.* New York: Academic Press, 1982.

Shanas, E. "Social Myth as Hypothesis: The Case of the Family Relations of Old People." *The Gerontologist* 19 (1979): 3-10.

Tindale, Joseph A. "Generational Conflict: Class and Cohort Relations Among Ontario Public Secondary School Teachers." Ph.D. diss., York University, 1980.

——. "Identity Maintenance Processes of Old Poor Men." In *Aging in Canada: Social Perspectives,* edited by V. W. Marshall. Toronto: Fitzhenry & Whiteside, 1980.

Troll, L. "The Family in a North American Context." In *Canadian Gerontological Collections III: The Family of Later Life,* edited by J. Crawford. Winnipeg: Canadian Association on Gerontology, 1980.

Woolcock, G. "The Tyranny of the Clock." In *An Introduction to Social Science,* edited by A. Naftalin et al. Chicago: Lippincott, 1953.

Sociology: Farms and Women

Abell, H. C. "The Women's Touch in Canadian Farm Work." *The Economic Annalist* 24 (1954): 37-38.

Bibliography

——. "The Rural Women's Perception of Urban and Rural Life." School of Urban and Regional Planning, University of Waterloo, 1970. Mimeo.

Bennett, John W. "Reciprocal Economic Exchanges Among North American Agricultural Operators." *Southwest Journal of Anthropology* 24 (1968): 276–309.

——. *Northern Plainsmen: Adaptive Strategy and Agrarian Life.* Chicago: Aldine, 1969.

Bennett, John W., and Seena B. Kohl. "Characterological, Institutional, and Strategic Interpretations of Prairie Settlement." In *Western Canada Past and Present*, edited by A. W. Rasporich. Calgary: The University of Calgary and McClelland & Stewart West, 1975.

——. "The Agrifamily System." Chap. 5 in *Of Time and the Enterprise: North American Family Farm Management in a Context of Resource Marginality*, edited by John W. Bennett. Minneapolis: University of Minnesota Press, 1979.

——. "A Longitudinal Cultural Ecology Study in Rural North America: The Saskatchewan Cultural Ecology Research Program." In *Anthropologists at Home: Towards an Anthropology of Issues in America*, edited by D. Messerschmitt. Cambridge: Cambridge University Press, 1981.

Brown, Rosemarie Geoffrion. "Farm Women." *Briarpatch* 9, no. 8 (1980): 10–11.

Buttell, Frederick H., and Gilbert W. Gillespie, Jr. "The Sexual Division of Farm Household Labor: An Exploratory Study of the Structure of On-Farm and Off-Farm Labor Allocation Among Farm Men and Women." *Rural Sociology* 49 (1984): 183–209.

Castillo, Gelia T. *The Changing Role of Women in Rural Societies: A Summary of Trends and Issues*. Seminar report no. 12. New York: Agricultural Development Council, 1977.

Elbert, Sarah. "The Challenge of Research on Farm Women." *The Rural Sociologist* 1 (1981): 387–90.

Flora, Cornelia Butler. "Farm Women, Farming Systems, and Agricultural Structure: Suggestions for Scholarship." *The Rural Sociologist* 1 (1981): 383–86.

——. "Farming Systems Research and Farm Management Research: What is the Difference?" *The Rural Sociologist* 3 (1983): 292–97.

Friedl, E. *Men and Women: An Anthropological View*. New York: Holt, Rinehart & Winston, 1975.

Bibliography

Hill, Frances. "Farm Women: A Challenge to Scholarship." *The Rural Sociologist* 1 (1981): 370-87.

Huffman, W. E. "The Value of the Productive Time of Farm Wives: Iowa, North Carolina, and Oklahoma." *American Journal of Agricultural Economics* 58 (1976): 836-41.

Kohl, Seena B. *Working Together: Women and Family in Southwestern Saskatchewan.* Toronto: Holt, Rinehart & Winston, 1976.

Kohl, Seena B., and John W. Bennett. "The Agrifamily Household" and "Succession, Enterprise Development, and the Role of the Wife." Chaps. 6 and 7 in *Of Time and the Enterprise: North American Family Farm Management in a Context of Resource Marginality*, edited by John W. Bennett. Minneapolis: University of Minnesota Press, 1979.

Koski, Susan E. *The Employment Practices of Farm Women.* Saskatoon: National Farmers Union, 1983.

Malone, Carl C., and Lucile Holaday Malone. *Decision Making and Management for Farm and Home.* Ames: Iowa State College Press, 1958.

Maret, Elizabeth, and James Cobb. "Some Recent Findings on the Economic Contribution of Farm Women." *The Rural Sociologist* 2 (1982): 112-15.

Oakley, Ann. *Women's Work: A History of the Housewife.* New York: Pantheon, 1974.

Pearson, Jessica. "Note on Female Farmers." *The Rural Sociologist* 44 (1979): 189-200.

Rowbotham, Sheila. *Hidden From History.* New York: Pantheon, 1975.

Sachs, Carolyn E. *The Invisible Farmers.* Totowa, N.J.: Rowman & Allanheld, 1983.

Sanday, P. R. "Towards a Theory of the Status of Women." *American Anthropologist* 75 (1973): 1682-1700.

Saskatchewan Department of Labour. *Farm Women.* Regina: Saskatchewan Women's Division, Department of Labour, 1977.

——. *This is the Law.* Regina: Saskatchewan Women's Division, Department of Labour, 1981.

Saskatchewan Royal Commission on Agriculture and Rural Life. *The Home and Family in Rural Saskatchewan.* Report no. 10. Regina: Queen's Printer, 1956.

Sawer, Barbara J. "Predictors of the Farm Wife's Involvement in General Management and Adoption Decisions." *Rural Sociology* 38 (1973): 412-26.

Scholl, Kathleen K. "Farm Women's Triad of Roles." *Family Economic Review* 1 (1983): 10-15.

Taylor, Norma. "All This for Three and a Half a Day: The Farm Wife." In *Women in the Canadian Mosaic*, edited by G. Matheson. Toronto: Peter Martin Associates, 1976.

Wilkening, Eugene A., and Lakshmi K. Bharadwaj. "Aspirations and Task Involvement as Related to Decision-Making Among Farm Husbands and Wives." *Rural Sociology* 33 (1968): 30-44.

Wilkening, Eugene A., Lakshmi K. Bharadwaj, and Sylvia Guerrero. "Consensus in Aspirations for Farm Improvement and Adoptions of Farm Practice." *Rural Sociology* 34 (1969): 183-96.

Sociology: Gender Studies

Balla, Bálint. *Soziologie der Knappheit. Zum Verständnis individueller und gesellschaftlicher Mangelzustände.* Stuttgart: Ferdinand Enke, 1978.

Bergmann, Werner. "Das Problem der Zeit in der Soziologie. Ein Literaturüberblick zum Stand der 'zeitsoziologischen' Theorie und Forschung." *Kölner Zeitschrift für Soziologie und Sozialpsychologie* 79 (1983): 462-504.

Brodie, M. Janine, and Jill McCalla Vickers. *Canadian Women in Politics: An Overview.* CRIAW paper no. 2. Ottawa: Canadian Research Institute for the Advancement of Women, 1982.

Calkins, Kathy. "Time: Perspectives, Marking and Styles of Usage." *Social Problems* 17 (1970): 487-501.

Clark, Susan, and Andrew S. Harvey. "The Sexual Division of Labour: The Use of Time." *Atlantis* 2, no. 1 (1976): 46-66.

Committee on Sexual Offenses Against Children and Youths. *Sexual Offenses Against Children.* 2 vols. Ottawa: Supply & Services, 1984.

Dumont, Micheline, Michèle Jean, Marie Lavigne, and Jennifer Stoddart. *L'Histoire des femmes au Québec depuis quatre siècles.* Montréal: Les Quinze, 1982.

Economic Council of Canada. *On the Mend: Twentieth Annual Review 1983.* Ottawa: Supply & Services, 1983.

Eichler, Margrit. "Women as Personal Dependents: A Critique of Theories of the Stratification of the Sexes and an Alternative Approach." In *Women in Canada*, edited by Marylee Stephenson. Toronto: New Press, 1973.

——. "Power, Dependency, Love and the Sexual Division of Labour. A Critique of the Decision-Making Approach to Family Power and an

Alternative Approach with an Appendix: On Washing My Dirty Linen in Public." *Women's Studies International Quarterly* 4 (1981): 201-19.

———. *Families in Canada Today: Recent Changes and their Policy Conse-quences*. Toronto: Gage, 1983.

———. "The Connection Between Paid and Unpaid Labour and its Implication for Creating Equality for Women in Employment." Paper prepared for the Royal Commission of Inquiry on Equality in Employment, 1984, forthcoming in vol. 2 of the commission report.

Fitzgerald, Maureen, Connie Guberman, and Margie Wolfe, eds. *Still Ain't Satisfied! Canadian Feminism Today*. Toronto: Women's Press, 1982.

Fortes, Meyer. Introduction to *The Developmental Cycle in Domestic Groups*, edited by Jack Goody. Cambridge: Cambridge University Press, 1958. This introduction is useful in the study of gender, household relationships, and time.

Friedman, Harriet. "World Market, State, and Family Farm: Social Bases of Household Production in the Era of Wage Labor." *Comparative Studies in Society and History* 20 (1978): 545-86. A useful study of time as it relates to gender and household relations.

Haney, Wava G., and Jane B. Knowles, eds. *Women and Farming Roles: Changing Structures*. Boulder, Colo.: Westview, 1988. A useful set of articles related to time, work, and gender studies.

Hess, Robert, and Gerald Handel. *Family Worlds*. Chicago: University of Chicago Press, 1959. Time, work, and gender studies related to families.

Meissner, Martin, Elizabeth W. Humphreys, Scott M. Meis, and William J. Scheu. "No Exit for Wives: Sexual Division of Labour and the Cumulation of Household Demands." *Canadian Review of Sociology and Anthropology* 12, pt. 1 (1975): 424-39.

Miles, Angela, and Geraldine Finn, eds. *Feminism in Canada: From Pressure to Politics*. Montreal: Black Rose Books, 1982.

Rogers, Susan Carol. "Female Forms of Power and the Myth of Male Domi-nance: A Model of Female/Male Interaction in Peasant Society." *American Ethnologist* 2 (1975): 727-56. A useful text in gender, work, and time studies.

Rosenfeld, Rachel. *Farm Women: Work Farm and Family in the U.S.* Chapel Hill, N.C.: University of North Carolina Press, 1985. An analysis of U.S. farm and farm women survey data related to work and time.

Rosaldo, Michelle. "Women, Culture and Society: A Theoretical Overview." In *Women, Culture and Society*, edited by Michelle Rosaldo and Louise

Bibliography

Lamphere. Stanford: Stanford University Press, 1974. A study related to women and culture in a temporal context.

Royal Commission on Equality in Employment. *Equality in Employment*. Vol. 1. Ottawa: Supply & Services, 1984.

Royal Commission on the Status of Women in Canada. *Report*. Ottawa: Information Canada, 1970.

Schneider, David M. *American Kinship: A Cultural Account*. Chicago: University of Chicago Press, 1968. A time-, gender-, and work-related study.

Schwartz, Barry. "Waiting, Exchange, and Power: The Distribution of Time in Social Systems." *American Journal of Sociology* 79 (1974): 841–70.

Smith, Dorothy E. "Women, the Family and Corporate Capitalism." In *Women in Canada*, edited by Mary Lee Stephenson. Toronto: New Press, 1973.

Wax, Rosalie. "Reciprocity in Fieldwork." In *Human Organization Research*, edited by R. N. Adams and J. J. Preiss. Homewood, Ill.: Dorsey, 1960.

III Artistic: Music, Literature, Fine Arts

Alkon, Paul K. *Defoe and Fictional Time*. Athens: University of Georgia Press, 1979.

Bank, J. A. *Tactus, Tempo and Notation in Mensural Music from the 13th to the 17th Century*. Amsterdam: Annie Bank, 1972. Published with the support of the Netherlands Organization for the Advancement of Pure Research (Z.W.O.), this work contains a "Conspectus of the Authorities from 1200–1620" and an "Index of Modern Authors from 1900–1970," both of which cite primary sources and other scholarly works dealing with these topics.

Bornstein, E. "Art Toward Nature." *The Structurist* 15/16 (1975–76): 142–57.

Buckley, J. H. *The Triumph of Time: A Study of Victorian Concepts of Time, History, Progress and Decadence*. Cambridge, Mass.: Belknap, 1967.

Cowley, M. "The Red Wagon." In *The View from Eighty*. New York: Viking, 1980.

Higdon, D. H. *Time and English Fiction*. London: Macmillan, 1977.

Lampl, Hans. "A Translation of *Syntagma musicum* III by Michael Praetorius." Ph.D. diss., University of Southern California, 1957, 149.

Lewis, Wyndham. *Time and Western Man*. Boston: Beacon, 1957.

——. *Patriarchs of Time: Dualism in Saturn-Cronus, Father Time, the Watch-maker God, and Father Christmas*. Athens: University of Georgia Press, 1988.

Bibliography

Mendilow, Adam A. *Time and the Novel.* New York: Humanities Press, 1952.

Meyerhoff, Hans. *Time in Literature.* Berkeley and Los Angeles: University of California Press, 1955.

Patrides, C. A. *Aspects of Time.* Manchester: Manchester University Press, 1976. A most valuable survey of literature on time with an outstanding bibliographical section (pp. 250-70). This text deals with such prominent literary figures as Faulkner, Sartre, James, Beckett, Eliot, and many others.

Praetorius, Michael. *Polyhymnia caduceatrix et panegyrica (1619).* In *Gesamtausgabe der Musikalischen Werke von Michael Praetorius,* edited by Wilibald Gurlitt. Vol. 17. Wolfenbüttel: Möseler Verlag, n.d.

———. *Syntagma musicum.* Vol. 3 of *Termini musici.* Wolfenbüttel, 1619. Facsimile edition edited by Wilibald Gurlitt, *Documenta Musicologica.* Cassel, Germany: Baerenreiter, 1958.

Sachs, Curt. *Rhythm and Tempo.* New York: W. W. Norton, 1953. An early study in music that provides information and advice for the listener/ performer who wishes to consider tempo within the context of history from the earliest times to the mid-twentieth century.

Tolstoy, Leo. *My Confessions.* Translated by L. Weiner. London: J. M. Dent, 1905. Tolstoy expresses his torment at the emptiness of life, the inevitability of death, and how he overcame these thoughts by reflecting on the simple faith of the uneducated.

Recordings

Ehmann, Wilhelm. "Polyhymnia caduceatrix et panegyrica: Christmas Music." Westphalian Ensemble. Nonesuch 71242.

Munrow, David. "Music of Praetorius." Early Music Consort. Angel S-37091.

The History of Music in Sound. Vol. 4. E.M.I. Records.

Index

Abell, H. C., 223n, 224n
Abortion, 10, 142–47
Act-omission, 139–40
Adams, K. J., 117n
Aeolus, 5
Agency, 52–54, 296, 303
Aging, 6–7, 66–67, 70–71, 73, 105–7, 118–19, 258
Alice in Wonderland, 2, 24, 306n
Anencephaly, 9, 126–29
Animism, 12, 184–85
Ansbacher, R., 175n
Aphrodite, 2
Archimedes, 296
Aristotle, 2, 6, 16, 252, 293–94, 296, 301, 303
Arndt, Johan, 239n
Arnold, Matthew, 34, 54
Art, 257–63
Aschenbaum, W. A., 109, 118n
Atherosclerosis, 69
Augustine, Saint, 2, 19, 37, 58, 285
Auschwitz, 282
Baby Doe case, 9, 11, 121, 123, 124–26, 165, 148n, 167–70, 178n
Balla, Bálint, 191, 203n
Banks, Robert, 3, 4–5, 40n, 42n, 55, 282, 304
Barker, S. F., 148n
Barr, J., 42n, 43n
Baudelaire, Charles, 34

Baxter, R., 42n
Beaumarchais, Pierre-Augustin Caron de, 254
Beckett, Samuel, 251
Beecher, Henry Ward, 61
Beethoven, Ludwig van, 292
Bell, W. J., 42n
Bellah, R. N., 292
Bengston, V. L., 118n
Bennett, John W., 212, 220, 222n, 223n, 225n
Bentham, Jeremy, 26, 41n, 150n
Bergmann, Werner, 189, 202n
Bergson, Henri, 5, 46, 300
Berk, Richard A., 229, 239n
Berk, Sarah F., 229, 239n
Berkhof, H. 43n
Bevans, G., 228, 238n
Bharadwaj, Lakshmi K., 224n
Bienfeld, M. A., 40n
Binstock, R., 118n
Biren, J. E., 118n
Bleak House (Dickens), 18, 273
Bliss, E. C., 42n
Bloch, N., 298
Bohr, N., 307n
Bornstein, Eli, 4, 17–18, 283
Boudin, Eugene, 261
Bouvia v. County of Riverside, 176n
Bouvia v. Supreme Court, 176n
Bradley, F. H., 281, 292
Brecht, Bertolt, 252
Brodie, M. Janine, 203n

Brohm, J. M., 41n
Brown, Rosemarie Geoffrion, 218, 224n
Buckley, J. H., 42n
Bunge, M., 298
Burnt Norton (Eliot), 255, 285
Buttell, Frederick H., 224n, 225n
Butterfield, Herbert, 30
Byron, (George Gordon Lord), 5
Cain, L. D., 117n
Calder, Robert, 4, 18-19, 283
Campbell, A. E., 40n, 248n
Camus, Albert, 5
Cancer, 69
Canterbury v. Spence, 161, 177n
Cardiovascular disease, 69
Carroll, John, 37, 43n
Carroll, Lewis, 1, 24, 289, 290, 293, 306n
Carlstein, T., 41n
Carlyle, Thomas, 257
Carter, James, 136
Casey, Lawrence, 132, 135-36, 137, 149n
Casserly, M. Catherine, 240n
Castillo, Gelia T., 223n
Calkins, Kathy, 203n
Catullus, 277-78
Cause, 301-2
Cerebrovascular disease, 69
Cézanne, Paul, 257, 259, 261-63
Change, 6, 58-59
Chaos, 2
Chapin, F. Stuart, 229, 239n, 240n, 241n, 245, 248n
Chaplin, Charlie, 261
Cheek, F., 40n
Chekhov, Anton, 251, 254
Cherry v. Borsman, 175n
Chopin, Frédéric, 54
Chronos, 2, 17, 284
Chudacoff, H. P., 118n
Cipolla, C., 40n
Cirrhosis, 69
Clark, J. P., 41n
Clark, Susan, 204n, 230, 240n
Cleese, John, 279
Clemenceau, George, 260

Clocks, 3, 23-24, 26-28, 31, 34, 35, 39, 40, 47, 58, 103, 116 (so-cial), 252, 284, 295, 300
Clockwise, 279
Cobb, James, 223n
Cobbs v. Grant, 161, 177n
Cohen, Ronald, 119n
"Comparison, A" (Cowper), 304
Computers, 300
Consent, 161-66
Converse, P. E., 40n, 239n, 243, 248n
Cook, R. J., 175n
Cote, Tony, 283
Cowgill, D. O., 108-9, 118n
Cowley, Malcolm, 18, 278-79, 292
Cranford, R. E., 178n
Csikszentmihalyi, M., 247, 248n
Cubism, 17, 260-63
Cullen, Ian, 227, 229, 237, 238n, 239n, 241n, 242n
Cullman, O., 43n
Culver, C., 177n
Curlender v. Bio-Science Laborato-ries, 174n
Curran, W. J., 179n
Dali, Salvador, 279
Dante (Alighieri), 3, 253
Darwin, Charles, 25, 301-2
da Vinci, Leonardo, 17
Dawson, Stephen, 10-11, 152, 161, 169-70
Dementia, 72
Demography, 75, 101, 104-11, 291
Denton, Frank T., 3, 7-8, 101, 291
Descartes, René, 60
Diabetes, 69, 130-31
Dickens, Bernard, 3, 9-11, 173n, 174n, 175n, 177n, 179n, 273, 291
Dickens, Charles, 18, 274, 283
Diderot, Denis, 254
Diet, 7
Dinnerstein, Shirley, 171-72, 179n
Divina Commedia (Dante), 253
Donovan, P., 175n
Dondi, Giovanni de, 3
Doudera, A. E., 178n

Down's syndrome, 9-11, 121-23, 131, 154, 165
Drama, 251-55
Drucker, P., 42n
Dumont, Micheline, 204n
Ecclesiastes, 34
Economics, 10, 13, 16, 96-100, 189-203, 227-42, 243-48, 282-83
Education, 12
Ehmann, Wilhelm, 270n
Eichler, Margrit, 4, 12-13, 203n, 204n, 274, 283
Einstein, Albert, 295, 300
Elbert, Sarah, 221, 225n
Elgar, Edward, 292
Eliot, George, 34
Eliot, T. S., 17, 285, 305
Elliot, David H., 230, 237, 240n, 241n
Ellul, Jacques, 39, 41n, 43n
Emphysema, 69
Engel, Friedrich, 42n
Enlightenment, 4, 25
Entropy, 25
Epistemology, 303
Equal worth, 5, 9-10, 122, 124, 128, 137, 284-86
Erikson, E., 7, 66
Esbenson, Steen, 283
Eternity, 2, 16, 255
Ethics committees, 11, 168-69
Euclid, 293
Euthanasia, 122, 132, 149
Evans, A. A., 40n
Event, 2, 45, 57, 245, 258, 297
Evolution, 4, 17, 262, 301
Exercise, 7
Existentialism, 5
Extraordinary means, 132-37, 149, 157, 160, 165
Faith, reconciliation with reason, 291
Family decisions, 167-68
Ferris, John (Judge), 136, 149n
Faulkner, William, 34
Feaver, Christine H., 75, 101
Feigenbaum, K., 248n
Ferge, Susan, 239n

Ferris, John, 136, 149n
Fertility, 8, 75-79
Feuerbach, Ludwig, 31
Finn, Geraldine, 203n
Fischer, D. H., 109, 118n
Fitzgerald, Maureen, 203n
Fletcher, Joseph, 137-38, 150n
Flora, Cornelia Butler, 224n
Foerster, James F., 229, 239n
Foner, Nancy, 118n
Fosmire v. Nicoleau, 176n
Foucault, Michel, 302
Four Quartets (Eliot), 290
Fracastoro, Girolamo, 67
Frankfurter, Felix, 274
Franklin, Benjamin, 33, 42n
Fraser, J. T., 41n, 42n
Freud, Sigmund, 31
Friedl, E., 223n
Friedman, M., 40n
Fries, J., 71
Fromm, Erich, 30, 41n
Fuchs, Victor R., 101

Gaea, 2
Gale, R., 306n
Gautier, Théophile, 259
Gender, 13, 103, 106, 189-202
Gerbert (later Pope Sylvester), 3
Gerhardi, William, 55
Gerr, B., 177n
Gesell, Gerhard, 129, 133
Gillespie, Gilbert W., 224n, 225n
Glasser, R., 40n, 42n
Gleitman v. Cosgrove, 174n, 175n
God, 12, 25, 32-33, 36-37, 47, 53-54, 56, 60-61, 186-87
Godson, V., 227, 237, 238n, 241n
Goethe, Johann Wolfgang von, 297
Goffman, E., 118n
Goodchild, M. F., 230, 240n
Gorovitz, S., 150n
Goudge, Thomas, 298, 302
Gould, Stephen Jay, 290, 297, 307n
Grad, J., 150n
Granville-Barker, Harley, 252-53
Graves, Frank, 240n
Gray, Thomas, 54
Grazia, S. de, 40n, 41n

Greschner, Donna, 4, 18, 283
Gremmo, Sigmund, 230, 239n, 240n, 241n
Grünbaum, Adolph, 295-97, 306n
Guberman, Connie, 203n
Guthrium, J. F., 118n
Guillen, Michael, 57
Gurlitt, Wilibald, 270n
Gutenschwager, G., 243, 248n
Haber, F. C., 41n
Habermas, J., 292
Haemophilia, 145
Hagerstrand, Torsten, 241n
Hamlet (Shakespeare), 16, 252-53
Handicapped, 10, 15, 121-42, 144-48, 165
Harbeson v. Parke-Davis, Inc., 174n, 175n
Hare, Richard, 145-47
Hareven, T., 111, 117n, 118n, 119n
Harrison, J., 295
Harvey, Andrew, 4, 15, 204n, 230n, 240n, 241n, 242n, 243, 283, 292
Havighurst, R. J., 248n
Hawes, Douglas K., 239n
Hawking, Stephen, 290, 297
Health costs, 100-101, 134, 152, 291
Heckler, Margaret, 149n
Hegel, Georg Wilhelm Friedrich, 293, 303
Heenan, John (Cardinal), 148n
Heidegger, Martin, 293-94, 303, 306n
Hempel, C., 298
Hentoff, Nat, 150n
Herrick, Robert, 278
Heschel, A., 42n
Hiebert, Paul, 65
Higdon, D. H., 42n
Hill, Frances, 222n, 223n, 224n
Hippocrates, 67
Hirsch, F. C., 40n, 41n
Hitler, Adolf, 282
Holder, A. R., 174n
Holmes, L. D., 108, 118n
Holt, K., 40n, 150n
Huffman, W. E., 223n, 224n
Hughes, Margaret, 118n, 283

Huizinga, Johan, 36, 43n
Huygen, C., 295
Hydrocephalic, 152
Ibsen, Henrik, 254
If You're Glad, I'll Be Frank (Stoppard), 279
Impressionism, 260-61
Industrial Revolution, 27-29, 109
Influenza, 68
Interim Final Rule, 125-26, 129
Intestinal deficiencies, 9, 127, 131
Intra-cranial haemorrhage, 9, 127, 130
Izumi, Shigechiyo, 69
Jackson, John, 283
Jakobovits, Immanuel, 122, 128, 148n
Janelle, D. G., 230, 240n
Javeau, Claude, 239n
Jean, Michèle, 204n
Jehovah's Witness, 158-59
Jesus, 39
John F. Kennedy Hospital v. Heston, 176n
Johnson, M., 42n
Johnson, Samuel, 66
Joyce, James, 34
Justice, 18; procedural, 273-75; natural, 273-75; distributive, 275
Kadish, Sanford, 122, 148n
Kairos, 2, 17, 284
Kant, Immanuel, 45, 293-94, 303
Kanungo, R. N., 241n
Keats, John, 5, 54
Keith, J., 118n, 119n
Kelly, Gerald, 134-35, 149n
Kempner, T., 41n
Kerr, W., 41n
Kertzer, D., 118n, 119n
Kew, Stephen, 150n
Keyserlingk, Edward H., 148n
Kierkegaard, Søren, 38
King, Cecil, 12, 283
King-Hele, D., 306n
Kinsley, Brian L., 231, 240n
Koch, Robert, 67

Kohl, Seena, 4, 14-15, 212, 222n, 225n, 283, 292
Kohli, M., 117n
Koop, C. Everett, 127-28, 149n
Koski, Susan E., 224n, 225n
Kretzmer, D., 173n
Krez, D., 178n
Kronos, 2
Kuhse, Helga, 3, 9-10
Labour-participation, 88-96
Lack, S., 148n
Lakoff, G., 42n
Lameron, R., 148n
Lampl, Hans, 270n
Landes, David S., 2-3, 19, 306n
Larkin, Philip, 253
Labaree, L. W., 42n
Larson, R., 248n
Laslett, P., 109, 118n
Laurence, Margaret, 18-19, 279, 292
Lavigne, Marie, 204n
Law, 18, 171-72, 173-79, 292
Law Reform Commission of Canada, 136
Lawrence, D. H., 34
Lawrence, N., 41n
Lawton, M. Powell, 239n
Lebhar, G. M., 42n
Lee, M. D., 241n
Leisure, 26, 29, 31, 36, 41-42, 228-38, 247-48, 252, 273-75
Levi, L., 40n
Levine, C., 178n
Life expectancy, 8, 65, 69-70, 73, 80-82, 106-7, 258
Lincoln, Abraham, 54
Linder, Staffan, 30, 41n, 241n
Lissitzky, E., 258
Literature, 18-19, 277-79
Living will, 11, 163-67
Locke, John, 138, 150n
Logic, 293-95, 298-301, 302-3, 308n
Lovelace, Richard, 278
Luce, G. G., 43n
Macdonald, W. Stephen, 230, 240n, 241n

MacNeil, Teresa, 283
Malette v. Shulman, 158, 176n, 177n
Malévy, E., 41n
Malone, Carl C., 223n
Malone, Lucile H., 223n
Maret, Elizabeth, 223n
Marey, Jules Étienne, 261
Marsh, J., 42n
Marshall, V. W., 117n, 118n, 119n
Marvell, Andrew, 278
Marx, Karl, 31, 33, 39, 42n, 293
Matsushima, Chiyono, 240n
Matthews, Vincent, 283
Mavor, Ronald, 4, 16-18, 283
Mayr, Ernst, 298-99, 300-303, 307n
McCormick, R. A., 179n
McCullough, Ernest, 4, 18-19, 283
McKay v. Essex Area Health Author-ity, 175n
McNab, Hilliard, 283
McPherson, Barry, 103, 117n
Medrich, Elliott A., 228, 239n
Meissner, Martin, 204n, 239n
Melbin, M., 41n
Mendilow, A., 25-26, 35, 41n, 43n
Messerschmitt, D., 222n
Metaphysics, 7, 19, 45
Metchnikoff, E., 66
Methodology, 243-48, 296
Meyerhoff, H., 42n, 43n
Meyersohn, R., 248n
Michelangelo, 292
Michelson, William, 239n, 240n
Miles, Angela, 203n
Moltmann, J., 43n
Monet, Claude, 17, 260-62, 292
Morgentaler v. The Queen, 175n
Morris, R., 306n
Morris, Thomas, 297
Moss, Miriam S., 239n
Mozart, Wolfgang Amadeus, 54, 252
Müller, G., 41n
Multivocal, 19, 283, 286, 293-95
Mumford, Lewis, 23, 40n
Munrow, David, 270n
Music, 18, 265-70
Nagel, E., 298
Nakanishi, Naomichi, 239n, 241n

Narrative, 50–54; and fiction, 279–82; and history, 263, 289–308; and Natives, 183–87, 292; and socio-historical time, 25–26, 108–11; and women's studies, 292

Natanson v. Kline, 161, 177n
Natives, 12, 183–87, 277
Necessity, 158–75
Needham, R., 3
Newton, Isaac, 26, 41n, 293
Nicolson, Nancy, 230, 240n
Nietzsche, Friedrich, 5, 292
Nilsson, M. P., 41n
Nissel, Muriel, 229, 239n
Now, 57, 303
Nutrition, 154
Nympheas (Monet), 260–61
Oakley, Ann, 206, 215, 223n
O'Donell, Terry, 231, 240n
Olympic Games, 29
Ordinary means, 132–37
Osler, William, 68
Osmond, H., 40n
Owen, J. O., 40n

Parfit, Derek, 143, 144–45
Park, D., 41n
Parker, O., 41n
Parmenides, 5, 45
Passmore, J., 308n
Patrushev, V. D., 227, 230, 240n
Pearson, Jessica, 224n
Perka v. The Queen, 175n
Person, 10, 19, 39, 50–52, 137, 140–44, 147, 150, 154, 184
Petkov, K., 230, 240n
Phelps, Elizabeth, 229, 239n, 241n, 242n
Philosophy, 18–19
Photography, 261
Picasso, Pablo, 5, 54
Pieper, Joseph, 36, 43n
Pineo, Peter C., 75
Pirandello, Luigi, 253
Plato, 2, 45, 56, 293
Pless, John E., 148n
Poincaré, H., 296

Polyglots, The (Gerhardi), 56
Polyhymnia caduceatrix et panegyrica (1619) (Praetorius), 18, 265–70
Popper, K., 298
Population, 8
Potential life, 139–48, 174
Praetorius, Michael, 18, 265–70
President's Commission, 136–37
Price, D., 3
Priestley, J. B., 34
Prigogine, Ilya, 281, 295
Procanik v. Cillo, 174n
Procos, Dimitri, 240n
Proposed Rule, 129
Proust, Marcel, 17, 34, 254–55
Public agencies, 170–71

Quadagno, Jill, 108, 118n
Quality of life, 135–37, 151–58
Quinlan, Joseph, 132
Quinlan, Karen, 10–11, 131–32, 135–36, 148n, 151–54, 160–61, 165, 168–69, 171, 173n, 174n, 175n, 177n, 178n, 179n

R. v. Arthur, 174n, 178n
R. v. Bourne, 175n
R. v. Dudley and Stephens, 175n
Raleigh, Sir Walter, 251
Ramsey, Paul, 123, 148n
Rationality, 51
Ray, Doug, 283
Reagan, Ronald, 124
Rectangular society, 71
Redman, Chief Richard, 283
Reformation, 25
Reibel v. Hughes, 161, 177n
Rescue, 158
Richardson, F. L., 40
Ricoeur, Paul, 303, 308n
Rights, 123–25, 138, 141, 157–61, 172–74
Robertson, Duncan, 3, 6–7, 282
Robinson, J. P., 40n, 239n, 242n, 243, 248n
Rodin, Auguste, 292
Rodríguez-Gomez, Juan Camilo, 241n
Roe v. Wade, 177n

Romaniuc, A., 101
Rosenman, R. H., 40n
Rousseau, Jean-Jacques, 34
Rowbotham, Sheila, 215, 223n
Russell, Bertrand, 57–58, 298
Ryle, Gilbert, 56, 293–94
Sachs, Carolyn E., 224n, 225n
Saikewicz case, 166, 171–72
Sanday, P. R., 223n
Sartre, Jean-Paul, 5
Saunders, D., 43n
Sawer, Barbara J., 224n
Schipp, P. A., 306n
Schloendorff v. Society of New York Hospital, 176n
Schneider, Annerose, 240n
Scholl, Kathleen K., 224n
Schopenhauer, Arthur, 51
Schwartz, B., 12–13, 189–91, 202n, 204n
Science, 281, 289, 291, 293–99, 300, 302
Selye, H., 40n
Seneca, 66
Seniority, 114–16
Septicemia, 68
Shakespeare, William, 16, 66, 251–52
Shanas, E., 110, 118n
Shaw, George Bernard, 61
Shaw, Susan M., 227, 238n
Siegel, Jacob S., 101
Singer, Peter, 3, 9–10, 274, 283, 284–85, 291
Sisyphus, 5, 48–51
Skelton, David, 3, 5–6
Skid row, 111–14
Skorgynski, Zigmunt, 239n
Sloane, R. B., 118n
Smith, G. P., 174n
Smoot, T. C., 41n
Solem, Robert, 4, 18, 283, 292
Somerville, M. A., 174n
South Africa, 6
Space, 245, 252, 262–63, 295–96
Spencer, Byron G., 3, 7–8, 101, 282, 291
Spina bifida, 145
Spinoza, Benedict de, 45

Sport, 26, 29, 31
Spring, Earle, 179n
Staikov, Zahari, 238n
Starkman, B., 175n
Steinbock, B., 149n
Stinson, Andrew, 143–47
Stinson, Jonathan, 144–47
Stinson, Peggy, 143–44, 147, 150n
Stinson, Robert, 144, 150n
Stoddart, Jennifer, 204n
Stokes, Roger, 3
Stone, Philip J., 230, 239n, 240n
Stone Angel, The (Laurence), 279
Stoppard, Tom, 279
Storrie, Kathleen, 283
Strange, Karl, 283
Stress, 6, 7, 24, 34, 36, 40, 58–59
Subjectivity, 130, 165, 254, 284, 305, 308n
Suicide, 157–59, 176
Swift, Daniel, 283
Sydenham, Thomas, 67
Syntagma musicum (Praetorius), 18, 265–70
Szalai, Alexander, 239n, 240n

Tagawa, B. K., 175n
Taylor, Norma, 223n
Taylor, Richard, 3, 55, 274, 282, 283, 285, 304
Technology, 6, 26–29, 39, 41
Tendler, Moshe, 148n
Terkel, Studs, 42n
Theology, 31–32, 35, 37–38
Thompson, E. P., 41n
Thrift, N., 41n
Through the Looking Glass (Carroll), 1, 290–91, 306n
Time: and motion studies, 26, 296; artistic, 1, 4, 6, 16, 18–19, 304, 305; cyclical, 4, 6, 12, 27, 47, 185–86, 284; decision-, 161–66; foundational, 1, 3, 16, 19, 304–5; functional, 4, 6, 10–12, 16, 19, 285–86, 290, 305; linear, 4, 116, 185–86, 297; management and use of, 32–33, 227–42, 243–48; Native concept of, 3, 183–87, 285; social, 1, 4, 6, 16,

(*Time, social concept of, cont.*):
19, 189-204, 304, 305; subjec-
tive, 34-35
Teachers, 114-16
Teleology, 301-2
Tindale, Joseph, 3, 8-9, 118n, 119n,
283
Tizard, J., 150n
Tooley, Michael, 138-39, 141, 143,
149n, 150n
Tournier, Paul, 37, 43n
Tovey, Donald, 251
Treas, J., 118n
Troll, L., 111, 118n
Tuberculosis, 68
Turpin v. Sortini, 174n
Typhoid, 68
United States v. Holmes, 175n
*United States v. University Hospital at
Stony Brook*, 178n, 179n
Univocal, 2, 19
Uranus, 2
Urinary incontinence, 72-73
Utility, 26

Vanek, Joann, 241n
van Gogh, Vincent, 292
van Leeuwen, A. T., 42n
Varga, Karoly, 240n
Vatican, 132
Veatch, Robert, 136, 149n, 178n,
179n
Veblen, Thorstein, 30, 42n
Vickers, Jill M., 203n
View from Eighty, The (Cowley),
278-79
Vries, S. de, 42n

Wachter, M. D., 176n
Wagner, Richard, 292
Walker, Kathryn E., 239n
Waller, Edmund, 278
Wallingford, Richard, 3
Weber v. Stony Brook Hospital, 178n
Welch, K., 41n
Wesley, John, 33, 42n
Westermarck, E., 150n
Whitehead, A. N., 300
Whitehouse v. Jordan, 174n
Whitlock, K. M., 179n
Whitrow, G. J., 41n, 295-96, 300,
303, 306n, 307n
Wilkening, Eugene A., 224n
Williams, Linda, 189
Wilson v. Swanson, 173n
Wills, G., 41n
Winner, A. E., 178n
Winter's Tale, A (Shakespeare), 251
Wittgenstein, Ludwig, 281, 283,
293-94
Wolfe, Margie, 203n
Wolfe, H., 43n
Women, 189-225; farm-, 205-25
Woods, Margaret E., 239n
Woolcock, G. A., 40n
Woolf, Henry, 255, 283
Woolf, Virginia, 34
Woolfolk, R. L., 40n
Yaker, H., 40n
Yeats, W. B., 16
Zelllick, G., 176n
Zeno, 45
Zeus, 2
Zuzanek, Jiri, 4, 15-16, 283, 292

Contributors

ROBERT BANKS is Associate Fellow, Zadok Centre for the Study of Christian-ity, Australian National University. Robert Banks has held teaching and research posts in history and in the history of ideas in Australian Universities, works extensively with lay resource centres, Christian communities, and vocational groups, and is presently Homer L. Goddard Professor of the Ministry of the Laity, School of Theology, Fuller Theological Seminary, Pasadena, California.

ELI BORNSTEIN was born in Milwaukee, Wisconsin, and studied in Saskatche-wan, Chicago, and Paris. He has taught at the University of Wisconsin and the University of Saskatchewan, Saskatoon, where he was the head of the Art Department from 1963–71. While living in Italy in 1957, he worked on a new constructed relief medium. In 1960 he founded the *Structurist*, an international art journal, and continues as editor/publisher. His works are exhibited widely; they can be seen at the National Art Gallery in Ottawa, the Walker Art Gallery in Minneapolis, and the Winnipeg airport, as well as various places in Saskat-chewan, among many other locations. He has exhibited in Europe and in North America in many major galleries, and was awarded the Allied Arts Medal by the Royal Architectural Institute of Canada in 1968 and the Governor General's Queen Elizabeth Medal in 1977.

ROBERT CALDER obtained his bachelor's (honours) and master's degrees in English at the University of Saskatchewan and his doctorate in English at the University of Leeds. Now Professor of English at the University of Saskat-chewan, he has been Head of the Department, Acting Head of the Department of Music, and Associate Dean (Fine Arts and Humanities) in the College of Arts and Science. Specializing in modern British fiction and drama, he has published on George Orwell, P. G. Wodehouse, Arthur Morrison, and John Arden. His critical study W. *Somerset Maugham and the Quest for Freedom* was published by William Heinemann in 1972, and his *Willie: The Life of W. Somerset Maugham* won the 1989 Governor General's Literary Award for Non-Fiction.

Contributors

FRANK T. DENTON is Professor of Economics at McMaster University (since 1968) and Director of the McMaster QSEP Program (the Program for Quantitative Studies in Economics and Population). Before coming to McMaster, he served for some fourteen years in research and administrative capacities with various government and private agencies. Previous positions include Senior Advisor on Research and Econometrics and Director of the Econometric Research staff at Statistics Canada, research consultant to the Economic Council of Canada, staff economist with the Senate of Canada Committee on Manpower and Employment, and economist with the Government of Ontario and with Philips Electronic Industries Limited. His undergraduate and graduate studies were carried out at the University of Toronto. He is a Fellow of the Royal Society of Canada, a Fellow of the American Statistical Association, and an elected member of the International Statistical Institute, the International Union for the Scientific Study of Population, and the National Bureau of Economic Research Conference on Income and Wealth. Dr. Denton has published extensively in the fields of economics, statistics, and demography and is the recipient of several major research grants.

BERNARD DICKENS is Professor in the Faculties of Law and Medicine, the Centre of Criminology, and the Centre for Bioethics at the University of Toronto. He earned his bachelor's of law from King's College, University of London, from which institution he also holds the degrees of master of laws and doctor of philosophy (the latter in the field of law and criminology) and doctor of laws (in medical jurisprudence). He is also a member of the English and Ontario bars and current (1990-91) President of the American Society of Law and Medicine.

MARGRIT EICHLER is Chair of the Department of Sociology in Education, Ontario Institute for Studies in Education, Toronto. She was educated at the University of Göttingen and the Free University of Berlin and earned her doctorate from Duke University, Chapel Hill, North Carolina. She is the author of *Martin's Father* (1971), *The Double Standard: A Feminist Critique of Feminist Social Science* (1980), and *Canadian Families Today* (1983), and the co-editor of *Women in Futures Research* (1982). Dr. Eichler is co-editor and founder of *Resources for Feminist Research* as well as a member of the Editorial Board of *Women's Studies International Quarterly*. She has received a number of research awards from government and the Social Sciences Research Council of Canada, and has written many articles and reviews on family and feminist issues.

DONNA GRESCHNER teaches constitutional law and legal theory at the College of Law, University of Saskatchewan. She is active in many women's organizations and has been a member of the Canadian Women's Studies Advisory Committee and the Canadian Human Rights Commission.

ANDREW HARVEY is Professor of Economics (and past chair of the Department of Economics), Saint Mary's University, Halifax; Adjunct Professor,

Henson College, Dalhousie University, Halifax; and President of Temporal-Spatial Research Inc. He has served as consultant to the FAO, the UN Statistical Office, and Statistics Canada, among other organizations. Dr. Harvey recently completed a document, "Guidelines for the Collection of Time Use Data," designed as a first step towards international standardization of the collection of such data, and is the author of numerous monographs, articles and reports.

CECIL KING is Director of Native Teacher Education, Faculty of Education, Queen's University, Kingston. He is former chair of the Indian and Northern Education Program, past director of the Indian Teacher Program, and former associate professor of the College of Education, University of Saskatchewan. Dr. King is a member of the Odawa First Nation, and was born on the Wikwe-mikong Indian Reserve, Manitoulin Island, Ontario.

SEENA KOHL earned her doctorate from Washington University, and teaches in the Department of Behavioral and Social Science, Webster University, Saint Louis, Missouri. She is a past coordinator of Women's Studies, Webster University, and has published numerous articles on family life, women's roles in agri-culture, and Saskatchewan farm life.

RONALD MAVOR was Professor and Head of the Drama Department, University of Saskatchewan, until June 1990. He graduated from Glasgow University in medicine and was a practising physician until 1957, when he became Drama Critic of the *Scotsman* newspaper in Edinburgh. He then became Director of the Scottish Arts Council, before moving to Saskatoon in 1977. He is the author of ten plays and a book about his father, the playwright James Bridie. He was appointed C.B.E in 1972 and now lives in Glasgow.

ERNEST MCCULLOUGH was graduated *magna cum laude* from the University of Notre Dame, South Bend, Indiana, and obtained his master's degree and doctorate from the University of Toronto. He is Associate Professor of Philos-ophy at Saint Thomas More College, University of Saskatchewan, where he has been Acting Principal and was Head of the Philosophy Department for some years. He specializes in mediaeval philosophy, the history of science, and ethics, with a special interest in the work of Albert the Great. He is presently interested in narrative notions of time, objective ideas, and analogy, and is writing a novel.

DUNCAN ROBERTSON is a specialist in geriatric and internal medicine current-ly located in Victoria, British Columbia. He was formerly a professor in the College of Medicine, University of Saskatchewan.

PETER SINGER was educated at the University of Melbourne and at Oxford University, where he gained his first teaching position. He has also taught at New York University, and has been a Fellow of the Woodrow Wilson Center for Scholars. He is now Professor of Philosophy and Director of the Centre for Human Bioethics at Monash University, Australia. Dr. Singer is a contributor to the *New York Review of Books*, *New York Times Magazine*, *The Nation*, and a variety of philosophical journals. He is also the author of *Democracy and Disobedience* (1973), *Animal Liberation* (1975), *Practical Ethics* (1979), *Marx* (1980), *The Expanding Circle* (1981), *Should the Baby Live?* (1985), and *In Defence of Animals* (1985).

DAVID SKELTON is former head of the Department of Geriatric Medicine, University of Alberta, Edmonton. He was born and educated in England, where he developed a community geriatric program at the University of Birmingham and a teaching program in geriatric medicine at the University of Southampton. He developed the first Canadian palliative care unit, at the Saint Boniface Hospital in Winnipeg. He is currently in private practice in geriatric medicine while holding an appointment in the Faculty of Medicine at the University of Alberta. He has published widely on health-care delivery, epidemiology, and dying, as well as on clinical and psycho-social aspects of aging. Dr. Skelton is also a priest in the Anglican Church of Canada.

ROBERT SOLEM is Professor of Music at the University of Saskatchewan, where he teaches music fundamentals and choral music and directs the University's Greystone Singers concert choir. He was graduated *magna cum laude* from Augustana College, Sioux Falls, South Dakota, and taught English at Missions-seminar Neuendettelsau, Germany, during 1957-58, following which he attended Princeton Seminary on a Rockefeller Theological Fellowship and pursued graduate studies, earning his master's degree in musicology in 1961 from the University of Minnesota. Doctoral studies followed; in 1962 he was appointed Special Lecturer in Music Education at the University of Saskatchewan.

BYRON G. SPENCER is Professor of Economics and a QSEP Research Associate at McMaster University, where he has been since 1966. He holds a bachelor's degree from Queen's University and a doctorate from Rice University. He has been a Senior Visitor at Cambridge University, England, and has served as Associate Chair of the McMaster Department of Economics, as a member of the Ontario Economic Council's Management Team for Social Services and Transfers, as Chair of the McMaster Arts Research Board, as a member of the Council of the Canadian Population Society, and in various other capacities. He is also a member of the International Union for the Scientific Study of Population. Dr. Spencer has published extensively in the form of books, monographs, and articles in professional journals, and is the recipient of several major research grants.

RICHARD TAYLOR has held professorships at Brown University, Columbia University, and the University of Rochester, and is currently Resident Distinguished Philospher at Hartwick College. His books include *Metaphysics* (1963), *Action and Purpose* (1966), *With Heart and Mind* (1973), *Freedom, Anarchy and the Law* (1973), *Good and Evil* (1984), and *Virtue Ethics* (1991).

Contributors

JOSEPH TINDALE is Associate Professor in the Department of Family Studies, College of Family and Consumer Studies, University of Guelph. He is also Chair of the University of Guelph Faculty Association and Co-ordinator of Projects on Gerontology for the Canadian Mental Health Association, as well as past chair of the Social Sciences Division of the Canadian Association on Gerontology. His research interests are intergenerational relations, older workers, and economic and health policy as they relate to older persons and their families in later life.

JIRI ZUZANEK is a Professor in the Department of Recreation and Leisure Studies, and the Department of Sociology, of the University of Waterloo. He served as Research Director of the European Centre for Leisure and Education in Prague, Czechoslovakia, and has taught at the University of Lund, Sweden, the City University of New York, and the University of Western Ontario. Dr. Zuzanek is the author of numerous articles in the area of leisure and cultural studies and of the book *Work and Leisure in the Soviet Union: A Time-Budget Analysis* (1980).